AQA Chemistry
Third edition

GCSE

Teacher Handbook

Sam Holyman
Series Editor: Lawrie Ryan

OXFORD
UNIVERSITY PRESS

OXFORD
UNIVERSITY PRESS

Great Clarendon Street, Oxford, OX2 6DP, United Kingdom

Oxford University Press is a department of the University of Oxford.
It furthers the University's objective of excellence in research,
scholarship, and education by publishing worldwide. Oxford is a
registered trade mark of Oxford University Press in the UK and in
certain other countries

© Oxford University Press 2016

The moral rights of the authors have been asserted

First published in 2016

All rights reserved. No part of this publication may be reproduced,
stored in a retrieval system, or transmitted, in any form or by any
means, without the prior permission in writing of Oxford University
Press, or as expressly permitted by law, by licence or under terms agreed
with the appropriate reprographics rights organization. Enquiries
concerning reproduction outside the scope of the above should be sent
to the Rights Department, Oxford University Press,
at the address above.

You must not circulate this work in any other form and you must
impose this same condition on any acquirer

British Library Cataloguing in Publication Data
Data available

978 0 19 835944 9

10 9 8 7 6 5 4 3 2 1

Paper used in the production of this book is a natural, recyclable
product made from wood grown in sustainable forests.
The manufacturing process conforms to the environmental regulations
of the country of origin.

Printed and Bound by CPI Group (UK) Ltd

Sam Holyman would like to acknowledge Annie Hamblin.

Lawrie would like to thank the following people for their help and
support in producing this teacher handbook. Each one has added value
to my initial efforts: Annie Hamblin, Sadie Garratt, Emma-Leigh Craig,
Amie Hewish, Andy Chandler-Grevatt.

Index compiled by INDEXING SPECIALISTS (UK) Ltd., Indexing house,
306A Portland Road, Hove, East Sussex, BN3 5LP United Kingdom.

Contents

This book has been written for the *AQA GCSE Chemistry* and *AQA GCSE Combined Science: Trilogy* courses, making them completely co-teachable. Chemistry only lessons are easily identifiable with their own black-bordered design, and are also formatted in italics in the below contents list for quick access.

Required practicals	v
Introduction	vi
Assessment and progress	viii
Differentiation and skills	x
Kerboodle	xii

1 Atoms, bonding, and moles — 2

Chapter C1 Atomic structure — 4
C1.1	Atoms	4
C1.2	Chemical equations	6
C1.3	Separating mixtures	8
C1.4	Fractional distillation and paper chromatography	10
C1.5	History of the atom	12
C1.6	Structure of the atom	14
C1.7	Ions, atoms, and isotopes	16
C1.8	Electronic structures	18
	C1 Checkpoint	20

Chapter C2 The periodic table — 22
C2.1	Development of the periodic table	22
C2.2	Electronic structures and the periodic table	24
C2.3	Group 1 – the alkali metals	26
C2.4	Group 7 – the halogens	28
C2.5	Explaining trends	30
C2.6	*The transition elements*	*32*
	C2 Checkpoint	34

Chapter C3 Structure and bonding — 36
C3.1	States of matter	36
C3.2	Atoms into ions	38
C3.3	Ionic bonding	40
C3.4	Giant ionic structures	42
C3.5	Covalent bonding	44
C3.6	Structure of simple molecules	46
C3.7	Giant covalent structures	48
C3.8	Fullerenes and graphene	50
C3.9	Bonding in metals	52
C3.10	Giant metallic structures	54
C3.11	*Nanoparticles*	*56*
C3.12	*Applications of nanoparticles*	*58*
	C3 Checkpoint	60

Chapter C4 Chemical calculations — 62
C4.1	Relative masses and moles	62
C4.2	Equations and calculations	64
C4.3	From masses to balanced equations	66
C4.4	The yield of a chemical reaction	68
C4.5	Atom economy	70
C4.6	Expressing concentrations	72
C4.7	*Titrations*	*74*
C4.8	*Titration calculations*	*76*
C4.9	*Volumes of gases*	*78*
	C4 Checkpoint	80

2 Chemical reactions and energy changes — 82

Chapter C5 Chemical changes — 84
C5.1	The reactivity series	84
C5.2	Displacement reactions	86
C5.3	Extracting metals	88
C5.4	Salts from metals	90
C5.5	Salts from insoluble bases	92
C5.6	Making more salts	94
C5.7	Neutralisation and the pH scale	96
C5.8	Strong and weak acids	98
	C5 Checkpoint	100

Chapter C6 Electrolysis — 102
C6.1	Introduction to electrolysis	102
C6.2	Changes at the electrodes	104
C6.3	The extraction of aluminium	106
C6.4	Electrolysis of aqueous solutions	108
	C6 Checkpoint	110

Chapter C7 Energy changes — 112
C7.1	Exothermic and endothermic reactions	112
C7.2	Using energy transfers from reactions	114
C7.3	Reaction profiles	116
C7.4	Bond energy calculations	118
C7.5	*Chemical cells and batteries*	*120*
C7.6	*Fuel cells*	*122*
	C7 Checkpoint	124

iii

3 Rates, equilibrium, and organic chemistry — 126

Chapter C8 Rates and equilibrium — 128
- C8.1 Rate of reaction — 128
- C8.2 Collision theory and surface area — 130
- C8.3 The effect of temperature — 132
- C8.4 The effect of concentration and pressure — 134
- C8.5 The effect of catalysts — 136
- C8.6 Reversible reactions — 138
- C8.7 Energy and reversible reactions — 140
- C8.8 Dynamic equilibrium — 142
- C8.9 Altering conditions — 144
- C8 Checkpoint — 146

Chapter C9 Crude oil and fuels — 148
- C9.1 Hydrocarbons — 148
- C9.2 Fractional distillation of oil — 150
- C9.3 Burning hydrocarbon fuels — 152
- C9.4 Cracking hydrocarbons — 154
- C9 Checkpoint — 156

Chapter C10 Organic reactions — 158
- C10.1 Reactions of the alkenes — 158
- C10.2 Structures of alcohols, carboxylic acids, and esters — 160
- C10.3 Reactions and uses of alcohols — 162
- C10.4 Carboxylic acids and esters — 164
- C10 Checkpoint — 166

Chapter C11 Polymers — 168
- C11.1 Addition polymerisation — 168
- C11.2 Condensation polymerisation — 170
- C11.3 Natural polymers — 172
- C11.4 DNA — 174
- C11 Checkpoint — 176

4 Analysis and the Earth's resources — 178

Chapter C12 Chemical analysis — 180
- C12.1 Pure substances and mixtures — 180
- C12.2 Analysing chromatograms — 182
- C12.3 Testing for gases — 184
- C12.4 Tests for positive ions — 186
- C12.5 Tests for negative ions — 188
- C12.6 Instrumental analysis — 190
- C12 Checkpoint — 192

Chapter C13 The Earth's atmosphere — 194
- C13.1 History of our atmosphere — 194
- C13.2 Our evolving atmosphere — 196
- C13.3 Greenhouse gases — 198
- C13.4 Global climate change — 200
- C13.5 Atmospheric pollutants — 202
- C13 Checkpoint — 204

Chapter C14 The Earth's resources — 206
- C14.1 Finite and renewable resources — 206
- C14.2 Water safe to drink — 208
- C14.3 Treating waste water — 210
- C14.4 Extracting metals from ores — 212
- C14.5 Life cycle assessments — 214
- C14.6 Reduce, reuse, and recycle — 216
- C14 Checkpoint — 218

Chapter C15 Using our resources — 220
- C15.1 Rusting — 220
- C15.2 Useful alloys — 222
- C15.3 The properties of polymers — 224
- C15.4 Glass, ceramics, and composites — 226
- C15.5 Making ammonia – the Haber process — 228
- C15.6 The economics of the Haber process — 230
- C15.7 Making fertilisers in the lab — 232
- C15.8 Making fertilisers in industry — 234
- C15 Checkpoint — 236

Answers — 238
Index — 253

Required practicals

As part of the *AQA GCSE Chemistry* course, students must complete eight Required practicals. Each Required practical is fully supported on Kerboodle with differentiated Practical sheets and accompanying Teacher and technician notes.

Required practicals		Topic
1	Preparation of a pure, dry sample of a soluble salt from an insoluble oxide or carbonate, using a Bunsen burner to heat dilute acid and a water bath or electric heater to evaporate the solution.	C5.5 C5.6
2	Determination of the reacting volumes of solutions of a strong acid and a strong alkali by titration. [H] Determination of the concentration of one of the solutions in mol/dm^3 and g/dm3 from the reacting volumes and the known concentration of the other solution.	C4.7
3	Investigate what happens when aqueous solutions are electrolysed using inert electrodes. This should be an investigation involving developing a hypothesis.	C6.4
4	Investigate the variables that affect temperature changes in reacting solutions such as, eg acid plus metals, acid plus carbonates, neutralisations, displacement of metals.	C7.1
5	Investigate how changes in concentration affect the rates of reactions by a method involving measuring the volume of a gas produced and a method involving a change in colour or turbidity. This should be an investigation involving developing a hypothesis.	C8.4
6	Investigate how paper chromatography can be used to separate and tell the difference between coloured substances. Students should calculate Rf values.	C12.2
7	Use of chemical tests to identify the ions in unknown single ionic compounds covering the ions.	C12.5
8	Analysis and purification of water samples from different sources, including pH, dissolved solids and distillation.	C14.2

Introduction

About the series

This is the third edition of the UK's number 1 course for GCSE Science. The student books have been approved by AQA, and our author teams and experts have been working closely with AQA to develop a blended suite of resources to support the new specifications.

All resources in this series have been carefully designed to support students of all abilities on their journey through GCSE Science. The demands of the new specifications are fully supported, with maths, practicals, and synoptic skills developed throughout, and all new subject content fully covered.

The series is designed to be flexible, enabling you to co-teach Foundation and Higher tiers, and Combined and Separate Sciences. Content is clearly flagged throughout the resources, helping you to identify the relevant content for your students.

Assessment is an important feature of the series, and is supported by our unique assessment framework, helping students to track and make progress.

The series is edited by Lawrie Ryan. Building on his vast experience as an author for much-loved titles such as Spotlight Science and the Chemistry for You Lawrie has become one of the best-known authors and editors of educational science books both nationally and internationally. A former Head of Science, Science Advisor, and Ofsted Inspector, he understands the demands of modern education and draws on his experience to deliver this new and innovative course that builds upon the legacy of previous editions

Your Teacher Handbook

This Teacher Handbook aims to save you time and effort by offering lesson plans, differentiation suggestions, and assessment guidance on a page-by-page basis that is a direct match to the Student Book.

With learning outcomes differentiated you can tailor the lessons and activities to suit your students and provide progression opportunities students of all abilities.

Lesson plans are written for 55-minute lessons but are flexible and fully adaptable so you can choose the activities that suit your class best.

Separate Science-only content is contained within whole topics and clearly flagged from the Combined Sciences content, enabling you co-teach using one Teacher Handbook.

Section opener

Overview

The Section opener provides an overview of the parts of the specification, required practicals, and maths skills covered in the section.

Specification links

This table provides an overview of the specification topics covered in the chapters of the section. It also gives an indication of which Paper each specification topic will be mainly assessed in.

Required practicals

This table indicated which required practicals are covered within this section. It also gives a list of Apparatus and techniques that could be assessed by that practical.

Key Stage 3 and GCSE Catch-up

This table outlines Key Stage 3 knowledge that is a pre-requisite for this section. Later Section Openers will also include GCSE knowledge from earlier in the course. Quick checkpoint activities, to assess students understanding of each statement, are provided

For each statement, a suggestion for how you can help students catch up is also provided, as well as an index of which topic each statement links to.

Maths skills

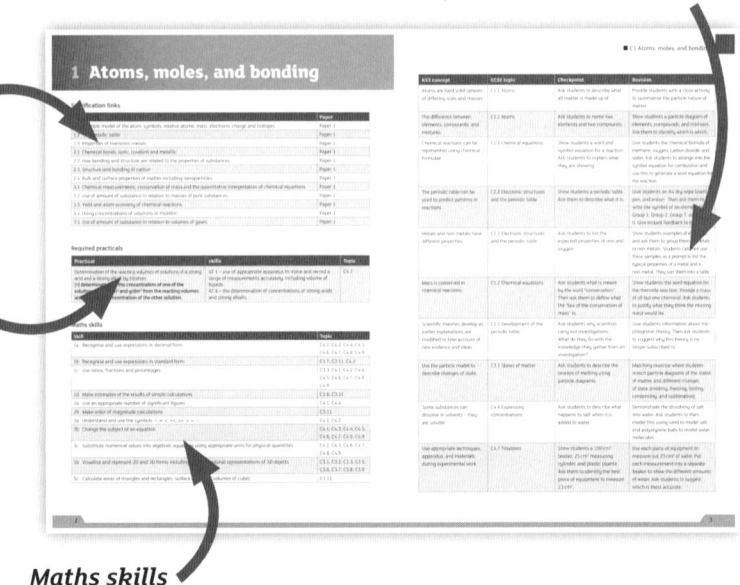

This table provides an overview of the maths skills covered in the chapters of the section.

Lesson

Specification links
This indicated the area of the AQA GCSE Chemistry (9–1) 2016 specification this lesson covers. Relevant Working scientifically and Mathematical requirements links are also provided.

Differentiated outcomes
This table summarises the possible lesson outcomes. They are ramped and divided into three ability bands. The three ability bands are explained in the Assessment and progress section. Each ability band has 2-3 outcomes defined, designed to cover the specification content for different ability levels

An index of questions and activities is given for each learning outcome, helping you to assess your students informally as you progress through each lesson

Key Stage 3 and GCSE Catch-up
These boxes provide equipment lists, an outline method, and safety requirements for any practicals in the lesson. Required practicals are flagged with the Required practical icon.
Although safety requirements are given, a fully-comprehensive risk assessment should be carried out before any practical activity is undergone.

Maths and literacy
These boxes provide suggestions of how Maths and Literacy skills can be developed in the lesson. Where relevant, the Maths skills are linked to the Mathematical requirements of the specification.

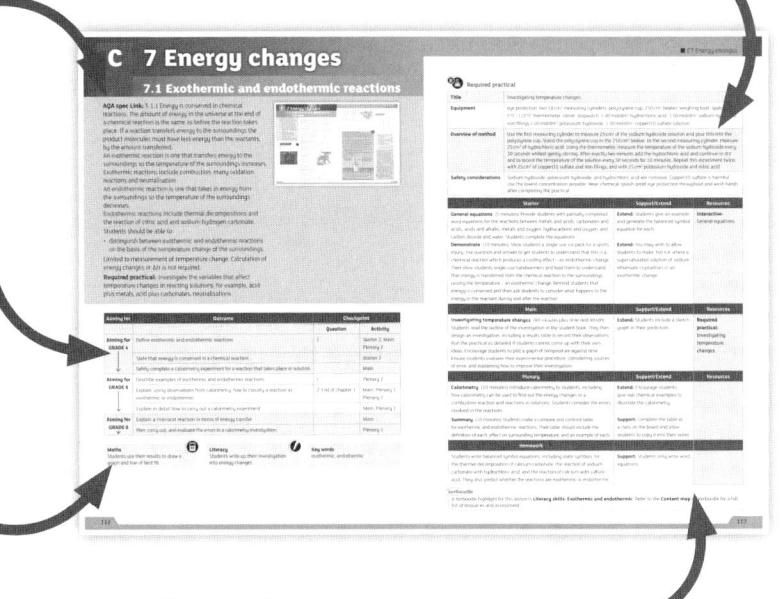

Suggested lesson plan
A suggested route through the lesson is provided, including ideas for support, extension, and homework. The right-hand column indicated where Kerboodle resources are available.

Checkpoint lesson

Overview
The Checkpoint Lesson is a suggested follow-up lesson after students have completed the automarked Checkpoint Assessment on Kerboodle. There are three routes through the lesson, with the route for each student being determined by their mark in the assessment. Each route aims to support students with progressing up an assessment band.

Checkpoint overview
This text provides a brief overview of the chapter, including the key concepts students should be confident with.

Checkpoint lesson plan
This table provides a differentiated lesson plan for the checkpoint follow-up lesson. This includes learning outcomes, starters and plenaries, supporting information for the follow-up worksheets (including any descriptions of relevant practicals), and progression suggestions to support students with progressing up a band.

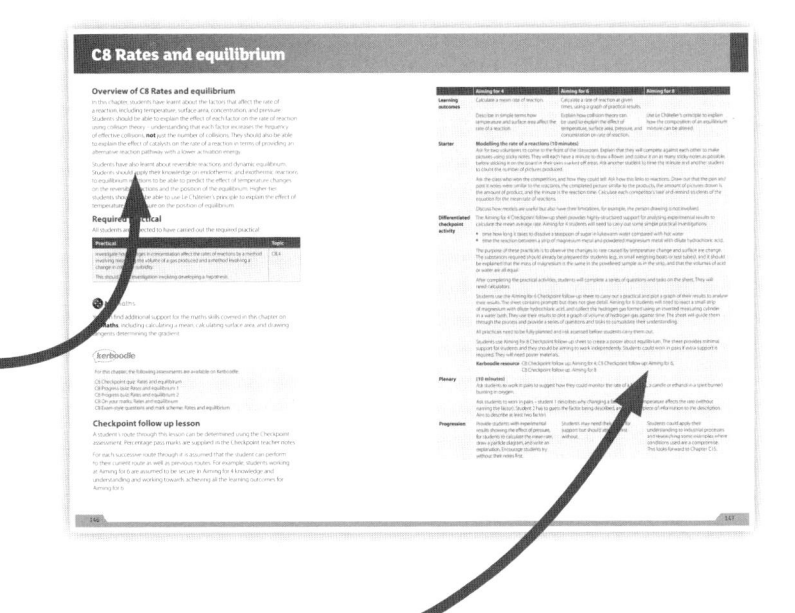

Assessment and progress

Dr Andrew Chandler-Grevatt

To ensure students are fully supported to make progress through the new linear exams, AQA GCSE *Sciences Third Edition* was developed in consultation with assessment consultant, Dr Andrew Chandler-Grevatt. Andrew worked with the team to develop an assessment framework that supports students and teachers in tracking and promoting progress through Key Stage 3 and GCSE.

Andrew is has a doctorate in school assessment, and a real passion for science teaching and learning. Having worked as a science teacher for ten years, of which five were spent as an AST, Andrew has a real understanding of the pressures and joys of teaching in the classroom. His most recent projects include *Activate for KS3 Science*, for which he developed a unique assessment framework to support schools in the transition away from levels.

The new GCSE grading system (9–1)

With the new specifications and criteria comes a new grading system. The old system of grades A*–G, is being replaced with a numerical system with grades 9–1. Grade 9 is the highest, and is designed to award exceptional performance.

The new grades are not directly equivalent to the old A*–C system, although some comparisons can be drawn:

- Approximately the same proportion of students will achieve a grade 4 or above as currently achieve a grade C or above.
- Approximately the same proportion of students will achieve a grade 7 as above as currently achieve an A or above.
- The bottom of grade 1 will be aligned with the bottom of grade G.

A 'good pass' is considered to be a grade 5 or above.

Throughout the course, resources and assessments have been designed to help students working at different grades to make progress.

5-year assessment framework

Purpose

The combination of the removal of levels, new performance measures, new grading system, and more demanding GCSEs makes it more important than ever to be able to track and facilitate progress from Year 7 and all the way through secondary. Assessment plays a key role in intervention and extension, and these are both vital in helping students of all abilities achieve their potential, and add value to their projected GCSE grade.

In the absence of levels, and as we learn more about the new GCSE grades, it is important that a framework is in place in order to inform learning, teaching, and assessment from Y7–Y11.

Framework

Throughout the 5 years, it is useful to define three ability bands, which can be used to inform the design of learning outcomes, learning resources, and assessments. By defining three bands, realistic and valuable intervention and extension can be designed and implemented to help students of all abilities make progress, and improve their grade projection.

At KS3, the model is designed with the aim of encouraging every student to gain a 'secure' grasp of each concept and topic, so that they are ready to progress. These students will be on track to secure a 'good pass' (grade 5 or above) at GCSE.

In the KS3 course Activate three bands have been defined:

- **Developing**, in which students are able to know and understand a concept, and demonstrate their knowledge in simple and familiar situations.
- **Secure**, in which students are able to apply their knowledge and skills to familiar

and some unfamiliar situations, undertake analysis, and understand more complex concepts.
- **Extending**, in which students are able to evaluate and create, apply their knowledge to complex and unfamiliar situations, and demonstrate advanced use of skills.

Using the framework throughout KS3 helps you to identify which students are ready to progress, and approximately what GCSE grades they should be aiming for.

At GCSE, students can then be differentiated into three bands, aiming for different grades.

- **Aiming for 4** is for students working at the lower grades 1–3, who would have been Developing at KS3, and aspiring to a Grade 4 at GCSE. Resources and assessments for these students are supportive, and focus on developing understanding of core concepts.
- **Aiming for 6** is for students working at grades 4–6, who would have been Secure at KS3. Resources and assessments for these students help to embed core concepts, by encouraging application and analysis, and beginning to explore more complex ideas and situations.
- **Aiming for 8** provides extension for students working at grades 7–9, who are able to grasp complex concepts, and demonstrate higher order skills, such as evaluation and creation in complex and unfamiliar situations.

The framework is summarised in the table below.

Key stage 3	Band	Developing		Secure		Extending	
	Level	3	4	5	6	7	8
GCSE	Band	Aiming for 4			Aiming for 6		Aiming for 8	
	Grades	1	2	3	4	5	6	7	8	9
	Demand	Low			Standard			High		

Informing learning outcomes

The assessment framework has informed the design of the learning outcomes throughout the course. Learning outcomes are differentiated, and there is a set of learning outcomes for every lesson for each ability band.

The checkpoint assessment system

This series includes a checkpoint assessment system for intervention and extension, designed to help students of all abilities make continuous progress through the course. The system also helps you and your students to monitor achievement, and ensure all students are on-track and monitored through the new linear assessments.

Checkpoint assessments are provided in Kerboodle. These are Automarked objective tests with diagnostic feedback. Once students have completed their assessment, depending on their results, they will complete one of three follow up activities, designed for intervention and extension. Students are supported with activity sheets, and lesson plans and overviews are provided for the teacher. The three follow-up routes are:

1. **Aiming for 4** is for students who achieved low score. These resources support students by helping to develop and embed core concepts.
2. **Aiming for 6** is for students who achieved a medium score. These resources encourage students to embed and extend core concepts, and begin to apply their knowledge in more complex or unfamiliar situations.
3. **Aiming for 8** is for students who have achieved a high score. These resources encourage extensive use of more complex skills, in more complex and unfamiliar situations, helping them to reach for the top grades.

The diagram below provides an overview of how the system works.

Differentiation and Skills

Maths skills and MyMaths

With the introduction of the introduction of the new GCSE competence in maths, the support and development of maths skills in a scientific context will be vital for success.

The Student Books contain a maths skills reference section that covers all the maths required for the specification, explained in a scientific context and with a worked example for reference. Where maths skills are embedded within the scientific content, the maths is demonstrated in a Using Maths feature providing a worked example and an opportunity for students to have a go themselves.

In Kerboodle you will find maths skills interactives that are automarked and provide formative feedback. Calculation sheets provide opportunities for practice of the maths skills and links to MyMaths are shown in the Lesson Player and Teacher Guide where additional resources exist that can be used to reinforce the maths skill. These include practice sheets and Invisi-pen worked examples.

Literacy skills

Literacy skills enable students to effectively communicate their ideas about science and access the information they need. Though the marks allocated for QWC are no longer present in the new specifications, a good degree of literacy is required to read and answer longer, structured exam questions, to access the more difficult concepts introduced in the new GCSE Programme of Study, to be able to effectively interpret and answer questions.

The student books flag opportunities to develop and practice literacy skills through the use of the pen icon. Key words are identified in the text and a glossary helps students get to grips with new scientific terms.

In Kerboodle, you will find Literacy Skills Interactives that help assess literacy skills, including the spelling of key words. Additional Literacy worksheets are available to reinforce skills learnt and provide practise opportunities.

The Teacher Guide flags literacy suggestions and opportunities relating to the lesson. All of these features will help to develop well-rounded scientists able to access information and communicate their ideas effectively.

Working Scientifically

Working Scientifically is new to the 2016 GCSE criteria. It is divided up into four areas and is integrated into the teaching and learning of Biology, Chemistry, and Physics. The four areas are:

1. Development of scientific thinking in which students need to be able to demonstrate understanding of scientific methods and the scientific process and how these may develop over time and their associated limitations
2. Experimental skills and strategies in which students ask scientific questions based on observations, make predictions using scientific knowledge and understanding, carry out investigations to test predictions, make and record measurements and evaluate methods
3. Analysis and evaluation in which students apply mathematical concepts and calculate results, present and interpret data using tables and graphs, draw conclusions and evaluate data, are able to accuracy, precision, repeatability and reproducibility
4. Scientific vocabulary, quantities, units, symbols and nomenclature in which students calculate results and manipulate data using scientific formulae using basic analysis, SI units and IUPAC chemical nomenclature where appropriate.

Working Scientifically is integrated throughout the Student Book with flagged Practical boxes, flagged Required Practical boxes, questions. A dedicated Working Scientifically reference chapter is also provided at the back of the Student Book to refer to during investigations, when answering Working Scientifically questions and to enable investigative skills to be developed.

In Kerboodle there are Practicals and Activities resources with their own Working Scientifically objectives, additional targeted Working Scientifically skills sheets as well as other resources such as simulations and Webquests to target specific skills areas. Questions are ramped in difficulty and opportunity to build up to and practice the practical based questions for the exam are provided.

For the required practicals the guidance provided to students acknowledges the differing degrees of support and independence required, with targeted support sheets to the key grade descriptors of Grade 4, 6, and 8, with a view to move the students over that Grade point onwards.

In the Teacher Guide lessons will often have a working scientifically focus in mind for the activities in that lesson. Working Scientifically Learning Outcomes, where specified, are differentiated to show the expectations for the differing ability levels.

For the purpose of the practical based questions in the examination, Required practicals are flagged and practice opportunities are provided through out the Student Book in the summary questions and exam-style questions.

Differentiation

Building upon the principles of *Activate* at Key Stage 3.

Differentiation using the checkpoint system

The end of chapter Checkpoint lessons will help you to progress students of every ability, targeting the key Grade boundaries of 4, 6, and 8 to enable students to review, consolidate and extend their understanding at each of the grade lesson points.

The tasks focused at students to become secure at Grades 4 and 6 are designed to help them become more secure in their understanding and consolidate the chapter. Teacher input will help them grasp important concepts from the chapter with the opportunity for some extension for Grade 6 students.

The tasks focused at students to become secure and extend at Grade 8 are designed to develop and challenge. Students will work more independently on these tasks to free up the teacher to be able to focus on those that found the chapter more challenging.

Teacher Guide

Lesson outcomes are differentiated and suggestions for activities throughout the lesson plans are accompanied by support and extension opportunities.

Student Book

Summary questions per lesson are ramped with a darker shading indicating a more challenging question. In the end of chapter summary questions and exam style questions, ramping occurs within the question (as would be seen in a typical exam question).

Practicals and Activities

All practicals and activities are differentiated. Where more complex areas are covered, additional support sheets may be provided to allow lower attaining students to access the activity.

For all required practicals (compulsory practicals) that may be assessed in an exam, specific support sheets are provided targeting the progression of students across the key Grades 4, 6 and 8.

Additional skills sheets may be used in conjunction with practicals to provide additional support in generic competencies such as constructing a graph etc.

Interactive Assessments

All interactive assessments are ramped in difficulty and support is provided in the feedback directing students where they can improve. In chapters with both levels of content, Higher and Foundation versions of assessment are available.

Written assessments

End of section tests and end of year tests have Foundation and Higher versions.

Kerboodle

AQA GCSE Sciences Kerboodle is packed full of guided support and ideas for running and creating effective GCSE Science lessons, and for assessing and facilitating students' progress. It is intuitive to use and customisable.

Kerboodle is online, allowing you and your students to access the course anytime, anywhere.

AQA GCSE Sciences Kerboodle consists of:
- lessons, resources, and assessment
- access to *AQA GCSE Science* Student books for both teachers and students.

Lessons, Resources, and Assessment

AQA GCSE Sciences Kerboodle offers new, engaging lesson resources, as well as a fully comprehensive assessment package, written to match the *AQA GCSE Science (9–1)* specifications.

Kerboodle offers comprehensive and flexible support for the *AQA GCSE Science (9–1)* specifications, enabling you to follow our suggested lessons and schemes of work or to create your own lessons and schemes and share them with other members of your department.

You can **adapt** many of the resources to suit your students' needs, with all non-interactive activities available as editable Word documents. You can also **upload** your own resources so that everything is accessed from one location.

Set homework and assessments through the Assessment system and **track** progress using the Markbook.

Lessons

Click on the **Lessons tab** to access the *AQA GCSE Sciences* lesson presentations and notes.

Ready-to-play lesson presentations complement every spread in the Teacher Handbook and Student Book. Each lesson presentation is easy to launch and features lesson objectives, starters, activity guidance, key diagrams, plenaries, and homework suggestions. The lesson presentations and accompanying note sections are 100% customisable. You can personalise the lessons by adding your own resources and notes, or build your own lesson plans using our resources.

Your lessons and notes can be accessed by your whole department and they are ideal for use in cover lessons.

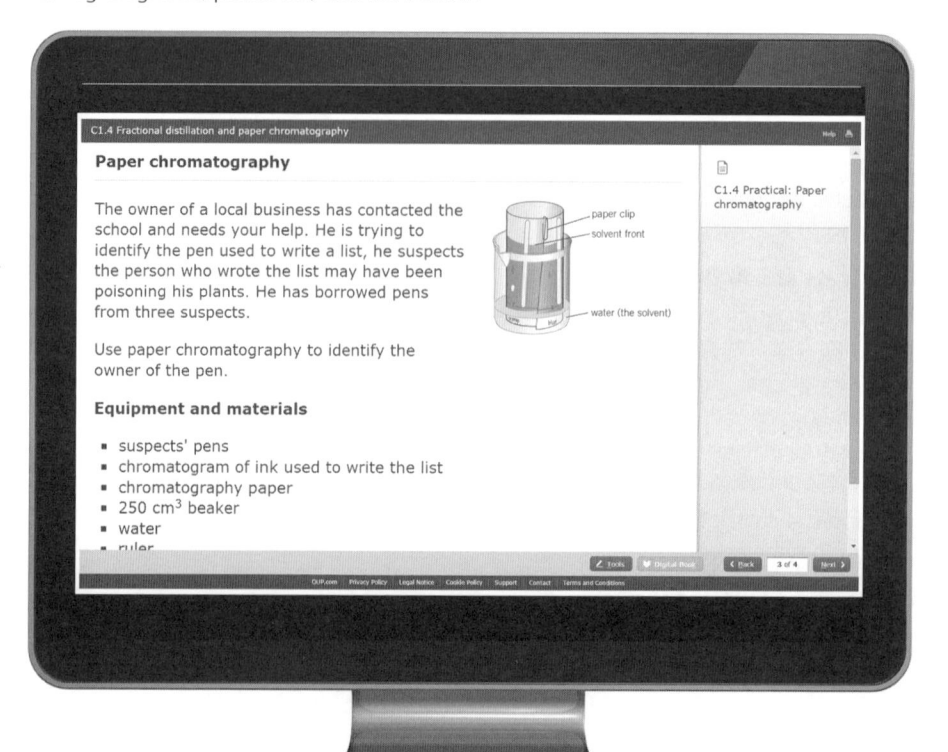

Resources

Click on the Resources tab to access the full list of AQA GCSE Sciences resources. Use the navigation panel on the left hand side to find resources for any lesson, chapter, or topic.

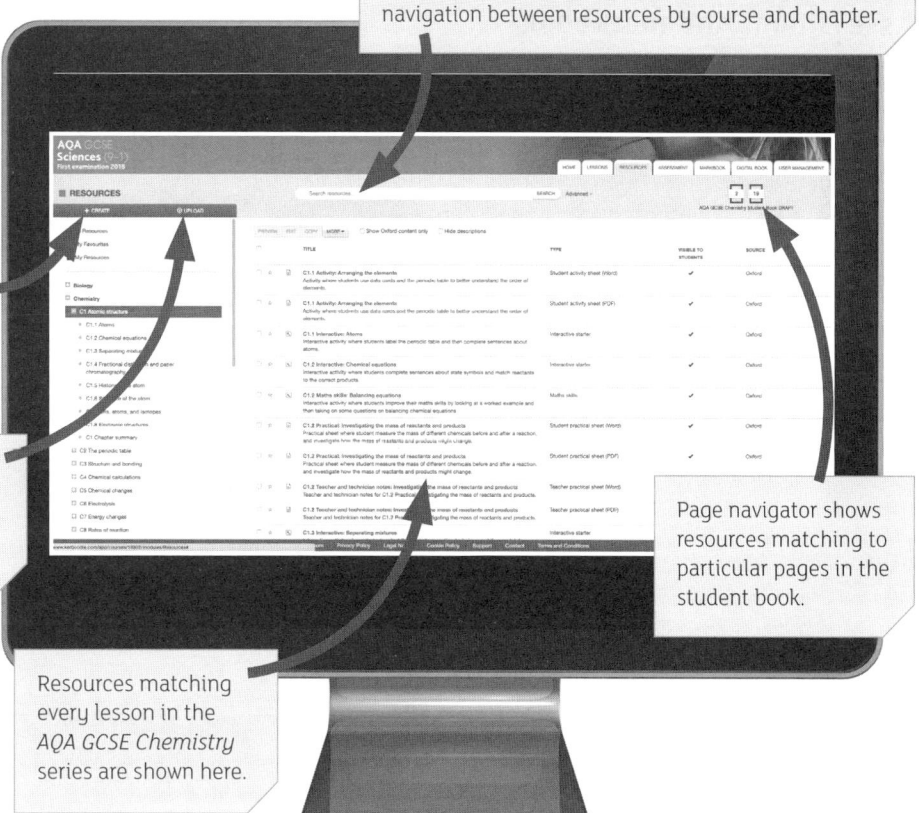

Fully customisable content to cater to all your classes. Resources can be created using the create button.

Existing resources can be uploaded on to the platform using the upload button.

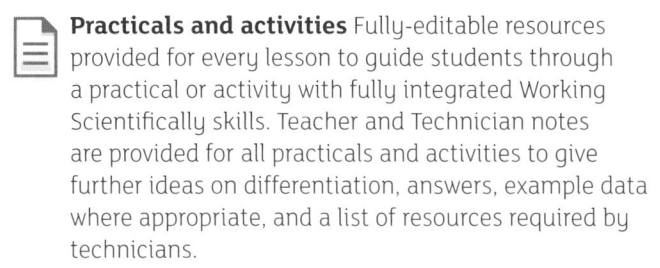

Navigation panel and search bar allow for easy navigation between resources by course and chapter.

Page navigator shows resources matching to particular pages in the student book.

Resources matching every lesson in the *AQA GCSE Chemistry* series are shown here.

Practicals and activities Fully-editable resources provided for every lesson to guide students through a practical or activity with fully integrated Working Scientifically skills. Teacher and Technician notes are provided for all practicals and activities to give further ideas on differentiation, answers, example data where appropriate, and a list of resources required by technicians.

Interactive starters or plenaries Accompany each lesson, and can be used front-of-class to maximise student participation.

Skills sheets Editable worksheets that target Maths, Literacy, and Working Scientifically skills. They provide guidance and examples to help students whenever they need to use a particular skill.

Skills interactives Auto-marked interactive activities with formative feedback that focus on key maths and literacy skills. You can use these activities in your class to help consolidate core skills relevant to the lesson, or they can be assigned as homework by accessing them through the Assessment tab.

Animations and videos Help students to visualise difficult concepts or to learn about real-life contexts, with engaging visuals and narration. They are structured to clearly address a set of learning objectives and are followed by interactive question screens to help consolidate key points and to provide formative feedback.

Simulations Allow students to control variables and look at outcomes for experiments that are difficult to carry out in the classroom or focus on tricky concepts.

Podcasts Available for every chapter to help review and consolidate key points. The podcast presents an audio summary with transcript, followed by a series of ramped questions and answers to assist students in their revision.

Targeted support sheets Available for the full ability range and are provided to help students progress as they complete their GCSE. **Bump up your Grades** target common misconceptions and difficult topics to securely move students over the key boundaries of Grades 4, 6, and 8. Extensions activities provide opportunities for higher-ability students to apply their knowledge and understanding to new contexts, whilst **Go Further** worksheets aim to inspire students to consider the subject at A Level and beyond.

WebQuests Research-based activities set in a real-life context. WebQuests are fun and engaging activities that can be carried out individually or within a group and are ideal for peer-review.

Checklists and chapter maps Self-assessment checklists for students of the key learning points from each chapter to aid consolidation and revision. For teachers there is an additional chapter-map resource that provides an overview of the chapter, specific opportunities to support and extend, and information on tackling common misconceptions.

Assessment and markbook

All of the assessment material in Kerboodle has been quality assured by our expert Assessment Advisor. Click on the **Assessment tab** to find the wide range of assessment materials to help you deliver a varied, motivating, and effective assessment programme.

Once your classes are set up in Kerboodle, you can assign them assessments to do at home or in class individually or as a group.

A **Markbook** with reporting function helps you to keep track of your students' results. This includes both auto-marked assessments and work marked by you.

Practice or test?

Many of the auto-marked assessment in the AQA GCSE Sciences Kerboodle is available in formative or summative versions.

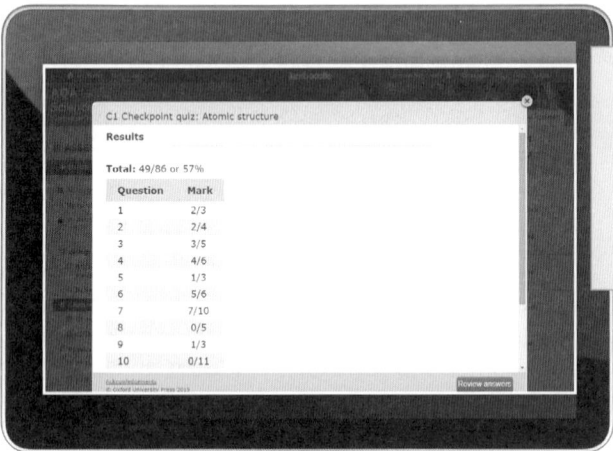

Test versions of the assessment provide feedback on performance at the end of the test. Students are only given one attempt at each screen but can review them and see which answers they get wrong after completing the activity. Marks are reported to the markbook.

Practice versions of the assessment provide screen-by-screen feedback, focusing on misconceptions, and provide hints for the students to help them revise their answer. Students are given the opportunity to try again. Marks are reported to the Markbook.

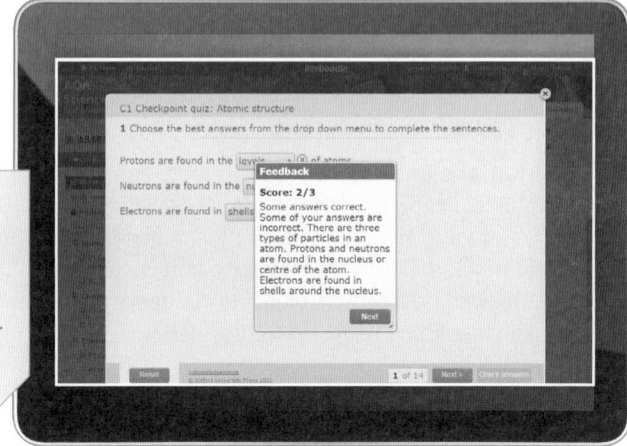

Assessment per chapter

Through each chapter there are many opportunities for assessment and determining/monitoring progress.

Progress quizzes Auto-marked assessments that focus on the content of the chapters. They are quick, engaging quizzes designed to be taken throughout the course to monitor progress and to focus revision.

Checkpoint assessments Auto-marked assessments designed to determine whether students have a secure grasp of concepts from the chapter. These assessments are ramped in difficulty and can be followed up by the differentiated Checkpoint Lesson activities.

On Your Marks Improve students' exam skills by analysing questions, looking at other students' responses, interpreting mark schemes, and answering exam-style questions.

Homework activities Auto-marked quizzes with ramped questions targeting the key Grades 4, 6, and 8 boundaries designed to help students apply and embed their knowledge and understanding from the classroom.

Formal testing

End-of-chapter tests Provide students with the opportunity to practise answering exam-style questions in a written format. There are differentiated Foundation and Higher versions, with separate options for the combined sciences and the separate sciences. Accompanied by a fully comprehensive mark scheme, data can be entered manually into the Markbook.

Mid-point and end-of-course written tests Provide students with the opportunity to practise answering exam-style questions in a full-length paper. There are differentiated Foundation and Higher versions, with separate options for the combined sciences and the separate sciences. Accompanied by a fully comprehensive mark scheme, data can be entered manually into the Markbook.

Kerboodle Book

The *AQA GCSE Sciences* Kerboodle Books are digital versions of the Student Books for you to use at the front of the classroom.

Access to the Kerboodle Book is automatically available as part of the Lessons, Resources, and Assessment package for both you and your students.

A set of tools is available with the Kerboodle Book so that you can personalise your book and make notes. Like all resources offered on Kerboodle, the Kerboodle Book can also be accessed using a range of devices.

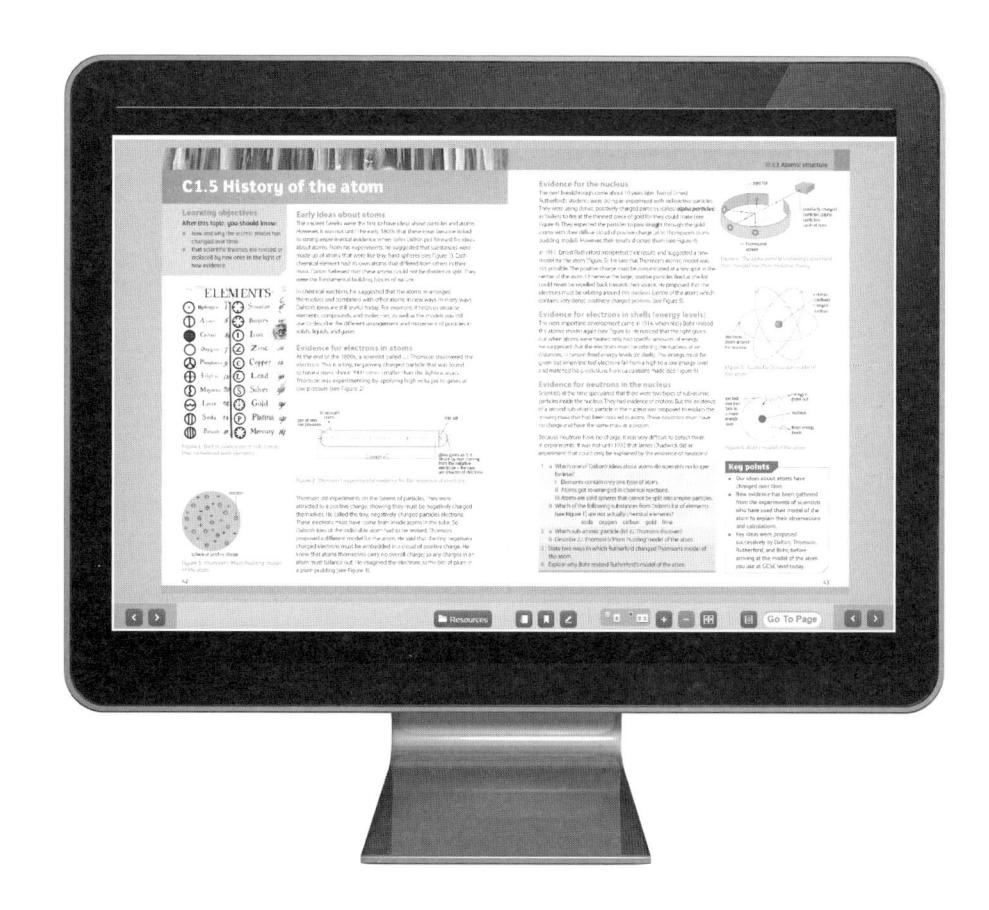

1 Atoms, moles, and bonding

Specification links

Topic	Paper
1.1 A simple model of the atom, symbols, relative atomic mass, electronic charge and isotopes	Paper 1
1.2 The periodic table	Paper 1
1.3 Properties of transition metals	Paper 1
2.1 Chemical bonds, ionic, covalent and metallic	Paper 1
2.2 How bonding and structure are related to the properties of substances	Paper 1
2.3 Structure and bonding of carbon	Paper 1
2.4 Bulk and surface properties of matter including nanoparticles	Paper 1
3.1 Chemical measurements, conservation of mass and the quantitative interpretation of chemical equations	Paper 1
3.2 Use of amount of substance in relation to masses of pure substances	Paper 1
3.3 Yield and atom economy of chemical reactions	Paper 1
3.4 Using concentrations of solutions in mol/dm^3	Paper 1
3.5 Use of amount of substance in relation to volumes of gases	Paper 1

Required practicals

Practical	skills	Topic
Determination of the reacting volumes of solutions of a strong acid and a strong alkali by titration. [H] determination of the concentration of one of the solutions in mol/dm^3 and g/dm^3 from the reacting volumes and the known concentration of the other solution.	AT 1 – use of appropriate apparatus to make and record a range of measurements accurately, including volume of liquids. AT 8 – the determination of concentrations of strong acids and strong alkalis.	C4.7

Maths skills

Skill	Topic
1a Recognise and use expressions in decimal form	C4.1, C4.2, C4.4, C4.5, C4.6, C4.7, C4.8, C4.9
1b Recognise and use expressions in standard form	C1.7, C3.11, C4.1
1c Use ratios, fractions and percentages	C3.3, C4.1, C4.2, C4.4, C4.5, C4.6, C4.7, C4.8, C4.9
1d Make estimates of the results of simple calculations	C1.6, C3.11
2a Use an appropriate number of significant figures	C4.1, C4.4
2h Make order of magnitude calculations	C3.11
3a Understand and use the symbols: =, =, <, <<, >>, >, ∝, ~	C4.1, C4.2
3b Change the subject of an equation	C4.1, C4.3, C4.4, C4.5, C4.6, C4.7, C4.8, C4.9
3c Substitute numerical values into algebraic equations using appropriate units for physical quantities	C4.2, C4.3, C4.6, C4.7, C4.8, C4.9
5b Visualise and represent 2D and 3D forms including two dimensional representations of 3D objects	C3.1, C3.2, C3.3, C3.5, C3.6, C3.7, C3.8, C3.9
5c Calculate areas of triangles and rectangles, surface areas and volumes of cubes	C3.11

C1 Atoms, moles, and bonding

KS3 concept	GCSE topic	Checkpoint	Revision
Atoms are hard solid spheres of differing sizes and masses.	C1.1 Atoms	Ask students to describe what all matter is made up of.	Provide students with a cloze activity to summarise the particle nature of matter.
The difference between elements, compounds, and mixtures.	C1.1 Atoms	Ask students to name two elements and two compounds.	Show students a particle diagram of elements, compounds, and mixtures. Ask them to identify which is which.
Chemical reactions can be represented using chemical formulae.	C1.2 Chemical equations	Show students a word and symbol equation for a reaction. Ask students to explain what they are showing.	Give students the chemical formula of methane, oxygen, carbon dioxide, and water. Ask students to arrange into the symbol equation for combustion and use this to generate a word equation for the reaction.
The periodic table can be used to predict patterns in reactions.	C2.2 Electronic structures and the periodic table	Show students a periodic table. Ask them to describe what it is.	Give students an A4 dry-wipe board, pen, and eraser. Then ask them to write the symbol of an element from Group 1, Group 2, Group 7, and Group 0. Give instant feedback to the class.
Metals and non-metals have different properties.	C2.2 Electronic structures and the periodic table	Ask students to list the expected properties of iron and oxygen.	Show students examples of elements and ask them to group them as metals or non-metals. Students can then use these samples as a prompt to list the typical properties of a metal and a non-metal. They sort them into a table.
Mass is conserved in chemical reactions.	C1.2 Chemical equations	Ask students what is meant by the word "conservation". Then ask them to define what the "law of the conservation of mass" is.	Show students the word equation for the thermite reaction. Provide a mass of all but one chemical. Ask students to justify what they think the missing mass would be.
Scientific theories develop as earlier explanations are modified to take account of new evidence and ideas.	C2.1 Development of the periodic table	Ask students why scientists carry out investigations. What do they do with the knowledge they gather from an investigation?	Give students information about the phlogiston theory. Then ask students to suggest why this theory is no longer subscribed to.
Use the particle model to describe changes of state.	C3.1 States of matter	Ask students to describe the process of melting using particle diagrams.	Matching exercise where students match particle diagrams of the states of matter and different changes of state (melting, freezing, boiling, condensing, and sublimation).
Some substances can dissolve in solvents – they are soluble.	C4.6 Expressing concentrations	Ask students to describe what happens to salt when it is added to water.	Demonstrate the dissolving of salt into water. Ask students to then model this using sand to model salt and polystyrene balls to model water molecules.
Use appropriate techniques, apparatus, and materials during experimental work.	C4.7 Titrations	Show students a 100 cm^3 beaker, 25 cm^3 measuring cylinder, and plastic pipette. Ask them to identify the best piece of equipment to measure 23 cm^3.	Use each piece of equipment to measure out 23 cm^3 of water. Put each measurement into a separate beaker to show the different amounts of water. Ask students to suggest which is most accurate.

C 1 Atomic structure
1.1 Atoms

AQA spec Link: 1.1.1 All substances are made of atoms. An atom is the smallest part of an element that can exist.

Atoms of each element are represented by a chemical symbol, for example, O represents an atom of oxygen, Na represents an atom of sodium.

There are about 100 different elements. Elements are shown in the periodic table.

Compounds are formed from elements by chemical reactions. Chemical reactions always involve the formation of one or more new substances, and often involve a detectable energy change. Compounds contain two or more elements chemically combined in fixed proportions and can be represented by formulae using the symbols of the atoms from which they were formed. Compounds can only be separated into elements by chemical reactions.

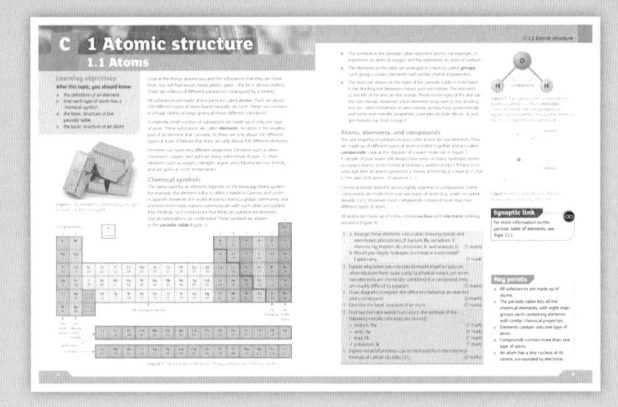

Aiming for	Outcome	Checkpoint	
		Question	Activity
Aiming for GRADE 4 ↓	Define the word element.		Starter 1
	Classify familiar substances as elements or compounds.		Main 2, Plenary 2
	Use the periodic table to find the symbols or names of given elements.		Main 1, Plenary 1
Aiming for GRADE 6 ↓	Describe the basic structure of an atom.	4, End of chapter 1	Starter 2
	Explain, including diagrams, the difference between a pure element, a mixture, and a compound.	2, 3	Plenary 2
	Name and give the chemical symbol of the first 20 elements in the periodic table.	End of chapter 3	Main 1, Plenary 1
Aiming for GRADE 8 ↓	Use chemical symbols of atoms to produce the chemical formulae of a range of elements and compounds.		Plenary 2
	Explain the significance of chemical symbols used in formulae and equations.	6	Main 2, Homework

Maths
Students identify patterns in element properties and sort the elements into groups to build their own version of a periodic table.

Literacy
Students research the alternative names of the groups of the periodic table.

Key words
atom, element, periodic table, group, compound, electron, nucleus

4

C1 Atomic structure

Starter	Support/Extend	Resources
Thumbs up or thumbs down? (5 minutes) Ask students to put their thumbs up if they think a statement is true, and thumbs down if they think a statement is false. • There are 1000 elements. *False* • All substances are made of atoms. *True* • Compounds are listed on the periodic table. *False* • Sulfur is a compound. *False* • Sodium is an element. *True* • An element contains only one type of atom. *True* **Thought shower** (10 minutes) Write the word atom on the board. Ask students to work in small groups to write as many facts as they can think of about atoms. Then invite each group to write one fact on the class thought shower. Look at the board and state how many misconceptions are written and through question and answer correct all the statements.	**Extend:** Ask students to correct the false statements.	

Main	Support/Extend	Resources
Arranging the elements (30 minutes) In small groups, give students the activity sheet with partially-completed information cards on a selection of elements – sodium, argon, gold, chlorine, potassium, neon, lithium, fluorine, hydrogen, carbon, oxygen, and bromine. Students complete the information cards and find as many ways as they can to group the elements. Ask students if they can find the symbols for each of the elements in the sample. Ask students to consider the basic structure of the atoms that make up elements, as in Figure 4 in the student book, and to speculate how the atoms of different elements might differ.	**Support:** Give students completed information cards of each element. **Extend:** Ask students to research the origin of any symbols that cannot be derived from the English name of the element.	**Activity:** Arranging the elements
Hydrogen, oxygen, and water (10 minutes) Have two bunged test tubes of hydrogen, two bunged test tubes of oxygen, and two bunged test tubes of water, all labelled with their contents. Wearing eye protection, put a glowing splint into each sample. Note observations (oxygen: splint re-lights, hydrogen: no effect, water: splint goes out). Repeat with a lighted splint (oxygen: splint burns slightly brighter, hydrogen: a squeaky pop is heard, water: splint goes out). Ask students to suggest how the properties of the elements relate to the compound that they make (no relation). Ask students to draw particle models to show hydrogen, oxygen, and water.	**Support:** Give students particle models that they can copy. **Extend:** Ask students to write a word or balanced chemical equation for making water from its elements. (hydrogen + oxygen → water $2H_2 + O_2 \rightarrow 2H_2O$)	

Plenary	Support/Extend	Resources
Show-me boards (5 minutes) Give students an A4 dry-wipe board, pen, and eraser. Ask students to write the correct symbol for one of the first 20 elements, or the symbol of one of the named elements you call out.	**Support:** Give students a simplified periodic table, with only some of the symbol tiles with information in.	
Atoms (10 minutes) Interactive where students label a periodic table then summarise the difference between atoms, elements, and compounds. Encourage students to give examples of elements and compounds.	**Extend:** Students include chemical formulae of the elements and compounds.	**Interactive:** Atoms

Homework		
Ask students to draw a particle model and word equation to show carbon, C, reacting with oxygen, O_2, to make carbon dioxide, CO_2. Students should identify the elements and compound in this reaction.	**Support:** Supply information as a cut and stick exercise. **Extend:** Ask students to write a balanced symbol equation with state symbols. ($C(s) + O_2(g) \rightarrow CO_2(g)$)	

C1.2 Chemical equations

AQA spec Link: 1.1.1 Chemical reactions can be represented by word equations or equations using symbols and formulae.

2.2.2 In chemical equations, the three states of matter are shown as (s), (l), and (g), with (aq) for aqueous solutions.

Students should be able to include appropriate state symbols in chemical equations for the reactions in this specification.

3.1.1 The law of conservation of mass states that no atoms are lost or made during a chemical reaction so the mass of the products equals the mass of the reactants.

This means that chemical reactions can be represented by symbol equations which are balanced in terms of the numbers of atoms of each element involved on both sides of the equation.

Students should understand the use of the multipliers in equations in normal script before a formula and in subscript within a formula.

3.1.3 Some reactions may appear to involve a change in mass but this can usually be explained because a reactant or product is a gas and its mass has not been taken into account. For example: when a metal reacts with oxygen the mass of the oxide produced is greater than the mass of the metal or in thermal decompositions of metal carbonates carbon dioxide is produced and escapes into the atmosphere leaving the metal oxide as the only solid product.

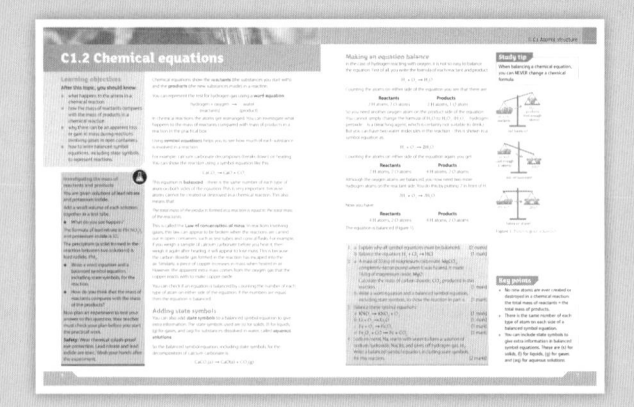

WS 1.2

Aiming for	Outcome	Checkpoint	
		Question	Activity
Aiming for GRADE 4 ↓	Describe familiar chemical reactions in word equations.	2	Main 1, Main 2
	State that mass is conserved in a chemical reaction.		Starter 1, Main 1, Main 2
Aiming for GRADE 6 ↓	Explain why mass is conserved in a chemical reaction.	1	Main 1
	Describe familiar chemical reactions with balanced symbol equations including state symbols.	2	Main 1, Main 2, Plenary 1, Plenary 2
	Balance given symbol equations.	1, 3, End of chapter 4	Starter 2, Plenary 2
Aiming for GRADE 8 ↓	Justify in detail how mass may appear to change in a chemical reaction.		Starter 1
	Describe unfamiliar chemical reactions with more complex balanced symbol equations, including state symbols.	4	Plenary 2
	Write balanced symbol equations.	4	Plenary 1, Homework

Maths
Students balance equations.

Literacy
Students write the steps for how to balance an equation.

Key words
reactants, products, word equation, balanced equation, law of the conservation of mass, state symbol, aqueous solution, precipitate

6

C1 Atomic structure

Practical

Title	Investigating the mass of reactants and products
Equipment	test tube, test-tube rack, test-tube bung, two dropping pipettes, splash-proof eye protection, potassium iodide solution, and lead nitrate solution, filter funnel, clamp stand and clamp, filter paper, watch glass, access to drying oven.
Overview of method	Place the test tube in the rack. Using a dropping pipette, add about 3 cm depth of potassium iodide solution to the test tube. Using the second dropping pipette add a similar volume of lead nitrate. The colourless solutions will form a yellow precipitate of lead iodide. This can be separated by filtration and dried in a drying oven.
Safety considerations	Wear splash-proof eye protection. Wash hands after the practical. Lead nitrate is toxic. Follow local disposal instructions and keep concentrations below 0.1 mol/dm^3. In case of pregnancy, lead compounds should not be used.

Starter	Support/Extend	Resources
Mass what? (5 minutes) Show students images of different experiments with the equation below the image. Ask students to suggest what happens to the mass and why, for example, iron rusting in an open beaker or a sealed test tube. **Chemical equations** (15 minutes) Use the interactive to revise the state symbols used in a balanced symbol equation. Then explain to students how to balance symbol equations. Students then match a list of reactants from balanced symbol equations with the products formed from the reaction.	**Support:** Ask students to write the word equation. **Extend:** Ask students to add state symbols.	**Interactive:** Chemical equations
Main	**Support/Extend**	**Resources**
Investigating the mass of reactants and products (30 minutes) Allow students to complete the investigation as outlined and get students to record the experiment in the form of word and balanced symbol equations. Then ask students to plan an experiment to investigate how mass changes in a chemical reaction. Once the plan has been checked you may wish to allow the students to complete the activity. **Molymod** (10 minutes) Ask students to make molecular models of hydrogen, chlorine, and hydrogen chloride. Ask them to write a word equation for this reaction that connects all of these chemicals. Explain that atoms are not made or lost in chemical reactions but are re-arranged and this is why symbol equations are balanced. Task students with balancing the atoms by making the appropriate models and then writing equations to represent the reaction.	**Support:** Ask students to verbally describe their plan. **Extend:** Ask students to add state symbols.	**Practical:** Investigating the mass of reactants and products
Plenary	**Support/Extend**	**Resources**
Steps to success (5 minutes) Ask students to write a list of successive steps for balancing an equation. Then to balance an equation using the steps to act as a worked example. **Balancing equations** (10 minutes) Students balance combustion equations of increasing difficulty.	**Support:** Give students the steps and allow them to cut and stick them into the correct order.	
Homework		
Ask students to find out the balanced symbol equation for respiration and photosynthesis.	**Extend:** Ask students to explain how the equations suggest the two processes are related.	

kerboodle

A Kerboodle highlight for this lesson is **Maths skills: Balancing equations**. Refer to the **Content map** on Kerboodle for a full list of resources and assessment.

C1.3 Separating mixtures

AQA spec Link: 1.1.2 A mixture consists of two or more elements or compounds not chemically combined together. The chemical properties of each substance in the mixture are unchanged.

Mixtures can be separated by physical processes such as filtration, crystallisation, and simple distillation. These physical processes do not involve chemical reactions.

Students should be able to:
- describe, explain, and give examples of the specified processes of separation
- suggest suitable separation and purification techniques for mixtures when given appropriate information.

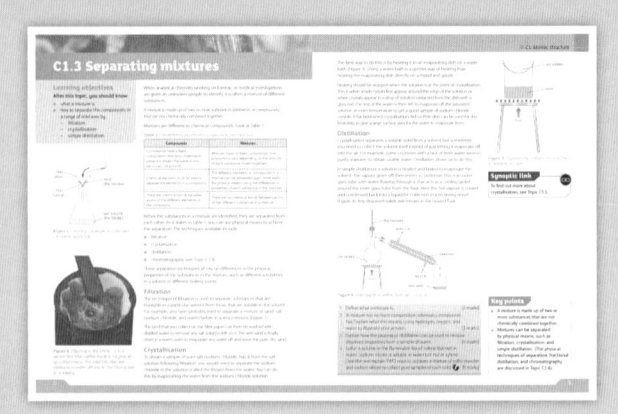

WS 2.2, 2.3
MS 5c

Aiming for	Outcome	Checkpoint	
		Question	Activity
Aiming for GRADE 4 ↓	Define the word mixture.	1, End of chapter 2	
	Identify a mixture and a compound.		Starter 2
	List different separation techniques.		Starter 1, Plenary 1
Aiming for GRADE 6 ↓	Explain the difference between a compound and a mixture.	2, End of chapter 2	Starter 2
	Explain how the chemical properties of a mixture relate to the chemical it is made from.		Main 2, Plenary 2
	Describe different separation techniques.	3, 4, End of chapter 2	Main 1, Plenary 1
Aiming for GRADE 8 ↓	Use experimental data to explain the classification of a substance as a compound or a mixture.		Main 2
	Suggest an appropriate separation or purification technique for an unfamiliar mixture.	4	Main 2, Plenary 2
	Explain in detail how multi-step separation techniques work.	4	Main 2, Plenary 2

Maths
Students explain how surface area affects the rate of filtering (5c).

Literacy
Students generate flow charts to explain how different separation techniques work.

Practical

Title	Sea water
Equipment	'sea water' (a mixture of sodium chloride, water, sand, small plant material), sieve, filter funnel, filter paper, conical flask, round bottom flask, bung with hole, delivery tube, test tube, Bunsen burner, flameproof mat, test-tube rack, stand, boss and clamp, condenser, thermometer, eye protection
Overview of method	Students sieve the water to remove the plant material. Collect the liquid and filter. The sandy residue can be washed by rinsing with distilled water and then dried in a drying oven. Distil the brine to leave the sodium chloride in the round bottom flask and collect pure water in the test tube.
Safety considerations	Do not drink the water. Wear eye protection during the distillation and wash hands after completing the practical.

C1 Atomic structure

Starter	Support/Extend	Resources
Separating mixtures (5 minutes) Use the interactive to show students a list of key words from the lesson and their definitions. Students match them up.	**Extend:** Ask students to write the chemical symbols or formulae for the elements and compounds featured.	**Interactive:** Separating mixtures
Sorting (10 minutes) Ask students to read the student book spread and classify every chemical as an element (hydrogen, oxygen and sulfur), a compound (sand, sodium chloride, salt, water, xylene and sodium nitrate) or a mixture (sand and salt and sea water).		

Main	Support/Extend	Resources
Flow chart (10 minutes) Ask students to write a flow chart to summarise how filtration, crystallisation, and simple distillation can separate a mixture and how to use melting or boiling point to show if a substance is a compound or a mixture.	**Support:** Show students the labelled diagrams of each technique. Encourage students to copy the diagram and then annotate with numbered stages to explain each technique.	
Sea water (30 minutes) Give students a sample of 'sea water' (a mixture of sodium chloride, water, sand, and small plant material). Ask students to use a series of separation techniques to separate out each part of the sea water and leave a sample of water that is safe to drink. Students should summarise their method and results in a table headed with mixture, separation technique, and outcome. Students should NOT drink the water. (Sieve then filter the sea water to remove any insoluble material (sand and plant material). Collect the filtrate solution and distil. Collect the distillate that boils at 100°C as this will be pure water.)	**Extend:** Ask students to write a full method for the purification of sea water, explaining how each step works.	**Practical:** Sea water

Plenary	Support/Extend	Resources
Match (5 minutes) Ask students to match the separation technique to the mixture. • Solution (where the solvent is to be collected) – simple distillation • Solution (where the solute is to be collected) – crystallisation • Insoluble compound from a liquid – filtration	**Extend:** Ask students to suggest a mixture which could be separated by each technique.	
Separation (10 minutes) Ask students to write an outline method of how they would extract carbon from copper sulfate crystals. (Add the mixture to water and filter. The residue is the carbon which could be washed by rinsing with distilled water and then dried in an oven. Evaporate off the water from the filtrate to form copper sulfate crystals.)	**Support:** Show students a sample of each chemical and images to help them determine the key properties. For example, copper sulfate crystals and solution (to show it is soluble) or a carbon block in water (to show it is not soluble).	

Homework		
Provide students with a sample of filter paper and ask them to suggest a method to fold it into a filter funnel to maximise the surface area.	**Extend:** Ask students to explain why fluting filter paper is better than folding it into a cone shape (surface area is maximised and all the paper is the same thickness so the flow rate is maximised and even).	

kerboodle
A Kerboodle highlight for this lesson is **Literacy sheet: Distillation**. Refer to the **Content map** on Kerboodle for a full list of resources and assessment.

C1.4 Fractional distillation and paper chromatography

AQA spec Link: 1.1.2 Mixtures can be separated by physical processes such as fractional distillation and chromatography. These physical processes do not involve chemical reactions.

Students should be able to:
- describe, explain, and give examples of the specified processes of separation
- suggest suitable separation and purification techniques for mixtures when given appropriate information.

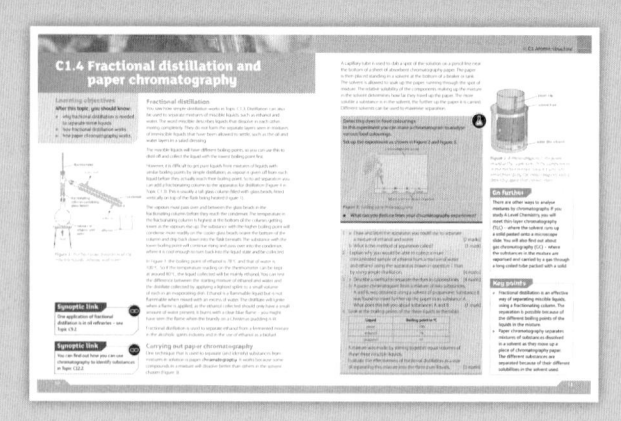

WS 2.2, 2.3

Aiming for	Outcome	Checkpoint	
		Question	Activity
Aiming for GRADE 4 ↓	State when fractional distillation would be used.	1	Main 1
	Safely make a paper chromatogram.		Main 2
Aiming for GRADE 6 ↓	Describe the process of fractional distillation.	1	Main 1
	Explain the main processes occurring in paper chromatography.	3	Main 2
Aiming for GRADE 8 ↓	Explain in detail how fractional distillation can separate miscible liquids with similar boiling points.	4	Main 1, Homework
	Evaluate separation or purification techniques for a given mixture.	4	

Maths
Students interpret chromatograms.

Literacy
Students follow a written method.

Key words
chromatography, biofuel

Practical

Title	Paper chromatography
Equipment	capillary tubes (one per food dye), selection of food dyes, chromatography paper, pencil, ruler, water, beaker, two paper clips, 250 cm³ beaker
Overview of method	Students draw a horizontal pencil line 1 cm from the bottom edge of a rectangular piece of chromatography paper. Put pencil crosses on the line, 1 cm apart and label for each food colouring. Using the capillary tubes, add three drops of each food colouring, allowing a little drying time between each drop, to the separate labelled crosses. Roll the chromatography paper into a cylinder and secure top and bottom with the paper clips. Add about 0.5 cm depth of water in a beaker. Insert the cylinder so that the bottom edge is in the water, but the pencil line is not below the water level. Leave the chromatogram to develop, so that the solvent line is above the dot that has moved the furthest. Remove the paper and uncoil, allow to dry.
Safety considerations	Some students may be allergic to food colouring.

C1 Atomic structure

Starter	Support/Extend	Resources
Key words (5 minutes) Use the interactive to give students the definitions of the key words miscible, condenser, fractionating column, simple distillation, and fractional distillation and ask them to suggest the key words.		**Interactive:** Key words
Distillation (10 minutes) Ask students to explain the use of distillation and how it works. Ask a few students to share their ideas.	**Support:** Ask students to work in small groups to generate the answer.	

Main	Support/Extend	Resources
Fractional distillation (25 minutes) Show students the equipment for fractional distillation and, if possible, demonstrate the separation of ethanol from water. Ask students to draw a diagram of the equipment and label each piece of equipment with its function and explain what is occurring. For example, round bottom flask containing the mixture of water and ethanol. Antibumping granules are added to ensure smooth boiling.	**Support:** Project a diagram of the equipment used in this experiment. Use question and answer to build up the labels as a class and allow students to record them on to their notes. **Extend:** Ask students to suggest how fractional distillation can be used to separate the gases in air. (Air must be cooled so that it liquefies, then fractional distillation can be used to separate the oxygen and nitrogen.)	
Paper chromatography (15 minutes) Ask students to complete a paper chromatogram as detailed in the practical box.	**Extend:** Ask students to suggest how a chromatogram could be used to identify a chemical and also separate a mixture.	**Practical:** Paper chromatography

Plenary	Support/Extend	Resources
Interpreting (5 minutes) Give students a chromatogram to study. Ask them to suggest which chemicals are pure (only have one spot), are mixtures (have more than one spot), contain x dyes (have x spots), contain the same dyes (spots rise to the same height above the baseline).	**Extend:** Show students chromatograms which have not developed correctly and ask them to evaluate the experiment (e.g., could have put the solvent above the baseline).	
Reflection (10 minutes) Ask students to think about one fact or skill that they revised in the lesson, and one that they have learnt. Encourage a few students to share their thoughts.	**Support:** Reinforce the learning outcomes and key points from the student book with a small group of students.	

Homework		
Explain how a condenser works. This should be a step-by-step logical explanation and include a fully labelled diagram to illustrate their prose.	**Extend:** Ask students to find out how bubble caps work in a fractionating column.	

kerboodle

A Kerboodle highlight for this lesson is **Literacy skills: Distillation**. Refer to the **Content map** on Kerboodle for a full list of resources and assessment.

C1.5 History of the atom

AQA spec Link: 1.1.3 New experimental evidence may lead to a scientific model being changed or replaced.

Before the discovery of the electron atoms were thought to be tiny spheres that could not be divided.

The discovery of the electron lead to the plum-pudding model of the atom. The plum-pudding model suggested that the atom was a ball of positive charge with negative electrons embedded in it.

The results from the alpha scattering experiments of Geiger and Marsden led to the plum-pudding model being replaced by the nuclear model.

Neils Bohr adapted the nuclear model by suggesting that electrons orbit the nucleus at specific distances. The theoretical calculations of Bohr agreed with experimental observations.

Later experiments led to the idea that the positive charge of any nucleus could be subdivided into a whole number of smaller particles, each particle having the same amount of positive charge. The name proton was given to these particles.

In 1932 the experimental work of James Chadwick provided the evidence to show the existence of neutrons within the nucleus.

Students should be able to:
- describe why the new evidence from the scattering experiment led to a change in the atomic model
- describe the difference between the plum-pudding model of the atom and the nuclear model of the atom.

Details of experimental work supporting the Bohr model are not required.

Details of alpha particle scattering experiments are not required.

Details of Chadwick's experimental work are not required.

WS 1.1, 1.2, 1.6

Aiming for	Outcome	Checkpoint	
		Question	Activity
Aiming for GRADE 4 ↓	List the significant models proposed for atoms.		Main 1, Main 2
	Identify the key parts of the plum-pudding model and the nuclear model of the atom.		Starter 1, Main 1, Main 2
Aiming for GRADE 6 ↓	Describe the differences between the plum-pudding model and the nuclear model of the atom.	2, 3	Main 1, Main 2, Homework
	Explain how evidence from scattering experiments changed the model of the atom.		Plenary 2
Aiming for GRADE 8 ↓	Justify why the model of the atom has changed over time.	4	Main 2, Plenary 2
	Evaluate the current model of an atom.		Main 2

C1 Atomic structure

Literacy
Students write a letter as a historical scientist about their contribution to the development of the theory of the structure of an atom.

Key words
electron, nucleus, proton, neutron

Starter	Support/Extend	Resources
Diagram (10 minutes) Show students a diagram of the nuclear model of the atom. Ask students to copy the diagram and label the key parts. **Crossword** (10 minutes) Ask students to complete a crossword for the key words that they are to use in this topic.	**Support:** Ask students to refer to Figure 4 in Topic C1.1 of the student book.	

Main	Support/Extend	Resources
Letter (20 minutes) Split the class into five groups and give them a scientist from Dalton, Thomson, Rutherford, Bohr, and Chadwick. Ask students to write a letter as one of the famous scientists to explain what they have discovered and how they think this affects the model of the atom. You may wish to 'age' the paper using used tea bags, or singe the edges with a candle flame.	**Support:** Give students the following writing frame for a letter: • Introduction – quick summary of what they think they've discovered • What their experiment was • What their results were • What they think this tells you about the atom • Conclusion	
Developing the atomic model (20 minutes) Ask students to make a timeline to show the development of the atomic model. They should include a labelled diagram of the model, the name of the scientist who suggested it, and the date.	**Extend:** Ask students to explain what evidence was collected and how it was used to generate the model.	**Activity:** Developing the atomic model

Plenary	Support/Extend	Resources
History of the atom (10 minutes) Interactive where students match the scientist with their discovery then complete a paragraph on how the atom was discovered.		**Interactive:** History of the atom
Evidence (10 minutes) Ask students to summarise where the evidence for the nuclear model has come from. • Electron – high voltage experiments on gases. • Nucleus – alpha (positively charge) radiation reflected by gold foil (showing a positive, dense centre to the atom). • Electron shells – light given out by heated atoms had specific energy. • Neutrons – explained the different masses of elements. Experimental evidence was not found until the early 1930s.	**Support:** Ask students to match up the model with the evidence.	

Homework		
Students complete the WebQuest where they research the changes in evidence that led to changes in the model of the atom. Alternatively, ask students to finish off the following sentences: The plum-pudding model and nuclear model are similar because… The plum-pudding model and nuclear model are different because…	**Support:** Give students some incomplete statements for them to complete and sort.	**WebQuest:** Models of the atom over time

C1.6 Structure of the atom

AQA spec Link: 1.1.4 The relative electrical charges of the particles in atoms are:

Name of particle	Relative charge
proton	+1
neutron	0
electron	−1

In an atom, the number of electrons is equal to the number of protons in the nucleus. Atoms have no overall electrical charge.

The number of protons in an atom of an element is its atomic number. All atoms of a particular element have the same number of protons. Atoms of different elements have different numbers of protons.

Students should be able to use the nuclear model to describe atoms.

1.1.5 Almost all of the mass of an atom is in the nucleus.

The relative masses of protons, neutrons, and electrons are:

Name of particle	Mass
proton	1
neutron	1
electron	very small

The sum of the protons and neutrons in an atom is its mass number.

WS 1.2
MS 1d

Aiming for	Outcome	Checkpoint	
		Question	Activity
Aiming for GRADE 4 ↓	State the relative charges and masses of sub-atomic particles.	1	Starter 2
	State that atoms have no overall charge (are neutral).		Starter 2, Plenary 1
	Label the sub-atomic particles on a diagram of a helium atom.		Starter 1
Aiming for GRADE 6 ↓	Describe atoms using the atomic model.	End of chapter 1	Main 2
	Explain why atoms have no overall charge.	3, End of chapter 1	Main 2
	Use atomic number and mass numbers of familiar atoms to determine the number of each sub-atomic particle.	4, End of chapter 1	Main 1
Aiming for GRADE 8 ↓	Use the periodic table to find atomic number and mass number data and use it to determine the number of each sub-atomic particle in any given atom.	4, End of chapter 3	Main 1
	Recognise and describe patterns in sub-atomic particles of elements listed in the periodic table.	2	Main 1
	Explain why we can be confident that there are no missing elements in the first 10 elements of the periodic table.		Main 1

C1 Atomic structure

Maths
Students use atomic number and mass number for elements to calculate the number of each sub-atomic particle.

Literacy
Students evaluate a model of an atom.

Key words
proton, neutron, electron, atomic number, mass number

Starter	Support/Extend	Resources
Explain (10 minutes) Ask students to work in pairs: one person verbally describes the nuclear model of the atom; the second person tries to draw the diagram. Then hold up the diagrams to show the class and vote on the best one and why. **Prose** (10 minutes) Give students the excerpt from the specification as detailed, but with the key words missing. Ask students to copy and complete the prose.	**Extend:** Ask students to describe and draw both the plum-pudding model and the nuclear model. **Support:** Give students a list of the missing words to select from.	

Main	Support/Extend	Resources
Table (20 minutes) Ask students to draw a table for the first 10 elements with the following column titles: Element, Symbol, Atomic number, Number of protons, Number of electrons, Number of neutrons. Demonstrate how to complete this for lithium and then encourage students to use the periodic table in the student book to complete the table. Students should then add another column titled "Mass number" and use their table to complete this column. **Model of an atom** (20 minutes) Students create a model of an atom of either ^{4}He, ^{7}Li, ^{12}C, ^{19}F, ^{16}O, or ^{23}Na. Students should add mass and charge information and label the nucleus. They should then evaluate their models.	**Support:** Provide a partially completed table for students to complete. **Extend:** Ask students to explain why we can be confident that there are no missing elements in the first 10 elements of the periodic table. **Extend:** Ask students to annotate information which explains why an atom has no charge, how an alpha particle can pass through an atom, and why electrons orbit a nucleus.	**Activity:** Model of an atom

Plenary	Support/Extend	Resources
Atomic structure (5 minutes) Interactive where students label an atom then complete sentences on protons, neutrons, and electrons. **Think, pair, square** (10 minutes) Ask students to think about the most important fact or skill they have learnt today. Then ask them to compare and agree with a neighbour and finally as a whole table. Get each table to report back to the class.	**Support:** Show students a list of the lesson objectives to help them remember what they have covered in the lesson.	**Interactive:** Atomic structure

Homework		
Ask students to complete the following: • List the symbols of three elements which have the same number of protons as neutrons in the atom. • Give the symbol of an element that does not have a neutron in the nucleus.	**Support:** Give a list of elements to choose from. **Extend:** Ask students to determine the number of each sub-atomic particle in the elements that they have chosen.	

kerboodle
A Kerboodle highlight for this lesson is **Literacy skills: More about atoms**. Refer to the **Content map** on Kerboodle for a full list of resources and assessment.

C1.7 Ions, atoms, and isotopes

AQA spec Link: 1.1.5 Atoms are very small, having a radius of about 0.1 nm (1×10^{-10} m).

The radius of a nucleus is less than 1/10 000 of that of the atom (about 1×10^{-14} m).

Almost all of the mass of an atom is in the nucleus.

Atoms of the same element can have different numbers of neutrons; these atoms are called isotopes of that element.

Atoms can be represented as shown in this example:

(mass number) $^{23}_{11}$Na
(atomic number)

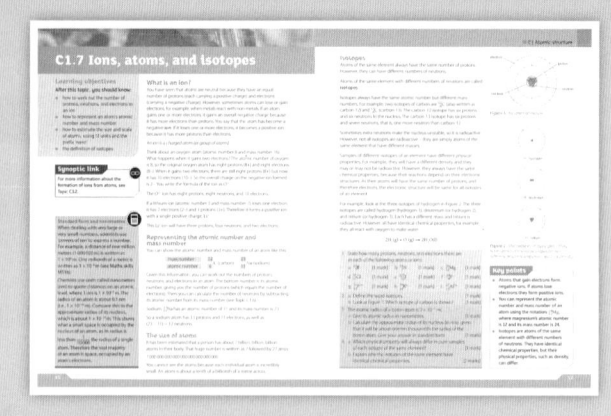

WS 4.3, 4
MS 1b

Aiming for	Outcome	Checkpoint	
		Question	Activity
Aiming for GRADE 4	State what an ion is.		Starter 1, Main 1
	Define an isotope.	2	Starter 1, Main 1, Plenary 1
	State the relative sizes of an atom and its nucleus.		Starter 2
Aiming for GRADE 6	Describe isotopes using the atomic model.	2, 4, End of chapter 4	Main 1
	Explain why ions have a charge.	2, End of chapter 1	Main 2
	Use atomic number and mass numbers of familiar ions to determine the number of each sub-atomic particle.	2, End of chapter 4	Main 2
Aiming for GRADE 8	Use the periodic table to find atomic number and use it to determine the number of each sub-atomic particle in an ion.	End of chapter 4	Main 2
	Use SI units and prefixes to describe the size of an atom and its nucleus in standard form.	3	Starter 2

Maths
Students calculate the number of each sub-atomic particle in atoms or ions. Students use standard form when writing quantities (1b).

Literacy
Students create a flow chart to explain how to determine the sub-atomic particles in atoms, ions, and isotopes.

Key words
isotope

C1 Atomic structure

Starter	Support/Extend	Resources
Definitions (5 minutes) Ask students to use the student book to define the following key words: • Ion – charged atom or molecule. • Isotope – an atom with the same number of protons but a different number of neutrons. • Atom – the smallest particle that can exist on its own. **Size** (10 minutes) Give students a selection of images and sizes, using SI units and prefixes. Ask students to group the information. For example: • electron microscope image of gold atoms, 0.1 nm, 1×10^{-10} m • alpha radiation, helium nuclei, 1/10 000 of an atom, 1×10^{-14} m. Using question and answer, ensure that students appreciate that electron microscopes can capture images of single atoms and that atoms are very small.	**Extend:** Ask students to give an example for each key word. **Support:** Give students a number line to give the idea of small and large in terms of SI units.	

Main	Support/Extend	Resources
Hydrogen isotopes (20 minutes) Show the atomic models of the three isotopes of hydrogen. Add information about the size of the radius of the atoms and the nuclei. Ask students to list the similarities (number of electrons, number of protons, electron arrangement, same atomic number, same atomic radius) and differences (number of neutrons, mass number). Then show students how to use the convention to detail atomic number, mass number, and symbol of an element for one isotope and ask them to draw it for the other isotopes. Students could then complete the Maths skills interactive for further practice in calculating the number of sub-atomic particles in atoms and ions. **Ideas about ions** (20 minutes) Ask students to make a flow chart to explain how you can use the atomic number and mass number to determine the sub-atomic particles in an ion. Then ask students to swap their flow charts with another student and they should use it to determine the sub-atomic particles in a variety of examples given on the activity sheet. Develop the flow chart by adding additional branches to explain how to determine the sub-atomic particles in a negative ion, positive ion, and an isotope.	**Extend:** Ask students to draw the atomic structure of helium isotopes and write the symbol with mass and atomic number detailed. **Support:** Give students the diagrams. Students can be given the list of similarities and differences, then using highlighters they can highlight in green the similarities and in pink the differences.	**Maths skills:** Ions and atoms **Activity:** Ideas about ions

Plenary	Support/Extend	Resources
Example (5 minutes) Show students the definitions of the key words and ask them to give an example to illustrate the key word. • An atom with the same number of protons but a different number of neutrons (isotope – hydrogen, deuterium, and tritium). • A charged atom (ion, e.g., O^{2-}). • A sub-atomic particle found in the nucleus of most atoms (neutron). **Ions, atoms, and isotopes** (10 minutes) Interactive where students identify the mass number and atomic number of lithium, oxygen, and sodium. They then complete a paragraph on isotopes.	**Support:** Give students a table headed – key word, definition, example and ask them to match up the pieces of information.	**Interactive:** Ions, atoms, and isotopes

Homework		
Ask students to draw and complete a table for the three carbon isotopes detailing the symbol and number of each sub-atomic particle.	**Extend:** Ask students to find out what property carbon-14 has and how it is used in archaeology.	

kerboodle

A Kerboodle highlight for this lesson is **Support: All about atoms**. Refer to the **Content map** on Kerboodle for a full list of resources and assessment.

C1.8 Electronic structures

AQA spec Link: 1.1.6 The electrons in an atom occupy the lowest available energy levels (innermost available shells). The electronic structure of an atom can be represented by numbers or by a diagram. For example, the electronic structure of sodium is 2,8,1 or

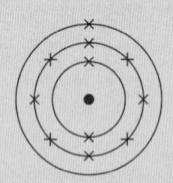

showing two electrons in the lowest energy level, eight in the second energy level, and one in the third energy level.

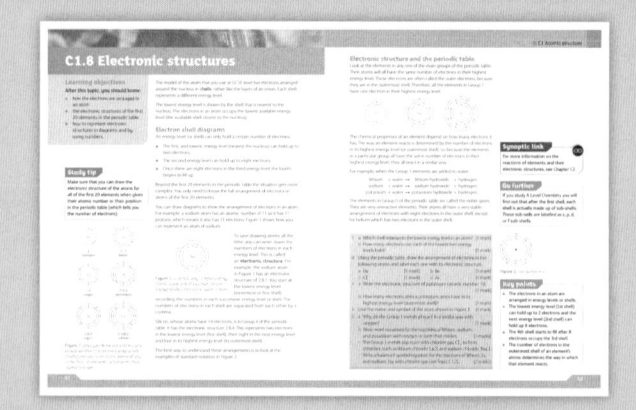

Aiming for	Outcome	Checkpoint	
		Question	Activity
Aiming for GRADE 4 ↓	State that electrons are found in energy levels of an atom.		Starter 2
	State the maximum number of electrons in the first three energy levels.	1	Starter 2
Aiming for GRADE 6 ↓	Write the standard electronic configuration notation from a diagram for the first 20 elements.		Main, Plenary 1
	Explain why elements in the same group react in a similar way.	5	Main
Aiming for GRADE 8 ↓	Use the periodic table to find atomic number and determine the electronic structure for the first 20 elements.	2, 3	Main, Plenary 1
	Make predictions for how an element will react when given information on another element in the same group.	5	Main

Maths
Students work out the number of electrons in each shell for a range of atoms.

Literacy
Students write a step-by-step guide, explaining how to work out the electronic structure of an element.

Key words
shells, electronic structure, noble gases

C1 Atomic structure

Starter	Support/Extend	Resources
Element bingo (5 minutes) As students enter the room give them each an element name written down on a piece of paper. Then ask questions and if their element answers the question they should hold up their piece of paper. For example: • Is it a liquid at room temperature (Hg and Br)? • Is it a Group 1 metal (Li, Na, K, Rb, Cs, Fr)? • Is it the element that has eight protons (O)?	**Extend:** Give students only the symbol of the element. **Support:** Give students a symbol tile from the periodic table.	
Label (10 minutes) Show students a diagram of an argon atom and ask them to label each sub-atomic particle. Explain that noble gases such as argon have very stable electronic structures. Then ask students to suggest how many electrons can fit in each electron shell (2,8,8).	**Extend:** Ask students to draw the structures of helium and neon using argon to help them.	

Main	Support/Extend	Resources
Electronic structures (40 minutes) Demonstrate how to build the electronic structure of an argon atom. Students then draw the electronic structures of lithium, carbon, neon, magnesium, fluorine, and chlorine. They then write a step-by-step guide, explaining how to work out the electronic structure of an element. Explain that the GCSE model breaks down after the 20th element. Encourage students to draw an outline of the periodic table for the first 20 elements, including the electronic structure of the first 20 elements in the diagram. Ask students to find a pattern between electronic structure and group number (or period number (number of electron shells)).	**Support:** Give students the diagrams to cut and stick into the correct places. **Support:** Ask students to complete Atomic structure worksheet, which gives students practice at extracting information about atoms from the periodic table. **Extend:** Introduce students to how the electrons are arranged in the sub-shells.	**Activity:** Electronic structure

Plenary	Support/Extend	Resources
Name that element (5 minutes) Give students the electronic structures and ask them to write the element that each represents. • 2 (He) • 2,1 (Li) • 2,8,8 (Ar) • 2,2 (Be) • 2,4 (C)	**Support:** Encourage students to use their diagrams from the main part of the lesson to help them.	
Electronic structures (10 minutes) Students summarise their learning from the lesson by using the interactive to complete sentences on electrons and the electron arrangement of chlorine and nitrogen.	**Support:** Give students the page references of the student book where they can find the information to help them answer the questions.	**Interactive:** Electronic structures

Homework		
Explain that chlorine has two isotopes – chlorine-35 and chlorine-37. Ask students to draw the electronic structure of both (2,8,7) and explain any differences in the electronic structures (none).		

kerboodle

A Kerboodle highlight for this lesson is **Go further: Sub-shells**. Refer to the **Content map** on Kerboodle for a full list of resources and assessment.

C1 Atomic structure

Overview of C1 Atomic structure

In this chapter, students have developed their understanding of atoms as fundamental chemical building blocks. They have seen how to interpret chemical formulae and extended their KS3 knowledge of the law of the conservation of mass, leading them to balance chemical equations. It is important that they understand that when balancing an equation, the formula of the substance must not change.

Students also develop their understanding of the differences between compounds and mixtures, and how mixtures can be separated using techniques such as filtration, crystallisation, distillation, and chromatography.

Finally, students learnt about the development of the atomic model, providing ample opportunity to foster their Working scientifically skills – specifically around the development and use of models within science. Students should be able to describe the evidence that lead to each new stage in the development of the atomic model. Studying the development of the atomic model should have led into the model currently accepted for GCSE, and students should be able to use this to write and draw electronic structures up to element 20.

MyMaths

You can find additional support for the maths skills covered in this chapter on **MyMaths**, including using standard form.

kerboodle

For this chapter, the following assessments are available on Kerboodle:

C1 Checkpoint quiz: Atomic structure
C1 Progress quiz: Atomic structure 1
C1 Progress quiz: Atomic structure 2
C1 On your marks: Atomic structure
C1 Exam-style questions and mark scheme: Atomic structure

Checkpoint follow up lesson

A student's route through this lesson can be determined using the Checkpoint assessment. Percentage pass marks are supplied in the Checkpoint teacher notes.

For each successive route through it is assumed that the student can perform to their current route as well as previous routes. For example, students working at Aiming for 6 are assumed to be secure in Aiming for 4 knowledge and understanding and working towards achieving all the learning outcomes for Aiming for 6.

	Aiming for 4	**Aiming for 6**	**Aiming for 8**
Learning outcomes	Recognise and name elements from their symbols.	Describe what information can be obtained from the periodic table, including the number of protons, neutrons, and electrons in atoms and the electronic structure of atoms.	Explain how the periodic table links to electronic structures of atoms.
	Describe the structure of an atom including the key properties of protons, neutrons, and electrons.	Explain how mass is conserved during reactions.	
	Describe the difference between compounds and mixtures, including how mixtures can be separated using filtration.	Describe reactions using word equations and simple balanced symbol equations.	Describe in detail how to balance symbol equations, including state symbols.

Starter

Quick-fire quiz (5 minutes)
Play a quick-fire quiz on the periodic table. Provide students with copies of the periodic table. Quiz questions should include asking for symbols for named elements, asking for element names from symbols, asking for numbers of electrons/protons/neutrons, definitions of group, period, isotope, asking for electronic structures. For Aiming for 4 students, focus on the first 20 elements of the periodic table. For Aiming for 6 and Aiming for 8 students, choose elements from the rest of the periodic table for them to name and find the symbols of and number of atomic particles. Do not ask for electronic structures of elements after the first 20 for any students.

Magnesium and oxygen (5 minutes)
Demonstrate the reaction between magnesium and oxygen by burning a small piece of magnesium ribbon in a Bunsen flame (appropriate safety precautions should be taken, including reminding students not to look directly at the flame). Ask students to give the word equation for the reaction. Write this on the board and then lead into discussing where reactants and products are found within an equation, writing a balanced symbol equation, and the concept of conservation of mass – which would be greater, the mass of magnesium reacted or magnesium oxide produced? Why?

Differentiated checkpoint activity

Aiming for 4 students use the Checkpoint follow-up sheet to produce a poster. The Aiming for 4 Checkpoint follow-up sheet provides structured tasks to support students with revising and summarising the information to include on their poster.	Aiming for 6 students use the Checkpoint follow-up sheet to produce a poster. The Aiming for 6 Checkpoint follow-up sheet provides students with questions to guide the content they include on their poster.	Aiming for 8 students use the Checkpoint follow-up sheet to produce a poster. The Aiming for 8 Checkpoint follow-up sheet provides fewer prompt questions and they cover more advanced content.
Students will need to be provided with the apparatus for filtering a mixture of sand and water and supported in carrying out this practical.		

Kerboodle resource Checkpoint follow up: Aiming for 4, C1 Checkpoint follow up: Aiming for 6, C1 Checkpoint follow up: Aiming for 8

Plenary

Poster review (5 minutes)
Ask students to lay their posters around the room. Students should then choose another person's poster to review. They should read the other person's poster and decide on two strong points about the poster and one point that could be improved on.

Revision (5 minutes)
Ask students to decide as a pair three key learning points from the chapter. Review these as a class. Address any misconceptions should they arise.

Progression

Students should identify the key points being covered in each task. Encourage them to write the key point as a question they then answer on their poster.	Provide students with a more challenging reaction, such as the complete combustion of decane from the Aiming for 8 Checkpoint follow-up.	Encourage students to balance more complicated symbol equations, such as the reactions of aluminium oxide with water and sodium hydroxide, including state symols.

C 2 The periodic table
2.1 Development of the periodic table

AQA spec Link: 1.2.1 The elements in the periodic table are arranged in order of atomic (proton) number and so that elements with similar properties are in columns, known as groups.

1.2.2 Before the discovery of protons, neutrons, and electrons, scientists attempted to classify the elements by arranging them in order of their atomic weights.

The early periodic tables were incomplete and some elements were placed in inappropriate groups if the strict order of atomic weights was followed.

Mendeleev overcame some of the problems by leaving gaps for elements that he thought had not been discovered and in some places changed the order based on atomic weights.

Elements with properties predicted by Mendeleev were discovered and filled the gaps. Knowledge of isotopes made it possible to explain why the order based on atomic weights was not always correct.

Students should be able to describe these steps in the development of the periodic table.

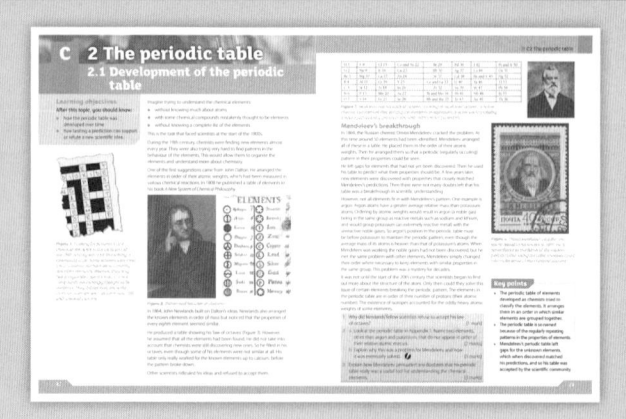

WS 1.1, 1.6

Aiming for	Outcome	Checkpoint	
		Question	Activity
Aiming for GRADE 4 ↓	List the significant models for ordering the elements.		Main 1, Main 2
	State how the elements are ordered in the periodic table.	End of chapter 1	Starter 1, Main 1, Main 2
Aiming for GRADE 6 ↓	Describe how the elements are arranged in groups and periods in the periodic table.		Main 1, Main 2
	Explain why the periodic table was a breakthrough in how to order elements.		Main 1, Main 2
Aiming for GRADE 8 ↓	Explain how and why the ordering of the elements has changed over time.	End of chapter 5	Main 1, Main 2

Maths
Students identify patterns in the periodic table.

Literacy
Students write a newspaper feature on the development and importance of the periodic table. They then appraise their work.

22

C2 The periodic table

Starter	Support/Extend	Resources
Geography of the periodic table (5 minutes) Students draw an outline of the periodic table and label metals, non-metals, alkali metals, halogens, transition metals, noble gases, group numbers, and period numbers.	**Support:** Show the outline on a board and use question and answer to build up the labelled diagram as a class. **Extend:** Ask students to highlight the metalloids.	
What I know table (10 minutes) Ask students to draw a table with three columns – what I know, what I want to know, and what I know now. Ask students to fill in the first column with bullet points about what they already know about the periodic table and in the second column, questions that they would like to have answered in the lesson.	**Support:** Ask students to work in small groups, with a higher ability student in each group to help support the team.	

Main	Support/Extend	Resources
The development of the periodic table (20 minutes) Students use secondary resources including the student book and the Internet to make a timeline to show how the elements were ordered in different ways. The timeline should include dates, the scientist who proposed the idea, and an outline of the idea (an image if available).	**Support:** Give students the information as a cut and stick activity. **Extend:** Ask students to explain why each model was replaced.	**Activity:** The development of the periodic table
Newspaper article (20 minutes) Students write a newspaper feature article to explain the development and importance of the periodic table.	**Support:** Give students questions to help structure their article. For example: • Introduction: what is the periodic table? • What were the problems with the first periodic tables? • How did Mendeleev's periodic table solve these? • Why is the periodic table important?	

Plenary	Support/Extend	Resources
The history of the periodic table (10 minutes) Interactive where students summarise their learning from the lesson by completing sentences on the work of chemists to arrange the elements.	**Support:** Give students some choices of comments that they could use.	**Interactive:** The history of the periodic table
What I know table revisited (10 minutes) Ask students to look back at their table from the starter. In a different colour, make any corrections in the first column, answer the questions in the second column and list any other information they have found out in the lesson in the last column.	**Extend:** Students can ask the teacher or other students any unanswered questions.	

Homework		
Students complete the WebQuest where they research the development of the modern periodic table. Alternatively, students compare Mendeelev's periodic table with the modern periodic table and list any differences.	**Extend:** Ask students to explain why the differences have occurred, for example, Group 0 are unreactive and Mendeelev did not predict their existence.	**WebQuest:** The early periodic table

kerboodle

A Kerboodle highlight for this lesson is **Extension: Development of the periodic table.** Refer to the **Content map** on Kerboodle for a full list of resources and assessment.

C2.2 Electronic structures and the periodic table

AQA spec Link: 1.2.1 The table is called a periodic table because similar properties occur at regular intervals.

Elements in the same group in the periodic table have the same number of electrons in their outer shell (outer electrons) and this gives them similar chemical properties.

Students should be able to:
- explain how the position of an element in the periodic table is related to the arrangement of electrons in its atoms and hence to its atomic number
- predict possible reactions and probable reactivity of elements from their positions in the periodic table.

1.2.3 Elements that react to form positive ions are metals. Elements that do not form positive ions are non-metals.

The majority of elements are metals. Metals are found to the left and towards the bottom of the periodic table. Non-metals are found towards the right and top of the periodic table.

Students should be able to:
- explain the differences between metals and non-metals on the basis of their characteristic physical and chemical properties.
- explain how the atomic structure of metals and non-metals relates to their position in the periodic table
- explain how the reactions of elements are related to the arrangement of electrons in their atoms and hence to their atomic number.

1.2.4 The elements in Group 0 of the periodic table are called the noble gases. They are unreactive and do not easily form molecules because their atoms have stable arrangements of electrons. The noble gases have eight electrons in their outer shell, except for helium, which only has two electrons. The boiling points of the noble gases increase with increasing relative atomic mass (going down the group).

Students should be able to:
- explain how properties of the elements in Group 0 depend on the outer shell of electrons of the atoms
- predict properties from given trends down the group.

WS 1.2

Aiming for	Outcome	Checkpoint	
		Question	Activity
Aiming for GRADE 4 ↓	Define a group and period in the periodic table.	1	Main
	Describe how electronic structure is linked to the periodic table.		Main
	State that noble gases are unreactive.		Main
Aiming for GRADE 6 ↓	Describe how the electronic structure of metals and non-metals are different.	2	Main
	Explain in terms of electronic structure how the elements are arranged in the periodic table.		Main
	Explain why the noble gases are unreactive and the trend in their boiling points.	5	Main
Aiming for GRADE 8 ↓	Explain how the electronic structure of metals and non-metals affects their reactivity.	4, End of chapter 6	Main
	Use the periodic table to make predictions about the electronic structure and reactions of elements.	5, End of chapter 3	Plenary 1
	Predict the electronic structure of stable ions for the first 20 elements.		Plenary 1

Maths
Students write the electronic structure and find patterns.

Literacy
Students write concise annotations describing the features of the periodic table.

24

C2 The periodic table

Starter	Support/Extend	Resources
The modern periodic table (10 minutes) Introduce the periodic table and how elements in the same group within the periodic table have similar properties. Students summarise the arrangement of elements in the periodic table, then identify some simple properties of groups of the periodic table.		**Interactive:** The modern periodic table
Diagrams (10 minutes) Ask students to draw the electronic structures of lithium, sodium, and potassium. Ask students what they all have in common and how their electronic structures relate to their position in the periodic table.	**Support:** Give students the electronic structures in notation form as reference.	

Main	Support/Extend	Resources
Electron structures and the periodic table (40 minutes) Give students a simplified version of the AQA periodic table photocopied onto an A3 sheet of paper, with plenty of space around the periodic table. Ask students to annotate the table to explain how electronic structure relates to position in the periodic table, how predictions of electronic structure can be made, why the noble gases are unreactive, the difference in electronic structures of simple ions of the first 20 elements, and the trend in boiling point of the noble gases. Their annotations should be illustrated with real examples, for example, Group 1 elements all have one electron in their outer shell (e.g., Li 2,1 and Na 2,8,1).	**Support:** Students complete the support worksheet about the modern periodic table to help them with their annotations. **Extend:** Students include annotations on the contributions Mendeleev made to the modern periodic table, including what he got wrong and how it was corrected.	**Activity:** Electron structures and the periodic table **Support:** The modern periodic table

Plenary	Support/Extend	Resources
Electronic structure (5 minutes) Ask students to suggest the symbol of: • positive ions with a 2,8 electron arrangement (Na^+, Mg^{2+}, Al^{3+}) • a neutral atom with a 2,8 electron arrangement (Ne) • negative ions with a 2,8 electron arrangement (F^-, O^{2-}, N^{3-}).	**Extend:** Ask the students to draw a diagram of each species including the number of protons and neutrons in the nucleus and the electronic structure.	
Jeopardy (10 minutes) Ask students to write a set of questions that are answered by each key point. Students should record their questions with the key points as answers in their exercise book.	**Support:** Give students five questions for which they then write the correct key fact that answers each question.	

Homework		
Explain why hydrogen could be considered to be a member of Group 1 (has one electron in the outer shell) or Group 7 (needs one electron to have the stable electronic structure of a noble gas, in this case He).	**Extend:** Students draw the electronic structure of the two ions that hydrogen can make (H^+ and H^-).	

C2.3 Group 1 – the alkali metals

AQA spec Link: 1.2.5 The elements in Group 1 of the periodic table are known as the alkali metals and have characteristic properties because of the single electron in their outer shell.

Students should be able to describe the reactions of the first three alkali metals with oxygen, chlorine, and water.

In Group 1, the reactivity of the elements increases going down the group.

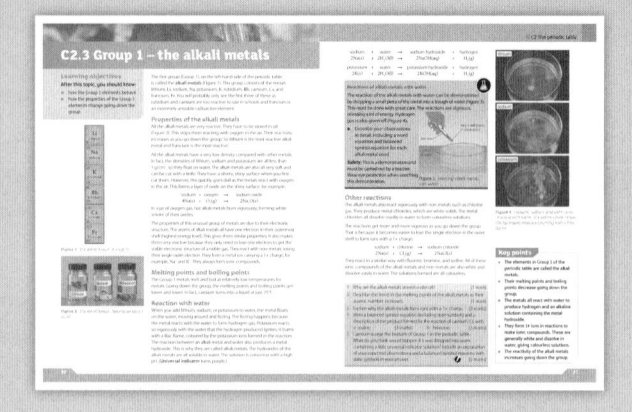

Aiming for	Outcome	Checkpoint	
		Question	Activity
Aiming for GRADE 4	Name the first three elements in Group 1.	End of chapter 1	Starter 1, Starter 2, Main
	Describe the Group 1 metals as having low densities.		Starter 2
	Write word equations from descriptions of how Group 1 metals react with water.		Main
Aiming for GRADE 6	Recognise trends in supplied data.	2, End of chapter 3	Starter 2, Main
	Explain why the elements in Group 1 react similarly and why the first three elements float on water.		Starter 2
	Describe how you can show that hydrogen and metal hydroxides are made when Group 1 metals react with water.		Main
Aiming for GRADE 8	Illustrate the reactions of Group 1 metals with balanced symbol equations.	4, 5	Main
	Explain how Group 1 metals form ions with a +1 charge when they react with non-metals.	3, End of chapter 3, 6	Starter 1
	Justify how Group 1 metals are stored and the safety precautions used when dealing with them.	1	Main

Maths
Students write the electronic structure, balance symbol equations, and plot a bar chart.

Literacy
Students create a visual summary.

Key words
alkali metals, universal indicator

Practical

Title	Reactions of alkali metals with water
Equipment	water trough, water, universal indicator solution, lithium, sodium, potassium, white tile, tweezers, scalpel, filter paper, safety screen, eye protection
Overview of method	Half fill the water trough with water and add enough universal indicator so that the water is clearly coloured green. Cut a small piece of lithium on a white tile and wipe the excess oil off the surface using a piece of filter paper. Using the tweezers, add the metal to the water and observe. Repeat with other Group 1 metals.
Safety considerations	Alkali metals are corrosive and highly flammable. Wear eye protection, including students. Use three screens to enclose trough, protecting students and teacher, with an additional one on the top to stop molten metal spitting over the top. Use no more than 5 mm piece of lithium, 4 mm of sodium, and 3 mm of potassium. Be aware that lithium tends to spit as it reacts with the water. You may wish to wear nitrile gloves. Universal indicator may be flammable.

■ C2 The periodic table

Starter	Support/Extend	Resources
Guess the alkali metal (5 minutes) Ask students to write the symbol of the elements and ions 2,1 (Li), 2,8 (Na$^+$), 2,8,8,1 (K), 2 (Li$^+$), 2,8,1 (Na), and 2,8,8 (K$^+$) **Bar Chart** (10 minutes) Ask students to plot a bar chart to show how the density of Group 1 metals changes as you go down the group. <table><tr><th>Element</th><th>Density in g/cm³</th></tr><tr><td>Li</td><td>0.53</td></tr><tr><td>Na</td><td>0.97</td></tr><tr><td>K</td><td>0.86</td></tr><tr><td>Rb</td><td>1.48</td></tr><tr><td>Cs</td><td>1.87</td></tr></table>	**Support:** Write the electronic structures and symbols onto a board. Have students match the symbol to the electronic structure. **Extend:** Ask students to state the trend in density and to try to explain this in terms of the packing of atoms within their structures and the mass of the atoms.	

Main	Support/Extend	Resources
Reactions of alkali metals with water (30 minutes) Show students the samples of Group 1 metals and explain why they are kept in oil. Demonstrate how easy it is to cut each metal, showing the speed of tarnishing and asking students to suggest how reactivity is changing as you go down the group. Demonstrate the metals reacting with water. You may wish to collect the hydrogen and test it (not with potassium as the hydrogen ignites in the reaction). Students should draw and complete a table with three columns (element, observations, equation). Students should complete the table as the demonstration progresses and reflect on the content using the student book to ensure all key information is recorded.	**Support:** Students should write a word equation for the reactions. **Extend:** Students above Year 9 with careful supervision can put Li into a half-filled 250 cm³ beaker of cold water. It is possible to collect the hydrogen produced by inverting a test tube over the reacting metal.	**Activity:** Reactions of alkali metals with water

Plenary	Support/Extend	Resources
Guess the metal (5 minutes) Ask students to suggest the symbol of: • the metal that floats as a molten ball of metal as it reacts with water – Na • the metal that floats as it reacts with water making a lilac flame – K • the metal that floats on water as it reacts to form LiOH – lithium Li • the gas made when a Group 1 metal reacts with water – hydrogen H$_2$. **Group 1** (10 minutes) Interactive where students summarise the electron arrangements and properties of the Group 1 elements. Students then complete a crossword of the key words from the lesson.	**Extend:** Ask the students to write statements to match the other members of Group 1.	**Interactive:** Group 1

Homework		
Ask students to find out the melting point of the Group 1 metals and draw a scatter graph (atomic number, melting point) and add a trend line.	**Extend:** Students state the trend and try to explain why the melting point changes as you go down the group.	

kerboodle

A Kerboodle highlight for this lesson is **Literacy sheet: Patterns and trends in Group 1**. Refer to the **Content map** on Kerboodle for a full list of resources and assessment.

C2.4 Group 7 – the halogens

AQA spec Link: 1.2.6 The elements in Group 7 of the periodic table are known as the halogens and have similar reactions because they all have seven electrons in their outer shell. The halogens are non-metals and consist of molecules made of pairs of atoms.

Students should be able to describe the nature of the compounds formed when chlorine, bromine, and iodine react with metals and non-metals.

In Group 7, the further down the group an element is the higher its relative molecular mass, melting point, and boiling point.

In Group 7, the reactivity of the elements decreases going down the group.

A more reactive halogen can displace a less reactive halogen from an aqueous solution of its salt.

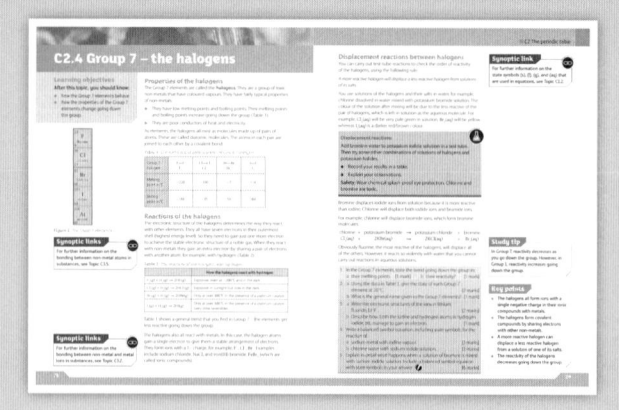

Aiming for	Outcome	Checkpoint	
		Question	Activity
Aiming for GRADE 4	Name the first four elements in Group 7.	2	Starter 2, Main 1, Main 2
	Recognise a halogen displacement reaction.		Main 1
	Describe the main properties of halogens.		Main 2, Plenary 2
Aiming for GRADE 6	Recognise trends in supplied data.	1, 2	
	Explain why the elements in Group 7 react similarly.		Main 2
	Explain how to complete a halogen displacement reaction and explain what happens in the reaction.	5	Main 1
Aiming for GRADE 8	Illustrate the reactions of Group 7 metals with balanced symbol equations.	4, 5	Main 1, Plenary 1
	Explain how Group 7 non-metals form ions with a −1 charge when they react with metals.	3	Starter 1, Plenary 2
	Explain in detail how to compare the reactivity of the Group 7 elements.		Main 1

Maths
Students balance equations.

Literacy
Students summarise information to form flash cards and write prose to explain the difference between a halogen and a halide.

Key words
halogen

Practical

Title	Displacement reactions
Equipment	test-tube rack, six test tubes, eye protection, bromine water, chlorine water, iodine water, potassium chloride solution, potassium bromide solution, potassium iodide solution, dropping pipettes
Overview of method	Add about a 2 cm depth of potassium chloride solution to two test tubes, 2 cm depth of potassium bromide to two further test tubes, and a 2 cm depth of potassium iodide to the last two test tubes. Add one full dropping pipette of chlorine water to potassium bromide and a second dropping pipette of chlorine water to potassium iodide. Then add one full dropping pipette of bromine water to potassium chloride and a second dropping pipette of bromine water to potassium iodide. Finally add one full dropping pipette of iodine water to potassium chloride and a second dropping pipette of iodine water to potassium bromide.
Safety considerations	Wear eye protection and complete the experiment in a well-ventilated room. Warn asthmatics to be aware of fumes. Bromine water is toxic and iodine water is harmful. Halogen waters should be kept in the fume cupboard. Potassium chloride, bromide, and iodide are harmful. Use solution strengths as low as possible. The risk can be reduced by completing the experiment on a microscale using dimple dishes and three drops of each solution.

C2 The periodic table

Starter	Support/Extend	Resources
Electronic structure (5 minutes) Ask students to write the electronic structure for fluorine (2,7), fluoride ion (2,8), chlorine (2,8,7), and chloride ion (2,8,8).	**Support:** Write the electronic structures and symbols onto a board. Ask students to match the symbol to the electronic structure.	
Diagrams (10 minutes) Show students samples of chlorine, bromine, and iodine in sealed containers. Explain that the elements are diatomic molecules. Ask students to use the particle model and draw a diagram of each of the elements in its state at room temperature.	**Support:** Show students particle models of each halogen and ask them to identify the halogen. **Extend:** Students predict the state of fluorine and astatine and then draw their particle diagrams.	

Main	Support/Extend	Resources
Displacement reactions (20 minutes) Ask students to design an appropriate results table where they can record their observations and write equations to illustrate any chemical reactions. Allow students to complete the experiment.	**Support:** Give students the results table and half-finished word equations already added. **Extend:** Students investigate the reactivity of halogens.	**Practical:** Displacement reactions
Flash cards (20 minutes) Ask students to use secondary resources such as the student book, data books, and the Internet to make flash cards for each halogen. They should include the name, symbol, electronic structure, state at room temperature, diagram of the element in a molecule, diagram of the electronic structure of the halogen and its halide ion (showing outer electrons only), and a fascinating fact.		

Plenary	Support/Extend	Resources
Complete the equation (5 minutes) Ask students to complete the following word and formula equations: • lithium iodide + bromine → (lithium bromide) + (iodine) • sodium chloride + iodine → (no reaction) • 2KI + (Cl$_2$) → 2KCl + (I$_2$)	**Extend:** Ask the students to write all the equations as balanced symbol equations with state symbols.	
Group 7 (10 minutes) Students fill in the gaps of a series of sentences that summarise the basic properties of Group 7 elements. Students then complete a crossword of key words from the lesson.		**Interactive:** Group 7

Homework		
Students explain the difference between a halogen and a halide.		

kerboodle
A Kerboodle highlight for this lesson is **Working scientifically: The boiling point of halogens**. Refer to the **Content map** on Kerboodle for a full list of resources and assessment.

C2.5 Explaining trends

AQA spec Link: 1.2.5 In Group 1, the reactivity of the elements increases down the group.

Students should be able to:
- explain how properties of the elements in Group 1 depend on the outer shell of electrons of the atoms
- predict properties from given trends down the group.

1.2.6 In Group 7, the reactivity of the elements decreases down the group.

Students should be able to:
- explain how properties of the elements in Group 7 depend on the outer shell of electrons of the atoms
- predict properties from given trends down the group.

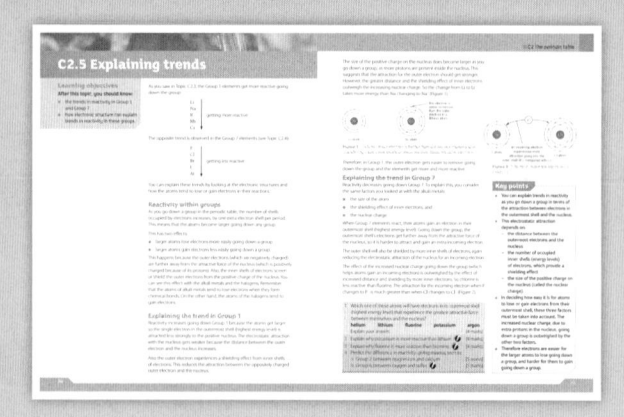

WS 1.2

Aiming for	Outcome	Checkpoint	
		Question	Activity
Aiming for GRADE 4	State the trend in reactivity in Group 1.		Starter 2, Main
	State the trend in reactivity in Group 7.		Starter 2, Main
Aiming for GRADE 6	Explain how electronic structure affects the trend in reactivity of Group 1 and Group 7 elements.	2, 3	Main
	Use the nuclear model to explain how the outer electrons experience different levels of attraction to the nucleus.	1	Main
Aiming for GRADE 8	Use electronic structure to explain the trends in physical and chemical properties of Group 1 and Group 7 elements.	End of chapter 2, 3	Main
	Apply knowledge of reactivity of Groups 1 and 7 to suggest and explain the trend in reactivity of Groups 2 and 6.	4	Main

Maths
Students draw electron diagrams and find patterns in data.

Literacy
Students make reasoned explanations of abstract concepts.

C2 The periodic table

Starter	Support/Extend	Resources
Products (5 minutes) Ask students to write an equation to summarise a reaction between: • a halogen and a Group 1 metal halide • a halogen and a Group 1 metal. **Clips** (10 minutes) Discuss the trends in reactivity of Group 1 and Group 7 as a class (or watch a video). Then ask students to summarise and describe the trend in each group in one sentence.	**Support:** Ask students to write word equations. **Extend:** Ask students to write balanced symbol equations with state symbols.	

Main	Support/Extend	Resources
Explaining trends (20 minutes) Remind students of some of the reactions of Group 1 and Group 7 elements, including how vigorous the reactions are depending on the element used. Students then sort a series of statements on the reactivity trends of Group 1 and Group 7 elements according to whether they describe Group 1 elements, Group 7 elements, or both groups. Students use this to make an infographic to explain the trends in reactivity of both groups.	**Extend:** Ask students to include information about how the reactivity of Group 2 compares with Group 1 and Group 6 with Group 7.	**Activity:** Explaining trends

Plenary	Support/Extend	Resources
Higher or lower (5 minutes) Give out the names of pairs of chemicals and ask students to suggest which is more reactive and why, for example, sodium or lithium – sodium is more reactive as it is a bigger atom and can lose its outer shell electron more easily. **Exam question** (10 minutes) Give students a five-mark past paper question. Ask them to write a mark scheme for the question, which should include the desirable answer, other accepted answers, and answers that are not to be accepted.	**Support:** Ask students to complete a sentence: Reactivity (increases) as you go down Group 1 as the outer (electrons) are (more) easily lost. Reactivity (decreases) as you go down Group 7 as it is (more) difficult to attract an (electron) to the outer shell. **Support:** Use an examination question from the Foundation tier.	

Homework		
Ask students to explain why it is not possible to suggest which reaction would be more vigorous: • sodium + chlorine • potassium + bromine (Potassium is more reactive than sodium but chlorine is more reactive than bromine.)	**Support:** Remind students of the trends in reactivity in the groups and encourage them to compare the metals in each and then the non-metals in each. **Extend:** Ask students to write balanced symbol equations with state symbols for each reaction.	

kerboodle

A Kerboodle highlight for this lesson is **Extension sheet: Putting the periodicity into the periodic table**. Refer to the **Content map** on Kerboodle for a full list of resources and assessment.

GCSE Chemistry Only

C2.6 The transition elements

AQA spec Link: 1.3.1 The transition elements are metals with similar properties which are different from those of the elements in Group 1.

Students should be able to describe the difference compared with Group 1 in melting points, densities, strength, hardness and reactivity with oxygen, water, and halogens.

Students should be able to exemplify these general properties by reference to Cr, Mn, Fe, Co, Ni, Cu.

1.3.2 Many transition elements have ions with different charges, form coloured compounds and are useful as catalysts.

Students should be able to exemplify these general properties by reference to compounds of Cr, Mn, Fe, Co, Ni, Cu.

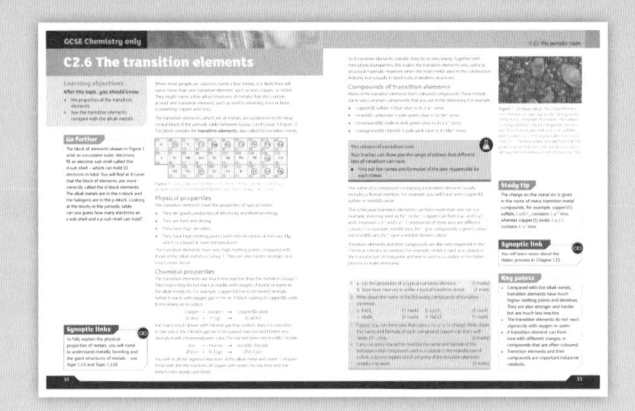

Aiming for	Outcome	Checkpoint	
		Question	Activity
Aiming for GRADE 4 ↓	List the typical properties of transition metals and their compounds.	1	Main
Aiming for GRADE 6 ↓	Describe how the properties of Group 1 metals compare with transition metals.	End of chapter 4	Main, Plenary 2
	Interpret the formula and names of familiar transition metal compounds.	2, 3, End of chapter 4	Main
Aiming for GRADE 8 ↓	Justify the use of a transition metal or its compound in terms of its chemical properties.	4	Main
	Suggest why Group 1 metals have different properties compared to transition metals.		Main

Maths
Students draw a Venn diagram of the properties of transition elements and Group 1 elements.

Literacy
Students research and explain, in terms of properties, the uses of transition metals and their compounds.

Key words
transition elements

Practical

Title	colours of vanadium
Equipment	Concentrated hydrochloric acid, zinc amalgam chips (or zinc dust if available), test tube, test-tube rack, 0.1 mol/dm³ ammonium metavanadate solution, spatula, two dropping pipettes, eye protection
Overview of method	Fill about a third of a test tube with concentrated hydrochloric acid and add one zinc chip. Then add a dropping pipette of ammonium metavanadate solution. Observe the colour change as the vanadium ions get reduced by the zinc.
Safety considerations	Concentrated hydrochloric acid is corrosive and ammonium metavanadate above 0.1 M concentration is toxic. Use lowest concentrations possible. Wear gloves when preparing solutions and chemical splash-proof eye protection during preparation and the experiment.

C2 The periodic table

Starter	Support/Extend	Resources
Feely box (5 minutes) Give students some samples of transition metals in sealed containers, labelled with the name and the symbol. Alternatively, project images of a sample of each metal. Ask students to look at the samples and suggest what the lesson is about. **Colours of vanadium** (10 minutes) Demonstrate how vanadium ions can change charge and each ion produces a different colour. Students produce a flow chart with the different ions detailed, including the colours of the ions.	**Support:** Try to use chromium, manganese, iron, cobalt, nickel, and copper as examples as these are listed in the specification. **Extend:** Give students a selection of transition metal compounds with several examples containing the same metal. **Extend:** Ask students to explain how this is reduction of vanadium (loss of oxygen / gain of electrons).	

Main	Support/Extend	Resources
Properties of transition elements (40 minutes) Ask students to draw a Venn diagram made of two circles that slightly overlap. Label one circle as Group 1 (alkali metals) and the second as transition metals. Students write the properties of Group 1 in the first circle. They then write the properties of transition metals in the second circle and write the common properties in the overlap. Using different coloured pens, students write examples of symbols and names of elements in the appropriate parts of the Venn diagram. Then ask students to focus on the properties of the transition metals and their uses. Students use the properties of the transition elements to justify why the uses of chromium, manganese, iron, cobalt, nickel, and copper.	**Support:** Give students the outline of the Venn diagram and show them the different properties for them to copy into the correct part of the Venn diagram. **Extend:** Encourage students to use examples outside those listed in the specification and to speculate why the alkali metals and transition elements differ.	**Activity:** Properties of transition elements

Plenary	Support/Extend	Resources
Reflection (5 minutes) Ask students to write down one fact that the lesson has reminded them of and one fact that was new to them today. **5, 4, 3, 2, 1** (10 minutes) Ask students to list five symbols of transition metals, four properties that all metals have, three symbols of magnetic elements, two properties that alkali metals have which are not shared by transition metals, and one metal that is a liquid at room temperature.	**Support:** Allow students to work in pairs.	

Homework		
Ask students to find the transition metals or their compounds which are catalysts for: • hydrogenation of margarine (nickel) • making sulfuric acid – Contact Process (V_2O_5) • making ammonia – Haber Process (iron) • making oxygen in the lab from hydrogen peroxide (MnO_2) • a catalytic converter in a car (platinum, rhodium, palladium).		

kerboodle

A Kerboodle highlight for this lesson is **Suport: Transition metals are marvellous**. Refer to the **Content map** on Kerboodle for a full list of resources and assessment.

C2 The periodic table

Overview of C2 The periodic table

In this chapter, students have learnt about the development of the periodic table, including the work of Dalton, Newlands, and Mendeleev. Within this, students should have built upon their understanding of the development of scientific models from *C1 Atomic structure*. Students should understand how each stage in the development of the periodic table was facilitated by new evidence becoming available. They should also be able to identify the importance of an inherent pattern to the elements and how this guided Mendeleev's thinking.

Students should also develop their understanding of electronic structures from *C1 Atomic structure*, and apply this to the arrangement of the periodic table and the chemical properties of Group 0, Group 1, and Group 7 elements. They should also be able to identify trends in properties and reactivity, and higher-tier students should be able to explain these in terms of the electronic structure of the elements.

Finally, students studying *AQA GCSE chemistry* were introduced to the properties and reactions of the transition elements. Students should be able to compare these with the elements of Group 1, identify that some transition elements can form many different ions, and recognise that they are used as catalysts.

MyMaths

You can find additional support for the maths skills covered in this chapter on **MyMaths**, including drawing a bar chart and finding patterns in data.

kerboodle

For this chapter, the following assessments are available on Kerboodle:

C2 Checkpoint quiz: The periodic table
C2 Progress quiz: The periodic table 1
C2 Progress quiz: The periodic table 2
C2 On your marks: The periodic table
C2 Exam-style questions and mark scheme: The periodic table

Checkpoint follow up lesson

A student's route through this lesson can be determined using the Checkpoint assessment. Percentage pass marks are supplied in the Checkpoint teacher notes.

For each successive route through it is assumed that the student can perform to their current route as well as previous routes. For example, students working at Aiming for 6 are assumed to be secure in Aiming for 4 knowledge and understanding and working towards achieving all the learning outcomes for Aiming for 6.

	Aiming for 4	**Aiming for 6**	**Aiming for 8**
Learning outcomes	Identify key parts of the periodic table.	Describe in detail how the periodic table is arranged.	Explain in detail how new evidence led to the development of the periodic table.
	Describe how the number of outer electrons is linked to the elements position in the periodic table.	Describe the key steps in the development of the periodic table.	
	Describe the changes in reactivity down Group 1 and Group 7.	Describe key reactions of Group 1 and Group 7 elements and explain how and why reactivity changes in these groups.	Explain the link between electronic structures, atomic radii, and chemical reactivity in Group 1 and Group 7.
Starter	**The periodic table (10 minutes)** Display a large periodic table that all students can see. Provide pupils with a selection of blank sticky notes. Ask students to write information that the periodic table can tell us onto a post it note. Students then stick their sticky note on the relevant area of the periodic table. For example, they may write "metals" and place this to the left hand side of the displayed periodic table. Discuss the information displayed on the periodic table, tackling any misunderstandings that may have been demonstrated. Then ask students to recall three key events that led to the modern periodic table looking that way it does now. Leave the periodic table and sticky notes displayed as it will be returned to in the plenary.		
Differentiated checkpoint activity	The Aiming for 4 Checkpoint follow-up sheet provides highly-structured guidance to support students with annotating a periodic table. A small scale demonstration or video clip showing the reactions of Group 1 metals should be carried out for Aiming for 4 students.	The Aiming for 6 Checkpoint follow-up sheet provides students with questions to guide their annotations of the periodic table. Aiming for 6 students could also watch the demonstration of the reactions of the Group 1 metals if necessary. Circulate around the room whilst students complete the relevant sheets. Focus help with Aiming for 4 and Aiming for 6 students predominantly.	The Aiming for 8 Checkpoint follow-up sheet provides fewer prompt questions and encourages students to write detailed explanations of the concepts. Aiming for 8 students will need to be provided with access to chemical data books and helped with finding the relevant physical data needed for the task (e.g., atomic radii). Aiming for 8 students could be provided with Internet access or textbooks to aid their research into developments of the periodic table.
	Kerboodle resource C2 Checkpoint follow up: Aiming for 4, C2 Checkpoint follow up: Aiming for 6, C2 Checkpoint follow up: Aiming for 8		
Plenary	**The periodic table – revisited (5 minutes)** Ask students to look again at the periodic table and accompanying sticky notes from the starter. Pairs of students take one sticky note (or share out if there is more than one note per pair), and to improve the detail that has been written down. Can they add more detail from the work they have carried out in the main part of the lesson?		
	Reviewing your work (5 minutes) Ask students to look at their partners work and identify one positive point, one point for improvement, and one piece of extra information that would be interesting to include.		
Progression	Encourage students to write word equations for the reactions of Group 1 and Group 7, giving support where necessary.	Students studying AQA GCSE Chemistry, students could be encouraged to compare the reactions of Group 1 with the reactions of transition elements.	Encourage students to apply their understanding to explaining the properties and reactivity of Group 2 elements.

C 3 Structure and bonding
3.1 States of matter

AQA spec Link: 2.2.1 The three states of matter are solid, liquid, and gas. Melting and freezing take place at the melting point, boiling and condensing take place at the boiling point. The three states of matter can be represented by a simple model. In this model, particles are represented by small solid spheres. Particle theory can help to explain melting, boiling, freezing, and condensing.

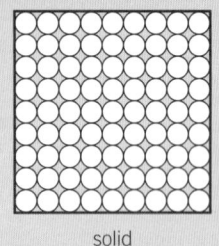

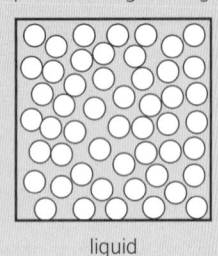

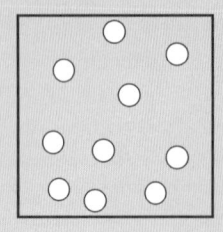

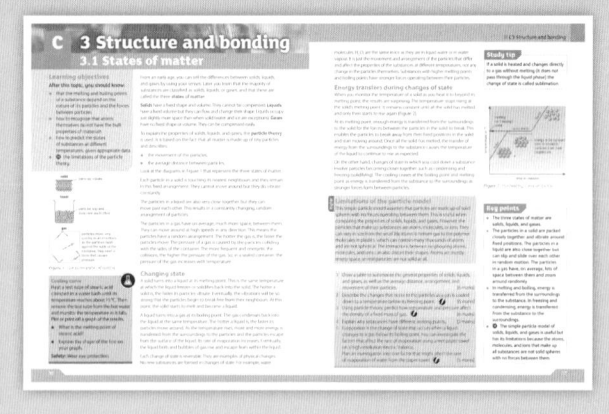

solid   liquid   gas

The amount of energy needed to change state from solid to liquid and from liquid to gas depends on the strength of the forces between the particles of the substance. The nature of the particles involved depends on the type of bonding and the structure of the substance. The stronger the forces between the particles the higher the melting point and boiling point of the substance.

H Limitations of the simple model above include that in the model there are no forces, that all particles are represented as spheres and that the spheres are solid.

Students should be able to:

- predict the states of substances at different temperatures given appropriate data
- explain the different temperatures at which changes of state occur in terms of energy transfers and types of bonding
- recognise that atoms themselves do not have the bulk properties of materials
- **H** explain the limitations of the particle theory in relation to changes of state when particles are represented by solid inelastic spheres which have no forces between them.

2.2.2 In chemical equations, the three states of matter are shown as (s), (l), and (g).

WS 2.2
MS 5b

Aiming for	Outcome	Checkpoint	
		Question	Activity
Aiming for GRADE 4	Identify the three states of matter and their state symbols.		Starter 1, Main
	Describe the process of melting, freezing, boiling, and condensing.	2	Starter 2, Main, Plenary 2
	Use the particle model to draw a representation of how particles are arranged in the three states of matter.	1	Main, Plenary 2
Aiming for GRADE 6	Use data to determine the state of a substance at a given temperature.	End of chapter 3	Starter 1, Main
	Explain, in terms of particles, the energy and temperature of a substance when it is at the melting point or boiling point.		Main, Plenary 2
	Describe the factors that affect rate of evaporation.	5	Plenary 1
Aiming for GRADE 8	Use the particle model to describe how energy, movement, and attraction between particles change as a substance is heated or cooled.	2, 3, 4	Main, Plenary 2
	Suggest why substances have different melting and boiling points from each other.	4	Plenary 1, Homework
	H Evaluate a model, explaining its limitations.		Main

Maths
Students visualise substances uses the particle model (5b) and also draw a line graph, including a line of best fit.

Key words
states of matter, solids, liquids, gases, particle theory

■ C3 Structure and bonding

Practical

Title	Cooling curve
Equipment	kettle, 250 cm³ beaker, water, boiling tube, -10°C to 110°C thermometer, stearic acid, stopwatch, boiling-tube rack, eye protection
Overview of method	Boil the kettle and half fill the beaker with water to make a warm water bath. Half fill a boiling tube with stearic acid and put in the water bath until the solid has melted. Insert the bulb of the thermometer into the stearic acid. Remove the boiling tube and put in a boiling-tube rack. Take the temperature of the stearic acid every 30 seconds for 10 minutes or until the chemical has been solidified for two minutes.
Safety considerations	Wear eye protection. Be aware that the kettle and hot water bath will be hot enough to burn skin.

Starter	Support/Extend	Resources
Sorting (5 minutes) Give students a selection of solids, liquids, and gases. (These could be elements as used in C1.1.) Ask teams of students to sort them by state and introduce the state symbols. **Solids, liquids, and gases** (10 minutes) Students use the interactive to identify if well known substances are solids, liquids, or gases. They then match the change of state key word to its description. Finally, provide students with a list of true or false statements about the properties solids, liquids, and gases. Students have to identify whether the statements are true or false.	**Support:** Use more everyday materials to sort into states. **Extend:** Give students items that cannot be easily classified, for example, hair gel or non-Newtonian fluids. **Extend:** Students should correct the false statements.	**Interactive:** Solids, liquids, and gases

Main	Support/Extend	Resources
Cooling curves (40 minutes) Students complete the practical to get temperature data from stearic acid as it cools. Encourage students to plot a cooling curve (temperature against time). Ask students to annotate the graph with the sections where the stearic acid is a liquid, freezing, and solid. Encourage students to use state symbol notation and draw annotated particle diagrams to show how the particles are moving and arranged in each section of the graph. **(H)** Once higher-tier students have completed their practical, they should evaluate the particle model and list some of its limitations.	**Support:** Allow students to use a data logger and print off the temperature graph. **Extend:** Ask students to predict the shape of the graph if the stearic acid had started at 380°C and cooled to 0°C. Stearic acid melting point: 69°C, boiling point: 376°C.	**Practical:** Cooling curves

Plenary	Support/Extend	Resources
Evaporation (10 minutes) Give students the structure and boiling point of a simple molecule such as oxygen (−183°C) and a giant ionic compound such as sodium chloride (1413°C). Ask students to suggest why these two substances have very different boiling points. **Predict** (10 minutes) Students sketch a graph to show what happens as water is heated from −10°C to 110°C. (Graph axes should be temperature against time. Temperature increases from −10°C to 0°C. Plateau at 0°C, where ice melts to liquid water. Temperature increases from 0°C to 100°C. Plateau at 100°C where liquid water turns to steam. Temperature increases from 100°C to 110°C.) Students should annotate their diagrams using particle diagrams.	**Support:** Give students the labelled axis.	

Homework		
Ask students to explain, in terms of the attraction of particles, why water boils at 100°C but ethanol boils at 78°C.		

kerboodle

A Kerboodle highlight for this lesson is **Interactive: States of matter.** Refer to the **Content map** on Kerboodle for a full list of resources and assessment.

C3.2 Atoms into ions

AQA spec Link: 2.1.1 There are three types of strong chemical bonds: ionic, covalent, and metallic. For ionic bonding the particles are oppositely charged ions. Ionic bonding occurs in compounds formed from metals combined with non-metals. For covalent bonding the particles are atoms which share pairs of electrons.

2.1.2 When a metal atom reacts with a non-metal atom electrons in the outer shell of the metal atom are transferred. Metal atoms lose electrons to become positively charged ions. Non-metal atoms gain electrons to become negatively charged ions. The ions produced by metals in Groups 1 and 2 and by non-metals in Groups 6 and 7 have the electronic structure of a noble gas (Group 0). The electron transfer during the formation of an ionic compound can be represented by a dot and cross diagram, for example, for sodium chloride:

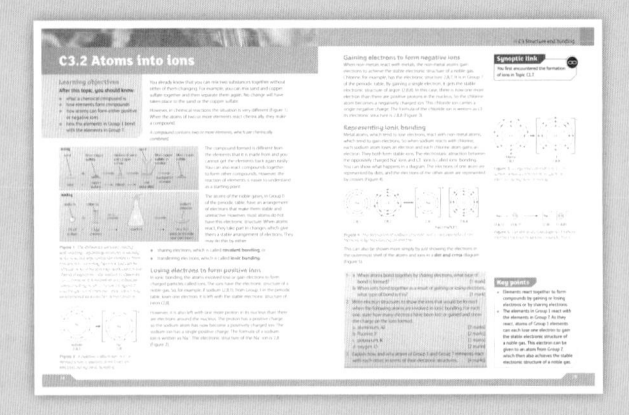

MS 5b

$$Na \bullet \ + \ {}^{xx}_{xx}Cl^{xx}_{xx} \longrightarrow [Na]^+ \ \left[{}^{xx}_{xx}Cl^{xx}_{xx}\right]^-$$
(2,8,1) (2,8,7)   (2,8)   (2,8,8)

Aiming for	Outcome	Checkpoint	
		Question	Activity
Aiming for GRADE 4 ↓	State the particles involved in ionic and covalent bonding.	1, End of chapter 3	Plenary
	Describe, with an example, how a Group 1 metal atom becomes a positive ion.	2, End of chapter 3	Starter 2, Main
	Describe, with an example, how a Group 7 non-metal atom becomes a negative ion.	2, End of chapter 3	Starter 2, Main
Aiming for GRADE 6 ↓	Draw dot and cross diagrams of compounds formed between Group 1 and Group 7 elements.		Main
	Explain how electron transfer allows ionic bonding to occur in the compound formed when a Group 1 metal reacts with a Group 7 non-metal.	3	Main
Aiming for GRADE 8 ↓	Draw dot and cross diagrams of unfamiliar ionic compounds.		Main
	Suggest and explain the charge of a monatomic ion based on its position in the periodic table.	2, End of chapter 2	Main

Maths
Students use the periodic table to determine the electronic configuration of atoms and ions. They also visualise atoms and ions using dot and cross diagrams (5b)

Literacy
Students explain why Group 1 metals and Group 7 elements react with each other.

Key words
covalent bonding, ionic bonding, dot and cross

■ C3 Structure and bonding

Starter	Support/Extend	Resources
Turning atoms into ions (5 minutes) Interactive where students match the definitions with the key terms atom and ion. They then sort chemical symbols to identify which are atoms and which are ions. **Label the diagram** (10 minutes) Give students a dot and cross diagram for the reaction of sodium and chlorine to form sodium chloride. Ask students to add the electronic structures of each particle and label which species are atoms and which species are ions.	**Extend:** Ask students to identify the anion (negative ion) and the cation (positive ion).	**Interactive:** Turning atoms into ions

Main	Support/Extend	Resources
Making sense of ions (40 minutes) Through question and answer with dot and cross diagrams, demonstrate how a lithium atom becomes a lithium ion and show this in a diagrammatic form. Then ask students to use this to draw the electronic structure of the Group 1 ions sodium and potassium. Students then draw dot and cross diagrams for atoms and ions of fluorine, oxygen, potassium, and magnesium forming potassium fluoride, potassium oxide, magnesium fluoride and magnesium oxide.	**Support:** Show students the electronic structures of the Group 7 atoms so all they have to do is add the extra electron, brackets and charge. **Extend:** Ask students to write the formula of the ions and compounds under the diagrams and draw dot and cross diagrams of other Group 1 halides.	**Activity:** Making sense of ions

Plenary	Support/Extend	Resources
Choose the bonding (5 minutes) Ask students to classify the bonding in the following compounds: • carbon dioxide (covalent) • nitrogen monoxide (covalent) • sodium bromide (ionic) • copper chloride (ionic) • sulfur dioxide (covalent) • silver nitrate (ionic between silver and nitrate, covalent in nitrate) **Flow chart** (10 minutes) Ask students to make a flow chart, including diagrams, to show how chlorine gains one electron from a sodium atom to become sodium chloride.	**Support:** Remind students that a metal bonded to a non-metal will be using ionic bonding, but non-metals only will be using covalent bonding.	

Homework		
Ask students to find the formula including charge of common molecular ions (hydroxide, nitrate, sulfate, carbonate, phosphate).		

C3.3 Ionic bonding

AQA spec Link: 2.1.2 The charge on the ions produced by metals in Groups 1 and 2 and by non-metals in Groups 6 and 7 relates to the group number of the element in the periodic table.

2.1.3 An ionic compound is a giant structure of ions. Ionic compounds are held together by strong electrostatic forces of attraction between oppositely charged ions. These forces act in all directions in the lattice and this is called ionic bonding.

The structure of sodium chloride can be represented in the following forms:

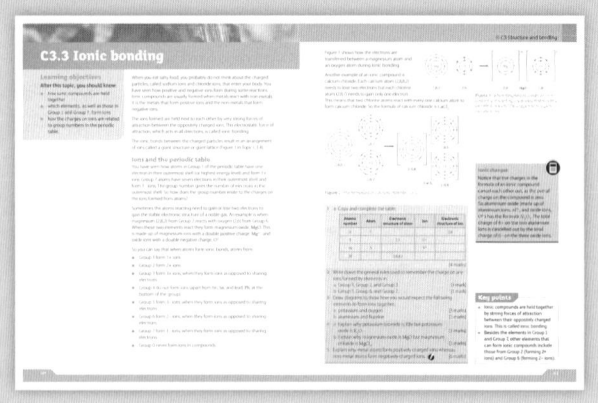

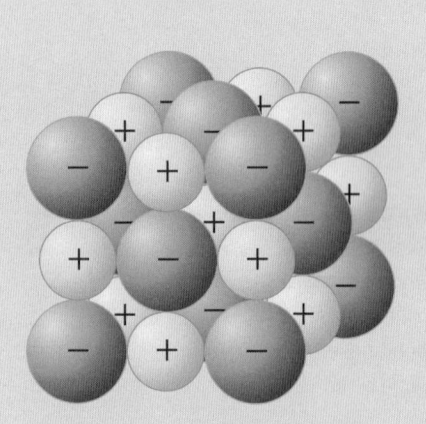

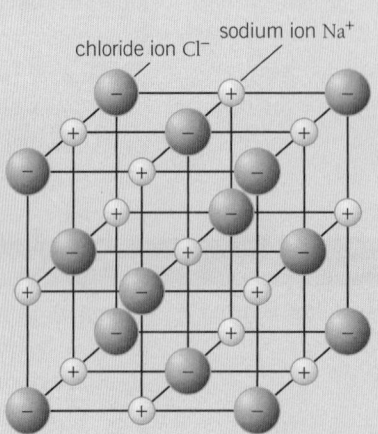

chloride ion Cl⁻   sodium ion Na⁺   MS 1c, 5b

Aiming for	Outcome	Checkpoint	
		Question	Activity
Aiming for GRADE 4 ↓	State that opposite charges attract.		Starter 1
	Write the charges of ions of Group 1, Group 2, Group 6, and Group 7 elements.	1, 3	Starter 1, Plenary 1
	Describe an ionic lattice.		Main 2
Aiming for GRADE 6 ↓	Explain how the position of an element in the periodic table relates to the charge on its most stable monatomic ion.	2	Main 1, Plenary 1
	Explain, in terms of electronic structure, how unfamiliar elements become ions.	5	Main 2
	Interpret the formulae of familiar ionic compounds to determine the number and type of each ion present.	4	Plenary 2
Aiming for GRADE 8 ↓	Suggest the charge on unfamiliar ions using the position of the element in the periodic table.		Main 1, Plenary 1
	Explain the ratio of metal and non-metal ions in compounds.	4	Main 2
	Generate the formulae of a wide range of ionic compounds when the charges of the ions are given.	End of chapter 5	Starter 1, Plenary 2, Homework

Maths
Students should be able to interpret and generate the formulae of ionic compounds and visualise ionic compounds using dot and cross diagrams and other models (5b).

Literacy
Students explain how ions are formed.

Key words
giant structure, giant lattice

■ C3 Structure and bonding

Starter	Support/Extend	Resources
List ions (5 minutes) Ask students to list an ion from Group 1, Group 2, Group 6, and Group 7. Ask students to explain what interaction they expect between the Group 1 and Group 2 ions and the Group 6 and Group 7 ions.	**Support:** Remind students that horizontal rows are called periods. **Extend:** Ask students to suggest formulae for the compounds that could form.	
Making ions (10 minutes) Ask students to draw a dot and cross diagram of a calcium atom and a calcium ion. They then annotate these diagrams to explain how and why calcium atoms become calcium ions. Then ask students to complete the same for oxygen atoms.	**Extend:** Ask students to draw a dot and cross diagram of calcium oxide and write the formula of the compound.	
Main	**Support/Extend**	**Resources**
What's the pattern? (15 minutes) Split the students into groups of three and give each team 20 sticky notes. Instruct the students to write the symbol (as in the periodic table) for each of the first 20 elements, each on separate sticky notes. Then add the electronic structure of the atom, formula of the ion, and the electronic structure of the ion (if they form a stable monatomic ion). Ask students to group the ions by charge and see if they can work out a pattern in the ion's charge and position in the periodic table.	**Support:** Give students part filled in information on the sticky notes. **Extend:** Ask students to explain why the noble gases and Group 4 elements do not commonly form stable monatomic ions.	**Activity:** What's the pattern?
Modelling ionic compounds (25 minutes) Show students some examples of 3D models of ionic compounds such as model kits and computer models. Then ask students to draw their own representation of an ionic lattice and label the positive ions, negative ions, electrostatic forces of attraction, and the formula of the compound. Discuss, or show students an animation of, the formation of sodium chloride from sodium and chlorine using dot and cross diagrams. Ask students to annotate their diagram further by explaining, using dot and cross diagrams, how the ions in the ionic lattice are formed from the atoms.	**Extend:** Encourage students to determine the formula of unfamiliar ionic compounds using percentage by mass of an element in a compound, and an element's relative atomic mass.	
Plenary	**Support/Extend**	**Resources**
Ions and group numbers (5 minutes) Interactive where students match monatomic ions to their group in the periodic table.		**Interactive:** Ions and group numbers
Ionic formulae (10 minutes) Provide students with a table showing the formula and charge of a series of ions. Students use the table to identify the chemical formula of some compounds.		
Homework		
Give students 10 compound names and ask them to complete the formulae. Ensure that the compound names get progressively harder, using unfamiliar ions, molecular ions (also known as compound ions), and brackets.	**Support:** Give students only monatomic ions to work out the formulae.	

kerboodle

A Kerboodle highlight for this lesson is **Calculation sheet: Ionic formulae**. Refer to the **Content map** on Kerboodle for a full list of resources and assessment.

C3.4 Giant ionic structures

AQA spec Link: 2.2.3 Ionic compounds have regular structures (giant ionic lattices) in which there are strong electrostatic forces of attraction in all directions between oppositely charged ions.

These compounds have high melting points and high boiling points because of the large amounts of energy needed to break the many strong bonds.

When melted or dissolved in water, ionic compounds conduct electricity because the ions are free to move and so charge can flow.

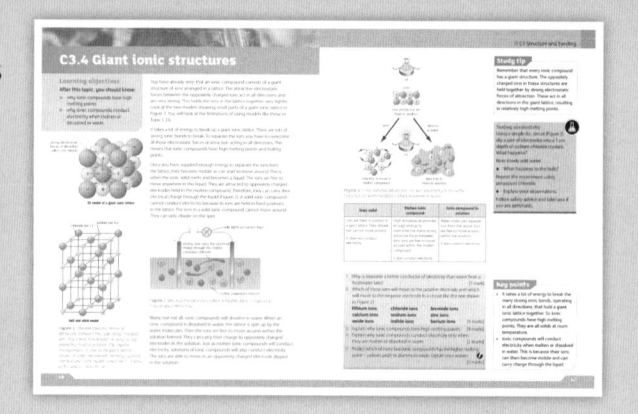

Aiming for	Outcome	Checkpoint	
		Question	Activity
Aiming for GRADE 4 ↓	State that ionic compounds have high melting points and can dissolve in water.		Plenary 1
	State that ionic compounds can conduct electricity when molten or dissolved in water.		Plenary 1
	Describe an ionic lattice.		Starter 2
Aiming for GRADE 6 ↓	Explain why ionic compounds have a high melting point.	3	Plenary 1
	Describe, in terms of ions, how an ionic compound can conduct electricity.	2	Main, Plenary 1
	Explain the movement of ions in solution or when molten.	4	Main, Plenary 1
Aiming for GRADE 8 ↓	Explain in detail why ionic compounds cannot conduct electricity when they are solid but can when molten or in solution.	4	Plenary 1
	Justify in terms of properties that a compound has ionic bonding.		Plenary 1, Homework
	Apply the ionic model to make predictions of the physical properties of ionic compounds.	3, 5	Plenary 1

Maths
Students will interpret and generate the formulae of ionic compounds.

Literacy
Students justify a prediction about the melting points of ionic compounds.

Practical

Title	Testing conductivity
Equipment	100 cm³ beaker, wash bottle with deionised water, two carbon electrodes, two crocodile clips, three wires, lamp, low voltage power supply, sodium chloride powder, potassium chloride powder, damp blue litmus paper
Overview of method	Add about a 1 cm depth of sodium chloride powder into the beaker and submerge the two electrodes, ensuring that they do not touch. Using crocodile clips and wires, connect the electrodes in series with the lamp and low voltage supply. Turn on the electricity and observe. Carefully add water to the beaker and observe. Repeat with potassium chloride.
Safety considerations	Complete in a fume cupboard as toxic chlorine gas is produced. Warn asthmatics not to breath in fumes and keep laboratory well ventilated. Wear chemical splash-proof eye protection as sodium or potassium hydroxide, a strong base, is made. The bulb may get hot, do not touch in case of thermal burns. Stop electrolysis if damp blue litmus paper detects acidic fumes. Wash hands after completing the experiment.

C3 Structure and bonding

Starter	Support/Extend	Resources
What's the connection? (5 minutes) Show students an image of a salt cellar, sodium chloride crystal, sodium chloride lattice, and gritting of roads. Ask students to suggest a connection (sodium chloride). **Labelling** (10 minutes) Give students a diagram of the sodium chloride lattice structure. Ask students to take one minute to label the diagram with key information that they can remember. Pass the paper on. The next person should have two minutes and they can amend previous work or add to the diagram. Repeat with a third person who should have three minutes. Then give to a fourth person who should stick the diagram in their book and make any final additions and amendments that are needed.	**Support:** Give students all the key terms and sentences to use on their diagram. **Extend:** Students should explain how an ionic lattice is formed.	

Main	Support/Extend	Resources
Testing conductivity (40 minutes) Give students the outline of the method to investigate the conductivity of ionic compounds as a powder and when dissolved in water. Students write a full method, including a risk assessment. They then complete the practical and draw their conclusions, using the ionic lattice model to explain their observations.	**Support:** Give students a writing frame and allow them to work in small groups to generate the method. **Extend:** In their conclusion, students explain in detail why ionic compounds can conduct electricity.	**Practical:** Testing conductivity

Plenary	Support/Extend	Resources
Giant ionic structures (10 minutes) Interactive where students complete a paragraph to describe the bonding and properties of ionic compounds. They then decide if descriptions of properties are true or false in describing ionic compounds. **Outline method** (10 minutes) Ask students to write an outline method to show that ionic compounds have high melting points.	**Support:** Give students a writing frame. For example: • Independent variable • Dependent variable • Equipment needed • Instructions Allow them to work in small groups to generate the method.	**Interactive:** Giant ionic structures

Homework		
Give students a piece of card in the shape of a bookmark. On the front they should explain what an ionic compound and giant lattice is. On the back they should list the properties and explain them in terms of the giant ionic lattice model. The focus should be on summarising the key information, including appropriate diagrams. The bookmark should be eye catching.	**Extend:** Ask students to then choose an ionic compound and illustrate the points that they have spoken about with that compound. **Support:** Give students the key points to include.	

kerboodle

A Kerboodle highlight for this lesson is **Extension sheet: Giant ionic structures**. Refer to the **Content map** on Kerboodle for a full list of resources and assessment.

C3.5 Covalent bonding

AQA spec Link: 2.1.4 When atoms share pairs of electrons, they form covalent bonds. These bonds between atoms are strong.

Covalently bonded substances may consist of small molecules, such as H_2, Cl_2, O_2, N_2, HCl, H_2O, NH_3, and CH_4.

Some covalently bonded substances have giant covalent structures, such as diamond.

The covalent bonds in molecules and giant structures can be represented in the following forms:

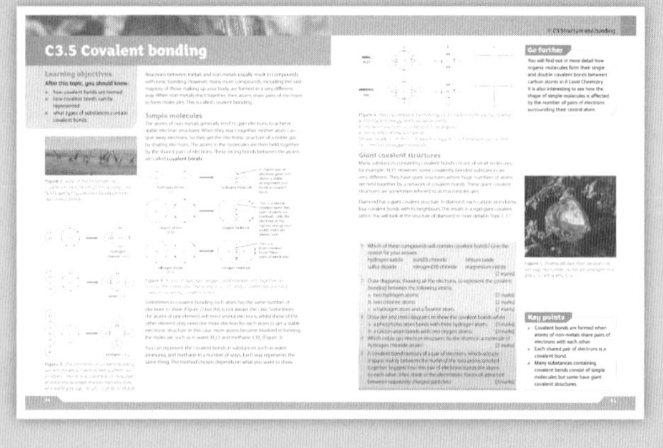

for ammonia, NH_3

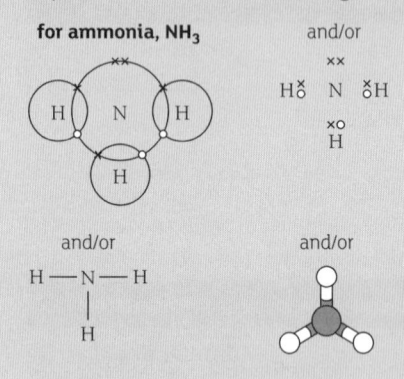

and/or

and/or

and/or

WS1.2
MS 5b

Students should be able to:
- draw dot and cross diagrams for the molecules H_2, Cl_2, O_2, N_2, Cl, HCl, H_2O, NH_3, and CH_4
- represent the covalent bonds in small molecules, using a line to represent a single bond.

Aiming for	Outcome	Checkpoint	
		Question	Activity
Aiming for GRADE 4	Describe a covalent bond.	5	Main 1
	Recognise a covalent compound from its formula, name, or diagram showing bonds.	1, End of chapter 3	Plenary 1
	Name familiar examples of small molecules which contain covalent bonds.		Main 1, Plenary 1
Aiming for GRADE 6	Explain how a covalent bond forms in terms of electronic structure.	4, 5	Main 1
	Draw dot and cross diagrams and ball and stick diagrams for H_2, Cl_2, O_2, N_2, HCl, H_2O, NH_3, and CH_4.	2, End of chapter 5	Main 2, Plenary 1, Homework
	Describe a double bond in a diatomic molecule.		Main 1, Plenary 2
Aiming for GRADE 8	Draw dot and cross diagrams and ball and stick diagrams for unfamiliar small molecules.	2, 3, End of chapter 5	Starter 1, Main 1, Main 2, Plenary 1
	Suggest how double and triple covalent bonds can be formed.		Main 1
	Suggest how the properties of a double covalent bond could be different to the properties of a single covalent bond.		Main 1

Maths
Students generate dot and cross diagrams of covalent molecules.

Literacy
Students explain what a covalent bond is.

Key words
covalent bonds

C3 Structure and bonding

Starter	Support/Extend	Resources
Diagrams (5 minutes) Students use the particle model to represent an atom, a chlorine gas molecule, and a water molecule. **Molecular model** (10 minutes) Ask students to work in pairs. Give them a molecular modelling kit and ask them to show an atom, a bond, a molecule made of an element, and a molecule made of a compound.	**Support:** Show students the diagrams and ask them to identify the substance and give their reasoning. **Extend:** Give students the balanced symbol equation for the formation of water from its elements. Ask them to represent this using the molecular modelling kit.	

Main	Support/Extend	Resources
Covalent bonding (30 minutes) Students work through the activity sheet to describe the covalent bonding in chlorine, oxygen, methane, and other simple molecules. Students then create an infomercial to advertise covalent bonds. Their advert should be no more than 30 seconds. **Formulae of covalent compounds** (10 minutes) Students work through the worked example then practise drawing dot and cross diagrams for simple covalent molecules.	**Support:** Give students key information that they must include in their infomercial. **Extend:** Students include information on double and triple bonds.	**Activity:** Covalent bonding **Calculation sheet:** Formulae of covalent compounds

Plenary	Support/Extend	Resources
Table (10 minutes) Students draw a table with four columns – molecule, formula, ball and stick, and dot and cross. Students fill in the table with H_2, O_2, H_2O, and CH_4. **Covalent bonding** (10 minutes) Interactive where students match the name and formula of a compound with its dot and cross diagram. They then complete a paragraph to describe covalent bonding.	**Support:** Provide students with the information so that they can sort it into the correct place within their table. **Extend:** Give students unfamiliar substances such as CO_2. **Extend:** Students extend the description of covalent bonding to also describe double and triple covalent bonds.	**Interactive:** Covalent bonding

Homework		
Students complete their table from plenary 1 with Cl_2, N_2, HCl, and NH_3. (If students did not do plenary 1, they should create the table, and include the molecules H_2, O_2, H_2O, and CH_4.) Students then classify the molecules as elements or compounds.	**Extend:** Include some unfamiliar small molecules, for example, ethane.	

kerboodle

A Kerboodle highlight for this lesson is **Bump up your grade: Covalent bonding**. Refer to the **Content map** on Kerboodle for a full list of resources and assessment.

C3.6 Structure of simple molecules

AQA spec Link: 2.2.4 Substances that consist of small molecules are usually gases or liquids that have relatively low melting points and boiling points. These substances have only weak forces between the molecules (intermolecular forces). It is these intermolecular forces that are overcome, not the covalent bonds, when the substance melts or boils. The intermolecular forces increase with the size of the molecules, so larger molecules have higher melting and boiling points. These substances do not conduct electricity because the molecules do not have an overall electric charge.

2.2.5 Polymers have very large molecules. The atoms in the polymer molecules are linked to other atoms by strong covalent bonds. The intermolecular forces between polymer molecules are relatively strong and so these substances are solids at room temperature.

2.1.4 Some covalently bonded substances have very large molecules, such as polymers.

Students should be able to:

- describe the limitations of using dot and cross, ball and stick, two and three-dimensional diagrams to represent molecules or giant structures
- deduce the molecular formula of a substance from a given model or diagram in these forms showing the atoms and bonds in the molecule.

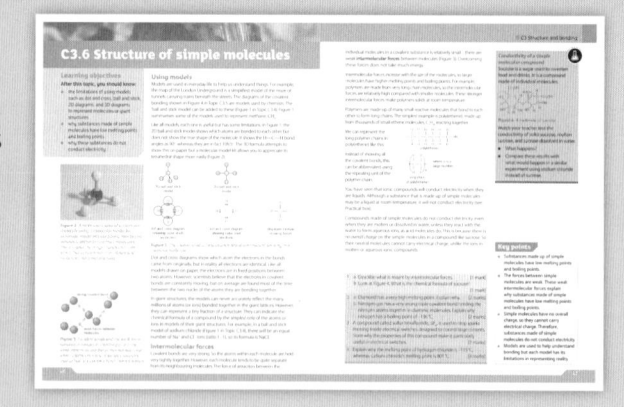

WS 1.2
MS 5b

Aiming for	Outcome	Checkpoint	
		Question	Activity
Aiming for GRADE 4 ↓	State that small molecules have low melting and boiling points.		Main 2, Plenary 2
	State that small molecules do not conduct electricity.	4	Main 1, Plenary 2
	Describe an intermolecular force.	1	Starter 1, Main 2
Aiming for GRADE 6 ↓	Explain how the size of molecules affects melting and boiling points.	3	Main 2, Plenary
	Explain why small molecules and polymers do not conduct electricity.		Main 1, Plenary
	Identify substances that would have weak intermolecular forces.	2	Starter 1
Aiming for GRADE 8 ↓	Predict the physical properties of unfamiliar covalently bonded substances.	3	Main 1, Plenary
	Compare and contrast the properties of substances with different bonding.	5	Starter 2
	Justify the use of a model to explain the physical properties of a small molecule and discuss the limitations of various molecular models.		Plenary 2

Maths
Students plot melting point and boiling point data as a bar chart or scatter graph. They use their graph to draw conclusions on melting point and boiling point trends.

Literacy
Students explain how the bonding in covalent and ionic molecules affects their melting points and boiling points.

Key words
intermolecular forces, polymers

46

C3 Structure and bonding

Practical

Title	Conductivity of a simple molecular compound
Equipment	100 cm³ beaker, wash bottle with deionised water, two carbon electrodes, two crocodile clips, three wires, lamp, low voltage power supply, sucrose powder
Overview of method	Add about a 1 cm depth of sucrose powder into the beaker and submerge the two electrodes, ensuring that they do not touch. Using crocodile clips and wires, connect the electrodes in series with the lamp and low voltage supply. Turn on the electricity and observe. Carefully add water to the beaker and observe. Repeat with sucrose dissolved in water and molten sucrose.
Safety considerations	Take care with what methods are used to melt sucrose.

Starter	Support/Extend	Resources
Intermolecular forces (10 minutes) Introduce inter molecular forces as the force of attraction between neighbouring molecules. Explain that the intermolecular forces *increase* with the *size* of the molecules. Show students molecular diagrams of oxygen, ethanol, and sucrose. Ask students to put the substances in order of strongest to weakest intermolecular forces. Then ask students to identify which substance is a solid, a liquid, and a gas.		
Sodium chloride versus sucrose (5 minutes) Show students an image of a sodium chloride giant lattice and a sucrose molecule. Tell students that sodium chloride is table salt and sucrose is commonly used as granulated sugar. Ask students to compare the two substances in terms of their bonding and properties.	**Support:** Tell students that sucrose is formed from covalent bonds and sodium chloride from ionic bonds.	

Main	Support/Extend	Resources
Conductivity of a simple molecular compound (20 minutes) Remind students of their experiment in Topic C3.4. Demonstrate to students that sucrose does not conduct electricity as a solid or when in solution. Ask students to explain their observation using the particle model.		
Displaying data (20 minutes) Provide students with the melting point and boiling point values for phosphorus, P_4, sulfur, S_8, chlorine, Cl_2, and argon, Ar. Students draw a ball and stick diagram to represent the element then plot a bar chart or scatter graph of the data (temperature against relative molecular mass). Ask students to draw conclusions consistent with the results, for example, melting points are always higher than boiling points and bigger molecules have higher melting and boiling points.	**Support:** Give students the phosphorus and sulfur ball and stick diagrams. **Extend:** Ask students to use diagrams to explain their observations.	**Activity:** Displaying data

Plenary	Support/Extend	Resources
Simple molecules (10 minutes) Students complete a crossword on bonding, intermolecular forces, and different properties of the states of matter. They then analyse a graph of molecular size against melting point and boiling point.		**Interactive:** Simple molecules
Models (10 minutes) Show students as many different ways of representing chlorine gas as you can find including 2D ball and stick, dot and cross diagrams, and 3D computer models. Ask students to evaluate the models and suggest which is best to describe each property studied in the lesson. Students justify their choice.	**Support:** Give a model and ask students to use it to illustrate a given property. **Extend:** Ask students to use the model to explain why most covalent compounds, such as hexane, do not dissolve in water.	

Homework
Students explain, using a labelled diagram, why ammonia has a low melting point.

C3.7 Giant covalent structures

AQA spec Link: 2.2.6 Substances that consist of giant covalent structures are solids with very high melting points. All of the atoms in these structures are linked to other atoms by strong covalent bonds. These bonds must be overcome to melt or boil these substances. Diamond and graphite (forms of carbon) and silicon dioxide (silica) are examples of giant covalent structures.

2.3.1 In diamond, each carbon atom forms four covalent bonds with other carbon atoms in a giant covalent structure, so diamond is very hard, has a very high melting point and does not conduct electricity.

2.3.2 In graphite, each carbon atom forms three covalent bonds with three other carbon atoms, forming layers of hexagonal rings and so graphite has a high melting point. The layers are free to slide over each other because there are no covalent bonds between the layers and so graphite is soft and slippery. In graphite, one electron from each carbon atom is delocalised. These delocalised electrons allow graphite to conduct thermal energy and electricity.

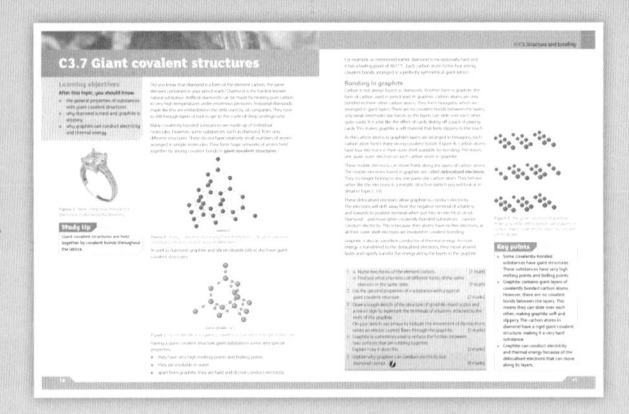

WS1.2
MS 5b

Aiming for	Outcome	Checkpoint	
		Question	Activity
Aiming for GRADE 4 ↓	List the main physical properties of diamond and graphite.	2	Main
	State that giant covalent structures have high melting points.	2	Main
	Describe the structure of graphite in terms of layers of carbon atoms.	3	Starter 2, Main, Plenary 1
Aiming for GRADE 6 ↓	Recognise the structure of diamond and graphite from information provided in written or diagrammatic form.		Starter 2
	Explain the properties of diamond in terms of its bonding.	4	Main
	Explain the properties of graphite in terms of its bonding.	4	Main
Aiming for GRADE 8 ↓	Use a molecular model of an unfamiliar giant covalent structure to predict and explain its physical properties.		Plenary 2, Homework
	Justify in detail a use for graphite based on its properties.	3	Main, Plenary 1
	Justify in detail a use for diamond based on its properties.	3	Main, Plenary 1

Maths
Students draw and interpret diagrams of giant covalent structures (5b).

Literacy
Students will explain how the structure and bonding of graphite and diamond affect their properties.

Key words
giant covalent structure, delocalised electrons

48

C3 Structure and bonding

Starter	Support/Extend	Resources
Link the items (5 minutes) Show students a carbon electrode, pencil, drill bit, graphite lubricant powder, carbon fingerprint powder, and a diamond (imitation). Ask students to suggest the connection (all carbon). **Giant covalent structures** (10 minutes) Give students the ball and stick diagrams of diamond and graphite. Ask students to label with key phrases such as carbon atom, covalent bond, free moving delocalised electrons, layers. Students then identify whether phrases describe the properties of graphite or diamond.	**Support:** Suggest to students that it is all the same element and ask them to suggest which one. **Support:** Show students the molecular models. **Extend:** Ask students to define the key phrases.	**Interactive:** Giant covalent structures

Main	Support/Extend	Resources
Carbon blogging (40 minutes) Introduce students to carbon, the bonding, properties, and uses of graphite, and the bonding, properties, and uses of diamond. Students then create a comparison table that includes the structure, describes the properties, and explains them in terms of structure and bonding. Students then use their comparison table to summarise the key points about carbon in the form of graphite and diamond as a blog article. Students should include a labelled diagram and links to at least one other interesting web page.	**Support:** Give the information as a cut and stick card sort. **Extend:** Ask students to include uses and justify which property makes them useful for that purpose. **Support:** Give students a writing frame to help them craft their article.	**Activity:** Carbon blogging

Plenary	Support/Extend	Resources
Uses of carbon (5 minutes) Give small groups of students a use of carbon, and then ask them to suggest which allotrope would be the best to use and then explain why. **Comparing structures** (10 minutes) Show students an image of a carbon dioxide molecule and the structure of silicon dioxide. Students explain the differences in properties between the two substances in terms of their structure and bonding.	**Support:** Give the uses and reasons for students to match up. **Extend:** Include other giant covalent compounds, for example, silicon dioxide.	

Homework		
Ask students to list and explain the properties of silicon dioxide.		

kerboodle

A Kerboodle highlight for this lesson is **Go further: Graphite**. Refer to the **Content map** on Kerboodle for a full list of resources and assessment.

C3.8 Fullerenes and graphene

AQA spec Link: 2.3.3 Graphene is a single layer of graphite and has properties that make it useful in electronics and composites. Students should be able to explain the properties of graphene in terms of its structure and bonding.

Fullerenes are molecules of carbon atoms with hollow shapes. The structure of fullerenes is based on hexagonal rings of carbon atoms but they may also contain rings with five or seven carbon atoms. The first fullerene to be discovered was Buckminsterfullerene (C_{60}) which has a spherical shape.

Carbon nanotubes are cylindrical fullerenes with very high length to diameter ratios. Their properties make them useful for nanotechnology, electronics and materials.

Students should be able to:

- recognise graphene and fullerenes from diagrams and descriptions of their bonding and structure
- give examples of the uses of fullerenes, including carbon nanotubes.

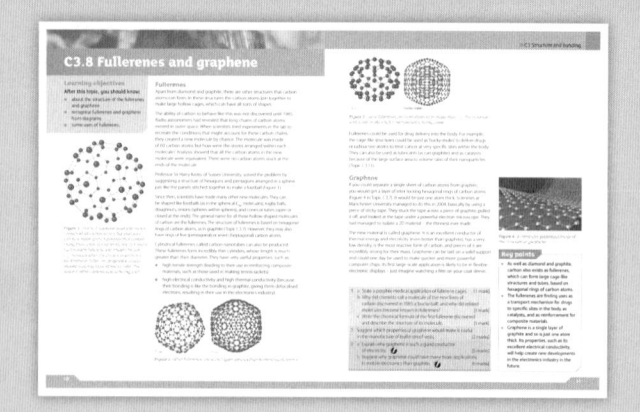

WS 1.2, 1.4
MS 5b

Aiming for	Outcome	Checkpoint	
		Question	Activity
Aiming for GRADE 4	Describe the relationship between graphite and graphene.		Starter 2
	List the main physical properties of fullerenes.		Main
	State the molecular formula of buckminsterfullerene.	1	Main, Plenary 1
Aiming for GRADE 6	Recognise the structure of a fullerene or nanotube in diagrams and prose.	1	Starter 2, Main, Plenary 1
	Explain the structure of fullerenes.		Main
	List the properties and consequent uses of fullerenes and carbon nanotubes.	1	Main, Plenary 2
Aiming for GRADE 8	Describe and explain the applications of fullerenes.	1	Main, Plenary 2
	Use molecular models of graphene, nanotubes, and fullerenes to explain their properties.	3	Homework
	Justify in detail a use for graphene, nanotubes, and fullerenes, based on their properties.	2, 3	Main, Plenary 2

Maths
Students interpret diagrams of fullernes and graphene (5b).

Literacy
Students differentiate between scientific facts and opinions. They also produce a newspaper article to summarise their understanding of fullerenes and graphene.

Key words
fullerenes

■ C3 Structure and bonding

Starter	Support/Extend	Resources
Odd one out (5 minutes) Show students diagrams of structures of graphite, diamond, fullerenes, and photographs of graphite, diamond, and coal. Ask students to suggest what they all have in common (all contain mainly carbon) and the odd one out (coal as it is not an allotrope of carbon as it is an impure form of carbon). **Making graphene** (10 minutes) Ask students to shade in a small section of their exercise book. Then stick a piece of sticky tape over the shaded area and carefully pull it off. Explain that the residue on the sticky tape is a sheet of graphene. Show students a ball and stick model of graphite and ask them to use it to model what graphene is.	**Support:** Use question and answer to demonstrate that the removal of one layer of graphite produces graphene.	

Main	Support/Extend	Resources
News articles (40 minutes) Give students some news articles about the discovery and use of fullerenes. Then ask them to highlight facts in green and opinion in pink. They then summarise their findings about this area of chemistry and produce a newspaper article of their findings.	**Support:** Use articles which are more focused on general interest. Provide students with a writing frame for their summaries. **Extend:** Give students more demanding articles.	**Activity:** News articles

Plenary	Support/Extend	Resources
Fullerenes and graphene (10 minutes) Interactive where students complete a summary of the structure and uses of graphene, fullerenes, and carbon nanotubes. **Properties and uses** (10 minutes) Give students a list of the properties of fullerenes and graphene. Students have to identify which substance the property describes. Students then use the properties to match fullerenes and graphene with some uses.	**Extend:** Students use the properties of graphene and fullerenes to justify their chosen applications.	**Interactive:** Fullerenes and graphene

Homework		
Students make a model of a bucky-ball. Their model should include a description of the properties of a bucky-ball and some potential uses.		

kerboodle

A Kerboodle highlight for this lesson is **Literacy skills: Graphene and fullerenes**. Refer to the **Content map** on Kerboodle for a full list of resources and assessment.

C3.9 Bonding in metals

AQA spec Link: 2.1.5 Metals consist of giant structures of atoms arranged in a regular pattern. The electrons in the outer shell of metal atoms are delocalised and so are free to move through the whole structure. The sharing of delocalised electrons gives rise to strong metallic bonds. The bonding in metals may be represented in the following form:

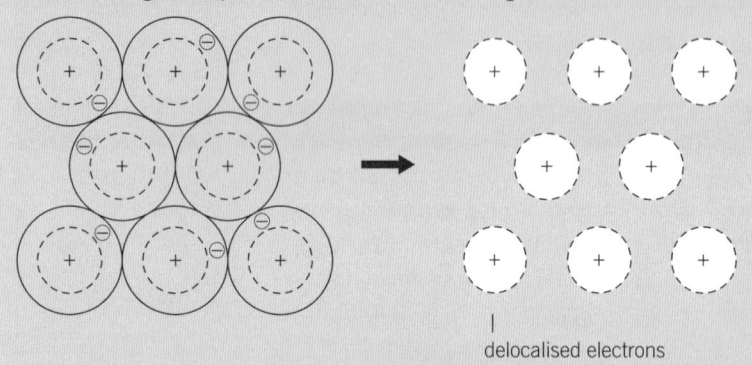

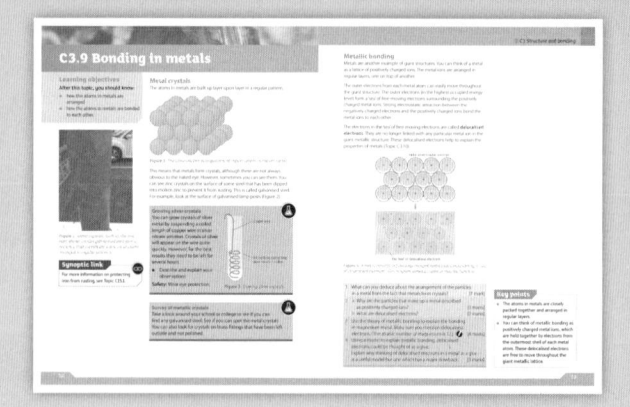

delocalised electrons

WS 1.2
MS 5b

Aiming for	Outcome	Checkpoint	
		Question	Activity
Aiming for GRADE 4 ↓	State that metals form a giant structure.	1	Starter 1
	Recognise metallic bonding in diagrams.		Starter 1, Starter 2, Plenary 1
Aiming for GRADE 6 ↓	Describe metallic bonding.	3	Main 1, Plenary 1, Plenary 2
	Recognise and represent metallic bonding diagrammatically.		Plenary 2
Aiming for GRADE 8 ↓	Explain how metal atoms form giant structures.	2, 3	Main 1, Plenary 2
	Evaluate different models of metallic bonding.	4	Plenary 1

Maths
Students draw the electronic structures of atoms and ions.

Literacy
Students describe their observations and the structure of the silver crystals produced in the practical.

Key words
delocalised electrons

Practical

Title	Growing silver crystals
Equipment	boiling tube, 10 cm length of copper wire, 0.4 mol/dm³ silver nitrate solution, wooden splint, boiling-tube rack, eye protection
Overview of method	Half fill the boiling tube with silver nitrate solution and stand it in the rack. Wind the copper wire into a corkscrew shape and wrap the end of the wire around the middle of a splint. Lower the wire into the boiling tube, so that at least half of the corkscrew shape is submerged. The splint should sit across the top of the boiling tube so that the wire can be removed from the liquid later.
Safety considerations	0.4 mol/dm³ silver nitrate solution is an irritant, wear splash-proof eye protection and wash hands after the experiment is completed. Follow CLEAPSS advice for disposal procedures.

C3 Structure and bonding

Starter	Support/Extend	Resources
Structure spotting (5 minutes) Show students diagrams of a giant covalent structure, a giant ionic structure, and a simple covalent molecule. Students describe each of the structures, list the types of bonding involved, and any properties they would expect the substance to have. Then show students a metallic structure. Ask students if this is a different type of bonding, and point out the differences from the other giant structures they have met. **Bonding in metals** (10 minutes) Students label a diagram of metallic bonding to show the key features. They then complete a matching exercise to briefly summarise the key features of the three types of bonding they have studied – ionic, covalent, and metallic.	**Extend:** Ask students to suggest how metal atoms bond to each other.	**Interactive:** Bonding in metals

Main	Support/Extend	Resources
Growing silver crystals (25 minutes) Ask students to draw a results table to note the appearance of the reactants. Run the experiment and students make observations after 10 minutes, then again after 20 minutes. Encourage students to write word and balanced symbol equations to illustrate the reaction. **Survey** (15 minutes) Allow students to tour the school in small groups to find examples of metal crystals in different structural materials. Galvanised steel and brass often allow the crystals to be seen. If possible, supply students with a digital camera and encourage them to take a digital image, annotate the image to highlight the crystal, and then add information to explain the bonding and structure in that image. Ensure students understand which parts of the site should not be visited and be given clear instruction of the time allowed for this activity. This activity could be carried out in between observations in the practical. Alternatively, supply students with images of galvanised steel and brass.	**Support:** Give students the results table and a descriptive word bank to help with their observations. **Extend:** Ask students to add state symbols to the equations. **Support:** Direct students to examples around the school.	**Practical:** Growing silver crystals

Plenary	Support/Extend	Resources
What's the connection? (5 minutes) Show students any models of metallic crystals that the school may have, a diagram, and 3D computer simulations. Ensure that students can pick out the key features of each model, for example, the metal ions and the electrons. **Silver crystals** (10 minutes) Ask students to look carefully at their silver crystals. Students use their knowledge of metallic bonding to explain the structure of the crystal in both prose and a labelled diagram.	**Extend:** Ask students to evaluate the models. Then to justify their selection of the best model for metallic bonding. **Support:** Give students the sentences to order and a diagram to label. **Extend:** Ask students to suggest other chemical reactions which would make silver crystals.	

Homework		
Students suggest and explain whether sodium or aluminium would have stronger metallic bonding.	**Support:** Give students the diagrams of the structure of each metal with the metal ion's charge clearly marked and the difference in electron density clear to see.	

C3.10 Giant metallic structures

AQA spec Link: 2.2.7 Metals have giant structures of atoms with strong metallic bonding. This means that most metals have high melting and boiling points.

In pure metals, atoms are arranged in layers, which allows metals to be bent and shaped. Pure metals are too soft for many uses and so are mixed with other metals to make alloys which are harder.

Students should be able to explain why alloys are harder than pure metals in terms of distortion of the layers of atoms in the structure of a pure metal.

2.2.8 Metals are good conductors of electricity because the delocalised electrons in the metal carry electrical charge through the metal. Metals are good conductors of thermal energy because energy is transferred by the delocalised electrons.

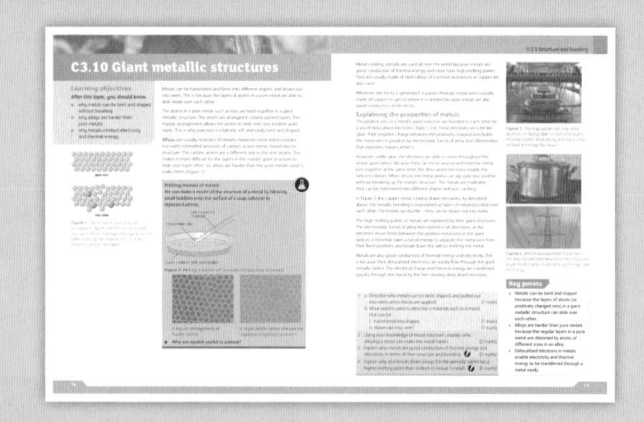

WS 1.2
MS 5b

Aiming for	Outcome	Checkpoint	
		Question	Activity
Aiming for GRADE 4 ↓	List the physical properties of metals.	1	Starter 2, Main
	Describe the structure of a pure metal.		Main
Aiming for GRADE 6 ↓	Explain key physical properties of metals using the model of metallic bonding.	1, 3, 4	Main
	Describe why metals are alloyed.	2	Main
Aiming for GRADE 8 ↓	Explain in detail, including labelled diagrams, how alloying affects the structure and bonding in metals and its effect on properties.	2	Main
	Justify in detail why alloys are more often used than pure metals.	2	Main

Maths
Students relate a 2D model to a 3D metallic structure (5b).

Literacy
Students explain the properties of metals.

Key words
alloys

Practical

Title	Making models of metals
Equipment	Petridish lid, soap solution, Pasteur pipette, eye protection
Overview of method	Half fill the lid of a Petridish with soap solution. Then using the Pasteur pipette blow bubbles which are equal in size. This models a pure metal crystal as the bubbles form layers which are uniformly arranged. Carefully push one line of bubbles and they rearrange without breaking. This models malleability and ductility. Using the Pasteur pipette introduce a few bubbles which are large in size. This models an alloy. Again push on a line of bubbles and notice how the bubbles resist motion. This models how an alloy is harder and stronger than a pure metal.
Safety considerations	Soap solution is an irritant, wear splash-proof eye protection and wash hands after the experiment is completed.

■ C3 Structure and bonding

Starter	Support/Extend	Resources
Periodic look up (5 minutes) Provide students with a periodic table. Ask students to find the symbol of copper, Cu, the atomic number of gold (79), the mass number of iron (56), and give the electronic structure of aluminium (2, 8, 3). **What do you know?** (10 minutes) Split the class into four groups and assign each group one of the metals copper, gold, iron, or aluminium. Ask each group to list the physical properties of their metal and any uses that they know of for that substance. Use question and answer to generate a common list of the physical properties of metals.	**Support:** Project a periodic table and circle the symbol tiles of the relevant elements to focus the attention of the students. **Extend:** Ask students if the pure metal is used for the purpose outlined and explore that it is often a mixture.	
Main	**Support/Extend**	**Resources**
Making models of metals (40 minutes) Explain that a model is a simplified version of what actually happens that helps scientists understand observations and make predictions. Run the practical as outlined. Ask students to explain malleability and ductility of a pure metal and an alloy by using labelled diagrams of the experiment. Students then complete a table with the three columns (metal property, explanation, illustrated use). Students should explain the key physical properties (ductile, malleable, thermal conductor, and electrical conductor) and illustrate a use for each property limited to copper, gold, iron, and aluminium. For example, copper is used in electrical wires because it is ductile and a good electrical conductor. Students develop their ideas of metallic bonding into a model and use this to explain some of the properties of metals and alloys.	**Support:** Allow students to film the experiment on their own devices so that they can re-play the key parts of the experiment. **Extend:** Ask students to investigate if it must always be a bigger atom introduced to the metal structure in an alloy to modify the properties. **Extend:** Ask students to include 'lustrous' and 'sonorous' in their table.	**Activity:** Making models of metals
Plenary	**Support/Extend**	**Resources**
Question time (5 minutes) Ask students to write five questions about the structure and bonding in metals. Encourage students to use the learning objectives to help them. Ask the students to swap their questions with a partner who should answer them for homework. **Metals and alloys** (10 minutes) Interactive where students complete a paragraph to explain the bonding and properties of metals. They then identify the reason why an alloy is sometimes used in place of a pure metal.	**Support:** Ask students to re-phrase the learning objectives as questions.	**Interactive:** Metals and alloys
Homework		
Ask students to answer the questions that have been generated in the plenary.		

kerboodle
A Kerboodle highlight for this lesson is **Extension sheet: Giant metallic structures**. Refer to the **Content map** on Kerboodle for a full list of resources and assessment.

GCSE Chemistry Only

C3.11 Nanoparticles

AQA spec Link: 2.4.1 Nanoscience refers to structures that are 1–100 nm in size, of the order of a few hundred atoms. Nanoparticles, are smaller than fine particles (PM$_{2.5}$), which have diameters between 100 and 2500 nm (1×10^{-7} m and 2.5×10^{-6} m). Coarse particles (PM$_{10}$) have diameters between 1×10^{-5} m and 2.5×10^{-6} m. Coarse particles are often referred to as dust.

As the side of a cube decreases by a factor of 10 the surface area to volume ratio increases by a factor of ten.

Nanoparticles may have properties different from those for the same material in bulk because of their high surface area to volume ratio. It may also mean that smaller quantities are needed to be effective than for materials with normal particle size.

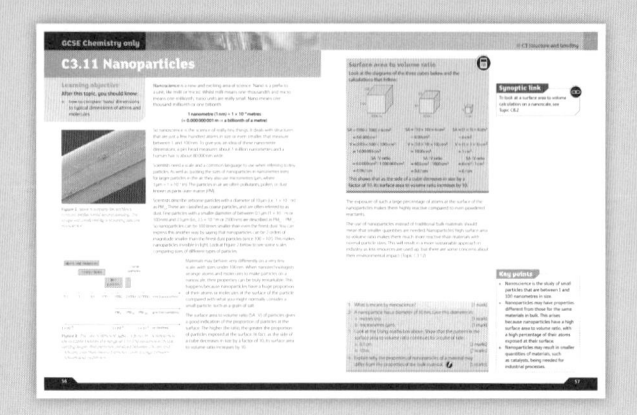

MS 1b, 1d, 2h, 5c

Aiming for	Outcome	Checkpoint	
		Question	Activity
Aiming for GRADE 4 ↓	State a definition of nanoscience.	1	Homework
	Describe how surface area to volume ratio increases as particle size decreases.		Main 2
	Recognise that the negative indices in standard form used in nanoscience represent very small numbers.		Starter 1, Plenary 2
Aiming for GRADE 6 ↓	Describe the size of nanoparticles.	2	Main 1, Plenary 2
	Explain why surface area to volume ratio increases as particle size decreases.		Starter 2, Main 2
	Convert lengths into standard form.	2	Starter 1, Plenary 2
Aiming for GRADE 8 ↓	Classify a particle as coarse, fine, or nanoparticle based on its size.		Plenary 1
	Quantitatively explain the relationship between surface area to volume ratio and particle size and its effect on properties.	3, 4	Starter 2, Main 2
	Convert standard form into a variety of length units.	2	Plenary 1

Maths
Students use standard form to express decimal numbers.

Literacy
Students write a safety briefing.

Key words
nanoscience

■ C3 Structure and bonding

Starter	Support/Extend	Resources
Standard form (5 minutes) Ask students to convert the following numbers into standard form: • 0.000 000 1 (1×10^{-7}) • 0.000 002 5 (2.5×10^{-6}) • 0.000 01 (1×10^{-5}) **Surface area demonstration** (10 minutes) Set up a Bunsen burner and safety equipment, including eye protection. Using metal tongs put a nail in the blue Bunsen flame and demonstrate that it just heats up rather than reacts with the oxygen in the air. Then dip the end of a wooden splint in water and then into iron powder. Put the end of the splint into the blue Bunsen flame. Oxidation occurs quickly as sparks of iron react. Use question and answer to ensure that students understand that as the surface area was increased this caused the reaction to occur much more quickly. So, the smaller particles had different properties to the larger particles.	**Support:** Show students a number line. **Extend:** Ask students to put the prefix instead of the standard form, for example, 1×10^{-7} m is 100 nanometres.	

Main	Support/Extend	Resources
Investigation (20 minutes) Explain to students that PM means particulate matter and the subscript represents the size in micrometres (10^{-6} m). Show students a CLEAPSS safety warning. Then ask them to prepare a similar briefing for a flour mill, discussing the difference between coarse dust particles and fine particles and how the latter could run the risk of explosion.	**Support:** Give students a writing frame. **Extend:** Ask students to include information on size as both metres in standard form and the PM scale.	
Nanoscience (20 minutes) Ask students to work in small groups. Give them 64 1-cm³ cubes that stick together (often found in mathematics departments). Ask students to make a cube 4×4×4 and record the volume and the surface area. Repeat for cubes 2×2×2 and 1×1×1. Students should record their results in an appropriate table. Ask students to add a column of surface area/volume. Explain that each the side length of cube is half the side length of the cube before and ask them to draw conclusions consistent with the results.	**Support:** Complete the calculations for the students. **Extend:** Ask students to use their mathematical knowledge to calculate the volume and surface area without making the cubes.	**Activity:** Nanoscience

Plenary	Support/Extend	Resources
Nanoparticles (5 minutes) Use the interactive to give students a variety of sizes of particle and ask them to classify them as coarse (dust), fine, or nanoparticle. Students then identify why nanoparticles have different properties from the same material in bulk.	**Support:** Only give values in standard form and write the definition on the board so that students can easily refer to it. **Extend:** Use a variety of length units, including metres in standard form and PM.	**Interactive:** Nanoparticles
Size and scale (10 minutes) Calculation sheet where students work through a worked example to compare nano dimensions to the dimensions of atoms and molecules, using numbers expressed in standard form. They then have further questions to practise.		**Calculation sheet:** Size and scale

Homework		
Ask students to write a tweet (max. 140 characters) to summarise their learning of nanoscience.		

kerboodle

A Kerboodle highlight for this lesson is **Calcuation: Surface area to volume**. Refer to the **Content map** on Kerboodle for a full list of resources and assessment.

GCSE Chemistry Only

C3.12 Applications of nanoparticles

AQA spec Link: 2.4.2 Nanoparticles have many applications in medicine for controlling drug delivery and in synthetic skin; in electronics; in cosmetics and sun creams; in the development of new catalysts for fuel cell materials; in deodorants and in fabrics to prevent the growth of bacteria. New applications for nanoparticulate materials are an important area of research.

Nanoparticles are being used in sun creams. Some of the benefits of nanoparticles in sun creams include better skin coverage and more effective protection from the sun's ultraviolet rays. Disadvantages include potential cell damage in the body and harmful effects on the environment.

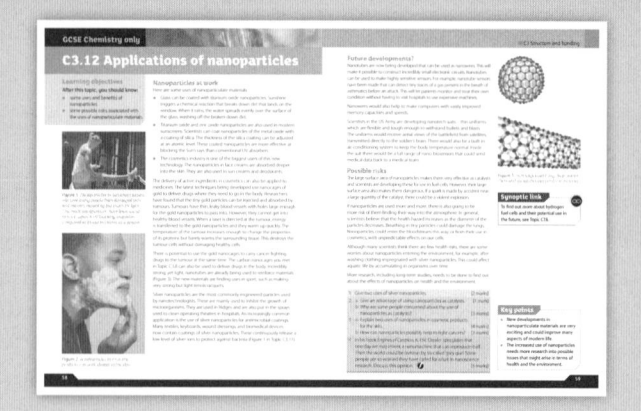

WS 1.3, 1.4, 1.5
MS 1b

Aiming for	Outcome	Checkpoint	
		Question	Activity
Aiming for GRADE 4 ↓	State that nanoparticles can be used in sun cream.		Starter 1, Main
	List a variety of uses of nanoparticles.	1, 2	Starter 1, Main
Aiming for GRADE 6 ↓	List the advantages and disadvantages of using nanoparticles.	2, End of chapter 7	Main, Plenary 2
	Explain why nanoparticles can have new applications.	3	Main
Aiming for GRADE 8 ↓	Evaluate the use of nanoparticles in their applications, including sun cream.	3	Main, Plenary 2
	Decide and justify in detail why nanotechnology research should continue.	4	Starter 1, Main, Plenary 1

Maths
Students need to understand and be able to use standard form when studying nanoparticles (1b).

Literacy
Students research the uses of nanoparticles and collate their information into a visual poster. There is also an opportunity for a debate on whether nanoparticles should be used.

58

■ C3 Structure and bonding

Starter	Support/Extend	Resources
What's the connection? (10 minutes) Show students a sample of sun cream, silver-coated plasters, cosmetics, and any other appropriate examples of nanotechnology. Ask students to suggest the connection. **Continuum** (10 minutes) Explain that one end of the classroom represents 100% agree and the opposite end is 0% agree, therefore in the middle students neither agree nor disagree. Ask students to stand where they feel about the use and development of nanoscience. Ask a few students to justify their choice.	**Extend:** After some initial discussion, tell students the link is nanoparticles. Students then start to make suggestions as to the role of nanoparticles in each example.	

Main	Support/Extend	Resources
Applications of nanoscience (40 minutes) Explain to students that nanoparticles have potential uses. Split the class into groups of five. Assign each member of the group one of the categories – fabrics, medicine, electronics, cosmetics, and sun creams. Each students researches the uses of nanoparticles within their category. The group then collates their information and creates a group poster, summarising the uses of nanoparticles. If time, groups could present their posters to the class, with each presentation lasting only a few minutes.		**Activity:** Applications of nanoscience

Plenary	Support/Extend	Resources
Continuum (5 minutes) Ask students to return to the continuum and stand where they now feel about the use and development of nanoscience. Ask students to raise their hands if they have not changed their viewpoint and ask for volunteers to justify that choice, and then repeat for the students who have changed their position. **Uses of nanoparticles** (5 minutes) Interactive where students sort the advantages and disadvantages of using nanoparticles in sun cream.	**Extend:** Students suggest further advantages and disadvantages.	**Interactive:** Uses of nanoparticles

Homework		
Students complete the WebQuest where they research some uses of nanotechnology. They use their research to produce a presentation to persuade some business people to invest in nanotechnology. Alternatively, ask students to make a poster to show the uses of nanotechnology and predict the future of this branch of science.		**WebQuest:** Nanoparticles

kerboodle

A Kerboodle highlight for this lesson is **Literacy sheet: Applications of nanoparticles**. Refer to the **Content map** on Kerboodle for a full list of resources and assessment.

C3 Structure and bonding

Overview of C3 Structure and bonding

In this chapter, students have developed their understanding of the states of matter from KS3. They have built upon their understanding of the particle model, using this to explain the energy transfers involved when substances change state.

Students have also learnt about the different types of bonding in substances. They should know that covalent bonding is the sharing of one or more pairs of electrons between non-metal atoms; ionic bonding involves a metal and non-metal atom, with the metal atom losing one or more electrons and the non-metal atom gaining one or more electron; and metallic bonding involves a delocalised sea of electrons surrounding the positive metal ions.

Students should have also learnt how the bonding of a substance affects its bulk properties. They should be able to describe the difference in bonding and properties of giant ionic structures, simple covalent molecules, and giant covalent structures (including different arrangements of carbon). Students should understand that covalent, metallic, and ionic bonding is strong, but that it is how the particles interact (intermolecular forces) that determines properties such as melting point, boiling point, and electrical conductivity.

Finally, students should have learnt about nanoparticles, their properties, and be able to explain how the surface area to volume ratio of nanoparticles is different to bulk material, and how this affects their uses.

MyMaths

You can find additional support for the maths skills covered in this chapter on **MyMaths**, including using standard form, calculating suface areas, and using ratios.

kerboodle

For this chapter, the following assessments are available on Kerboodle:

C3 Checkpoint quiz: Structure and bonding
C3 Progress quiz: Structure and bonding 1
C3 Progress quiz: Structure and bonding 2
C3 On your marks: Structure and bonding
C3 Exam-style questions and mark scheme: Structure and bonding

Checkpoint follow up lesson

A student's route through this lesson can be determined using the Checkpoint assessment. Percentage pass marks are supplied in the Checkpoint teacher notes.

For each successive route through it is assumed that the student can perform to their current route as well as previous routes. For example, students working at Aiming for 6 are assumed to be secure in Aiming for 4 knowledge and understanding and working towards achieving all the learning outcomes for Aiming for 6.

	Aiming for 4	Aiming for 6	Aiming for 8
Learning outcomes	Recognise and describe the three main types of bonding.	Describe the main types of bonding and related structures. Explain what occurs when each type of substance is melted or boiled.	Use experimental results to identify bonding types present.
Starter	**Molecular models (5 minutes)** Show molecular models of simple covalent structures (e.g., a molecule of oxygen), giant covalent structures (e.g., diamond) and ionic substances (e.g., sodium chloride). An animation of the delocalised electrons within metallic bonding could also be shown. Discuss with students what is happening within each type of bonding in terms of electron sharing/transfer and the properties of each type of substance. **Dot-and-cross diagrams (5 minutes)** Model how dot-and-cross diagrams can be used to represent the bonding in substances, for example, by drawing the dot-and-cross diagram for sodium chloride, NaCl, and methane, CH_4. Ensure that you highlight that dots and crosses represent electrons, and the number in the outer shell of elements corresponds to the group number for each element. Describe how electrons are shared in covalent molecules and so these diagrams are shown with overlapping outer 'shells', how in ionic substances outer electrons are transferred so each ion is shown in square brackets with charges, and dots and crosses can show where electrons have come from.		
Differentiated checkpoint activity	The Aiming for 4 Checkpoint follow-up sheet provides a highly-structured fact sheet on the different types of bonding for students to complete.	The Aiming for 6 Checkpoint follow-up sheet provides students with tasks that will support students with producing their own fact sheet on bonding.	Aiming for 8 students analyse experimental data to identify the bonding and structure of a series of substances. If Aiming for 8 students are very capable, once they have completed the task they could be given a selection of substances to experiment on to determine the bonding and structures present, e.g., by testing conduction, solubility, and by researching their melting and boiling points.
	Kerboodle resource C3 Checkpoint follow up: Aiming for 4, C3 Checkpoint follow up: Aiming for 6, C3 Checkpoint follow up: Aiming for 8		
Plenary	**Bonding (10 minutes)** Draw four columns on a whiteboard or flipchart. Give the columns the headings simple covalent, giant covalent, ionic, and metallic bonding respectively. Ask pairs or small groups to come up with three facts on each type of bonding. Then ask them to compare with neighbouring groups before then discussing points as a class. Address any misconceptions that have arisen. Ask students to then describe, or draw using a simple cartoon style drawing, what happens when each type of substance is melted or boiled.		
Progression	Encourage students to use their notes from the chapter and the student book to add more detail into their fact sheet.	Provide students with the data from the Aiming for 8 sheet and allow them to use their fact sheet to identify the bonding of the substances.	Provide students with a substance that completely fit into the patterns that have been analysing, for example, carbon dioxide (a simple molecule) dissolves in water but has a melting point of −56.6 °C and is a colourless gas.

C 4 Chemical calculations
4.1 Relative masses and moles

AQA spec Link: 3.1.2 The relative formula mass M_r of a compound is the sum of the relative atomic masses of the atoms in the numbers shown in the formula.

3.2.1 **H** Chemical amounts are measured in moles. The symbol for the unit mole is mol.

The mass of one mole of a substance in grams is numerically equal to its relative formula mass.

One mole of a substance contains the same number of the stated particles, atoms, molecules, or ions as one mole of any other substance.

The number of atoms, molecules, or ions in a mole of a given substance is the Avogadro constant. The value of the Avogadro constant is 6.02×10^{23} per mole.

Students should understand that the measurement of amounts in moles can apply to atoms, molecules, ions, electrons, formulae, and equations, for example that in one mole of carbon, C, the number of atoms is the same as the number of molecules in one mole of carbon dioxide, CO_2.

Students should be able to use the relative formula mass of a substance to calculate the number of moles in a given mass of that substance and vice versa.

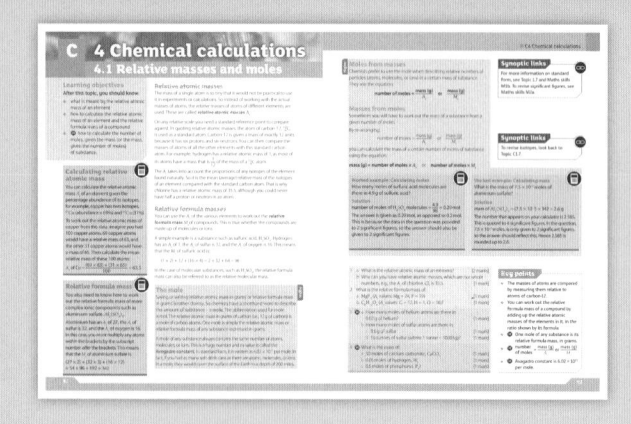

MS 1a, 1b, 1c, 2a, 3a, 3b

Aiming for	Outcome	Checkpoint	
		Question	Activity
Aiming for GRADE 4	Use the periodic table to identify the relative atomic mass for the first 20 elements.	1	Starter 1
	Calculate the relative formula mass for familiar compounds when the formula is supplied and is without brackets.	2, End of chapter 1	Main, Plenary 2
Aiming for GRADE 6	Use the periodic table to find the relative atomic mass of all elements.		Starter 1, Main, Plenary 2
	Calculate the relative formula mass for unfamiliar compounds when the formula is given.	2, End of chapter 1	Plenary 2
	H State the units for the amount of substance.		Starter 2, Main, Plenary 1, Plenary 2
Aiming for GRADE 8	Explain why relative atomic masses may not be a whole number.	5	Plenary 1
	Explain why some elements have the same relative atomic mass as each other.	3	Plenary 1
	H Calculate the number of moles or mass of a substance from data supplied.	3, 4, End of chapter 2	Starter 2, Main, Plenary 1, Plenary 2

Maths
Students use Avogadro's constant (1b) to calculate relative formula mass or moles (3b).

Literacy
Students produce a revision guide page, summarising information from the topic and the previous chapter.

Key words
relative atomic mass A_r, relative formula mass M_r, mole, Avogadro constant.

C4 Chemical calculations

Starter	Support/Extend	Resources
Fingers (5 minutes) Ask students to use their fingers to demonstrate the mass of the first four elements. Ask questions which encourage the students remember key information about the periodic table, for example, what is the relative atomic mass of the element with the symbol H? What is the relative atomic mass of the element in Group 0 of Period 1? What is the relative atomic mass of the element at the top of Group 2? **Looking at Avogadro** (10 minutes) **H** Give the students sealed samples of a mole of various safe elements such as 56 g iron or 32 g sulfur. Tell students that a mole of helium would occupy 24 dm³ at room temperature and pressure. Ask the students what they all have in common (they are all elements). Then ask them to think about particles and explain that every sample has the same number of particles. Then ask students to suggest why each sample has a different mass (each atom has a different mass). Introduce the idea that all the samples contain a mole.	**Support:** Remind students of the definitions of the key words that you are planning to use in your questions. **Extend:** Ask students to suggest the relative mass of a hydrogen molecule.	

Main	Support/Extend	Resources
Amount of substance (40 minutes) Using a molecular modelling kit, ask small groups of students to make a model of a hydrogen molecule. Through question and answer, ascertain that the relative atomic mass of hydrogen is 1 and as a molecule of hydrogen is made up of two hydrogen atoms, H_2, the relative mass of a molecule of hydrogen would be 2. Repeat for oxygen, nitrogen, and then water. Students then complete the activity sheet where they calculate the relative molecular mass of a series of molecules. **H** Explain the concept of Avogadro's constant and the mole. Ask students to suggest how many atoms are in a mole of hydrogen atoms (6.02×10^{23}), and how many atoms are in a mole of hydrogen molecules (12.04×10^{23}), and then how many hydrogen atoms are in a mole of water molecules (12.04×10^{23}). Students then use the activity sheet to carry out further calculations involving the mole.	**Extend:** Give students mole calculation to complete, including calculating relative formula mass, moles, and mass of compounds.	**Activity:** Amount of substance

Plenary	Support/Extend	Resources
Atomic mass and isotopes (5 minutes) Show students an A Level periodic table. Ask them to explain why the relative atomic masses are not whole numbers. Then ask students to suggest why the relative atomic mass of cobalt and nickel is the same in the periodic table of the student book, but not in the A Level periodic table. **Information from the periodic table** (10 minutes) Interactive where students label the mass number, atomic number, and symbol of lithium. **H** They then sort given masses of elements according to how many moles of the element the mass represents.		**Interactive:** Information from the periodic table

Homework
Students produce a page for a revision guide, summarising the structure of the atom, isotopes, and how calculate relative formula mass. Their revision page should include a one worked example to explain what relative formula mass is and how it can be calculated. Higher tier students should also include information on the mole.

kerboodle

A Kerboodle highlight for this lesson is **Bump up your grade: Inside compounds**. Refer to the **Content map** on Kerboodle for a full list of resources and assessment.

Higher tier

C4.2 Equations and calculations

AQA spec Link: 3.2.2 The masses of reactants and products can be calculated from balanced symbol equations.

Chemical equations can be interpreted in terms of moles.
For example:

$Mg + 2HCl \longrightarrow MgCl_2 + H_2$

shows that one mole of magnesium reacts with two moles of hydrochloric acid to produce one mole of magnesium chloride and one mole of hydrogen gas.

Students should be able to:
- calculate the masses of substances shown in a balanced symbol equation
- calculate the masses of reactants and products from the balanced symbol equation and the mass of a given reactant or product.

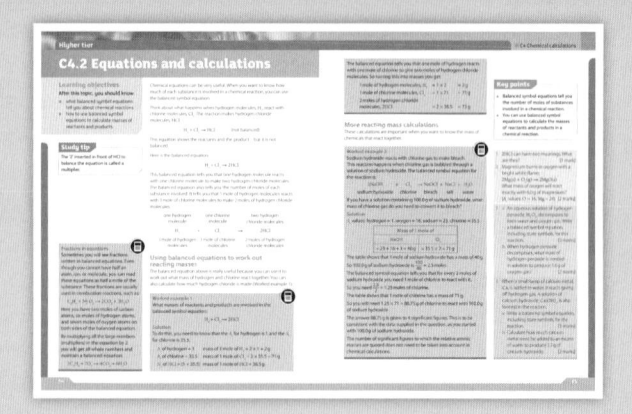

MS 1a, 1c, 3b, 3c

Aiming for	Outcome	Checkpoint	
		Question	Activity
Aiming for GRADE 6 ↓	Explain why chemical equations must be balanced.		Main 1, Plenary 2
	Calculate the relative formula mass for one substance when the relative formula masses are given for all the other substances in a balanced symbol equation.		Main 1, Main 2, Plenary 2
Aiming for GRADE 8 ↓	Interpret balanced symbol equations in terms of mole ratios.	1, End of chapter 5	Main 2, Plenary 2
	Use balanced symbol equations to calculate reacting masses.	2, 3, 4, End of chapter 5, 7	Main 2, Plenary 2

Maths
Students calculate relative formula mass, moles, or reacting masses (3b, 3c) and balance chemical equations (1c).

Literacy
Students describe what happens to the atoms in a chemical reaction, using the concept of moles in their description.

Practical

Title	Magnesium and hydrochloric acid
Equipment	test tube, test-tube rack, boiling tube, 1 mol/dm³ hydrochloric acid, 1 cm length magnesium ribbon, splint, Bunsen burner and safety equipment, eye protection
Overview of method	Half fill the test tube with hydrochloric acid and add the piece of magnesium ribbon. Quickly put the boiling tube over the top of the test tube and support in the rack. Remove the boiling tube, keeping open end downwards, and test the gas with a lighted splint.
Safety considerations	Hydrochloric acid is an irritant, magnesium ribbon is highly flammable, and hydrogen is explosive. Wear eye protection and keep magnesium away from the naked flame. Do not make more than a boiling tube of hydrogen gas.

C4 Chemical calculations

Starter	Support/Extend	Resources
Balancing equations (5 minutes) Use the interactive to show students chemical equations of familiar chemical reactions, without the balancing numbers. Students balance them, then use the balanced symbol equation of the reaction of magnesium and hydrochloric acid to choose the correct words to complete a paragraph on the reaction. **Mass** (10 minutes) Demonstrate the magnesium and dilute hydrochloric acid reaction outlined, without trapping the hydrogen gas in a boiling tube. Ask students to predict (suggest what would happen and why) to the mass of the chemicals in the reaction. Use question and answer to illicit that the mass would drop as one of the reactants is lost to the atmosphere. Then ask students to suggest what would happen to the mass if this experiment was completed in sealed pressure-stable container (mass remains the same).	**Support:** Allow students to use a molecular modelling kit to help them kinaesthetically work out the answers. **Extend:** Ask students to add state symbols to the balanced equation and to suggest another method to collect the hydrogen gas.	**Interactive:** Balancing equations

Main	Support/Extend	Resources
Magnesium and hydrochloric acid (20 minutes) Students carry out the practical then write a word equation and a balanced symbol equation for the reaction. Students describe the ratio of chemicals in terms of individual atoms or molecules. Then remind students about what a mole is. Ask them to write a new paragraph explaining the ratio of the chemicals in terms of moles. Students then explain the ratio of reactant and products in terms of mass if they were given 24 g of magnesium to react with excess hydrochloric acid. **Moles and mass** (20 minutes) Students summarise the individual steps in the worked examples of the student book as tasks to complete to help them work out a calculation.	**Support:** Give students the formula for each substance so that they only need to balance the equation. **Extend:** Ask students to complete reacting mass calculations using the mole concept.	**Practical:** Magnesium and hydrochloric acid

Plenary	Support/Extend	Resources
Important (5 minutes) Ask students to think of a reason why reacting mass calculations could be useful in everyday life/industry. Then ask students to share their ideas in small groups and encourage each group to give a different reason. **Predict** (10 minutes) Explain to students that calcium is also a Group 2 metal and reacts in a similar way to magnesium with hydrochloric acid. Ask them to write a balanced symbol equation for this reaction and suggest what mass of calcium is needed to make 2 g of hydrogen gas.	**Support:** Give students the word equation and the formulae for the substances. **Extend:** Ask students to use moles in their calculations.	

Homework		
Ask students to complete reacting mass calculations for the thermal decomposition of 100 g of calcium carbonate to make calcium oxide and carbon dioxide.	**Support:** Give students the word equation and the formulae for the substances. **Extend:** Give the starting mass of calcium carbonate as 50 tonnes.	

kerboodle

A Kerboodle highlight for this lesson is **Calculation sheet: Moles and masses**. Refer to the **Content map** on Kerboodle for a full list of resources and assessment.

Higher tier

C4.3 From masses to balanced equations

AQA spec link: 3.2.3 The balancing numbers in a symbol equation can be calculated from the masses of reactants and products by converting the masses in grams to amounts in moles and converting the numbers of moles to simple whole number ratios.

Students should be able to balance an equation given the masses of reactants and products. Students should be able to change the subject of a mathematical equation.

3.2.4 In a chemical reaction involving two reactants, it is common to use an excess of one of the reactants to ensure that all of the other reactant is used. The reactant that is completely used up is called the limiting reactant because it limits the amount of products.

Students should be able to explain the effect of a limiting quantity of a reactant on the amount of products it is possible to obtain in terms of amounts in moles or masses in grams.

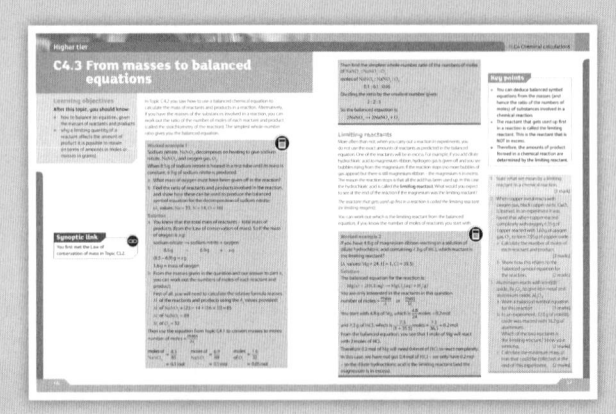

MS 3b, 3c

Aiming for	Outcome	Checkpoint	
		Question	Activity
Aiming for GRADE 6 ↓	Explain why chemical equations must be balanced.		Starter 2, Main
	Identify the limiting reactant in a chemical reaction.	3	Plenary 1, Main
Aiming for GRADE 8 ↓	Explain the effect of a limiting reactant on the amount of product made.		Main
	Use balanced symbol equations to calculate reacting masses when there is a limiting reactant.	2, 3	Main

Maths
Students calculate relative formula mass, moles, and reacting masses (3b, 3c).

Literacy
Students write their own revision podcast to explain the importance of balanced symbol equations.

Key words
limiting reactant

66

C4 Chemical calculations

Starter	Support/Extend	Resources
Balanced? (5 minutes) Give students a series of balanced and unbalanced symbol equations. Students sort them, then complete a paragraph on limiting reactants. **Interpret the equations** (10 minutes) Students look carefully at the following equations: 1. copper sulfate + magnesium → magnesium sulfate + copper 2. $CuSO_4 + Mg \rightarrow MgSO_4 + Cu$ 3. $2CuSO_4 + 2Mg \rightarrow 2MgSO_4 + 2Cu$ 4. $\frac{1}{2}CuSO_4 + \frac{1}{2}Mg \rightarrow \frac{1}{2}MgSO_4 + \frac{1}{2}Cu$ 5. $CuSO_4(aq) + Mg(s) \rightarrow MgSO_4(aq) + Cu(s)$ Ask students to identify the similarities (all represent the same reaction) and differences (word equation has no ratios, last equation also has state symbols). Explain to students that as long as the mole ratios remain the same, different multipliers can be used to balance equations. Ask students to suggest why it is important that formula equations are balanced.	**Extend:** Students correctly balance the equations that are unbalanced.	**Interactive:** Balanced?

Main	Support/Extend	Resources
Equations and calculations (40 minutes) Students use the worked example from the student book to create a flow chart that summarises how to balance a symbol equation when given reacting masses. They use a second colour to annotate their flow chart with the worked example. Students then create a second flow chart to summarise the steps involved in calculating reacting masses when given a balanced symbol equation, using the worked example on the activity sheet. They annotate their flow chart with the worked example in a second colour. Students then use their flow charts to answer a series of questions involving these calculations.		**Activity:** Equations and calculations

Plenary	Support/Extend	Resources
Reactant definitions (5 minutes) Ask students to define limiting reactant and reactant in excess. Then give students some descriptions of a reaction and ask them to identify the limiting reactant and the reactant in excess. **Podcast** (10 minutes) Students work in small groups to write a podcast. Their podcast should explain the importance of balanced symbol equations, how they can be generated from reacting masses, and what a limiting reactant is. (Podcasts could be recorded if the school has this facility or if students are able to use their own devices such as smart phones.)	**Support:** Students each match word to its definition.	

Homework		
Ask students to think about the reaction between calcium carbonate in indigestion tablets and hydrochloric acid in the stomach. Students should predict which reagent is the limiting reagent.	**Extend:** Ask students to calculate the maximum mass of hydrochloric acid that can be neutralised by a dose of 4.00 g of calcium carbonate (expect an answer given to three significant figures).	

kerboodle

A Kerboodle highlight for this lesson is **Maths skills: Using masses to balance equations**. Refer to the **Content map** on Kerboodle for a full list of resources and assessment.

GCSE Chemistry Only

C4.4 The yield of a chemical reaction

AQA spec Link: 3.3.1 Even though no atoms are gained or lost in a chemical reaction, it is not always possible to obtain the calculated amount of a product because:

- the reaction may not go to competition because it is reversible
- some of the product may be lost when it is separated from the reaction mixture
- some of the reactants may react in ways different to the expected reaction.

The amount of a product obtained is known as the yield. When compared with the maximum theoretical amount as a percentage, it is called the percentage yield.

$$\% \text{ yield} = \frac{\text{mass of product actually made}}{\text{maximum theoretical mass of product}} \times 100$$

Students should be able to:

- calculate the theoretical amount of a product from a given amount of reactant and the balanced equation for the reaction
- calculate the percentage yield of a product from the actual yield of a reaction.

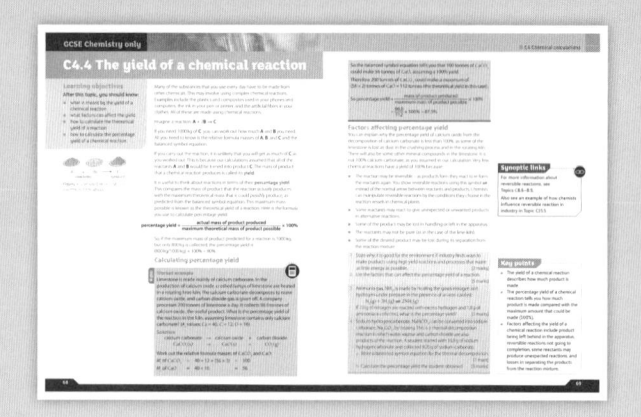

MS 1a, 1c, 2a, 3b

Aiming for	Outcome	Checkpoint	
		Question	Activity
Aiming for GRADE 4 ↓	State the definition of theoretical yield, actual yield, and percentage yield.		Starter 1
	Calculate percentage yield when actual yield and theoretical yield are given.		Main 1, Main 2, Plenary 1
Aiming for GRADE 6 ↓	Calculate percentage yield when the actual yield is given and the mass of the limiting reactant is given.	3, 4, End of chapter 4	Plenary 1
	List reasons why actual yield is often lower than theoretical yield.	2	Starter 2
Aiming for GRADE 8 ↓	Calculate the percentage yield using a variety of units and conversions.	End of chapter 5	Main 1, Main 2
	Justify why percentage yield can never be above 100%.	End of chapter 5	Plenary 2

Maths
Students calculate theoretical yield and percentage yield (1c).

Key words
yield, percentage yield

Practical

Title	Finding the percentage yield
Equipment	eye protection, crucible with well-fitting lid, tongs, pipe-clay triangle, Bunsen burner, tripod, heatproof mat, emery paper, 10 cm lengths of magnesium ribbon, balance
Overview of method	Weigh the crucible and its lid and record the mass in the Results table. Use the emery paper to clean the surface of your piece of magnesium ribbon. Coil the ribbon loosely and put it in the crucible. Replace the crucible lid and weigh the crucible, lid, and magnesium together. Set up a tripod and a pipe-clay triangle on the heatproof mat. Put the crucible in the middle of the pipe-clay triangle and make sure that it is stable. Light the Bunsen burner and begin to heat the crucible. Once the crucible is hot, use the tongs to gently lift the lid a little. Keep heating the crucible and lifting the lid until you see no further reaction. At this point, remove the lid, and heat for another couple of minutes. Put the lid back on if it appears that you are losing some product. Turn off the Bunsen burner, replace the lid, and allow the apparatus to cool. Reweigh the crucible containing the product together with the lid.

■ C4 Chemical calculations

Safety considerations	The most significant hazard in this experiment is the hot apparatus. Warn students that it will take some time (at least 15 minutes) for the crucible and lid to cool down and that they should not try and pick them up until cool enough to handle. Students should wear eye protection whilst carrying out the experiment. The students should be encouraged not to stare at the burning magnesium when they raise the crucible lid. Give each group of students a piece of magnesium. Do not allow them to take it themselves.

Starter	Support/Extend	Resources
Key terms (5 minutes) Students use the interactive to match the key terms actual yield, theoretical yield, and percentage yield with their definitions. They then sort a series of statements describing scenarios which can cause a percentage yield greater than 100% and less than 100%. **Industry** (10 minutes) Show students a photograph of a lime kiln. (Alternatively, you may be able to find a clip on the Internet of a lime kiln in action.) Explain to students that limestone is thermally decomposed to make calcium oxide and carbon dioxide. The calcium oxide is an important feedstock for the construction industry. Ask students to suggest why the percentage yield is below 100%. Create a list using question and answer. Then highlight the difference between processing loss (e.g., not transferring all the chemicals) and the chemical reasons (e.g., not all of the limestone is calcium carbonate).	**Extend:** Ask students to choose a chemical reaction of their choice and illustrate the different yields with a worked example. **Support:** You may wish to hand out samples in sealed containers (or show photos) of limestone and calcium carbonate so that they can see that limestone is an impure chemical.	**Interactive:** Key terms

Main	Support/Extend	Resources
Finding the percentage yield (25 minutes) Complete the practical in which students heat magnesium ribbon in a crucible, record the mass of magnesium ribbon used, and the mass of magnesium oxide produced. They then use the mass of magnesium to calculate the theoretical yield of the reaction and compare this with the actual mass of magnesium oxide found by experiment to calculate the percentage yield. Move on to the next activity whilst students wait for the apparatus to cool before they can weigh the crucible and magnesium oxide produced. **Calculating percentage yield** (15 minutes) Discuss the worked example of a lime kiln that is outlined in the student book. Students then work through the calculation sheet for further practice on calculating percentage yield and reacting masses.	**Support:** Students should work in small groups to complete this activity.	**Practical:** Finding the percentage yield **Calculation sheet:** Calculating percentage yield

Plenary	Support/Extend	Resources
Percentage yield (5 minutes) Explain to students that copper carbonate thermally decomposes in a similar way to calcium carbonate. In a chemical reaction 123.5 g of copper carbonate was heated and 37.3 g of copper oxide was made. Ask students to calculate the percentage yield of this reaction. **More than 100%?** (10 minutes) It is usual to consider that the percentage yield will always be less than 100%, however, on occasion the percentage yield could appear to be greater than 100%. Ask students to suggest reasons for the errors that could cause such an anomaly.	**Extend:** Ask students to write a balanced symbol equation with state symbols for this reaction. **Support:** You may need to give students scenarios to help them, for example, copper sulfate crystals that are made by evaporation. The yield appeared to be 110% because the crystals were wet and some of the paste was water.	

Homework		
Students complete the WebQuest where they are given an unfamiliar desired product and the amount needed. They research how the product is made, give a balanced equation, and carry out some calculations around the reaction. They use their research to produce an instruction sheet for a chemical company. Alternatively, ask students to generate three questions which are each answered by the key points in the student book.		**WebQuest:** Creating compounds

GCSE Chemistry Only

C4.5 Atom economy

AQA spec Link: 3.3.2 The atom economy (atom utilisation) is a measure of the amount of starting materials that end up as useful products. It is important for sustainable development and for economic reasons to use reactions with high atom economy.

The percentage atom economy of a reaction is calculated using the balanced symbol equation for the reaction as follows:

$$\frac{\text{relative formula mass of desired product from equation}}{\text{sum of relative formula masses of all reactants from equation}} \times 100$$

Students should be able to:

- calculate the atom economy of a reaction to form a desired product from the balanced equation
- **(H)** explain why a particular reaction pathway is chosen to produce a specified product given appropriate data such as atom economy (if not calculated), yield, rate, equilibrium position, and usefulness of by-products.

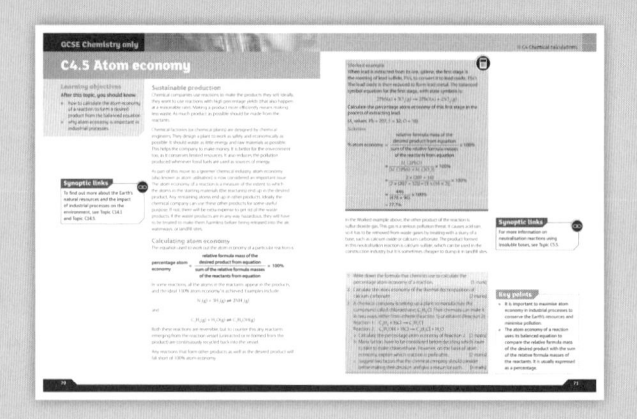

MS 1a, 1c, 3b

Aiming for	Outcome	Checkpoint	
		Question	Activity
Aiming for GRADE 4 ↓	Calculate the formula mass of substances when the formula is given.		Starter 2
	Balance simple chemical equations.		Main
	State a definition of atom economy.	1	Main
Aiming for GRADE 6 ↓	Calculate the atom economy for a given chemical reaction.	2, 3	Main
	Explain why using reactions with high atom economy is important.		Main
Aiming for GRADE 8 ↓	Evaluate different reactions to decide the best production method of a chemical.	3	Main
	Explain why the sum of the formula masses of the reactants is the same as the sum of the formula masses of the products.		Plenary 1

Maths
Students calculate formula mass and atom economy (1c, 3b).

Literacy
Students suggest and explain factors that can influence the method a company chooses for the synthesis of a chemical.

■ C4 Chemical calculations

Starter	Support/Extend	Resources
Annotate (5 minutes) On the board write: $$\frac{\text{relative formula mass of desired product from equation}}{\text{sum of relative formula masses of all reactants from equation}} \times 100$$ Through question and answer, ensure that students understand what relative formula mass, desired product, and reactant mean. **Atom economy** (10 minutes) Students match the compounds ethene, water, ethanol, sugar, and carbon dioxide with their chemical formula and relative formula mass. They then choose the correct words to complete a paragraph on atom economy.	**Support:** Give students the definitions and have them identify what key phrase it relates to. **Extend:** Use the sigma symbol Σ in the formula, and make sure students understand what it means.	**Interactive:** Atom economy

Main	Support/Extend	Resources
Atom economy (40 minutes) Explain to students that there are two common industrial methods for making ethanol. Ethanol is an important feedstock chemical used as a solvent and to make other products. Explain that one method is by fermentation, where yeast converts sugar into ethanol and carbon dioxide only. Ask students to write the word equation and then the balanced symbol equation for this reaction. Then they should calculate the atom economy for this reaction. Explain that a different method is the hydration of ethene. This makes only ethanol. Again ask students to write equations and calculate the atom economy. Students then look through the specification and write the balanced symbol equations for the important industrial processes that they will study (Haber process, aluminium oxide electrolysis, and iron oxide reduction with carbon). Students should then use these equations to calculate the atom economy for each process.	**Extend:** Ask students to use state symbols in the equation. Then ask them to justify which manufacturing process is best. **Extend:** You may wish to give other examples such as the Contact process, making hydrogen for the Haber process, and making nitric acid.	**Activity:** Atom economy

Plenary	Support/Extend	Resources
Choosing a reaction pathway (10 minutes) 🄷 Provide students with two theoretical reaction pathways to produce a useful product. One reaction pathway should have a low yield of the desired product but some useful by-products. The other reaction pathway should have a high yield for the desired product but some toxic by-products that are not useful. Students choose which reaction pathway they would use on an industrial scale and justify their answer. **Atom economy** (10 minutes) Students use the calculation sheet to practise calculating the atom economy of a reaction.		**Calculation sheet:** Atom economy

Homework		
Ask students to summarise in bullet points the importance of a high atom economy in an industrial process.		

kerboodle
A Kerboodle highlight for this lesson is **Literacy skills: Atom economy**. Refer to the **Content map** on Kerboodle for a full list of resources and assessment.

C4.6 Expressing concentrations

AQA spec Link: 3.2.5 Many chemical reactions take place in solutions. The concentration of a solution can be measured in mass per given volume of solution, for example, grams per dm³ (g/dm³).

Students should be able to:

- calculate the mass of solute in a given volume of solution of known concentration in terms of mass per given volume of solution
- **H** explain how the mass of a solute and the volume of a solution is related to the concentration of the solution.

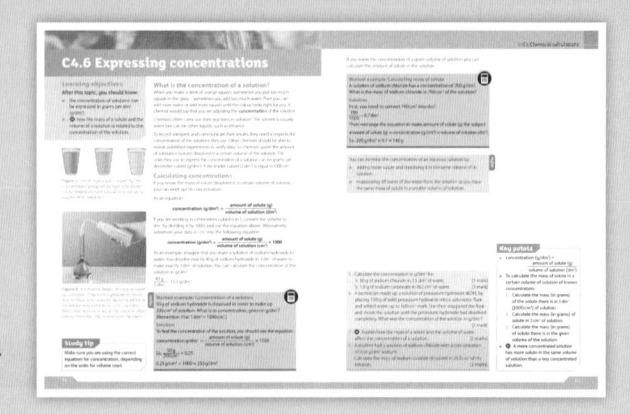

MS 1c, 3b

Aiming for	Outcome	Checkpoint	
		Question	Activity
Aiming for GRADE 4 ↓	Describe what the concentration of a solution is.		Starter 2, Plenary 2
	Calculate the concentration of a solution in g/dm³ when given the mass of solute in g and volume of solution in dm³.	1, 2	Main 1, Main 2
Aiming for GRADE 6 ↓	**H** Explain how concentration of a solution can be changed.	3	Starter 2, Main 1, Plenary 2
	Calculate the mass of solute (in g) in a solution when given the concentration in g/dm³ and volume in dm³ or cm³.	4	Main 1
Aiming for GRADE 8 ↓	Calculate the mass of a chemical when any volume and concentration is given.	4	Main 1
	Explain the concentration of a solution in terms of particles.	3	Plenary 2

Maths
Students calculate concentration and mass (3b).

Literacy
Students explain the terms concentration and dilute by relating it to squash. They also write an explanation applying their understanding of concentration and calculating concentration to an unfamiliar situation – medicinal drug drip bags.

Key words
concentration

Practical

Title	Making a standard solution
Equipment	250 cm³ volumetric flask, 100 cm³ beaker, stirring rod, anhydrous sodium hydrogensulfate powder, de-ionised water, dropper, weighing bottle, funnel, eye protection
Overview of method	Weigh out between 2.7 g and 3.3 g anhydrous sodium hydrogensulfate and pour the contents of the weighing bottle into a beaker. Add approximately 100 cm³ of de-ionised water and stir until all of the sodium hydrogensulfate dissolves. Using a funnel, add the solution into the volumetric flask. Make the volumetric flask up to the graduated mark by carefully adding de-ionised water from the wash bottle. Stopper the volumetric flask and shake it thoroughly to mix the contents of the flask.
Safety considerations	Sodium hydrogensulfate is harmful. Wear eye protection and wash hands after making the solution.

C4 Chemical calculations

Starter	Support/Extend	Resources
Equation triangle (5 minutes) Show students the equation triangle to calculate the concentration of a solution in g/dm³. Then ask them to use it to write three formulae with each term as the subject of the equation. **Squash** (10 minutes) Show students a 'double' concentrated bottle of squash, a 'normal' bottle of squash, and a 'ready to drink' bottle of squash. Ask students to put them in order of most concentrated to least concentrated, then most dilute to least dilute. Then ask students to define the terms concentrated and dilute in terms of squash.	**Support:** You may need to demonstrate how to use the equation triangle to determine the formula. **Extend:** Ask students to add the units in the formula for each term.	

Main	Support/Extend	Resources
Making a standard solution (25 minutes) Demonstrate how to make a standard solution. Then allow students in small groups to make their own standard solution. Encourage students to use the worked example in the student book to calculate the concentration of the solution that they have made in g/dm³. In order to calculate this value they will need to note the mass of solid used and convert the volume into dm³. **Concentrations of solutions** (15 minutes) Ask students to copy out the key points from the student book and illustrate each one with a explanation and a worked example	**Extend:** Students to suggest ways that they could improve the procedure to ensure that the concentration is more accurate, for example, weighing by difference, including rinsing of the equipment. **Extend:** Read each line of working for each worked example and use question and answer to get the class to classify which key point it relates to.	**Practical:** Making a standard solution

Plenary	Support/Extend	Resources
Algebra (5 minutes) Ask students to show mathematically that: mass = concentration × volume × relative formula mass Then provide students with some volumes and concentrations of solutions. Students calculate the amount of solute in the solution. **Diagrams** (10 minutes) Ask students to draw particle diagrams of a concentrated solution made of 20 acid particles (red circles) and 20 water molecules (blue circles). Ask students to draw a diagram with half the concentration of acid.	**Support:** Remind students that $$\text{moles} = \frac{\text{mass}}{\text{relative formula mass}}$$ and moles = concentration × volume **Extend:** Ask students to put terms into the equation to change cm³ to dm³ and kg to g.	

Homework		
Students write an explanation of why it is important that pharmacists understand how to calculate concentrations when they are preparing drugs to put in drip bags.	**Extend:** Give students a concentration calculation of a saline drip (e.g., 9 g/dm³).	

kerboodle

A Kerboodle highlight for this lesson is **Extension sheet: Expressing concentrations**. Refer to the **Content map** on Kerboodle for a full list of resources and assessment.

GCSE Chemistry Only

C4.7 Titrations

AQA spec Link: 3.2.5 The volumes of acid and alkali solutions that react with each other can be measured by titration using a suitable indicator.

Students should be able to:

- describe how to carry out titrations using strong acids and strong alkalis only (sulfuric, hydrochloric, and nitric acids only) to find the reacting volumes accurately.

Required practical: Determination of the reacting volumes of solutions of a strong acid and a strong alkali by titration.

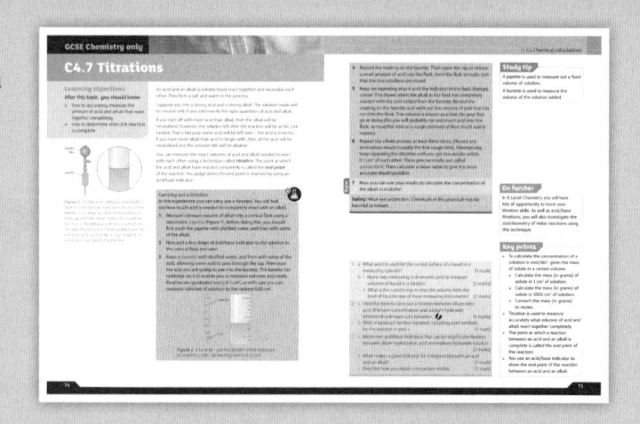

MS 1a, 1c, 2b, 3b, 3c

Aiming for	Outcome	Checkpoint	
		Question	Activity
Aiming for GRADE 4 ↓	Accurately read the volume on a burette to 1 decimal place.	1	Starter 1, Main
	Identify concordant results.		Starter 1, Main
Aiming for GRADE 6 ↓	Calculate a titre.		Main
	Describe how an indicator can be used to determine the end point.		Main, Plenary 1
	Explain how accuracy can be improved in a titration.	1, 2	Main, Plenary 2
Aiming for GRADE 8 ↓	Justify the use of a pipette and burette for a titration, evaluating the errors involved in reading these instruments.		Main, Plenary 2
	Explain how precise results are obtained in a titration.		Main, Plenary 2
	Justify the use of an indicator in an acid–base titration.	3	Main, Plenary 1, Homework

Maths
Students read a scale on a burette and calculate the mean of repeat titres (2b).

Literacy
Students provide an evaluation of their results.

Key words
titration, end point, pipette, burette, concordant

Required practical

Title	Carrying out a titration
Equipment	50 cm³ burette, stand, burette holder, 25 cm³ pipette, pipette filler, white tile, 250 cm³ conical flask, wash bottle of distilled water, funnel, eye protection, 0.1 mol/dm³ sodium hydroxide solution, 0.1 mol/dm³ hydrochloric acid, phenolphthalein indicator, 100 cm³ (waste) beaker
Overview of method	Wash the pipette with distilled water, and then with some of the alkali. Wash the burette with distilled water, and then some dilute hydrochloric acid. Fill the burette to 0 cm³ with hydrochloric acid. Use the pipette to transfer 25 cm³ of sodium hydroxide solution into the conical flask. Add a few drops of phenolphthalein indicator to the solution in the flask and swirl. Then place the conical flask on the white tile directly below the burette. Record the reading on the burette. Then open the tap to release a small amount of acid into the flask. Swirl the flask to make sure that the two solutions are mixed. Keep adding small amounts of acid and swirling until the indicator in the flask changes colour. Record the reading on the burette and work out the volume of acid run into the flask. Repeat the whole process at least three times. Discard any anomalous results (usually the first rough titre). Then calculate a mean value to give the most accurate results possible. Alternatively, keep repeating the titration until you get two results within 0.1 cm³ of each other (concordant results) and calculate the mean of these two results.

C4 Chemical calculations

Safety considerations	Sodium hydroxide is an irritant. Use the lowest concentration of hydrochloric acid possible. Wear eye protection. Do not fill the burette above head height, do not suck solutions into the pipette by mouth, and wash hands after making the solution.

Starter	Support/Extend	Resources
Titration apparatus (5 minutes) Students use the interactive to label the equipment in a diagram of the experimental setup of a titration. They then put a series of phrases in the correct order to describe an outline method for a titration. **Neutralisation** (10 minutes) Remind students of the concentration in g/dm³ calculations they met in Topic C4.6 by asking them to calculate the concentration of a solution of 3.63 g of solute dissolved fully in 0.20 dm³ $\left(\frac{3.63}{0.20} = 18.15 \text{ g/dm}^3\right)$.	**Extend:** Ask students to write the ionic equation for this reaction.	**Interactive:** Titration apparatus

Main	Support/Extend	Resources
Carrying out a titration (40 minutes) Demonstrate how to use burettes and pipettes (including reading from the bottom of the meniscus, touching the tip on the side of the conical flask, and how it is normal for a tiny amount of solution to remain in the pipette). Allow students to practise using the glassware with water only. Demonstrate how to complete a titration. Students then carry out their own titration. Then ask students to draw a pictorial flow chart to show the titration procedure. Higher-tier students will carry out further analysis on their data in Topic C4.8.	**Extend:** Ask students to suggest ways that they could improve the procedure to ensure that the value of titre is more accurate. **Extend:** Ask students to use their knowledge from the Topic C4.6 to work out the number of moles of sodium hydroxide used.	**Required practical:** Carrying out a titration

Plenary	Support/Extend	Resources
Phenolphthalein (5 minutes) Ask students to explain the purpose of the phenolphthalein in the titration experiment. **Evaluation of the results** (10 minutes) Ask students to comment on the reproducibility and repeatability of their results. Then ask students to comment on the accuracy of their results.	**Support:** Remind students of the definition of reproducibility (i.e., when your results are similar to another group), repeatability (i.e., when your results show close agreement each time), and accuracy (i.e., close to the true value).	

Homework
Students explain why universal indicator is not a suitable indicator for a titration.

kerboodle

A Kerboodle highlight for this lesson is **Literacy sheet: Titrations**. Refer to the **Content map** on Kerboodle for a full list of resources and assessment.

GCSE Chemistry Only — Higher tier

C4.8 Titration calculations

AQA spec Link: 3.4 The concentration of a solution can be measured in mol/dm³.

The amount in moles of solute or the mass in grams of solute in a given volume of solution can be calculated from its concentration in mol/dm³.

If the volumes of two solutions that react completely are known and the concentration of one solution is known, the concentration of the other solution can be calculated.

Students should be able to explain how the concentration of a solution in mol/dm³ is related to the mass of the solute and the volume of the solution.

4.2.5 Students should be able to:
- calculate the chemical quantities in titrations involving concentrations in mol/dm³ and in g/dm³.

Required practical: Determination of the concentration of one of the solutions in mol/dm³ and g/dm³ from the reacting volumes and the known concentration of the other solution.

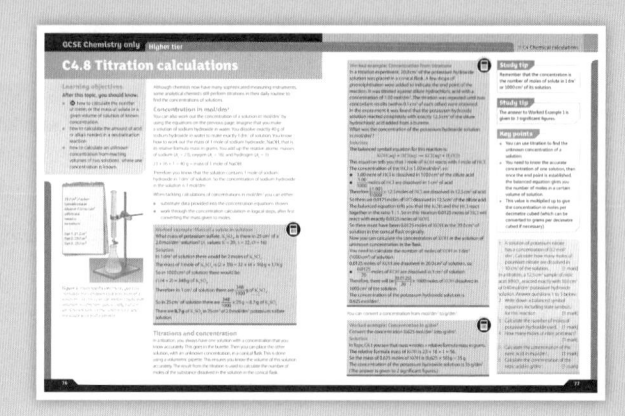

MS 1a, 1c, 2b, 3b, 3d

Aiming for	Outcome	Checkpoint	
		Question	Activity
Aiming for GRADE 6 ↓	Calculate the concentration of a solution in mol/dm³ when given the amount of solute in moles and volume of solution in dm³.	6	Starter 2, Main
	Calculate the amount of acid or alkali needed in a neutralisation reaction.	2, 4	Main, Plenary 2
	Calculate the mole and mass of solute (in g) in a solution when given the concentration in mol/dm³ and volume in dm³ or cm³.	6, End of chapter 6	Starter 2, Main, Plenary 2
Aiming for GRADE 8 ↓	Calculate the unknown concentration of a reactant in a neutralisation reaction when the volumes are known and the concentration of one reactant is also known.	5, End of chapter 6	Main, Plenary 2
	Extract data from given information to perform multi-step calculations independently.		Main, Plenary 2

Maths
Students use titration results to calculate a mean (2b) and the concentration of an acid (3d). They also create their own practice question and mark scheme on titration that includes some maths skills.

Literacy
Students analyse a practice question, answer, and marking guidance. They also write their own practice question.

■ **C4 Chemical calculations**

Starter	Support/Extend	Resources
Remember moles (5 minutes) Ask students to recall the three different formulae that they have met to calculate moles.	**Support:** All students to complete three equation triangles. **Extend:** Ask students to include the common conversion of cm^3 to dm^3 into their formulae.	
Mole equations (10 minutes) Interactive where students identify the equations to calculate amount of substance (mole), relative formula mass, and concentration in mol/dm^3 and g/dm^3. They then complete a paragraph describing an acid–base titration to remind themselves of the practical from Topic C4.7.		**Interactive:** Mole equations

Main	Support/Extend	Resources
Titration calculations (15 minutes) Remind students of the unit of concentration g/dm^3. Give students a simple example to calculate. Then introduce that concentration can also be measuring in mol/dm^3. and give students a couple example calculations to reinforce using mol/dm^3. Students then work through the worked examples, using a red pen to highlight the information relating to the acid and a blue pen to highlight the information for the alkali. This can help reduce transposition errors. Then allow students to practise their calculations using the calculation sheet. Students then use their data from the required practical in Topic C4.7 to determine the concentration of sodium hydroxide in their titration.		**Calculation sheet:** Titration calculations **Required practical:** Carrying out a titration – part 2

Plenary	Support/Extend	Resources
Algebra (5 minutes) Explain to students to assume that one mole of acid reacts with one mole of alkali. Then ask students to explain the following formula: $C_{(acid)} \times V_{(acid)} = C_{(alkali)} \times V_{(alkali)}$	**Extend:** Ask students to generate a similar expression if the mass of the acid was known.	
On your marks (10 minutes) Students analyse examination questions by looking at a sample student answer along with marking comments. Alternatively students answer a practice question and swap their answers with a partner to mark.	**Support:** Allow students to work in pairs to discuss the sample student answers.	**On your marks:** Titrations

Homework		
Students write their own titration question for the reaction of nitric acid with potassium hydroxide. Their question should include a maths skills element and a practical skills element. They should also supply a mark scheme for their work.		

kerboodle
A Kerboodle highlight for this lesson is **Maths skills: Titrations**. Refer to the **Content map** on Kerboodle for a full list of resources and assessment.

GCSE Chemistry Only — Higher tier

C4.9 Volumes of gases

AQA spec Link: 3.5 Equal amounts in moles of gases occupy the same volume under the same conditions of temperature and pressure.

The volume of one mole of any gas at room temperature and pressure (20 °C and 1 atmosphere pressure) is 24 dm^3.

The volume of gaseous reactants and products can be calculated from the balanced equation for the reaction.

Students should be able to:

- calculate the volume of a gas at room temperature and pressure from its mass and relative formula mass
- calculate volumes of gaseous reactants and products from a balanced equation and a given volume of a gaseous reactant or product.

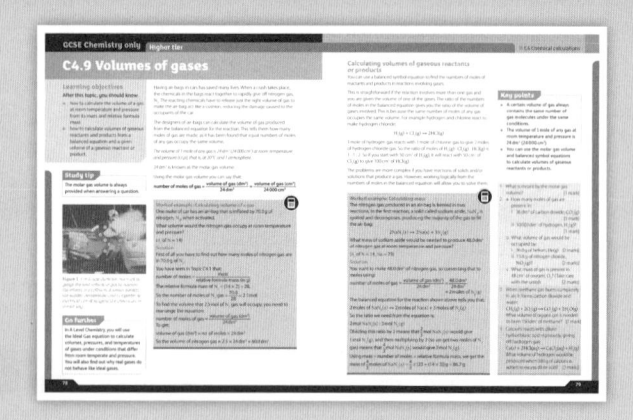

MS 1a, 1c, 3b, 3c

Aiming for	Outcome	Checkpoint	
		Question	Activity
Aiming for GRADE 6 ↓	Calculate the amount in moles of gas in a given volume at room temperature and pressure.	2	Main 1
	Convert units.	2	Main 1
Aiming for GRADE 8 ↓	Suggest how the volume of gas would change when temperature or pressure was changed.		Main 2
	Calculate the moles or volume of a gaseous substance involved in a chemical reaction.	3, 4, End of chapter 7, 8	Main 1

Maths
Students calculate mass, volume, and moles (3b).

Literacy
Students write a prediction.

Practical

Title	Molar volume of a gas
Equipment	100 cm^3 gas syringe, delivery tube and bung, top-pan balance, weighing boat, specimen tube, boiling tube, 2 mol/dm^3 hydrochloric acid, sodium hydrogencarbonate, eye protection
Overview of method	Put around 0.30 g of sodium hydrogencarbonate into a boiling tube and record the exact mass. Fill the specimen tube with hydrochloric acid. Put the specimen tube into the boiling tube, stopper with the bung, and use the delivery tube to connect the boiling tube to the gas syringe. Tip the apparatus so the acid then mixes and reacts with the sodium hydrogencarbonate. When the reaction is complete, record the volume of gas produced.
Safety considerations	Hydrochloric acid is an irritant. Wear eye protection.

C4 Chemical calculations

Starter	Support/Extend	Resources
Moles of gas (5 minutes) Explain to students that the volume of one mole of any gas at room temperature and pressure is 24 dm^3. Ask students to represent this as a formula. Then ask students to write the expression with volume as the subject of the equation.	**Support:** Ask students to generate a formula triangle. **Extend:** Ask students to suggest the conversion factor to change from cm^3 to dm^3 or litres.	
Think (10 minutes) Show students a photograph of a chemical plant with sealed vessels. Then ask students to suggest why the volume of a gas produced in a chemical reaction is important for chemical engineers in industry. Use question and answer to illicit that gas production can cause explosions, the reactors need to be stronger to cope with the pressure, and the staff need more training.		

Main	Support/Extend	Resources
Molar volume of a gas (30 minutes) Students carry out the practical to work out the volume occupied by one mole of carbon dioxide gas.		**Practical:** Molar volume of a gas
The volume of gases (10 minutes) Remind students that the volume a gas takes up is the same no matter what the gas is. Then ask students to predict what would happen to the molar gas volume if the temperature was increased, and then decreased under room pressure. Then ask students to predict the effect on the molar gas volume when pressure is increased, and then decreased at room temperature. Students should use labelled particle diagrams in their predictions.	**Support:** You may wish to remind students of the concept of the mole and the Avogadro constant.	

Plenary	Support/Extend	Resources
Algebra (5 minutes) Ask students to link the expression for calculating the mass of a gas when the volume, temperature, and pressure is given.	**Support:** Remind students that moles = $\dfrac{\text{mass}}{\text{relative formula mass}}$	**Interactive:** Volumes of gases
Volumes of gases (10 minutes) Interactive where students complete a paragraph about the moles of a gas.		
Students then sort statements on the volume and moles that describe two balloons of the same volume – one filled with hydrogen and one filled with helium.		

Homework		
Ask students to explain why the relative formula mass for oxygen gas is greater than for hydrogen gas but the gas volume will be the same at room temperature and pressure.	**Support:** Remind students that the volume that a gas takes up is the same no matter what the gas is.	

kerboodle

A Kerboodle highlight for this lesson is **Calculation sheet: Molar volumes of gases**. Refer to the **Content map** on Kerboodle for a full list of resources and assessment.

C4 Chemical calculations

Overview of C4 Chemical calculations

In this chapter, students will build upon their understanding of the structure of atoms and sub-atomic particles to understand relative atomic mass and relative formula mass. Students should be able to use relative atomic massess to calculate relative formula masses of compounds.

For higher-tier students, this was then related to the mole and Avogadro's constant, and the relevant calculations introduced. Students should be able to use the equation number of moles = mass (g) / A_r and use moles to balance symbol equations and calculate reacting masses. Students studying *AQA GCSE Chemistry* have also learnt how to calculate the percentage yield and percentage atom economy of a reaction.

Students then applied their understanding of relative atomic mass, relative formula mass, and moles to concentrations. All students should be able to carry out calculations with concentrations in g/dm^3, and students studying *AQA GCSE Chemistry* should also be confident with concentrations in mol/dm^3 and with calculating moles in gases. These students should also have carried out a titration as part of the required practical, with higher-tier students using their results to calculate the concentration of an unknown solution.

Required practical

All students studying *AQA GCSE Chemistry* are expected to have carried out the required practical:

Practical	Topic
Determination of the reacting volumes of solutions of a strong acid and a strong alkali by titration.	C4.7
H Determination of the concentration of one of the solutions in mol/dm^3 and g/dm^3 from the reacting volumes and the known concentration of the other solution.	**H** C4.8

Students studying *AQA GCSE Combined science: Trilogy* do not need to carry out this required practical.

MyMaths

You can find additional support for the maths skills covered in this chapter on **MyMaths**, including percentages, using standard form, and rearranging equations.

kerboodle

For this chapter, the following assessments are available on Kerboodle:

C4 Checkpoint quiz: Chemical calculations
C4 Progress quiz: Chemical calculations 1
C4 Progress quiz: Chemical calculations 2
C4 On your marks: Chemical calculations
C4 Exam-style questions and mark scheme: Chemical calculations

Checkpoint follow up lesson

A student's route through this lesson can be determined using the Checkpoint assessment. Percentage pass marks are supplied in the Checkpoint teacher notes.

For each successive route through it is assumed that the student can perform to their current route as well as previous routes. For example, students working at Aiming for 6 are assumed to be secure in Aiming for 4 knowledge and understanding and working towards achieving all the learning outcomes for Aiming for 6.

	Aiming for 4	**Aiming for 6**	**Aimin for 8**
Learning outcomes	Recognise the relative atomic mass from element symbols.	Calculate the relative formula mass of compounds	Use the number of moles to calculate experimental masses, concentrations, and gas volumes of substances.
	Calculate the relative formula mass of simple compounds.	Calculate the number of moles present in a solution, using titration results from a familiar reaction.	Calculate the number of moles present in a solution using titration results from an unfamiliar reaction.
	Decide whether simple equations are balanced.	Balance simple formula equations	Explain the calculations carried out in titration reactions.
	Calculate the percentage yield of a reaction when provided with the actual yield and the theoretical yield.	Calculate the theoretical and percentage yield of a reaction.	
Starter	**Definitions (5 minutes)** Students work in small groups to provide definitions from memory for the following key words – relative atomic mass, relative formula mass, equation, moles, mass, volume, concentration. **Key word links (5 minutes)** Display the key words in spread out manner on either an interactive whiteboard or a blank piece of poster paper. Ask students to link any words that they think are related. They should explain why they are related. Higher-tier students may begin to give the formula that link some of these words but verbal explanations can also be given, for example, the relative atomic mass is he number of grams that one mole of a substance would weigh. Address any misconceptions that arise and draw out the concept of what a mole is – it may be useful to show a picture or physical examples of what one mole of various substances looks like, for example, 12 g of carbon, or 64 g of copper.		
Differentiated checkpoint activity	The Aiming for 4 Checkpoint follow-up sheet provides a worked example before students attempt each question. Students should work alone to complete their calculations as they will peer review the calculations during the plenary.	The Aiming for 6 Checkpoint follow-up sheet provides students with a series of calculation questions from the chapter. Students should work alone to complete their calculations as they will peer review the calculations during the plenary. Aiming for 6 students would benefit from watching a simple titration demonstration to remind them of the key steps, especially the fact that the titration is stopped when the end point is reached, and this represents the point at which all the substances have completely reacted.	The Aiming for 8 Checkpoint follow-up sheet encourages students to explain the concepts behind titration experiments and calculations. Students should work alone to complete their calculations as they will peer review the calculations during the plenary. Aiming for 8 students may also want to watch the titration demonstration.
	Kerboodle resource C4 Checkpoint follow up: Aiming for 4, C4 Checkpoint follow up: Aiming for 6, C4 Checkpoint follow up: Aiming for 8		
Plenary	**Reviewing their work (10 minutes)** Ask students to peer review the work of someone else following the same route. • They should consider the following points: • Has the person got the same answer as you? • If they have, did they follow the same steps? • If they have not, why not? • Can you spot any errors in their working? • Can you suggest one way they could improve their calculations? • (Aiming for 8 students only) Have they clearly explained the link between no of moles, mass, concentration and volume? Have they formulae to show these links?		
Progression	Once students have completed the sheet, provide them with more questions and encourage them to attempt them without the worked example.	Provide students more difficult questions and encourage them to answer without using any notes.	Students use titration results to calculate other quantities, for example, provide students with solution concentrations and ask them to calculate the volume that would titrate together.

81

2 Chemical reactions and energy changes

Specification links

Topic	Paper
4.1 Reactivity of metals	Paper 1
4.2 Reaction of acids	Paper 1
4.3 Electrolysis	Paper 1
5.1 Exothermic and endothermic reactions	Paper 1
5.2 Chemical cells and fuel cells	Paper 1

Required practicals

Practical	skills	Topic
Preparation of a pure, dry sample of a soluble salt from an insoluble oxide or carbonate, using a Bunsen burner to heat dilute acid and a water bath or electric heater to evaporate the solution.	AT 2 – safe use of appropriate heating devices and techniques including use of a Bunsen burner and a water bath or electric heater. AT 3 – use of appropriate apparatus and techniques for conducting chemical reactions, including appropriate reagents. AT 4 – safe use of a range of equipment to purify and/or separate chemical mixtures including evaporation, filtration, crystallisation. AT 6 – safe use and careful handling of liquids and solids, including careful mixing of reagents under controlled conditions.	C5.6
Investigate what happens when aqueous solutions are electrolysed using inert electrodes. This should be an investigation involving developing a hypothesis.	AT 3 – use of appropriate apparatus and techniques for conducting and monitoring chemical reactions. AT 7 – use of appropriate apparatus and techniques to draw, set up and use electrochemical cells for separation and production of elements and compounds. AT 8 – use of appropriate qualitative reagents and techniques to analyse and identify unknown samples or products including gas tests for hydrogen, oxygen and chlorine.	C6.4
Investigate the variables that affect temperature changes in reacting solutions such as, for example, acid plus metals, acid plus carbonates, neutralisations, displacement of metals.	AT 1 – use of appropriate apparatus to make and record a range of measurements accurately, including mass, temperature, and volume of liquids. AT 3 – use of appropriate apparatus and techniques for conducting and monitoring chemical reactions. AT 5 – making and recording of appropriate observations during chemical reactions including changes in temperature. AT 6 – safe use and careful handling of gases, liquids and solids, including careful mixing of reagents under controlled conditions, using appropriate apparatus to explore chemical changes.	C7.1

Maths skills

Skill	Topic
1a Recognise and use expressions in decimal form.	C7.3, C7.4
1b Recognise and use expressions in standard form.	C7.4
1c Use ratios, fractions and percentages.	C6.1
2a Use an appropriate number of significant figures.	C7.4
2h Make order of magnitude calculations.	C5.7, C5.8
3b Change the subject of an equation.	C7.4
4a Translate information between graphical and numeric form.	C7.3

C2 Chemical reactions and energy changes

KS3 concept	GCSE topic	Checkpoint	Revision
Metals have different reactivity and can be written as a list from most to least reactive.	C5.1 Reactivity series	Ask students to recall the reactivity series.	Students should work in small groups to create a mnemonic to help them remember the reactivity series.
A more reactive element will take the place of a less reactive element from its compound.	C5.2 Displacement reactions	Give students a selection of metal and metal compounds and ask students to predict if a reaction would take place.	Ask students to outline an experiment to form a reactivity series using metals and metal solutions only.
Salts are made in a neutralisation reaction.	C5.6 Making more salts	Ask students to define a salt and outline a method to make one.	Give students the chemical formula of common acids and salts made from those acids. Students should then match them together and use this to define a salt.
Indicators can be used to determine the pH of a solution.	C5.7 Neutralisation and the pH scale	Show students a Universal indicator pH scale and ask them to label it with weak, strong, acid, base, and neutral.	Allow students to use pH indicator paper and colour chart to test the pH of some chemicals and then classify them as acid, alkali or neutral.
Some compounds can dissolve in water and make aqueous solutions.	C6.4 Electrolysis of aqueous solutions	Ask students to define the term aqueous solutions and give the state symbol.	Give students a particle diagram of an aqueous solution and ask them to add a key to show the solution, solute and solvent.
Chemical reactions sometimes get hot and sometimes get cold.	C7.1 Exothermic and endothermic reactions	Ask students to suggest how you monitor a chemical reaction to classify it as exothermic or endothermic.	Give students a hand warmer and a sports cooling pack. Explain that both are chemical reactions but one gives out energy (exothermic) and one takes in energy (endothermic). Then ask students to write a tweet to differentiate between the two terms.
Batteries are cells connected in series.	C7.5 Chemical Cells and batteries	Ask students explain how a battery can be made from cells.	Show students circuit symbols for cells and batteries and ask them to name the circuit symbol. Draw their attention that a battery symbol is made of more than one cell and explain that this is because a battery is made from more than one cell.

C 5 Chemical changes
5.1 The reactivity series

AQA spec Link: 4.1.1 Metals react with oxygen to produce metal oxides. The reactions are oxidation reactions because metals gain oxygen.

Students should be able to explain reduction and oxidation in terms of loss or gain of oxygen.

4.1.2 When metals react with other substances the metal atoms form positive ions. The reactivity of a metal is related to its tendency to form positive ions. Metals can be arranged in order of their reactivity in a reactivity series. The metals potassium, sodium, lithium, calcium, magnesium, zinc, iron, and copper can be put in order of their reactivity from their reactions with water and dilute acids.

Students should be able to:

- recall and describe the reactions, if any, of potassium, sodium, lithium, calcium, magnesium, zinc, iron, and copper with water or dilute acids and where appropriate, to place these metals in order of reactivity
- deduce an order of reactivity of metals based on experimental results.

The reactions of metals with water and acids are limited to room temperature and do not include reactions with steam.

Aiming for	Outcome	Checkpoint	
		Question	Activity
Aiming for GRADE 4	List the order of common metals in the reactivity series.		Plenary 2
	Use general equations to write specific word equations for metals listed in the reactivity series reacting with oxygen, water, and acid.		Starter 1
	Safely make and record observations.		Main
Aiming for GRADE 6	Describe oxidation and reduction in terms of gain or loss of oxygen.	End of chapter 1	Starter 1
	Write word equations for the metals listed in the reactivity series reacting with oxygen, water, and acid, and balance given symbol equations.	1, 2, End of chapter 1	Starter 2, Main, Homework
	Predict observations for the metals listed in the reactivity series reacting with oxygen, water, and acid.	2, End of chapter 1	Starter 2
Aiming for GRADE 8	Justify uses of metals in the reactivity series based on their chemical reactivity.	3, 4	Plenary 1
	Write balanced symbol equations, with state symbols, for the metals listed in the reactivity series reacting with oxygen, water, and acid.	1, 2, End of chapter 1	Main, Homework
	Evaluate in detail the investigation of metals plus acid, assessing the control of variables and the validity of conclusions drawn from the data collected.		Main

Maths
Students use a scale to measure solutions and masses.

Literacy
Students define what the reactivity series is, and explain how it can be generated and investigated.

Key words
ores, oxidised, reduced, reactivity series

C5 Chemical changes

Practical

Title	The reactivity series
Equipment	coarse-grained filings of copper, aluminium, zinc, iron, and magnesium, eye protection, 0.1 mol/dm³ hydrochloric acid, dropping pipette, spatula, balance, weighing boat, five test tubes, test-tube rack, 10 cm³ measuring cylinder
Overview of method	Using the measuring cylinder add 2 cm³ of acid into each test tube. Add half a spatula of each metal to separate test tubes and observe. This experiment can also be carried out with water. You may wish to measure the mass of the metal before it is added to the acid. Use a weighing boat and weigh by difference.
Safety considerations	Magnesium is highly flammable, aluminium, zinc, and iron filings are also flammable. Hydrochloric acid is an irritant. Keep the metals away from any naked flames. Wear eye protection and wash hands after completing the practical.

Starter	Support/Extend	Resources
General equations (5 minutes) Ask students to complete the following general equations: metal + oxygen → (metal oxide) metal + water → (metal hydroxide + hydrogen) metal + acid → (metal salt + hydrogen) **Metals and water** (10 minutes) Explain to students that when lithium is put in water it reacts vigorously but when magnesium is put in water there is no observable reaction. Then explain that calcium's reactivity is between these two metals. Ask students to predict what observations they would therefore expect to see.	**Support:** Ask students to match up the reactants with the products. **Extend:** Ask students how you could prove that hydrogen was formed. **Support:** Demonstrate or show videos of the reactions. **Extend:** Students write word and balanced symbol equations for the reactions.	

Main	Support/Extend	Resources
Metals and acids (40 minutes) Ask students to plan an investigation to determine the order of reactivity between copper, aluminium, zinc, iron, and magnesium when reacted with acid. Encourage students to write word and balanced symbol equations for all of the metals that react. They should also write a list of the metals from most to least reactive. If there is time, students could carry out part of their investigation.	**Extend:** Students give a detailed evaluation of their investigation.	**Practical:** Metals and acids

Plenary	Support/Extend	Resources
Bridges (10 minutes) Show students a picture of a steel bridge and an iron bridge. Ask students to justify the use of each material for the purpose (strong, malleable). Then ask students to suggest why the maintenance of the iron bridge is greater than the steel bridge (iron reacts with the environment to form rust, steels are an alloy of iron and other elements and some types can resist rusting).	**Support:** Give students a sample of stainless steel cutlery and a rusty nail. **Extend:** Ask students to suggest why aluminium is sometimes used for a bridge but is more reactive than iron.	
The reactivity series (10 minutes) Interactive where students sort metals according to whether they react with water. They then put the metals of the reactivity series in order.	**Support:** Work as a class to come up with a mnemonic to remember the order of the reactivity series.	**Interactive:** The reactivity series

Homework		
Students write equations to show the reaction between magnesium and hydrochloric acid, and the reaction between magnesium and sulfuric acid.	**Support:** Remind students of the general equation. **Extend:** Ask students to write balanced symbol equations with state symbols.	

C5.2 Displacement reactions

AQA spec Link: 4.1.2 The non-metals hydrogen and carbon are often included in the reactivity series.

A more reactive metal can displace a less reactive metal from a compound.

Students should be able to:

- explain how the reactivity of metals with water or dilute acids is related to the tendency of the metal to form its positive ion.

4.1.4 ⓗ Oxidation is the loss of electrons and reduction is the gain of electrons.

Student should be able to:

- write ionic equations for displacement reactions.

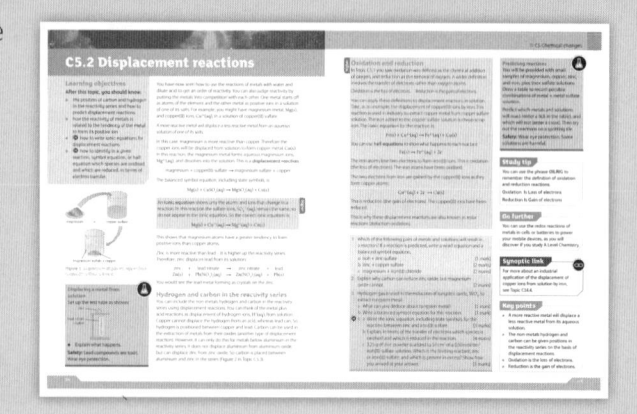

Aiming for	Outcome	Checkpoint	
		Question	Activity
Aiming for GRADE 4	Recall a definition of a displacement reaction.	End of chapter 3	Starter 2, Main
	Use the reactivity series to determine whether a reaction between a metal and a different metal salt will occur.	1, End of chapter 2	Main, Plenary 2
	Safely make and record observations.		Main
Aiming for GRADE 6	Explain why a displacement reaction occurs.	2, 3	Homework
	Write word equations and straightforward balanced symbol equations for displacement reactions.	End of chapter 2, 3	Starter 2, Main, Plenary 2
	Predict observations for the metals listed in the reactivity series reacting with a different metal salt.	End of chapter 1, 3	Starter 2, Main
Aiming for GRADE 8	ⓗ Describe displacement reactions using an ionic equation.	4	Starter 2, Main
	Write balanced symbol equations, with state symbols, for displacement reactions.	1, 3, End of chapter 1, 2, 3	Starter 2, Main
	ⓗ Determine and explain which species is oxidised and which species (metal atom or ion) is reduced in a displacement reaction in terms of electron transfer.	4, End of chapter 1	Plenary 1

Maths
Students generate balanced symbol and ionic equations.

Literacy
Students use their understanding of the reactivity series to explain why some reactions will not occur.

Key words
displacement reaction, ionic equation, half equation

Practical

Title	Displacing a metal from solution
Equipment	test tube, test-tube rack, eye protection, zinc sheet (0.5 cm width by 10 cm length), lead nitrate solution, eye protection
Overview of method	Half fill a test tube with lead nitrate solution and put in a test-tube rack. Insert the lead into the liquid and observe.
Safety considerations	Lead compounds are toxic. Follow CLEAPSS advice for disposal procedures. Wear chemical splash-proof eye protection and wash hands after completing the practical.

■ C5 Chemical changes

Title	Predicting reactions
Equipment	coarse-grained filings of magnesium, copper, zinc, and iron, 0.5 mol/dm³ magnesium sulfate solution, 0.5 mol/dm³ copper(II) sulfate solution, 0.5 mol/dm³ zinc sulfate solution, 0.5 mol/dm³ iron(II) sulfate solution, four dropping pipettes, eye protection, spotting tile
Overview of method	Using the dropping pipette put three drops of each solution into four separate dimples of the spotting tile. Put a single grain of magnesium in each dimple and observe. Repeat with all the metals.
Safety considerations	Magnesium, zinc, and iron filings are highly flammable. Copper sulfate, zinc sulfate, and iron sulfate are harmful. Keep the metals away from any naked flames. Wear eye protection and wash hands after completing the practical.

Starter	Support/Extend	Resources
Classify (5 minutes) Students use the student book to classify the statements to define oxidation and reduction: • Gain of oxygen (oxidation) • Loss of oxygen (reduction) • Gain of electrons (reduction) • Loss of electrons (oxidation) **Displacing a metal from solution** (10 minutes) Set up the the practical to displace lead from lead nitrate solution with zinc. Encourage students to predict what will happen by writing word and balanced symbol equations with state symbols. 🄗 Higher-tier students should write ionic equations for this reaction.	**Support:** Only higher-tier attaining students need to identify oxidation and reduction by the transfer of electrons. **Extend:** Ask students to suggest how oxidation and reduction could be described in terms of hydrogen.	

Main	Support/Extend	Resources
Predicting reactions (40 minutes) Students complete the displacement reactions of metals investigation. Encourage students to write the equations for the reactions that occur.	**Support:** Encourage students to put a tick or cross in the results table to show whether they think a reaction will occur. **Extend:** Ask students to predict the observations when silver is put into copper sulfate solution.	**Practical:** Predicting reactions

Plenary	Support/Extend	Resources
Displacing a metal from solution revisited (5 minutes) Revisit the displacement of lead from lead nitrate solution by zinc. Discuss what has happened. 🄗 Have students determine and explain which species has been oxidised and which has been reduced in terms of electron transfer. **Displacement reactions** (10 minutes) Students use the interactive to complete a series of word equations describing displacement reactions. Students then choose the correct chemical formula symbols to complete some balanced symbol equations for displacement reactions.	**Support:** Write the word equation on the board. **Extend:** Ask students to write a balanced ionic equation. **Extend:** Ask students to write balanced symbol equations for the reactions. **Extend:** Higher attaining students should explain which species has been oxidised and which has been reduced.	**Interactive:** Displacement reactions

Homework		
Ask students to explain why there is no reaction between silver nitrate solution and silver and no reaction between aluminium oxide and carbon.		

kerboodle
A Kerboodle highlight for this lesson is **Go further: Mobile devices**. Refer to the **Content map** on Kerboodle for a full list of resources and assessment.

87

C5.3 Extracting metals

AQA spec Link: 4.1.3 Unreactive metals such as gold are found in the Earth as the metal itself but most metals are found as compounds that require chemical reactions to extract the metal. Metals less reactive than carbon can be extracted from their oxides by reduction with carbon. Reduction involves the loss of oxygen.

Knowledge and understanding are limited to the reduction of oxides using carbon.

Knowledge of the details of processes used in the extraction of metals is not required.

Students should be able to:

- interpret or evaluate specific metal extraction processes when given appropriate information
- identify the substances which are oxidised or reduced in terms of gain or loss of oxygen.

4.1.4 (H) **Oxidation is the loss of electrons and reduction is the gain of electrons.**

Student should be able to:

- write ionic equations for displacement reactions
- identify in a given reaction, symbol equation, or half equation which species are oxidised and which are reduced.

Aiming for	Outcome	Checkpoint	
		Question	Activity
Aiming for GRADE 4 ↓	Define oxidation and reduction in terms of oxygen.		Main 1, Main 2
	Describe how metals can be extracted.		Main 1, Main 2, Plenary 2
Aiming for GRADE 6 ↓	Identify species that are being oxidised and reduced in a chemical reaction.	4	Main 1, Main 2
	Explain why some metals are found uncombined in the Earth's crust.	2, 3	Starter 1, Main 1, Plenary 2
Aiming for GRADE 8 ↓	Explain how carbon or hydrogen can be used to reduce an ore.	4	Starter 2, Main 1, Main 2
	Evaluate the extraction process to obtain a metal from its ore.		Main 1, Homework

Maths
Students generate balanced symbol and ionic equations.

Literacy
Students write a report or presentation about the different forms of metal extraction.

Key words
metal ore, electrolysis

Practical

Title	Reduction by carbon
Equipment	two boiling tubes, boiling-tube rack, eye protection, copper oxide, lead oxide, carbon powder, boiling-tube holders, spatula, two evaporating dishes, two pieces of paper, Bunsen burner and safety equipment
Overview of method	Fold the paper in half and then open it out. Put one spatula of copper oxide and two spatulas of carbon powder in the fold. Use the spatula to mix the powders well. Then use the fold of the paper to help tip the powder into the boiling tube. Heat in the blue flame for a few minutes. Remove from the flame and tip the contents into the evaporating dish to observe. Repeat using lead oxide and carbon.
Safety considerations	Lead oxide is toxic, copper oxide is harmful. Follow CLEAPSS advice for disposal procedures. Carry out in a well-ventilated room. Wear eye protection and wash hands after completing the practical.

C5 Chemical changes

Starter	Support/Extend	Resources
Copper (5 minutes) Show students a selection of copper ores, for example, malachite, cuprite, chalcopyrite, and some native copper. Ask students to suggest the connection (all different forms that copper can be found in the Earth's crust).	**Support:** Explain to students that all the samples contain the same element – ask them to suggest which one. **Extend:** Ask students to suggest why copper can be found native and in ores.	
Extracting metals (10 minutes) Students complete a paragraph to introduce the concept that some metals have to be extracted from their ores and that carbon is sometimes used in the extraction process.	**Extend:** Ask students to justify why carbon is used to reduce copper oxide in an ore rather than hydrogen.	**Interactive:** Extracting metals

Main	Support/Extend	Resources
Reduction by carbon (25 minutes) Students extract copper from copper oxide using the method outlined. Encourage students to write word and symbol equations for the reduction reaction. **H** Higher-tier attaining students should also write ionic equations, underlining the species that is being oxidised in one colour and the species that is being reduced in another colour. Students should include a key so that they can revise from their notes.	**Extend:** Give students copper carbonate and ask them to write the equations for the two reactions which result in the copper being formed.	**Practical:** Reduction by carbon
Researching metal extraction (15 minutes) Students use the student book to write some revision notes on methods of metal extraction. Their notes should include a list of metals (and two non-metals, carbon and hydrogen), arranged in order of their chemical reactivity, and explain how their selected metals are extracted. Their explanations should include reference to each metal's position in the reactivity series. Students could use the Internet or other secondary resources to research their methods of metal extraction.	**Extend:** Ensure students include balanced symbol equations with state symbols in their answer.	

Plenary	Support/Extend	Resources
On your marks (10 minutes) Show students a practice question, example answer, and the mark scheme. Ask students to identify where the answer could be improved. Alternatively, students can answer a practice question then swap with a partner to mark.		**On your marks:** Extracting metals
Extracting metals (5 minutes) Students explain why gold was the first metal to be used to make jewellery.	**Extend:** Students also suggest why some metals are more expensive to extract from their ores.	

Homework		
Students complete the WebQuest where they research the extraction of metals from ore using carbon. They then summarise their research in a presentation or report. Alternatively, explain to students that titanium easily reacts with carbon to make titanium carbide which is brittle. Ask students to explain why theoretically titanium could be extracted from its ore using carbon, but is actually displaced from titanium tetrachloride with a more reactive metal like sodium.		**WebQuest:** Find an extraction, ore else

kerboodle

A Kerboodle highlight for this lesson is **Animation: Extracting metals**. Refer to the **Content map** on Kerboodle for a full list of resources and assessment.

C5.4 Salts from metals

AQA spec Link: 4.2.1 Acids react with some metals to produce salts and hydrogen.

(H) Students should be able to:

- explain in terms of gain or loss of electrons, that these are redox reactions.

4.2.3 Soluble salts can be made from acids by reacting them with solid insoluble substances such as metals. The solid is added to the acid until no more reacts and the excess solid is filtered off to produce a solution of the salt.

Salt solutions can be crystallised to produce solid salts.

Students should be able to describe how to make pure, dry samples of named soluble salts from information provided.

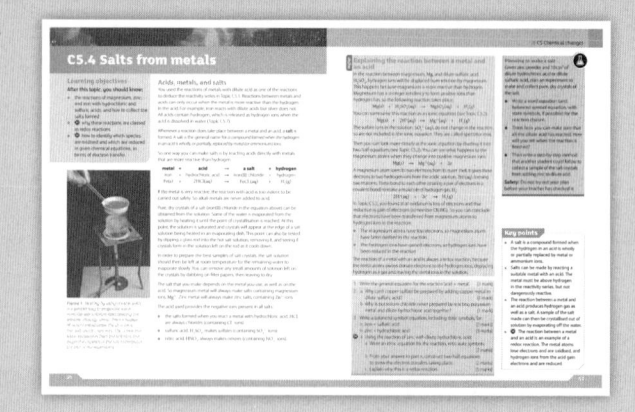

Aiming for	Outcome	Checkpoint	
		Question	Activity
Aiming for GRADE 4	Recall a definition of a salt.		Plenary 1
	Name a salt formed between a metal and sulfuric acid or hydrochloric acid.		Starter 2, Plenary 2, Homework
	Recall a general equation for a metal reacting with an acid and use it to write specific word equations.	1	Main 1, Plenary 1, Homework
Aiming for GRADE 6	Describe how to make a salt by reacting a metal with an acid.		Main 1
	Write a balanced symbol equation to describe a reaction between a metal and sulfuric acid or hydrochloric acid.	4, End of chapter 6	Main 1, Plenary 2
	Identify the chemical formula of the salt produced from the reaction between an acid and a metal.		Starter 2, Main 1
Aiming for GRADE 8	(H) Explain the reaction between a metal and an acid.	2	Main 2
	(H) Write ionic and half equations, including state symbols, to describe a reaction between a metal and sulfuric acid or hydrochloric acid.	4	Main 2, Homework
	(H) Identify and explain in detail which species is oxidised and which is reduced.	4	Main 2, Homework

Maths
Students generate balanced symbol and ionic equations.

Literacy
Students plan and write a method for preparing a soluble salt.

Key words
salt

Practical

Title	Planning to make a salt
Equipment	zinc powder, spatula, 10 cm³ measuring cylinder, 100 cm³ beaker, dilute hydrochloric acid or dilute sulfuric acid, filter paper, funnel, 100 cm³ conical flask, stirring rod, evaporating dish, eye protection, Bunsen burner and safety equipment, tripod and gauze, access to a drying oven, tongs
Overview of method	Measure 10 cm³ of acid into the beaker. Add half a spatula of zinc power into the acid and stir. Continue adding the zinc until there is no more fizzing. Filter the mixture and discard the residue. Pour the filtrate into an evaporating dish. Heat the solution until the volume is halved. Remove from the heat and leave in a warm place to crystallise. Then put the evaporating basin in a drying oven or pat dry with absorbent paper.
Safety considerations	Zinc powder is highly flammable and the acids are irritants. Keep the zinc away from naked flames and wear eye protection throughout. Wash hands after completing the practical.

■ C5 Chemical changes

Starter	Support/Extend	Resources
Diagram (5 minutes) Draw a labelled diagram to show how to separate a sample of dry salt that has been dissolved in water to form a solution. **Salts from metals** (10 minutes) Interactive where students complete the general word equation for the reaction of an acid and a metal to form a salt and hydrogen. They then order sentences to explain how salts are made.	**Support:** Show students the equipment that you would need to use. **Extend:** Ask students to suggest how to remove any unreacted insoluble reactant from the solution before the salt is collected from the solution.	**Interactive:** Salts from metals

Main	Support/Extend	Resources
Planning to make a salt (30 minutes) Students plan a method for making a zinc salt from reacting zinc with an acid. Ensure that the plan is checked then allow students to make a sample of the dry zinc salt. The final drying and collection of the crystals can take place next lesson or plans can be collected and checked this lesson before the practical is tackled next lesson. Students should write the word equation and balanced symbol equation for the reaction they investigate. This practical could be used for Required practical 1, however differentiated Required practical resources are not available on Kerboodle. **Explaining** (20 minutes) ❿ This activity can be done whilst students' crystals are drying. Wearing eye protection, demonstrate magnesium (highly flammable) reacting with sulfuric acid (irritant) by putting 5 cm length of ribbon into half a test tube of dilute sulfuric acid. Put a boiling tube over the end to collect the gas and perform the squeaky pop test for hydrogen. Then discuss the explanation of the reaction between magnesium and sulfuric acid, given in the student book. Students then predict what would happen when calcium (highly flammable) is put into hydrochloric acid. Demonstrate this reaction. Ask students to explain the reaction in terms of oxidation and reduction illustrating their answer using word, balanced symbol equations with state symbols, ionic equations, and half equations.	**Support:** Give students the method outline. Then ask them to draw a diagrammatic flow chart to show the stages of the method.	**Practical:** Planning to make a salt

Plenary	Support/Extend	Resources
Finish the sentence (5 minutes) Ask students to complete the following sentences: • A salt is… • When sulfuric acid reacts with a metal… • A spectator ion is… **Extracting metals** (10 minutes) Students complete equations to describe the following reactions: • iron reacting with hydrochloric acid • magnesium reacting with sulfuric acid.	**Support:** Allow students to work in pairs to discuss the answers. **Support:** Students should write word and balanced symbol equations. **Extend:** Students should write ionic and half equations.	

Homework		
Students write three general equations for a metal, M (which forms a 1+ ion) reacting with sulfuric acid and hydrochloric acid.	**Support:** Write word equations only. **Extend:** Students should label the species that is oxidised and the species that is reduced.	

kerboodle

A Kerboodle highlight for this lesson is **Extension sheet: Salts from metals**. Refer to the **Content map** on Kerboodle for a full list of resources and assessment.

C5.5 Salts from insoluble bases

AQA spec Link: 4.2.2 Acids are neutralised by bases (e.g., insoluble metal hydroxides and metal oxides) to produce salts and water.

The particular salt produced in any reaction between an acid and a base depends on:

- the acid used (hydrochloric acid produces chlorides, nitric acid produces nitrates, sulfuric acid produces sulfates)
- the positive ions in the base.

Students should be able to:

- predict products from given reactants
- use the formulae of common ions to deduce the formulae of salts.

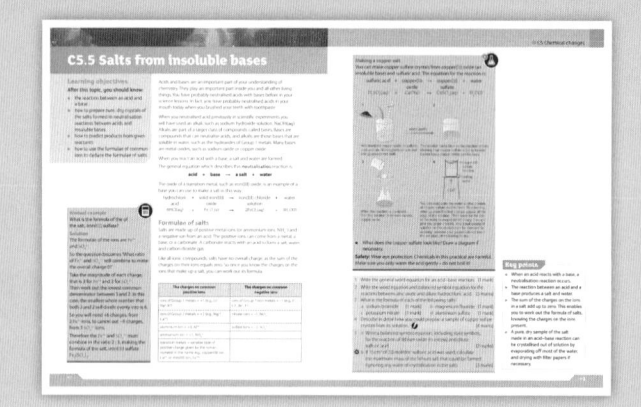

Aiming for	Outcome	Checkpoint	
		Question	Activity
Aiming for GRADE 4	Safely prepare a pure, dry sample of a soluble salt from an insoluble base and a dilute acid.		Main
	Name a salt formed between a metal hydroxide or metal oxide and sulfuric acid or hydrochloric acid.	End of chapter 5	Starter 1
	Recall a general equation for a base reacting with an acid and use it to write specific word equations.	1, 2	Main 2
Aiming for GRADE 6	Describe a method to prepare a pure, dry sample of a soluble salt from an insoluble substance and a dilute acid.	4	Main
	Write a balanced symbol equation to describe a reaction between a metal hydroxide or oxide and sulfuric acid or hydrochloric acid.	5, End of chapter 5, 6	Starter 1, Main
	Explain why the reaction between a base and a dilute acid is a neutralisation reaction.	End of chapter 5	Plenary 1
Aiming for GRADE 8	**H** Explain the reaction between a metal oxide or metal hydroxide and an acid, including an ionic equation.		Main, Plenary 1
	Generate the formulae of salts given the names of the metal or base and the acid	3	Starter 1
	Explain how alkalis are a subgroup of bases.		Starter 2

Maths
Students generate balanced symbol equations and the formulae of salts.

Literacy
Students write a risk assessment.

Key words
neutralisation

Practical

Title	Making a copper salt
Equipment	copper oxide powder, spatula, 1 mol/dm³ sulfuric acid, 20 cm³ measuring cylinder, 100 cm³ beaker, evaporating dish, filter paper, funnel, stirring rod, eye protection, Bunsen burner and safety equipment, tripod and gauze, access to a drying oven, tongs

C5 Chemical changes

Overview of method	Measure 20 cm³ of sulfuric acid into the beaker. Add half a spatula of copper oxide power to the acid and stir. Gently warm the breaker on a tripod and gauze. Do not allow the acid to boil. Continue adding the copper oxide until there is some black powder suspended. Allow the beaker to cool. Filter the mixture and discard the residue (unreacted copper oxide). Pour the filtrate into an evaporating dish. Heat the solution until the volume is halved or the point of crystallisation is reached. Remove from the heat and leave in a warm place to crystallise. Then put the evaporating dish in a drying oven or pat dry with absorbent paper.
Safety considerations	Copper oxide powder is harmful and sulfuric acid is an irritant. Wear eye protection throughout. Wash hands after completing the practical.

Starter	Support/Extend	Resources
Salts from insoluble bases (5 minutes) Provide students with a list of acid and metal oxide reactions. Students identify the name and formula of the salt that will be formed. **Alkalis and bases** (10 minutes) Draw a table with three headings – bases, alkalis, both bases and alkalis. Students sort the following into the appropriate column of the table. • Dissolve in water (alkali) • React with acids (both bases and alkalis) • NaOH (alkalis) • Metal hydroxides (both bases and alkalis) • Copper oxide (bases) • Have a pH greater than 7 (both bases and alkalis)	**Extend:** Students write a balanced symbol equation for each reaction. **Extend:** Give only the names of the salts. **Extend:** Students use the sorted table to write a paragraph explaining the similarities and differences between alkalis and bases.	**Interactive:** Salts from insoluble bases

Main	Support/Extend	Resources
Making a copper salt (40 minutes) Give students the method for making copper sulfate crystals. Students write their own risk assessment and then complete the practical to make a sample of the dry copper salt. This practical could be used for Required practical 1, however, differentiated Required practical resources are not available on Kerboodle.	**Extend:** Ask students to write the balanced symbol equation with state symbols. High attaining students should also write an ionic equation.	**Practical:** Making a copper salt

Plenary	Support/Extend	Resources
Equations (5 minutes) Ask students to write word equations and balanced symbol equations for all the reactions met in the lesson. Students then use their equations to explain why the reaction of a base and a dilute acid is a neutralisation reaction. **H** High-tier students should also write ionic equations. **Explaining procedure** (10 minutes) Ask students to review the method to make a copper salt and explain the following: • Copper oxide was in excess (the black reactant left over in a suspension, as all the acid needed to be neutralised). • The residue is discarded (this is the unreacted copper oxide and as such is an impurity in the preparation). • The filtrate is heated and volume reduced by half (to create a hot saturated solution, which on cooling will crystallise out into larger, well-formed crystals of the hydrated salt).	**Support:** Students use the general equation for the reaction of bases and acids to write their equations. **Support:** Use question and answer to ensure that all students understand these key parts of the method. **Extend:** Students should explain why copper sulfate cannot be made by reacting copper and sulfuric acid directly.	

Homework		
Students suggest how the method would need to be modified so that the percentage yield of copper sulfate could be calculated.	**Support:** Show students the formula for calculating percentage yield as detailed in Topic C4.4.	

kerboodle
A Kerboodle highlight for this lesson is **Literacy sheet: Making salts**. Refer to the **Content map** on Kerboodle for a full list of resources and assessment.

C5.6 Making more salts

AQA spec Link: 4.2.2 Acids are neutralised by alkalis (e.g., soluble metal hydroxides) to produce salts and water, and by metal carbonates to produce salts, water, and carbon dioxide.

The particular salt produced in any reaction between an acid and a base or alkali depends on:

- the acid used (hydrochloric acid produces chlorides, nitric acid produces nitrates, sulfuric acid produces sulfates)
- the positive ions in the alkali or carbonate.

Students should be able to:

- predict products from given reactants
- use the formulae of common ions to deduce the formulae of salts.

4.2.3 Soluble salts can be made from acids by reacting them with solid insoluble substances, such as metal oxides, hydroxides, or carbonates. The solid is added to the acid until no more reacts and the excess solid is filtered off to produce a solution of the salt.

Salt solutions can be crystallised to produce solid salts.

Students should be able to describe how to make pure, dry samples of named soluble salts from information provided.

Required practical: preparation of a pure, dry sample of a soluble salt from an insoluble substance and a dilute acid.

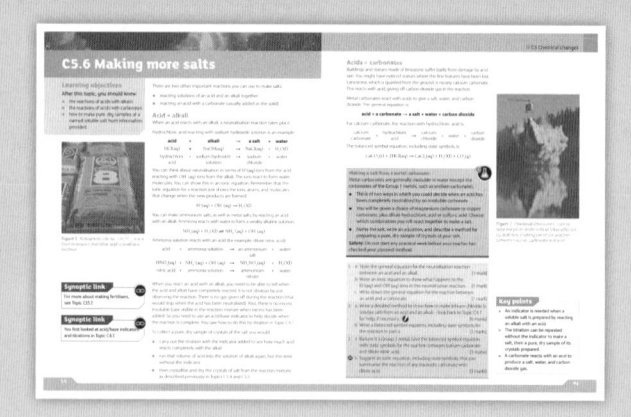

4.2.4 In neutralisation reactions between an acid and an alkali, hydrogen ions react with hydroxide ions to produce water. This reaction can be represented by the equation:

$$H^+(aq) + OH^-(aq) \rightarrow H_2O(l)$$

Aiming for	Outcome	Checkpoint	
		Question	Activity
Aiming for GRADE 4 ↓	Safely make a salt by reacting a metal carbonate with a dilute acid.		Main
	Write a general word equation for metal carbonates and alkalis reacting with dilute acids and use this to make specific word equations.	1	Starter 2
Aiming for GRADE 6 ↓	Describe how to make a dry sample of a salt from reacting a metal carbonate or an alkali with a dilute acid.	2	Main 1, Homework
	Write balanced symbol equations for neutralisation reactions.		Main 1, Homework
Aiming for GRADE 8 ↓	Explain the reaction between ammonia and dilute acids to produce salts and the agricultural importance of the salts.		Plenary 2, Homework
	Describe neutralisation using ionic equations, including the ionic equation for a carbonate plus an acid.	1, 3	Plenary 1

Maths
Students write balanced symbol equations and ionic equations.

Literacy
Students write a method for making a salt. They also write a magazine article to explain the importance of ammonium salts in agriculture.

Required practical

Title	Making a salt from a metal carbonate
Equipment	magnesium carbonate powder, copper carbonate powder, spatula, 1 mol/dm³ hydrochloric acid, 1 mol/dm³ sulfuric acid, 20 cm³ measuring cylinder, 100 cm³ beaker, evaporating dish, filter paper, funnel, stirring rod, eye protection, Bunsen burner and safety equipment, tripod and gauze, access to a drying oven, tongs

■ C5 Chemical changes

Overview of method	Measure 20 cm³ of one acid into the beaker. Add half a spatula of one of the metal carbonate powders into the acid and stir. Continue adding the same metal carbonate until there is no effervescence. It may be necessary to filter the mixture and discard the residue (unreacted metal carbonate). Pour the filtrate into an evaporating basin. Heat the solution until the volume is halved or until the point of crystallisation is reached. Remove from the heat and leave in a warm place to crystallise. Then put the evaporating basin in a drying oven or pat dry with absorbent paper.
Safety considerations	Copper carbonate powder is harmful and the acids are irritants. Wear eye protection throughout. Wash hands after completing the practical.

Starter	Support/Extend	Resources

Making more salts (10 minutes) Interactive where students complete a crossword to summarise all the reactions that can be used to make metal salts.
H Higher-tier students can then choose the correct species to complete an ionic equation to describe a neutralisation reaction.
General equations (10 minutes) Ask students to use the following equations to generate a general word equation for the reaction.
a) sodium hydroxide + hydrochloric acid → sodium chloride + water
  $KOH + HNO_3 \rightarrow KNO_3 + H_2O$
  $OH^- + H^+ \rightarrow H_2O$
  (acid + alkali → salt + water)
b) calcium carbonate + hydrochloric acid →
     calcium chloride + water + carbon dioxide
  $CuCO_3 + H_2SO_4 \rightarrow CuSO_4 \quad + \quad H_2O \; + \; CO_2$
  (metal carbonate + acid → salt + carbon dioxide + water)
	Extend: Ask students to classify the types of equation represented.	**Interactive:** Making more salts

Main	Support/Extend	Resources
Making a salt from a metal carbonate (40 minutes) Demonstrate a metal carbonate reacting with an acid in a boiling tube. Ask students to make their observations. Then ask them to write a method for making a salt from a metal carbonate reacting with a dilute acid. Students should illustrate the reaction with an equation. Encourage students to explain the observations that they could make which shows all of the acid has reacted. They then carry out the practical, collecting the pure, dry crystals next lesson.	**Support:** Give students the method from above and ask them to write word equations for the reaction. **Extend:** Ask students to modify the method to show that carbon dioxide gas was produced.	**Required practical:** Making a salt from a metal carbonate

Plenary	Support/Extend	Resources
Explain (5 minutes) Ask students to explain neutralisation by annotating a balanced symbol equation. They should highlight the 'acid particle' in red, the 'alkali particle' in blue, and water molecule in green. **Justify** (10 minutes) Ammonium sulfate (($NH_4)_2SO_4$) and ammonium nitrate (NH_4NO_3) can both be used as fertilisers. Ask students to justify which fertiliser they would choose.	**Extend:** Ask students to write the ionic equation for the neutralisation reaction. **Support:** Demonstrate the reaction again.	

Homework		
Ask students to write a magazine article for a 'Sunday Supplement' which explains the importance of ammonium salts in agriculture and how they can be made. Students should outline how to make an ammonium salt from the neutralisation of a dilute acid with ammonium hydroxide.	**Support:** Show examples of 'Sunday Supplement' articles. **Extend:** Students explain how ammonia gas becomes ammonium hydroxide and represent this with an ionic equation.	

kerboodle
A Kerboodle highlight for this lesson is **Calculation sheet: Calculating percentage yield**. Refer to the **Content map** on Kerboodle for a full list of resources and assessment.

# C5.7 Neutralisation and the pH scale

AQA spec Link: 4.2.4 Acids produce hydrogen ions, H^+, in aqueous solutions.

Aqueous solutions of alkalis contain hydroxide ions, OH^-.

The pH scale, from 0 to 14, is a measure of the acidity or alkalinity of a solution, and can be measured using universal indicator or a pH probe.

A solution with pH 7 is neutral. Aqueous solutions of acids have pH values of less than 7 and aqueous solutions of alkalis have pH values greater than 7.

Students should be able to:
- describe the use of universal indicator or a wide range indicator to measure the approximate pH of a solution
- use the pH scale to identify acidic or alkaline solutions.

MS 2h

Aiming for	Outcome	Checkpoint	
		Question	Activity
Aiming for GRADE 4 ↓	Safely use universal indicator to classify a solution as acidic or alkaline.		Main
	Describe the pH scale.		Starter 2
	Recall an example of an alkaline, neutral, basic, and acidic chemical.		Starter 1
Aiming for GRADE 6 ↓	Describe how universal indicator can be used to classify a chemical as acidic or alkaline.		Main
	Describe how solutions can be acidic or alkaline.	2	Main
	Describe the relationship between alkalis and bases.	1	Plenary 1
Aiming for GRADE 8 ↓	Evaluate how universal indicator or a data logger can be used to determine the approximate pH of a solution.	3, 5	Plenary 2
	Use ionic equations to explain how solutions can be acidic or alkaline.	1, 2	Main
	Explain how the pH of a solution changes as acid or alkali is added.	4	Main

Maths
Students write balanced ionic equations. They also understand the pH scale in terms of the changes in order of magnitude between each value (2h)

Literacy
Students evaluate an experimental method.

Key words
alkalis, bases, acids, neutral, pH scale

Practical

Title	Obtaining a pH curve
Equipment	0.5 mol/dm^3 hydrochloric acid, 0.5 mol/dm^3 sodium hydroxide, 20 cm^3 measuring cylinder, burette, burette holder, stand, pH sensor, 100 cm^3 beaker, eye protection
Overview of method	Fill a burette to 0 cm^3 with hydrochloric acid and using a burette clamp hold in place over the beaker. Measure 20 cm^3 of sodium hydroxide and add to the beaker. Use the pH probe to measure the pH. Add 1 cm^3 of hydrochloric acid from the burette. Swirl the mixture and using the pH probe record the pH. Repeat with additions of 1 cm^3 of hydrochloric acid until 25 cm^3 of acid has been added.
Safety considerations	Hydrochloric acid and sodium hydroxide are corrosive. Wear chemical splash-proof eye protection throughout. Do not fill the burette above head height, and do not suck solutions into the pipette by mouth. Wash hands after completing the practical.

C5 Chemical changes

Title	pH scale
Equipment	14 test tubes, two test-tube racks, two 100 cm³ beakers, two 10 cm³, measuring cylinders, two dropping pipettes, universal indicator solution, 0.1 mol/dm³ hydrochloric acid, 0.1 mol/dm³ sodium hydroxide, deionised water, eye protection
Overview of method	Add hydrochloric acid to a test tube until it is two-thirds full. Using a dropping pipette take 1 cm³ of the acid from the first test tube and put into the second test tube, then add 9 cm³ of deionised water. Mix the liquids. Remove 1 cm³ of the acid from the second test tube and put into the third test tube, then add 9 cm³ of deionised water. Mix the liquids well. Repeat for the first six test tubes. Fill the seventh test tube with deionised water. Add sodium hydroxide to the 14th test tube. Using a dropping pipette take 1 cm³ of the sodium hydroxide from the 14th test tube and put into the 13th test tube, then add 9 cm³ of deionised water. Mix the liquids. Repeat until all of the test tubes have a dilution in them. Now add universal indicator to each test tube and the full colour range should be observed.
Safety considerations	Hydrochloric acid and sodium hydroxide are irritants. Universal indicator is flammable. Wear eye protection throughout. Wash hands after completing the practical.

Starter	Support/Extend	Resources
Guess the pH (5 minutes) Ask students to write the word equation for the reaction of hydrochloric acid with sodium hydroxide. They should then annotate their predictions of the pH for each chemical–hydrochloric acid (pH 1), sodium hydroxide (pH 14), and sodium chloride solution/water (pH 7). **pH scale** (10 minutes) The pH scale is a logarithmic scale. Choose students to aid with demonstrating the pH scale practical to illustrate the difference in concentration of each number on the pH scale.	**Support:** Have samples of each chemical and use universal indicator to demonstrate the pH. **Extend:** Ask students to write a balanced symbol equation with state symbols and an ionic equation for this reaction.	

Main	Support/Extend	Resources
Obtaining a pH curve (40 minutes) Explain to students that they are going to add hydrochloric acid to sodium hydroxide. They should predict how the pH changes as the 1 cm³ increments are added. Then allow students to complete the practical outlined. Students should draw a line graph with a line of best fit to display their results.	**Support:** Allow students to use a data-logger which records the data and this can be automatically plotted on a graph. **Extend:** Ask students to annotate their graph to explain why the pH changes in terms of which ion is in excess.	**Practical:** Obtaining a pH curve

Plenary	Support/Extend	Resources
The pH scale (5 minutes) Call out pH values, colours of universal indicator, and other statements that describe acids and alkalis. Students have to classify whether each statement or value is describing an acid or an alkali. **Justify** (10 minutes) Ask students to work in small groups to evaluate the method for generating a pH curve and suggest improvements. Then ask each group to feed back one of their ideas.	**Support:** Ask students to compare the method they used with using a data logger and explain why a data logger would be an improvement.	**Interactive:** The pH scale

Homework		
Ask students to predict the shape of a pH curve when potassium hydroxide is added to nitric acid. They should illustrate the reaction with equations.		

kerboodle

A Kerboodle highlight for this lesson is **Maths skills: Plotting a pH curve**. Refer to the **Content map** on Kerboodle for a full list of resources and assessment.

Higher tier

C5.8 Strong and weak acids

AQA spec Link: 4.2.6 A strong acid is completely ionised in aqueous solution. Examples of strong acids are hydrochloric acid, nitric acid, and sulfuric acid.

A weak acid is only partially ionised in aqueous solution. Examples of weak acids are ethanoic acid, citric acid, and carbonic acid.

For a given concentration of aqueous solutions, the stronger an acid, the lower the pH.

As the pH decreases by one unit, the hydrogen ion concentration of the solution increases by a factor of 10.

Students should be able to:

- use and explain the terms dilute and concentrated (in terms of amount of substance), and weak and strong (in terms of the degree of ionisation) in relation to acids
- describe neutrality and relative acidity in terms of the effect on hydrogen ion concentration and the numerical value of pH (whole numbers only).

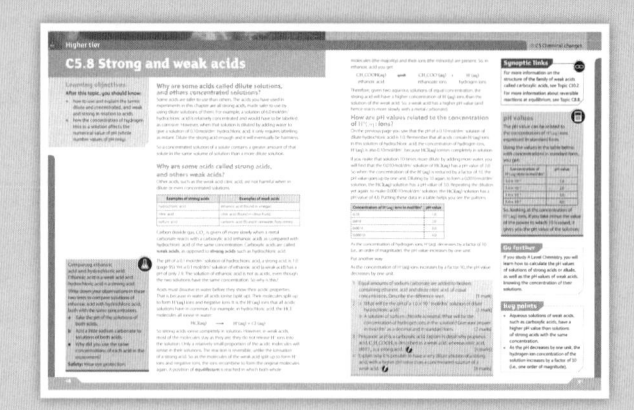

MS 2h

Aiming for	Outcome	Checkpoint	
		Question	Activity
Aiming for GRADE 6	Recall examples of strong and weak acids.		Starter 1
	Describe how an acid or alkali can be concentrated or dilute.		Starter 2, Main 1, Main 2, Plenary 1, Plenary 2
	Describe how an acid or alkali can be weak or strong.	1	Starter 1
Aiming for GRADE 8	Explain the difference between concentration and strong or weak in terms of acids and alkalis.	4	Main 1, Main 2, Plenary 1, Plenary 2
	Use ionic equations to explain how acids can be strong or weak.	3	Starter 2
	Quantitatively explain how the concentration of hydrogen ions relates to the pH number.	2, End of chapter 7	Plenary 1

Maths
Students calculate concentrations and recognise that a change of one unit in the pH scale is a change in the order of magnitude of the concentration of H^+ ions (2h).

Literacy
Students use scientific understanding and terminology to describe why a H^+ ion is also known as a proton.

Key words
strong acids, weak acids

Practical

Title	Comparing acids
Equipment	0.5 mol/dm³ hydrochloric acid, 0.5 mol/dm³ ethanoic acid, sodium carbonate powder, 10 cm³ measuring cylinder, four test tubes, test-tube holders, universal indicator with colour chart, spatula and eye protection
Overview of method	Add 3 cm³ of hydrochloric acid to the first test tube. Add a few drops of universal indicator and compare with the colour chart to determine the pH of the solution. Repeat for ethanoic acid using the second test tube. In the third test tube, add 3 cm³ of hydrochloric acid. Add half a spatula of sodium carbonate power and observe. Repeat for ethanoic acid using the fourth test tube.
Safety considerations	The acids are corrosive and the sodium carbonate powder is an irritant. Wear chemical splash-proof eye protection throughout. Wash hands after completing the practical. Universal indicator may be flammable.

C5 Chemical changes

Starter	Support/Extend	Resources
Strong and weak acids (5 minutes) Students complete the paragraph to describe the difference between strong and weak acids, and how the pH of an acid is affected by acid strength and concentration. Then give students a list of acids to classify as strong or weak acids. For example: • Hydrochloric acid (strong) • Citric acid (weak) • Ethanoic acid (weak) • Sulfuric acid (strong) • Nitric acid (strong)	**Extend:** Give students the formula for each example and ask them to write balanced symbol equations to illustrate the ionisation when the acid is in solution.	**Interactive:** Strong and weak acids
Acids: formulae and equations (10 minutes) Ask students to write an equation to show the ionisation in water of ethanoic acid and hydrochloric acid.	**Extend:** Draw the dot and cross diagrams of HCl gas and ethanoic acid.	

Main	Support/Extend	Resources
Comparing acids (30 minutes) Ask students to design a results table to record their observations. Allow students to investigate the two acids and then ask them to conclude which is the stronger acid and to explain how they know.	**Support:** Explain to the students that the concentration of both acids is the same and therefore a control variable. **Extend:** Ask students to outline how a reactive metal like magnesium could be used to classify the strength of an acid.	**Practical:** Comparing acids
pH and H⁺ concentration (10 minutes) Students use the calculation sheet to work through some calculations on H⁺ concentration and pH values.		**Calculation sheet:** pH and H⁺ concentration

Plenary	Support/Extend	Resources
Concentrated and dilute (5 minutes) Wearing eye protection put 10 cm³ of 0.1 mol/dm³ hydrochloric acid into a 250 cm³ beaker. Then add water to dilute the acid, using a pH probe to monitor the pH. Ask students to explain this observation.	**Extend:** Encourage students to use numbers to explain the dilution observed and the relationship with the pH number. **Support:** Ask students to compare the method they used with using a data logger and explain why a data logger would be an improvement.	
Diagram (10 minutes) Ask students to use the particle model to depict the following situations: • Dilute weak acid • Concentrated weak acid • Dilute strong acid • Concentrated strong acid Water particles could be shown as blue circles, the acid as a red particle labelled HA, the H⁺ as a red particle, and the negative ion as a white particle labelled A⁻.		

Homework		
Ask students to explain why H⁺ is also known as a proton.	**Extend:** Ask students to justify why sulfuric acid is known as a diprotic acid or a dibasic acid.	

kerboodle

A Kerboodle highlight for this lesson is **Literacy skills: Strong and weak acids**. Refer to the **Content map** on Kerboodle for a full list of resources and assessment.

C5 Chemical changes

Overview of C5 Chemical changes

In this chapter, students have revised and developed their understanding of the reactivity series from KS3. They have studied the reactions of the metals potassium, sodium, lithium, calcium, magnesium, zinc, iron, and copper with water and acids and should be able to recall and describe these reactions. They have applied their understanding of the reactivity series to displacement reactions and the extraction of metals, as well as introducing higher-tier students to the concepts of oxidation and reduction as the loss and gain of electrons respectively.

Students also learnt about salts and how they are prepared, including from metals and acids, acids and bases, and acids and carbonates. Students should be able to prepare a pure, dry sample of a salt from an insoluble metal oxide or carbonate as part of the required practical.

Finally, students have learnt about the pH scale. Higher-tier students should be able to explain how pH relates to H^+(aq) ion concentration and the difference between strong and weak acids.

Required practical

All students are expected to have carried out the required practical:

Practical	Topic
Preparation of a pure, dry sample of a soluble salt from an insoluble oxide or carbonate, using a Bunsen burner to heat dilute acid and a water bath or electric heater to evaporate the solution.	C5.4 C5.5 C5.6

MyMaths

You can find additional support for the maths skills covered in this chapter on **MyMaths**, including using standard form and orders of magnitude.

kerboodle

For this chapter, the following assessments are available on Kerboodle:

C5 Checkpoint quiz: Chemical changes
C5 Progress quiz: Chemical changes 1
C5 Progress quiz: Chemical changes 2
C5 On your marks: Chemical changes
C5 Exam-style questions and mark scheme: Chemical changes

Checkpoint follow up lesson

A student's route through this lesson can be determined using the Checkpoint assessment. Percentage pass marks are supplied in the Checkpoint teacher notes.

For each successive route through it is assumed that the student can perform to their current route as well as previous routes. For example, students working at Aiming for 6 are assumed to be secure in Aiming for 4 knowledge and understanding and working towards achieving all the learning outcomes for Aiming for 6.

	Aiming for 4	**Aiming for 6**	**Aiming for 8**
Learning outcomes	Use experimental results to state the reactivity series of metals.	Link the reactivity series to reactions of metals, including displacement.	Plan a method to produce a salt.
	State the name of a salt.	Use symbol equations to represent reactions of metals and their compounds with acids.	Explain the underlying scientific concepts that dictate how metals and their compounds react with acids.
	Write word equations to represent reactions between metals and their compounds with acids	Explain reactions of metals and their compounds with acids in terms of oxidation and reduction.	
Starter	**Reactivity series (15 minutes)** Demonstrate the reaction between three or four metals and dilute hydrochloric acid. Provide Aiming for 4 and Aiming for 6 students with a in which to record observations.		
	Discuss with students how observations can be used as clues to the metal's reactivity. Draw up a reactivity series and recap that metals at the top of the series are most reactive and metals at the bottom are least reactive.		
	Discuss with students that metals are able to displace elements below it in the reactivity series from their compounds – explain that hydrogen and carbon can be included in the series, and if a metal is more reactive than hydrogen it will be able to displace it from the acid when it is reacted with acid, and this is why hydrogen gas is formed. Ask students to suggest which of the metals they just observed must be more reactive than hydrogen.		
Differentiated checkpoint activity	The Aiming for 4 Checkpoint follow-up sheet provides highly-structured questions to support students with revising the content of the chapter.	The Aiming for 6 Checkpoint follow-up sheet provides prompt questions to support students with revising the content of the chapter.	Students use Aiming for 8 Checkpoint follow-up sheet to plan a detailed method for the production of a salt. Aiming for 8 students should be allowed to work predominantly independently and should be provided with 'hazcards' to use when considering risks associated with the practical investigations they plan. You may wish to let Aiming for 8 students skip the lesson starter and move immediately into the main task.
	Make the student books available to students.	Aiming for 6 students may need assistance in working out the formulae of metal nitrates and sulfates in order to attempt to balance formulae equations. Make the student books available to students.	
	Kerboodle resource C5 Checkpoint follow up: Aiming for 4, C5 Checkpoint follow up: Aiming for 6, C5 Checkpoint follow up: Aiming for 8		
Plenary	**Sharing learning (5 minutes)** Ask all pupils to list two things they have learnt, or understood more clearly, through completing the main task. Then ask them to then list one thing that they would still like to find out more about, and how they think they could do this. Ask for some students to volunteer their suggestions – when they give their area for improvement, ask if anyone else had this as a point they had learnt/ understood more. If such a match is found, ask the confident student to summarise.		
Progression	Provide students with the reactivity series and ask them to write word equations for the displacement reactions that were not demonstrated.	Ask students to summarise the method demonstrated in the starter, including any safety precautions taken. Students then suggest three more metals that could be tested and give the expected result.	The sheet provides minimal support for students and they should be aiming to work independently. Students could work in pairs if extra support is required.

C 6 Electrolysis
6.1 Introduction to electrolysis

AQA spec Link: 4.3.1 When an ionic compound is melted or dissolved in water, the ions are free to move about within the liquid or solution. These liquids and solutions are able to conduct electricity and are called electrolytes.

Passing an electric current through electrolytes causes the ions to move to the electrodes. Positively charged ions move to the negative electrode (the cathode), and negatively charged ions move to the positive electrode (the anode). Ions are discharged at the electrodes producing elements. This process is called electrolysis.

ⓗ Throughout Section 4.3 higher-tier students should be able to write half equations for the reactions occurring at the electrodes during electrolysis, and may be required to complete and balance supplied half equations.

4.3.2 When a simple ionic compound (e.g., lead bromide) is electrolysed in the molten state using inert electrodes, the metal (lead) is produced at the cathode and the non-metal (bromine) is produced at the anode.

Students should be able to predict the products of the electrolysis of binary ionic compounds in the molten state.

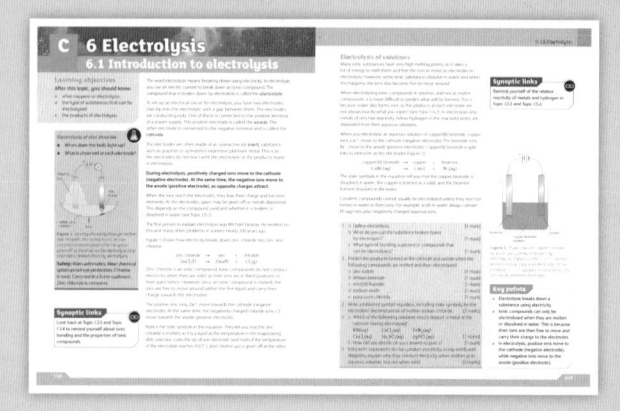

WS 1.2, 2.4, 3.5
MS 1c

Aiming for	Outcome	Checkpoint	
		Question	Activity
Aiming for GRADE 4 ↓	Define electrolysis.	1	Starter 2
	Write a word equation to describe the electrolysis of a molten ionic compound.		Main
Aiming for GRADE 6 ↓	Describe electrolysis in terms of movement of ions.	End of chapter 1, 2	Starter 2, Main, Plenary 2
	Write a balanced symbol equation including state symbols for the overall electrolysis of a molten ionic compound.	3	Main
	Predict the products at each electrode for the electrolysis of a molten ionic compound.	2	Main, Homework
Aiming for GRADE 8 ↓	Explain why electrolysis can only occur when an ionic compound is molten or in aqueous solution.	5	Main, Plenary 1, Plenary 2
	ⓗ Describe electrolysis with half equations at the electrodes.	End of chapter 2	Main
	Explain the classification of the reactions at each electrode as oxidation or reduction.		Main

Maths
Students balance ionic equations.

Literacy
Students use their understanding of electrolysis to write a story from the point of view of an electrolyte.

Key words
electrolyte, anode, cathode, inert

Practical

Title	Electrolysis of zinc chloride
Equipment	ceramic crucible, anhydrous zinc chloride powder, spatula, tongs, Bunsen burner and safety equipment, two carbon electrodes, bung with two holes, clamp and stand, ammeter, three wires, two crocodile clips, low voltage power supply, tripod, pipe-clay triangle, beaker filled with water, universal indicator paper

C6 Electrolysis

Overview of method	Half fill the crucible with zinc chloride and balance it in a pipe-clay triangle on a tripod. Submerge the ends of the electrodes into the powder, making sure they do not touch. Connect the electrodes into a series circuit with the ammeter and the low voltage power supply. Put the Bunsen burner under the crucible and heat moderately until the zinc chloride melts. At the anode, bubbles of chlorine vapour can be seen. Run the electrolysis for up to 15 minutes. Once finished, let the crucible cool. Using the tongs, put the cooled crucible into the beaker of water and let any leftover zinc chloride dissolve. Filter the water to get the metallic zinc.
Safety considerations	Zinc chloride is corrosive and chlorine is toxic. Carry out in a fume cupboard. Take care with any students who have breathing problems. Wear chemical splash-proof eye protection throughout and wash hands after demonstration.

Starter	Support/Extend	Resources
Formula (5 minutes) Explain to students that zinc forms 2+ ions. Ask them to determine the formula of zinc chloride and state the bonding present. **Electrolysis** (10 minutes) Set up a simple electrolysis circuit made of about 1 cm depth of sodium chloride in a 100 cm^3 beaker, with two carbon electrodes connected in series to a low voltage lamp and a low voltage power supply. Demonstrate that the bulb does not light up when sodium chloride is a solid. Add water and the bulb will light up, showing there is a flow of current. Ask students to suggest which type of particles is carrying the charge between the electrodes in the beaker and why in a solid the ionic compound cannot conduct (ions are not free to move).	**Support:** Encourage students to look back at their work on bonding and the definitions of the different bonding types.	

Main	Support/Extend	Resources
Electrolysis of zinc chloride (40 minutes) Show students samples of zinc, zinc chloride, and chlorine. Encourage students to note the difference in appearance of the chemicals. Explain the process of electrolysis and encourage students to predict the products at each electrode. Demonstrate the electrolysis of zinc chloride as outlined. Use question and answer to ensure students make all the relevant observations. Students should draw a labelled diagram and then add information to explain how the ions move to each electrode and how they become the elements.	**Support:** Allow students to use prose to explain what is happening to the ions at each electrode. **Extend:** 🄷 Ensure students write half equations and classify the reaction as oxidation or reduction (see Topic C6.2). **Extend:** Discuss how this process could be used to coat metal items with copper.	**Practical:** Electrolysis of zinc chloride

Plenary	Support/Extend	Resources
Electrolysis (5 minutes) Interactive where students complete a paragraph to explain how ionic compounds conduct electricity in solution and when molten. Students then label a diagram of an electrolysis experiment to identify the different species involved, the anode, and the cathode. **Personification of electrolysis** (10 minutes) Ask students to imagine that they are an electrolyte that is first melted and then electrolysed. They should write a brief story to describe what happens to them.		**Interactive:** Electrolysis

Homework		
Ask students to predict, including equations, the products of the electrolysis of lead bromide, copper chloride, and copper bromide.	**Extend:** Include half equations with state symbols at each electrode (see Topic C6.2).	

kerboodle
A Kerboodle highlight for this lesson is **Literacy skills: Electrolysis**. Refer to the **Content map** on Kerboodle for a full list of resources and assessment.

C6.2 Changes at the electrodes

AQA spec Link: 4.3.1 (H) **Throughout Section 4.3 higher-tier students should be able to write half equations for the reactions occurring at the electrodes during electrolysis, and may be required to complete and balance supplied half equations.**

4.3.4 The ions discharged when an aqueous solution is electrolysed using inert electrodes depend on the relative reactivity of the elements involved.

At the negative electrode (cathode), hydrogen is produced if the metal is more reactive than hydrogen.

At the positive electrode (anode), oxygen is produced unless the solution contains halide ions when the halogen is produced.

This happens because in the aqueous solution water molecules break down producing hydrogen ions and hydroxide ions that are discharged.

Students should be able to predict the products of the electrolysis of aqueous solutions containing a single ionic compound.

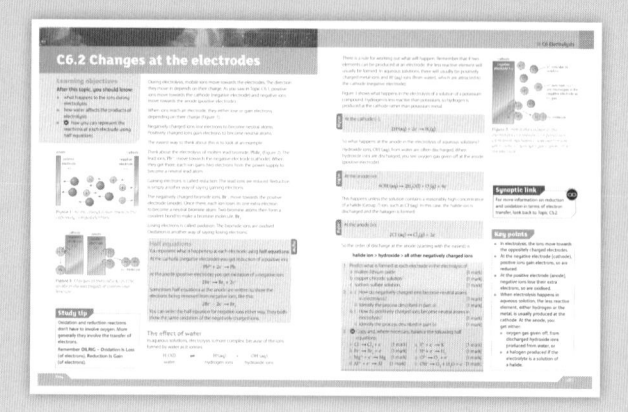

WS 1.2

Aiming for	Outcome	Checkpoint	
		Question	Activity
Aiming for GRADE 4	State that oxygen can be produced at the anode when some solutions are electrolysed.		Main 1, Main 2
	State that hydrogen can be produced at the cathode when some solutions are electrolysed.		Main 1, Main 2
	Write a word equation to describe electrolysis of a solution.		Main 1, Main 2
Aiming for GRADE 6	Describe electrolysis of solutions in terms of movement of ions.	2, End of chapter 1, 2	Main 1, Main 2, Plenary 2
	Write a balanced symbol equation including state symbols for the overall electrolysis of a solution.		Main 1, Main 2, Plenary 2
	Predict the products at each electrode for the electrolysis of a molten ionic compound or its solution.	1	Main 1, Main 2, Plenary 2
Aiming for GRADE 8	Explain how hydrogen ions and hydroxide ions can be present in solutions, including a balanced symbol equation with state symbols, for the reversible reaction in which water ionises.	End of chapter 4	Starter 2, Main 1, Main 2, Plenary 2
	(H) **Describe electrolysis with half equations at the electrodes.**	3, End of chapter 5	Main 1, Main 2, Plenary 2
	Explain the classification of reactions at the electrodes as oxidation or reduction.	2, End of chapter 6	Main 1, Main 2, Plenary 1, Plenary 2

Maths
Students balance chemical equations and half equations.

Literacy
Students discuss the arrangement of electrons in a hydrogen ion and a hydroxide ion. Students also compare and contrast anodes and cathodes and the reactions that occur at them. Students predict products of electrolysis reactions and explain their predictions.

Key words
half equation

C6 Electrolysis

Starter	Support/Extend	Resources
List your particles (5 minutes) Ask students to list the particles present in a sample of lithium bromide solution and to give their symbols (Li$^+$, Br$^-$, H$_2$O, H$^+$, and OH$^-$).	**Extend:** Ask students to draw the dot and cross diagrams of the lithium ion, bromide ion, hydrogen ion, and water molecule.	
Water (10 minutes) Ask students to draw the dot and cross diagram of water. Then ask students to work in small groups to discuss how the electrons could be arranged to make a hydrogen ion and a hydroxide ion. Use question and answer to ensure that students recognise that a very small proportion of water molecules break up and form these ions.	**Support:** Show students the dot and cross diagram of water and use molecular models to demonstrate how the bond in water could be broken.	

Main	Support/Extend	Resources
Electrolysis of potassium bromide (20 minutes) Ask students to consider a solution of potassium bromide. Which ions would be attracted to each electrode? Students explain why hydrogen gas is made at the cathode rather than potassium metal (remind students of the reaction of potassium with water). Then ask students to explain why bromine is made at the anode rather than oxygen. Students write a word and symbol equation for the reactions at the electrodes.	**Extend:** 🄷 Students write half equations for the reactions at the electrodes and classify as oxidation or reduction.	**Activity:** Electrolysis of potassium bromide
Explaining ions (20 minutes) Ask students to make a table to compare and contrast each electrode. Each time they write anode, positive, or the symbol/name of a positive ion they should use a red pen. Each time they write cathode, negative, or the symbol/name of a negative ion they should use a blue pen. Any species that has no charge should be written in green pen. They should include information about reduction, oxidation, and which ions are attracted to each electrode and use appropriate vocabulary.	**Extend:** 🄷 Ask students to write half equations for each electrode.	

Plenary	Support/Extend	Resources
Oxidation or reduction (5 minutes) Ask students to classify the following statements as oxidation or reduction: • At the cathode (reduction) • At the anode (oxidation) • Metal ions becoming metal atoms (reduction) • Non-metal ions becoming atoms (oxidation) • Electrolysis (neither as it is actually an example of both, i.e., redox)	**Support:** Remind students of the definition of oxidation and reduction.	**Interactive:** Oxidation or reduction
Predict (10 minutes) Students predict the products if water was electrolysed and explain how they are produced.	**Extend:** Ask students to write balanced chemical equations and half equations in their work.	

Homework		
Students predict, including equations, the products of the electrolysis of solutions of copper chloride, copper sulfate, and sulfuric acid using carbon electrodes.	**Extend:** Ask students to write balanced half equations.	

kerboodle
A Kerboodle highlight for this lesson is **Literacy sheet: Electroplating**. Refer to the **Content map** on Kerboodle for a full list of resources and assessment.

C6.3 Extraction of aluminium

AQA spec Link: 4.3.1 (H) Throughout Section 4.3 higher-tier students should be able to write half equations for the reactions occurring at the electrodes during electrolysis, and may be required to complete and balance supplied half equations.

4.3.3 Metals can be extracted from molten compounds using electrolysis. Electrolysis is used if the metal is too reactive to be extracted by reduction with carbon or if the metal reacts with carbon. Large amounts of energy are used in the extraction process to melt the compounds and to produce the electrical current.

Aluminium is manufactured by the electrolysis of a molten mixture of aluminium oxide and cryolite using carbon as the positive electrode (anode).

Students should be able to:

- explain why a mixture is used as the electrolyte
- explain why the positive electrode must be continually replaced.

4.3.5 (H) During electrolysis, at the cathode (negative electrode), positively charged ions gain electrons and so the reactions are reductions.

At the anode (positive electrode), negatively charged ions lose electrons and so the reactions are oxidations. Reactions at electrodes can be represented by half equations, for example:

$$2H^+ + 2e^- \rightarrow H_2$$

and

$$4OH^- \rightarrow O_2 + 2H_2O + 4e^- \quad \text{or} \quad 4OH^- - 4e^- \rightarrow O_2 + 2H_2O$$

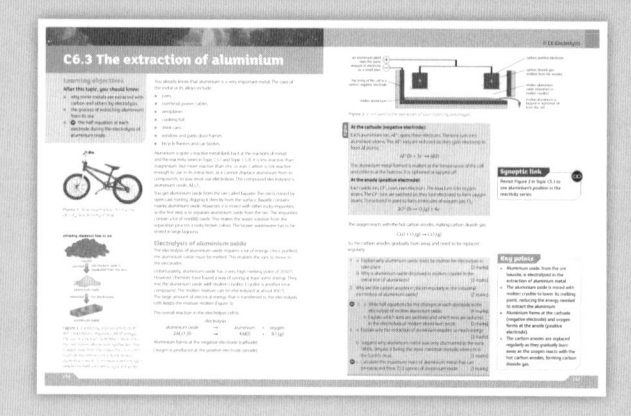

WS 1.2, 1.4, 1.5

Aiming for	Outcome	Checkpoint	
		Question	Activity
Aiming for GRADE 4 ↓	State that aluminium can be extracted from aluminium oxide using electrolysis.		Main 1, Plenary 2
	Write a word equation to describe the electrolysis of aluminium oxide.		Main 1, Plenary 2
Aiming for GRADE 6 ↓	Describe the electrolysis of aluminium oxide.		Main 1, Plenary 2
	Explain why electrolysis is an expensive metal extraction method and illustrate this with the extraction of aluminium.	1, 2, 4	Main 1, Plenary 2
	Explain why cryolite is added to aluminium oxide in the industrial extraction of aluminium.	1	Main 1, Plenary 2
Aiming for GRADE 8 ↓	Explain why electrolysis is used to extract aluminium from compounds.		Main 1, Plenary 2
	(H) Describe electrolysis with half equations at the electrodes.	3	Main 1, Main 2, Plenary 2
	(H) Explain the classification of the reactions at each electrode as oxidation or reduction.	3	Main 1, Plenary 2

C6 Electrolysis

Maths
Students balance symbol and ionic equations.

Literacy
Students prepare a presentation on the extraction of aluminium.

Starter	Support/Extend	Resources
Aluminium uses (5 minutes) Give students a tray of aluminium items, for example, foil, drinks can, drinks cup, saucepan. Then ask students to suggest what they all have in common. **Dot and cross diagrams** (10 minutes) Ask students to draw the dot and cross diagram of an aluminium atom, oxygen molecule, and aluminium oxide compound.	**Extend:** Ask students to suggest which property of aluminium makes it a desirable material for each particular use. **Support:** Give students the formulae for oxygen and aluminium oxide.	

Main	Support/Extend	Resources
The extraction of aluminium (30 minutes) Introduce the electrolytic cell. Show students an unlabelled diagram of the electrolytic cell for aluminium production. Ask students to annotate the diagram to: • describe electrolysis of aluminium oxide in terms of ions moving • write an equation to summarise the electrolysis • explain why cryolite is added • explain why carbon electrodes need to be replaced frequently. A labelled diagram of the electrolytic cell is available in the student book. **Writing half equations** (H) (10 minutes) Students use the maths skills interactive for further practice on writing half equations for electrolysis reactions.	**Support:** You may wish to show students a video of the industrial electrolysis of aluminium. **Extend:** (H) Ensure students write half equations for the reactions at the electrodes and classify them as oxidation or reduction.	**Activity:** The extraction of aluminium **Maths skills:** Writing half equations

Plenary	Support/Extend	Resources
Extraction of aluminium (5 minutes) Students complete sentences to describe the process of aluminium extraction. They then identify whether the reactions at the anode and cathode are reduction reactions or oxidation reactions. **Flow chart** (10 minutes) Ask students to use the student book to make a flow chart to describe how aluminium is extracted from the Earth. (H) The flow chart should include equations for the electrolysis of aluminium and classifications of each of the reactions as oxidation or reduction.	**Extend:** Students could annotate their flow chart to dicuss environmental, economic, and social issues of mining aluminium ore and the extraction of aluminium metal.	**Interactive:** Extraction of aluminium

Homework		
Students complete their flow chart from Plenary 2		

kerboodle
A Kerboodle highlight for this lesson is **WebQuest: Extracting aluminium**. Refer to the **Content map** on Kerboodle for a full list of resources and assessment.

107

C6.4 Electrolysis of aqueous solutions

AQA spec Link: 4.3.1 (H) Throughout Section 4.3 higher-tier students should be able to write half equations for the reactions occurring at the electrodes during electrolysis, and may be required to complete and balance supplied half equations.

4.3.4 The ions discharged when an aqueous solution is electrolysed using inert electrodes depends on the reactivity of the elements involved.
At the negative electrode (cathode), hydrogen is produced if the metal is more reactive than hydrogen.
At the positive electrode (anode), oxygen is produced unless the solution contains halide ions when the halogen is produced.
This happens because in the aqueous solution water molecules break down producing hydrogen ions and hydroxide ions that are discharged.
Students should be able to predict the products of the electrolysis of aqueous solutions containing a single ionic compound.

Required practical: Investigate what happens when aqueous solutions are electrolysed using inert electrodes. This should be an investigation involving developing a hypothesis.

4.3.5 (H) During electrolysis, at the cathode (negative electrode), positively charged ions gain electrons and so the reactions are reductions.
At the anode (positive electrode), negatively charged ions lose electrons and so the reactions are oxidations.
Reactions at electrodes can be represented by half equations, for example:

$$2H^+ + 2e^- \rightarrow H_2$$

and

$$4OH^- \rightarrow O_2 + 2H_2O + 4e^- \quad \text{or} \quad 4OH^- + 4e^- \rightarrow O_2 + 2H_2O$$

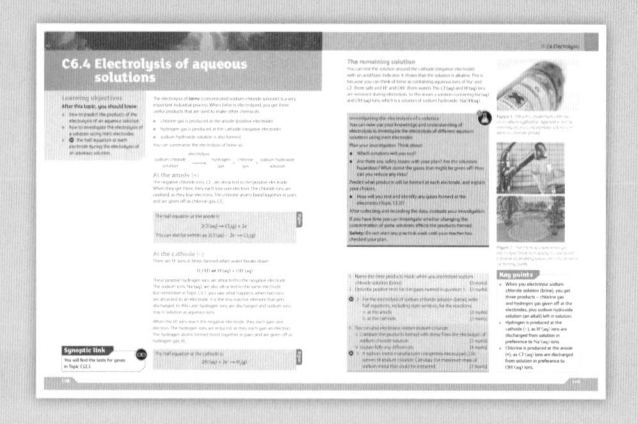

WS 1.2

Aiming for	Outcome	Checkpoint	
		Question	Activity
Aiming for GRADE 4	State the products of the electrolysis of brine and a use for each.	1	Starter 2, Main, Plenary 1
	Safely electrolyse a solution, with guidance provided.		Main
Aiming for GRADE 6	Describe how to electrolyse brine in terms of ions moving.		Main, Plenary 1
	Predict the products of electrolysis of a solution.	End of chapter 3	Starter 2, Main
	Plan and carry out an electrolysis investigation.		Main
Aiming for GRADE 8	(H) Explain the electrolysis of brine using half equations, classifying reactions at the electrode as oxidation or reduction.	2, End of chapter 3	Main, Plenary 1, Plenary 2
	Evaluate in detail an investigation they have planned and carried out, commenting on their methodology and quality of the data collected.		Main
	Compare and contrast the electrolysis of a compound in solution with its electrolysis as a molten compound.	3	Plenary 1

Maths
Students write balanced half equations.

Literacy
Students write an outline plan with predictions for investigating the electrolysis of solutions.

Key words
brine

C6 Electrolysis

Required practical

Title	Investigating the electrolysis of solutions
Equipment	two ignition tubes with bungs, two carbon electrodes, two wires, two crocodile clips, low voltage lab pack, selection of solutions to electrolyse all 1 mol/dm³, 100 cm³ measuring cylinder, eye protection, plastic cylinder with bung, stand, boss and clamp, nitrile gloves
Overview of method	Put two holes in the bung and push through the carbon electrodes so that 2 cm are protruding above the bung. Put the bung into the plastic cylinder. Using a stand, boss and clamp, hold the electrolytic cell upright and half fill with the solution to be electrolysed. Connect the electrodes to a low voltage lab pack. If a gas is likely to be collected wear nitrile gloves, then fill ignition tubes with electrolytic solution, and hold over the electrodes to collect the gas by displacement. Turn on the low voltage power supply.
Safety considerations	Hazard is dependent on the solution to be electrolysed. However, general advice would be wear chemical splash-proof eye protection throughout, wear nitrile gloves to collect the gas by displacement, and complete the practical in a well-ventilated room or fume cupboard. Take care with any students who have breathing problems. Wash hands after completing the practical.

Starter	Support/Extend	Resources
Electrolysis of aqueous solutions (10 minutes) Interactive where students complete a crossword to summarise what they have learnt so far about electrolysis. **Predict the products** (10 minutes) Ask students to predict the products at the electrodes for the following electrolyses: • Iron(II) sulfate solution (iron and oxygen) • Copper(II) nitrate solution (copper and oxygen) • Iron(III) chloride solution (iron and chlorine) • Sodium chloride solution (hydrogen and chlorine) **H** Students should write a half equation for each product that demonstrates how it is made, classify each as oxidation or reduction, and state at which electrode the change occurs.	**Support:** Remind students that hydrogen is made if a reactive metal is in the electrolyte. If a halide is in the electrolyte, a halogen is made, if not then oxygen is produced.	**Interactive:** Electrolysis of aqueous solutions

Main	Support/Extend	Resources
Investigating the electrolysis of solutions (40 minutes) Split the class into small groups. Introduce the investigation and ask students to write an outline plan, highlighting the dependent and control variables and predictions. If the plan is safe allow students to complete their investigation, recording their observations in a table. Encourage students to write a conclusion and evaluation.		**Required practical:** Investigating the electrolysis of solutions

Plenary	Support/Extend	Resources
Copper chloride (5 minutes) Ask students to predict the products of the electrolysis of copper chloride as a liquid and as a solution. Students should then explain the difference and similarities in the products. **Explaining observations** (10 minutes) Demonstrate the electrolysis of brine in a Petri-dish, adding universal indicator. Ask students to explain their observations. Bubbles demonstrate that a gas is made, universal indicator turns colourless around the anode as chlorine is produced, and universal indicator turns purple as sodium hydroxide, an alkali, is made.	**Extend: H** Ask students to write the half equations for each electrolysis. **Support:** Focus attention on the experiment that they have completed and relate this to these observations.	

Homework		
Ask students to explain how the electrolysis of brine produces hydrogen, chlorine, and sodium hydroxide.	**Extend: H** Students should use equations in their explanations.	

kerboodle
A Kerboodle highlight for this lesson is **Bump up your grade: Electrolysis of aqueous solutions**. Refer to the **Content map** on Kerboodle for a full list of resources and assessment.

C6 Electrolysis

Overview of C6 Electrolysis

In this chapter, students were introduced to electrolysis. They build upon their knowledge from *Chapter C3* to explain why ionic compounds can undergo electrolysis when molten or in solution. They should also be able to explain the movement of particles during electrolysis, and the reactions that occur at the electrodes.

Students then applied their understanding of electrolysis to the extraction of aluminium, and learnt how to investigate the electrolysis of a solution. They should be able to predict the products of electrolysis and higher-tier students should be able to write balanced half equations.

Required practical

All students are expected to have carried out the required practical:

Practical	Topic
Investigate what happens when aqueous solutions are electrolysed using inert electrodes. This should be an investigation involving developing a hypothesis.	C6.4

kerboodle

For this chapter, the following assessments are available on Kerboodle:

C6 Checkpoint quiz: Electrolysis
C6 Progress quiz: Electrolysis 1
C6 Progress quiz: Electrolysis 2
C6 On your marks: Electrolysis
C6 Exam-style questions and mark scheme: Electrolysis

Checkpoint follow up lesson

A student's route through this lesson can be determined using the Checkpoint assessment. Percentage pass marks are supplied in the Checkpoint teacher notes.

For each successive route through it is assumed that the student can perform to their current route as well as previous routes. For example, students working at Aiming for 6 are assumed to be secure in Aiming for 4 knowledge and understanding and working towards achieving all the learning outcomes for Aiming for 6.

	Aiming for 4	**Aiming for 6**	**Aiming for 8**
Learning outcomes	Describe what happens to an ionic substance when it is electrolysed.	Describe what happens during electrolysis.	Predict, using half equations, what would happen when a given substance is electrolysed
	Describe what happens at the anode and the cathode to form elements.	Explain what happens at the electrodes using the terms reduction and oxidation.	
Starter	**Electrolysis in action (10 minutes)** Show a video clip of electrolysis in action. Emphasise that electrolysis occurs because when ionic substances are molten or dissolved their ions become mobile, and that they will be attracted to the oppositely charged electrodes. Recap that ions gain or lose electrons at the electrodes to form neutral elements. This could be role modelled by students, using counters to represent electrons.		
Differentiated checkpoint activity	The Aiming for 4 Checkpoint follow-up sheet provides various cut and stick activities that students can use to create their revision poster. Aiming for 4 students will need to be provided with scissors and glue as the follow-up sheet contains pictures they can cut out and stick on their poster to help explain what happens during electrolysis.	The Aiming for 6 Checkpoint follow-up sheet provides prompt questions to support students with the content their poster should cover.	Students use Aiming for 8 Checkpoint follow-up sheet provides questions to support students with the content their poster should cover. The content is of a higher demand than the Target 6 sheet.
	Kerboodle resource C6 Checkpoint follow up: Aiming for 4, C6 Checkpoint follow up: Aiming for 6, C6 Checkpoint follow up: Aiming for 8		
Plenary	**Electrolysis song (10 minutes)** Ask students to think of an easy poem or song to help them remember what happens during electrolysis, specifically at each electrode. Then ask some students to demonstrate their songs or poems to the rest of the class.		
Progression	Provide students with some further prompt questions and ask them to add further annotations to their poster using the student book and their notes from the chapter.	Encourage students to write balanced half equations for the electrolysis of lead bromide.	Provide students with an unfamiliar electrolysis experiment and ask them to predict and explain what would happen. Encourage them to do so without their posters.

C 7 Energy changes

7.1 Exothermic and endothermic reactions

AQA spec Link: 5.1.1 Energy is conserved in chemical reactions. The amount of energy in the universe at the end of a chemical reaction is the same as before the reaction takes place. If a reaction transfers energy to the surroundings the product molecules must have less energy than the reactants, by the amount transferred.

An exothermic reaction is one that transfers energy to the surroundings so the temperature of the surroundings increases. Exothermic reactions include combustion, many oxidation reactions and neutralisation.

An endothermic reaction is one that takes in energy from the surroundings so the temperature of the surroundings decreases.

Endothermic reactions include thermal decompositions and the reaction of citric acid and sodium hydrogen carbonate.

Students should be able to:

- distinguish between exothermic and endothermic reactions on the basis of the temperature change of the surroundings.

Limited to measurement of temperature change. Calculation of energy changes or ΔH is not required.

Required practical: Investigate the variables that affect temperature changes in reacting solutions, for example, acid plus metals, acid plus carbonates, neutralisations.

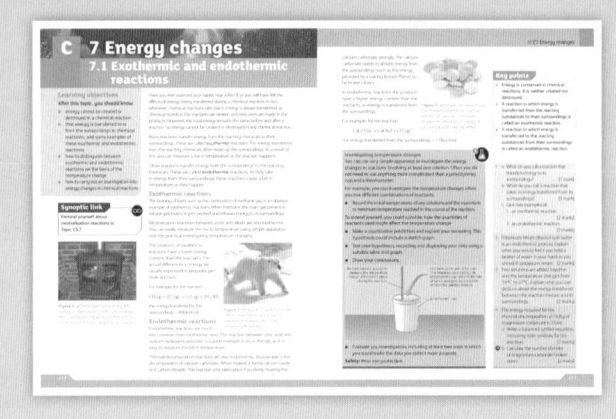

Aiming for	Outcome	Checkpoint	
		Question	Activity
Aiming for GRADE 4 ↓	Define exothermic and endothermic reactions.	1	Starter 2, Main, Plenary 2
	State that energy is conserved in a chemical reaction.		Starter 2
	Safely complete a calorimetry experiment for a reaction that takes place in solution.		Main
Aiming for GRADE 6 ↓	Describe examples of exothermic and endothermic reactions.	1	Plenary 2
	Explain, using observations from calorimetry, how to classify a reaction as exothermic or endothermic.	2, End of chapter 1	Main, Plenary 1, Plenary 2
	Explain in detail how to carry out a calorimetry experiment.		Main, Plenary 1
Aiming for GRADE 8 ↓	Explain a chemical reaction in terms of energy transfer.		Main
	Plan, carry out, and evaluate the errors in a calorimetry investigation.		Plenary 1

Maths
Students use their results to draw a graph and line of best fit.

Literacy
Students write up their investigation into energy changes.

Key words
exothermic, endothermic

C7 Energy changes

Required practical

Title	Investigating temperature changes
Equipment	eye protection, two 50 cm^3 measuring cylinders, polystyrene cup, 250 cm^3 beaker, weighing boat, spatula, 0 °C–110 °C thermometer, stirrer, stopwatch, 1.00 mol/dm^3 hydrochloric acid, 1.00 mol/dm^3 sodium hydroxide, iron filings, 1.00 mol/dm^3 potassium hydroxide, 1.00 mol/dm^3 copper(II) sulfate solution
Overview of method	Use the first measuring cylinder to measure 25 cm^3 of the sodium hydroxide solution and pour this into the polystyrene cup. Stand the polystyrene cup in the 250 cm^3 beaker. In the second measuring cylinder, measure 25 cm^3 of hydrochloric acid. Using the thermometer, measure the temperature of the sodium hydroxide every 30 seconds whilst gently stirring. After exactly two minutes add the hydrochloric acid and continue to stir and to record the temperature of the solution every 30 seconds for 10 minutes. Repeat this experiment twice: with 25 cm^3 of copper(II) sulfate and iron filings, and with 25 cm^3 potassium hydroxide and nitric acid.
Safety considerations	Sodium hydroxide, potassium hydroxide, and hydrochloric acid are corrosive. Copper(II) sulfate is harmful. Use the lowest concentration possible. Wear chemical splash-proof eye protection throughout and wash hands after completing the practical.

Starter	Support/Extend	Resources
General equations (5 minutes) Provide students with partially completed word equations for the reactions between metals and acids, carbonates and acids, acids and alkalis, metals and oxygen, hydrocarbons and oxygen, and carbon dioxide and water. Students complete the equations. **Demonstrate** (10 minutes) Show students a single-use ice pack for a sports injury. Use question and answer to get students to understand that this is a chemical reaction which produces a cooling effect – an endothermic change. Then show students single-use handwarmers and lead them to understand that energy is transferred from the chemical reaction to the surroundings, raising the temperature – an exothermic change. Remind students that energy is conserved and then ask students to consider what happens to the energy in the reactant during and after the reaction.	**Extend:** Students give an example and generate the balanced symbol equation for each. **Extend:** You may wish to allow students to make 'hot ice' where a supersaturated solution of sodium ethanoate crystallises in an exothermic change.	**Interactive:** General equations

Main	Support/Extend	Resources
Investigating temperature changes (40 minutes plus time next lesson) Students read the outline of the investigation in the student book. They then design an investigation, including a results table to record their observations. Run the practical as detailed if students cannot come up with their own ideas. Encourage students to plot a graph of temperature against time. Ensure students evaluate their experimental procedure, considering sources of error, and explaining how to improve their investigation.	**Extend:** Students include a sketch graph in their prediction.	**Required practical:** Investigating temperature changes

Plenary	Support/Extend	Resources
Calorimetry (10 minutes) Introduce calorimetry to students, including how calorimetry can be used to find out the energy changes in a combustion reaction and reactions in solutions. Students consider the errors involved in the reactions. **Summary** (10 minutes) Students make a compare and contrast table for exothermic and endothermic reactions. Their table should include the definition of each, effect on surrounding temperature, and an example of each.	**Extend:** Encourage students give real chemical examples to illustrate the calorimetry. **Support:** Complete the table as a class on the board and allow students to copy it into their notes.	

Homework		
Students write balanced symbol equations, including state symbols, for the thermal decomposition of calcium carbonate, the reaction of sodium carbonate with hydrochloric acid, and the reaction of calcium with sulfuric acid. They also predict whether the reactions are exothermic or endothermic.	**Support:** Students only write word equations.	

kerboodle
A Kerboodle highlight for this lesson is **Literacy skills: Exothermic and endothermic**. Refer to the **Content map** on Kerboodle for a full list of resources and assessment.

C7.2 Using energy transfers from reactions

AQA spec Link: 5.1.1 An exothermic reaction is one that transfers energy to the surroundings so the temperature of the surroundings increases.

Everyday uses of exothermic reactions include self-heating cans and hand warmers.

An endothermic reaction is one that takes in energy from the surroundings so the temperature of the surroundings decreases.

Some sports injury packs are based on endothermic reactions.

Students should be able to:

- evaluate uses and applications of exothermic and endothermic reactions given appropriate information.

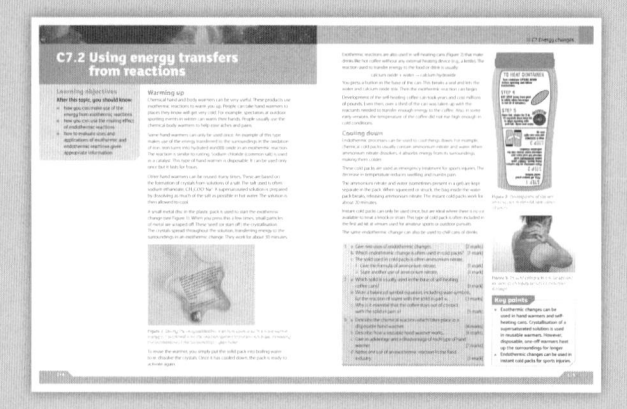

Aiming for	Outcome	Checkpoint	
		Question	Activity
Aiming for GRADE 4 ↓	State a use of an exothermic reaction and an endothermic reaction.	1, 2, 3	Main, Plenary 1, Plenary 2
	Write word equations for familiar reactions.		Starter 1, Plenary 1, Plenary 2
Aiming for GRADE 6 ↓	Explain how an energy change from a chemical reaction can be used.	2, 3	Main, Plenary 1, Plenary 2
	Write balanced symbol equations for familar reactions.		Plenary 2
Aiming for GRADE 8 ↓	Suggest a chemical reaction for a specific purpose based on the energy change for the reaction.	2	Main, Plenary 1, Plenary 2
	Evaluate in detail the uses of exothermic and endothermic reactions.	2, 3	Main, Plenary 1

Maths
Students balance symbol equations and draw a line graph.

Literacy
Students produce a spider diagram of the key ideas about self-heating cans. Students also produce a risk assessment for the use of self-heating cans.

Practical

Title	Supersaturated solution sodium ethanoate
Equipment	boiling tube, anhydrous sodium ethanoate powder, spatula, dropping pipette, distilled water, hot water bath, boiling-tube holder, temperature probe
Overview of method	Half fill a boiling tube with sodium ethanoate powder and add four drops of water. Put the boiling tube in a hot water bath for about five minutes, agitating occasionally. Add water dropwise, with one minute of heating between additions until all of the solid has dissolved. Remove the boiling tube from the water and carefully allow to cool without moving the boiling tube unnecessarily.
Safety considerations	This should be carried out as a teacher-led demonstration only. Wear eye protection.

■ C7 Energy changes

Starter	Support/Extend	Resources
Completing equations (5 minutes) Students use the interactive to complete the following word equations: • iron + (oxygen) → iron(III) oxide • calcium oxide + (water) → calcium hydroxide • (sodium ethanoate solution) → solid sodium ethanoate • ammonium nitrate solid + water → (ammonium nitrate solution) They then put sentences in the correct order to describe how hand warmers work.	**Support:** Encourage students to use the student book text to find the answers. **Extend:** Ask students to write balanced symbol equations for these reactions, including state symbols.	**Interactive:** Completing equations
Supersaturated sodium ethanoate solution (10 minutes) Have a supersaturated solution of sodium ethanoate in a boiling tube. Put a temperature probe into the solution and then start recording the temperature. Show students the data captured in a graphical form. Ask students to classify the reaction as exothermic or endothermic and suggest a use for this reaction.	**Extend:** Ask students to suggest the physical change which is occurring in this practical.	

Main	Support/Extend	Resources
Using energy transfers from a reaction (40 minutes) Introduce uses of exothermic reactions. Ask students to work in small groups to make a list of the key features for a self-heating can. Using question and answer, build up a spider diagram of the features. Then ask students to draw a cross section of their self-heating can, labelling where the food will be held and the chemicals for the exothermic reaction, and to explain how the reaction will begin.	**Support:** You may wish to demonstrate a self-heating can such as those from and outdoor equipment shop.	**Activity:** Using energy transfers from a reaction
Introduce uses of endothermic reactions. Demonstrate the use of commercially available ice packs. In groups and wearing eye protection, students cut one side of the ice pack and carefully remove the contents. They put the solid into a beaker and burst the water bag into the beaker, then record the temperature every 30 seconds for 10 minutes. Students could then plot a line graph of this data.	**Extend:** Evaluate single-use sports packs such as those using ammonium nitrate compared to re-usable gel ice packs.	

Plenary	Support/Extend	Resources
Diagram (5 minutes) Show students a diagram of a re-usable hand warmer. Ask them to suggest labels to explain how it works. Then encourage students to list the pros and cons of this method of hand warmer.		
Uses of exothermic and endothermic reactions (10 minutes) Ask students to write a table with two columns, one labelled exothermic and the second labelled endothermic. Students write two real-life uses for each type of reaction. They should include word equations and balanced symbol equations to illustrate the reactions used.	**Extend:** Ask students to evaluate each reaction for its use.	

Homework		
Students write a risk assessment for a self-heating can using the hydration of calcium oxide to heat the food.	**Support:** Show students a bottle of calcium oxide and its hazard symbols.	

kerboodle

A Kerboodle highlight for this lesson is **Extension sheet: Using energy transfers from reactions**. Refer to the **Content map** on Kerboodle for a full list of resources and assessment.

C7.3 Reaction profiles

AQA spec Link: 5.1.2 Chemical reactions can occur only when reacting particles collide with each other and with sufficient energy. The minimum amount of energy that particles must have to react is called the activation energy.

Reaction profiles can be used to show the relative energies of reactants and products, the activation energy, and the overall energy change of a reaction.

Students should be able to:

- draw simple reaction profiles (energy level diagrams) for exothermic and endothermic reactions showing the relative energies of reactants and products, the activation energy, and the overall energy change, with a curved line to show the energy as the reaction proceeds
- use reaction profiles to identify reactions as exothermic or endothermic
- explain that the activation energy is the energy needed for a reaction to occur
- calculate energy changes.

5.1.3 (H) During a chemical reaction:
- **energy must be supplied to break bonds in the reactants**
- **energy is released when bonds in the products are formed.**

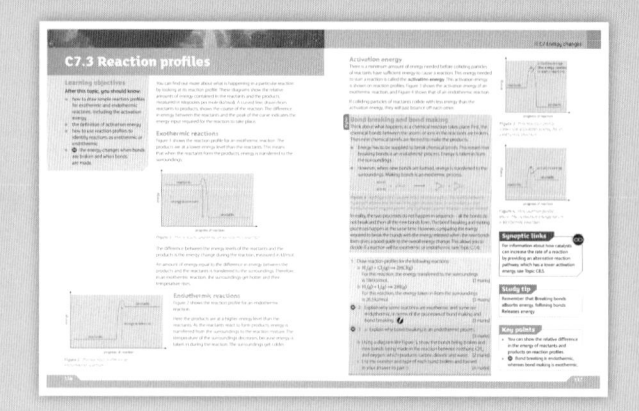

WS 1.2
MS 1a, 4a

Aiming for	Outcome	Checkpoint	
		Question	Activity
Aiming for GRADE 4	Define activation energy.		Starter 1, Main 1, Main 2, Plenary 1, Plenary 2
↓	Sketch a generic reaction profile diagram for an exothermic or endothermic reaction.		Main 1, Main 2, Plenary 1, Plenary 2
Aiming for GRADE 6	Label activation energy on a reaction profile diagram.		Main 1, Main 2, Plenary 1, Plenary 2
	Generate a specific reaction profile diagram for a given chemical reaction when its energy change is also supplied.	1, End of chapter 2	Main 1, Main 2, Plenary 2
↓	(H) Identify bonds broken in reactants and new bonds made in products of a reaction.	2	Main
Aiming for GRADE 8	Explain why chemical reactions need activation energy to start them.	2	Main 1, Main 2, Plenary 1, Plenary 2
	Use the particle model to explain how a chemical reaction occurs.	2, 3, End of chapter 3	Main 2
↓	(H) Explain energy change in terms of the balance between bond making and bond breaking.	3	Main 2

Maths
Students draw reaction profile diagrams (4a) and balance symbol equations.

Key words
activation energy

■ C7 Energy changes

Practical

Title	Reaction profiles
Equipment	rubber balloon, hydrogen cylinder and regulator with hose, cotton string, 1 kg mass, metre rule, splint, elastic band, match and match box eye protection
Overview of method	Fill a rubber balloon with hydrogen and tie the neck tight. Then tie a 1 m length of cotton to the knot and attach the 1 kg mass to the other end. Secure the splint to the end of the metre rule with an elastic band. Wearing eye protection, ignite the splint and hold at arm's length on the metre rule to explode the hydrogen in the balloon.
Safety considerations	Wear chemical splash-proof eye protection. Hydrogen is extremely flammable. Ignite the balloon at arm's length and ensure that the balloon is at least two metres from students and not near any ceiling tiles or other objects.

Starter	Support/Extend	Resources
Copy and complete (5 minutes) Ask students to complete these sentences: • In a (chemical) change, reactant bonds are (broken) and new substances are made as product bonds are (formed). • Breaking bonds (takes in) energy from the surroundings and this is an (endothermic) change. • Making bonds (releases) energy to the surroundings and this is an (exothermic) change.	**Support:** Give students the list of words to put into the prose.	
Energy changes (10 minutes) Interactive where students complete a paragraph on the energy changes involved in the making and breaking of bonds. They then label two reaction profile diagrams as endothermic or exothermic, identifying the reactants, products, and activation energy.		**Interactive:** Energy changes

Main	Support/Extend	Resources
Reaction profiles (burning hydrogen) (20 minutes) Demonstrate a hydrogen explosion as detailed. Then allow students to test the gas on a small scale themselves. Prepare a boiling tube of hydrogen with a bung in the top. Students should wear chemical splash-proof eye protection and put a lighted splint into the open mouth of the boiling tube. They should observe a pop. This demonstration must be carefully monitored by a teacher or technician. Ask students to write equations for the reaction and then illustrate the reaction in a reaction profile diagram. They should annotate the activation energy and describe this as the energy provided by the flame, and add the actual chemicals which are the reactants and the products.	**Support:** You may wish to use question and answer to complete the task on the board before students copy the information into their notes. **Extend:** Ensure students write balanced symbol equations with state symbols.	**Practical:** Reaction profiles
Reaction profiles (burning methane) (20 minutes) Light a Bunsen burner and turn it to the blue flame. Ask students to write an equation to illustrate this reaction. Then give students a molecular modelling kit. Encourage students to work in small groups to illustrate the combustion of methane by making the models of the reactants and then forming the products. Ask students to explain why energy is needed to break the bonds and then why energy is released when bonds are made. Students should then sketch the reaction profile for this reaction.	**Support:** Supply the balanced symbol equation. Ask students to make the reactants and then rearrange the atoms to make the products. **Extend:** Give each group of students a different chemical reaction to model.	

Plenary	Support/Extend	Resources
Reaction profiles (10 minutes) Students use the calculation sheet to analyse reaction profiles to determine if they are exothermic or endothermic reactions.	**Extend:** Students label reactants, products, activation energy, and energy change of the reaction.	**Calculation sheet:** Reaction profiles
Modelling (10 minutes) Choose the group that included the highest level chemistry in modelling the combustion of methane in Main 2 to share and explain their model with the rest of the class.	**Extend:** Ask students to assess their peers using the science department marking policy.	

Homework		
Ask students to draw a reaction profile diagram for the hydration of ammonium nitrate in a single-use sports cold pack.		

kerboodle

A Kerboodle highlight for this lesson is **Bump up your grade: How do catalysts work?**. Refer to the **Content map** on Kerboodle for a full list of resources and assessment.

Higher tier

C7.4 Bond energy calculations

AQA spec Link: 5.1.3 During a chemical reaction:
- energy must be supplied to break bonds in the reactants
- energy is released when bonds in the products are formed.

The energy needed to break bonds and the energy released when bonds are formed can be calculated from bond energies. The difference between the sum of the energy needed to break bonds in the reactants and the sum of the energy released when bonds in the products are formed is the overall energy change of the reaction.

In an exothermic reaction, the energy released from forming new bonds is greater than the energy needed to break existing bonds. In an endothermic reaction, the energy needed to break existing bonds is greater than the energy released from forming new bonds.

Students should be able to calculate the energy transferred in chemical reactions using bond energies supplied.

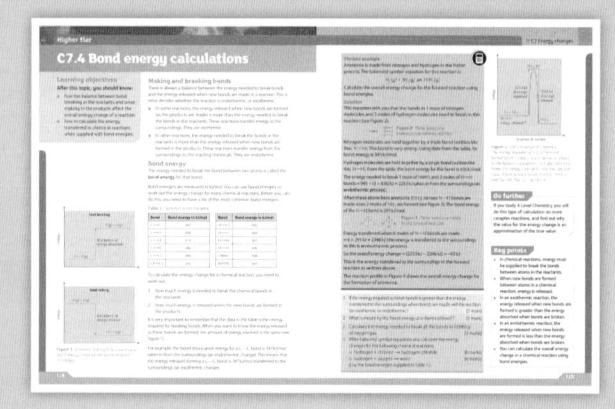

MS 1a, 1b, 2a, 3b

Aiming for	Outcome	Checkpoint	
		Question	Activity
Aiming for GRADE 6	Explain, using the particle model, how reactants become products in a chemical reaction.		Main
	Explain why bond breaking is endothermic and bond making is exothermic.	End of chapter 3, 4	Starter 2, Main, Plenary 2
	Define bond energy and identify all the bonds that break and are made in a chemical reaction.	2, 4	Main
Aiming for GRADE 8	Calculate the energy needed to break the reactant bonds and the energy released when the product bonds are made.	4, End of chapter 4	Main, Plenary 2
	Calculate the energy change for a reaction, including the correct unit.	4, End of chapter 4	Main, Plenary 2
	Explain in terms of bond energies how a reaction is either exothermic or endothermic.	1, End of chapter 3	Main

Maths
Students rearrange equations (3b) and use appropriate units when carrying out bond energy calculations. They also use standard form (1b), decimal form (1a), and an appropriate number of significant figures (2a).

Literacy
Student summarise the steps to calculate energy change and explain the energy change of a reaction in terms of bond breaking and bond making.

Key words
bond energy

118

C7 Energy changes

Starter	Support/Extend	Resources
Sketch (5 minutes) Ignite a Bunsen burner. Using question and answer, establish the word and symbol equation for the reaction. Ask students to justify whether the reaction is exothermic or endothermic and explain whether energy is being released or taken in by the system. Students should then use this information to sketch a reaction profile. **Predict** (10 minutes) Ask students to consider carbon. It can form bonds with itself, for example, C—C in alkanes, C=C in alkenes, and C≡C in alkynes. Ask students to predict, with an explanation, which type of carbon bond would take: • the most energy to break • the least energy to break • the most energy transferred to the surroundings when made • the least energy transferred to the surroundings when made.	**Support:** Bullet point the key information on the board to allow students to use this to generate their sketch. **Support:** Show students molecular models of ethane, ethene, and ethyne.	

Main	Support/Extend	Resources
Calculating bond energies (40 minutes) Go through the worked example in the student book of calculating the energy change in the Haber Process. Students use the worked example to summarise the steps in performing this calculation: • Draw displayed formulae for the balanced symbol equation. • Total each type of bond on the reactants side. • Total each type of bond on the product side. • Calculate the energy required to break the reactant bonds. • Calculate the energy transferred to the surroundings when the product bonds are made. • Energy change = energy required to break product bonds − energy transferred to the surroundings when products are made. Students then use their summary to answer further questions.	**Extend:** Students suggest the energy change for the reverse reaction of the Haber Process. **Support:** Give students a molecular modelling kit. Encourage them to work in small groups to illustrate the Haber process by making the models of the reactants and then forming the products.	**Activity:** Calculating bond energies

Plenary	Support/Extend	Resources
Thought shower (5 minutes) Explain to students that the calculated energy change of a reaction using average bond energy values are usually different to the measured amount. Ask students to discuss in small groups the reasons for this. **Energy calculations** (10 minutes) Students label a reaction profile, identify true and false statements about breaking and making bonds, and calculate the energy change for some reactions when the balanced symbol equation and mean bond energies are given.	**Extend:** Ask students to classify the reasons as practical (e.g. heat loss to the surroundings) or calculation error (e.g., using average bond energy values rather than specific values for that molecule). **Extend:** Students correct the statements that are false.	**Interactive:** Energy calculations

Homework		
Ask students to consider ethane, C_2H_6. They should write a word equation and a symbol equation for the combustion of this chemical to make carbon dioxide and water only. Using the bond energy data in the student book they should calculate the energy change for the complete combustion of ethane.		

kerboodle

A Kerboodle highlight for this lesson is **Maths skills: Bond energies**. Refer to the **Content map** on Kerboodle for a full list of resources and assessment.

GCSE Chemistry Only

C7.5 Chemical cells and batteries

AQA spec Link: 5.2.1 Cells contain chemicals which react to produce electricity.

The voltage produced by a cell is dependent upon a number of factors including the type of electrode and electrolyte.

A simple cell can be made by connecting two different metals in contact with an electrolyte.

Batteries consist of two or more cells connected together in series to provide a greater voltage.

In non-rechargeable cells and batteries the chemical reactions stop when one of the reactants has been used up. Alkaline batteries are non-rechargeable.

Rechargeable cells and batteries can be recharged because the chemical reactions are reversed when an external electrical current is supplied.

Students should be able to interpret data for relative reactivity of different metals and evaluate the use of cells.

Students do not need to know details of cells and batteries other than those specified.

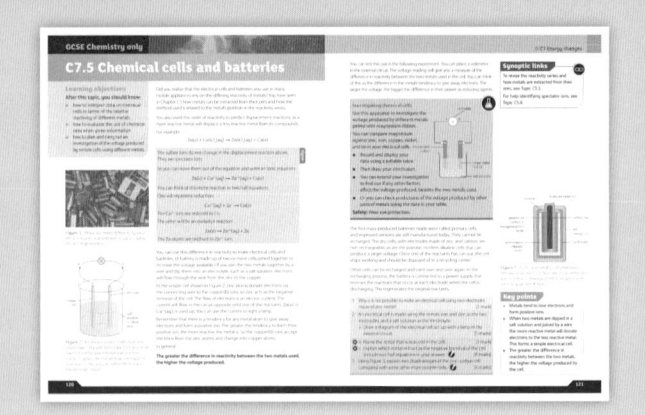

Aiming for	Outcome	Checkpoint	
		Question	Activity
Aiming for GRADE 4	Describe a simple cell.	2	Starter 1, Starter 2, Plenary 1
	Describe a battery.		Starter 1
	Give an example of a non-rechargeable battery.		Plenary 2, Homework
Aiming for GRADE 6	Explain how potential difference can be changed in a cell.		Starter 2, Main
	Interpret data from an electrochemical cell to determine the reactivity of the metals involved.	1, End of chapter 5	Main
	Explain why non-rechargeable batteries stop working.		Plenary 2, Homework
Aiming for GRADE 8	Describe an electrochemical cell with half equations and ionic equations.	2	Main, Plenary 2, Homework
	Explain why the reactions in an electrochemical cell are redox reactions and determine which species is oxidised or reduced in an electrochemical cell.	2	Main, Plenary 2, Homework
	Evaluate the use of non-rechargeable cells.	3	Plenary 2, Homework

Maths
Students write balanced half equations and ionic equations, and design a table to record their results.

Literacy
Students make a presentation about primary and secondary cells. Student also apply their knowledge of electrochemical cells to explain how an archaeological discovery could be an early cell.

■ C7 Energy changes

Practical

Title	Investigating chemical cells
Equipment	voltmeter (or multimeter), two wires, two crocodile clips, strips of magnesium, zinc, iron, copper, and tin, electrolyte (e.g., sodium chloride solution), eye protection, 100 cm^3 beaker
Overview of method	Half fill a beaker with the electrolyte. Connect two different metals in series with the voltmeter. Submerge half of each electrode in the electrolyte. Ensure that the two pieces of metal do not touch. Record the potential difference. Repeat with different combinations of metals.
Safety considerations	Electrolytes are often irritants as are zinc and nickel. Magnesium is flammable. Wear chemical splash-proof eye protection throughout and wash hands after completing the practical. Take care of any students who are asthmatic.

Starter	Support/Extend	Resources
Circuit symbols (5 minutes) Ask students to match the circuit symbols to their meaning for a cell, battery, low voltage power supply, voltmeter, ammeter, and lamp. Students then sort statements according to whether they describe a primary cell or a secondary cell. **Fruit clock** (10 minutes) Demonstrate a fruit clock. Using an LED clock display, attach it in series using two wires with crocodile clips on one end to a piece of magnesium ribbon and a piece of copper. Push the metals into a piece of fruit. Ask students to suggest what is happening. Explain to the students that the more reactive metal is giving electrons to the less reactive metal. Ask students to classify this type of reaction (redox).	**Support:** You may have a commercial potato clock available to show students. **Extend:** Ask students to write the half equations and the ionic equations for this reaction.	**Interactive:** Circuit symbols

Main	Support/Extend	Resources
Investigating chemical cells (40 minutes) Ask students to design a suitable results table. Run the practical investigation. Students then use the data to create a reactivity series.	**Extend:** Demonstrate lead with a few metals and ask students to insert this metal into their reactivity series. Wear gloves during this demonstration.	**Practical:** Investigating chemical cells

Plenary	Support/Extend	Resources
Baghdad battery (5 minutes) Explain to students that an archaeologist has found a ceramic pot, with a copper cylinder inside. This houses a corroded iron nail which fits into the cylinder. Historians believe that the cylinder was filled with grape juice. Many researchers believe that this was an early cell used to gold plate artefacts. Ask students to explain, using their knowledge of electrochemical cells, how this set-up could be used to produce a current. (Reaction between iron and copper in an acid electrolyte to produce a current.) **Primary and secondary cells** (10 minutes) Split the class in half, and ask each half to write simple sentences on either primary (non-rechargeable) cells or secondary (rechargeable) cells. Then have students share their points with each other to build up a comparison for primary and secondary cells. Encourage students to correct any errors that are shared.	**Extend:** There are many news articles and clips available to share with the class.	

Homework		
Students prepare a presentation on primary (non-rechargeable) and secondary (rechargeable) cells. Their presentations should include what primary and secondary cells are, listing their advantages and disadvantages, and some uses for the cells. Students could work in small groups to generate a presentation on their findings.	**Extend:** Encourage students to give examples and include balanced equations to illustrate them.	

kerboodle

A Kerboodle highlight for this lesson is **Extension sheet: Chemical cells and batteries**. Refer to the **Content map** on Kerboodle for a full list of resources and assessment.

GCSE Chemistry Only

C7.6 Fuel cells

AQA spec Link: 5.2.2 Fuel cells are supplied by an external source of fuel (e.g., hydrogen) and oxygen or air. The fuel is oxidised electrochemically within the fuel cell to produce a potential difference.

The overall reaction in a hydrogen fuel cell involves the oxidation of hydrogen to produce water.

Hydrogen fuel cells offer a potential alternative to rechargeable cells and batteries.

Students should be able to:

- evaluate the use of hydrogen fuel cells in comparison with rechargeable cells and batteries
- ⓗ write the half equations for the electrode reactions in the hydrogen fuel cell.

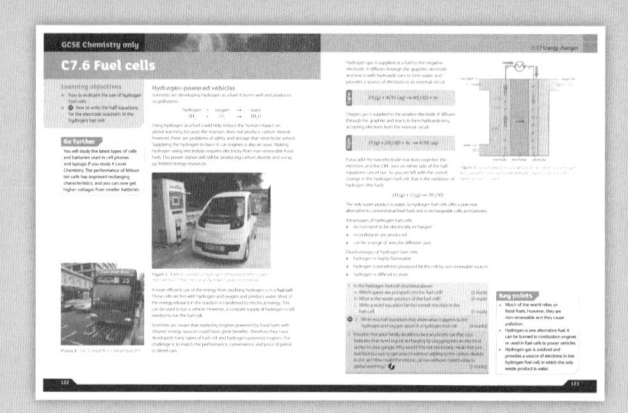

Aiming for	Outcome	Checkpoint	
		Question	Activity
Aiming for GRADE 4	Describe a hydrogen fuel cell.	1, End of chapter 6	Main, Plenary 1, Plenary 2
	State some uses for hydrogen fuel cells.		Main, Plenary 2
	State that hydrogen fuel cells could be an alternative to rechargeable cells and batteries.		Main
Aiming for GRADE 6	Explain how a hydrogen fuel cell produces electricity.	2	Main, Plenary 2
	List the advantages and disadvantages of hydrogen fuel cells.	End of chapter 6	Starter 2, Main, Plenary 2
	Explain why hydrogen fuel cells are an alternative to rechargeable cells and batteries.		Main
Aiming for GRADE 8	ⓗ Describe the reactions in fuel cells using balanced symbol and half equations.	2, End of chapter 6	Starter 1, Main, Plenary 2
	Evaluate the use of hydrogen fuel cells instead of rechargeable cells and batteries.	3	Main, Plenary 2
	Determine and explain which species is oxidised and which is reduced in a hydrogen fuel cell.	End of chapter 6	Main, Plenary 2

Maths
Students balance symbol and ionic equations.

Literacy
Students evaluate hydrogen fuel cells, creating a visual summary of the key ideas. Students also prepare a report on using hydrogen as a fuel or write a letter to an MP to persuade them to provide more funding for research into hydrogen fuel cells. Students can extract key ideas from news reports and articles for these tasks.

Key words
fuel cell

Practical

Title	Hydrogen/oxygen explosion
Equipment	hydrogen gas, oxygen gas, party balloon, cotton string, 1 kg mass, metre rule, elastic band, splint, matches and match box, eye protection

■ C7 Energy changes

Overview of method	Fill no more than 300 cm³ volume of a rubber party balloon with a stoichiometric ratio of oxygen and hydrogen. Then tie closed and attach a 1 m length of cotton and anchor with a 1 kg mass. Use a rubber band to secure a splint at the end of a metre rule. Wearing chemical splash-proof eye protection and ear defenders, light the splint and put the flame over the stretched section of the rubber balloon.
Safety considerations	Oxygen and hydrogen are extremely flammable and oxygen is also oxidising. Use no more than 300 cm³ volume of the mixture of the gases. Ensure observers are at least 5 m away and wear chemical splash-proof eye protection. Keep balloon away from ceiling tiles or any other objects.

Starter	Support/Extend	Resources
Hydrogen/oxygen explosion (5 minutes) If not shown previously, allow students to observe the experiment outlined. Encourage students to write a word equation for the reaction. 🄷 Higher-tier students should write balanced symbol equations. **Fuelling a car** (10 minutes) Show students a hydrogen fuel cell car image. Students work in small groups to list the pros and cons for hydrogen fuel cell cars. You may wish to look at news websites to find clips of hydrogen fuel cells being discussed.	**Extend:** Students determine which species was oxidised and which was reduced. **Support:** Show students a small-scale squeaky pop test and use question and answer to illicit the pros and the cons.	

Main	Support/Extend	Resources
Hydrogen fuel cells (40 minutes) Show students the diagram of the hydrogen fuel cell in the student book. Use question and answer to build up the equations at each electrode and the overall equation. Ask students to discuss in small groups whether they think hydrogen fuel cells could soon replace other batteries in everyday uses. Ask students to write a visual summary of the hydrogen fuel cell theory, application, drawbacks, and benefits. Then explain to students that cars can be powdered using electricity from a rechargeable battery charged from mains electricity or from hydrogen fuel cells. Ask students to compare and contrast the two methods of providing electricity for powering a car.	**Support:** Students only produce word equations. **Extend:** 🄷 Students produce balanced symbol equations. **Extend:** Students should justify which they think is the best method for providing electricity to power a car.	**Activity:** Hydrogen fuel cells

Plenary	Support/Extend	Resources
Hydrogen fuel cell (5 minutes) Students use the interactive to sort advantages and disadvantages of using hydrogen fuel cells in cars. Then show students an unlabelled diagram of a hydrogen fuel cell. Ask them to label the key parts. They then write equations and highlight which species is being oxidised and which is being reduced. **Application** (10 minutes) Show students a diagram of a methanol fuel cell. Ask them to suggest the fuel and to write the overall equation for the reaction knowing that methanol will react to produce carbon dioxide and water only. 🄷 Higher-tier students should produce balanced symbol equations.	**Extend:** Ask students to justify whether they think a hydrogen fuel cell or a methanol fuel cell is most environmentally friendly.	**Interactive:** Hydrogen fuel cell

Homework		
Students complete the WebQuest where they research the advantages and disadvantages of using hydrogen as a fuel. They use their research to prepare a report. Alternatively, ask students to draft a letter to an MP about research into hydrogen-powered vehicles. Students should make a persuasive argument for extra funding being made available for it, stress the problems that will arise if the present situation continues, and the problems that the research needs to solve.		**WebQuest:** Is hydrogen the perfect fuel?

kerboodle
A Kerboodle highlight for this lesson is **Literacy sheet: Fuel cells**. Refer to the **Content map** on Kerboodle for a full list of resources and assessment.

123

C7 Energy changes

Overview of C7 Energy changes

In this chapter, students have learnt about the energy transfers that occur during chemical reactions. They should understand that an exothermic reaction transfers energy from the system to the surroundings, and an endothermic reaction transfers energy from the surroundings to the system. This is a key concept that students should be confident with. Students should be able to interpret experimental data to identify if a reaction is exothermic or endothermic and should be able to describe some uses of exothermic and endothermic reactions.

Students further developed their qualitative understanding of the energy transfers in a reaction into a quantitative understanding. They should be confident with sketching and interpreting reaction profile diagrams and higher-tier students should be able to use bond energies to calculate overall energy changes for a reaction, identifying if it is exothermic or endothermic.

Students should also have applied their understanding of the reactivity series and electrolysis to chemical cells and fuel cells.

Required practical

All students are expected to have carried out the required practical:

Practical	Topic
Investigate the variables that affect temperature changes in reacting solutions such as, for example, acid plus metals, acid plus carbonates, neutralisations, displacement of metals.	C7.1

MyMaths

You can find additional support for the maths skills covered in this chapter on **MyMaths**, including drawing and interpreting graphs and substituting numerical values into algebraic equations.

kerboodle

For this chapter, the following assessments are available on Kerboodle:

C7 Checkpoint quiz: Energy changes
C7 Progress quiz: Energy changes 1
C7 Progress quiz: Energy changes 2
C7 On your marks: Energy changes
C7 Exam-style questions and mark scheme: Energy changes

Checkpoint follow up lesson

A student's route through this lesson can be determined using the Checkpoint assessment. Percentage pass marks are supplied in the Checkpoint teacher notes.

For each successive route through it is assumed that the student can perform to their current route as well as previous routes. For example, students working at Aiming for 6 are assumed to be secure in Aiming for 4 knowledge and understanding and working towards achieving all the learning outcomes for Aiming for 6.

	Aiming for 4	**Aiming for 6**	**Aiming for 8**
Learning outcomes	Recognise endothermic and exothermic reactions.	Explain what endothermic and exothermic reactions are.	Explain how a hydrogen fuel cell works.
	Draw a simple energy profile for an endothermic and an exothermic reaction.	Represent endothermic and exothermic reactions using energy profiles.	Writ half equations for the reactions that takes place within a hydrogen fuel cell.
		Explain how endothermic and exothermic reactions are useful.	
Starter	**Definitions (5 minutes)** Students work in pairs to give definitions for endothermic and exothermic reactions. Ask for examples from students, discuss and address any misconceptions that arise, and draw out a general definition.		
	Reaction profile diagrams (5 minutes) Sketch a reaction profile onto an interactive whiteboard or dry-wipe board. Ask students to give the key labels for the profile, and to identify if it shows an endothermic reaction or an exothermic reaction. Discuss what a reaction profile shows and how it differs for endothermic and exothermic reactions.		
Differentiated checkpoint activity	The Aiming for 4 Checkpoint follow-up sheet provides a practical circus for students to investigate energy transfers during reactions. Work with Target 4 students to complete the suggested practical circus. These are suggested ideas only and will require a full risk assessment and plan for any practical used:		
	• Add a spatula of ammonium chloride to a boiling tube of water and monitoring the temperature throughout. • Add equal quantities of dilute acid and dilute alkali together in a test tube and monitoring the temperature throughout. • Activate a single use hand-warmer. • Activate a single use instant ice-pack.		
	Students use the Aiming for 6 Checkpoint follow-up sheet to produce a leaflet summarising exothermic and endothermic reactions. The sheet contains prompt questions to guide students with what to include. Provide text books for additional support.		
	Students use Aiming for 8 Checkpoint follow-up sheet to create a leaflet about hydrogen fuel cells. The sheet provides minimal support for students and they should be aiming to work independently. Students could work in pairs if extra support is required. They should include any relevant half equations. Provide text books for additional support. They may also benefit from access to the Internet.		
	Kerboodle resource C7 Checkpoint follow up: Aiming for 4, C7 Checkpoint follow up: Aiming for 6, C7 Checkpoint follow up: Aiming for 8		
Plenary	**Key facts (5 minutes)** Ask students to list three key facts about endothermic and exothermic reactions. Compare their list with another pupil and give one suggestion that would improve the list.		
	Labelling a reaction profile diagram (5 minutes) Ask pupils to sketch a reaction profile for an endothermic reaction, including as many labels or descriptions as possible without referring to any revision aids or lesson notes. Give 30 seconds only. Then award a point for each correct label students give. Students should include axes labels, identifying the reactants and products, activation energy, and an indication of the overall energy change.		
Progression	Provide students with prose that describes reactions, giving activation energy. Students use this to draw fully-labelled reaction profile diagrams.	Students should include in their leaflet instructions for calculating bond energies and the overall energy change during a reaction.	Students could include a detailed evaluation of fuel cells, including advantages and disadvantages.

3 Rates, equilibrium, and organic chemistry

Specification links

Topic	Paper
6.1 Rate of reaction	Paper 2
6.2 Reversible reactions and dynamic equilibrium	Paper 2
7.1 Carbon compounds as fuels and feedstock	Paper 2
7.2 Reactions of alkenes and alcohols	Paper 2
7.3 Synthetic and naturally occurring polymers	Paper 2

Required practicals

Practical	skills	Topic
Investigate how changes in concentration affect the rates of reactions by a method involving measuring the volume of a gas produced and a method involving a change in colour or turbidity. This should be an investigation involving developing a hypothesis.	AT 1 – use of appropriate apparatus to make and record a range of measurements accurately, including mass, time, temperature, and volume of liquids and gases. AT 3 – use of appropriate apparatus and techniques for conducting and monitoring chemical reactions. AT 5 – making and recording of appropriate observations during chemical reactions including the measurement of rates of reaction by a variety of methods such as production of gas and colour change. AT 6 – safe use and careful handling of gases, liquids and solids, including careful mixing of reagents under controlled conditions, using appropriate apparatus to explore chemical changes.	C8.4

Maths skills

Skill	Topic
1a Recognise and use expressions in decimal form.	C8.1, C8.2, C8.4, C8.5, C9.1
1b Recognise and use expressions in standard form.	C8.2, C8.3, C8.4
1c Use ratios, fractions and percentages.	C8.1, C8.2, C8.3, C8.4, C8.6, C8.9, C9.2, C9.3, C9.4, C10.1, C10.3, C10.4, C11.4
1d Make estimates of the results of simple calculations.	C8.1
2a Use an appropriate number of significant figures.	C8.3, C8.4, C8.5
2b Find arithmetic means.	C8.4, C8.5
2c Construct and interpret frequency tables and diagrams, bar charts and histograms.	C9.2
3a Understand and use the symbols: $=, <, \ll, \gg, >, \propto, \sim$.	C8.2, C8.4
3b Change the subject of an equation.	C8.3, C8.4
3c Substitute numerical values into algebraic equations using appropriate units for physical quantities.	C8.2, C8.3, C8.4
4a Translate information between graphical and numeric form.	C8.1, C8.2, C8.3, C8.4, C8.5
4b Understand that $y = mx + c$ represents a linear relationship.	C8.1
4c Plot two variables from experimental or other data.	C8.1, C8.2, C8.3, C8.4, C8.5
4d Determine the slope and intercept of a linear graph.	C8.1
4e Draw and use the slope of a tangent to a curve as a measure of rate of change.	C8.1, C8.2, C8.3, C8.4, C8.5
5b Visualise and represent 2D and 3D forms including two dimensional representations of 3D objects.	C8.2, C10.1, C10.2, C11.1, C11.2, C11.3

C3 Rates, equilibrium, and organic chemistry

KS3 concept	GCSE topic	Checkpoint	Revision
Different chemical reactions happen at different speeds.	C8.1 How fast?	Ask students give examples of slow chemical reactions e.g. rusting, fast chemical reactions e.g. combustion and very fast reactions e.g. explosions.	Provide students with a sorting activity, where they group chemical reactions as slow, fast and very fast.
Changes both chemical and physical can be speeded up by heating.	C8.3 The effect of temperature	Ask students to suggest why putting magnesium in cold water takes a long time to make hydrogen that you can test, but in warm water it is much faster.	Ask students to complete the missing words in a cloze passage about chemical and physical change and the effect of raising the temperature on the rate.
In chemical reactions a new product is made. If the product can become the reactants under the same conditions, it is a reversible reaction.	C8.6 Reversible reaction	Ask students to explain why litmus indicator can illustrate a reversible chemical change.	Give students a crossword with clues which are the definitions of the key words (chemical change, physical change, reactant, product, reversible reaction, pH indicators).
Mixtures made from different liquids can be separated by distillation.	C9.2 fractional distillation	Ask students to label a distillation set up and then annotate in a different colour to explain how it separates a mixture.	Give students statements for them to order to correctly explain how distillation separates liquids.
Combustion is the science word for burning and is when oxygen combines with a fuel which is heated to release chemical energy in a usable form.	C9.3 Burning hydrocarbon fuels	Ask students label the combustion triangle and explain what this shows.	Ask students to write a fictitious 'job specification' for a fuel.
Combustion of fossil fuels releases carbon dioxide and water.	C9.3 Burning hydrocarbon fuels	Ask students to outline an experiment where they could test the products of combustion to show that carbon dioxide and water have been made.	Provide students with a selection of part finished word and symbol equations. Ask students to complete them.
Recall the general properties of polymers (qualitative).	C11.1 Addition polymerisation	Ask students to draw a spider diagram to illustrate the general properties of polymers. They could then add examples of polymers and uses justifying them based on the properties.	Give students some examples of plastics and ask them to handle them. Give students a list of properties and ask them to select the general properties of plastics from the list.
Describe a simple model of DNA including the part played by Watson, Crick, Wilkins and Franklin in the development of the DNA model.	C11.4 DNA	Ask students to write a newspaper feature article to describe how the current model of DNA has been generated.	Give students a story board about the development of the model of DNA. Ask students to draw cartoons to illustrate the information.

C 8 Rates and equilibrium
8.1 Rate of reaction

AQA spec Link: 6.1.1 The rate of a chemical reaction can be found by measuring the quantity of a reactant used or the quantity of product formed over time:

$$\text{mean rate of reaction} = \frac{\text{quantity of reactant used}}{\text{time taken}}$$

$$\text{mean rate of reaction} = \frac{\text{quantity of product formed}}{\text{time taken}}$$

The quantity of reactant or product can be measured by the mass in grams, by a volume in cm^3.

The units of rate of reaction may be given as g/s or cm^3/s.

H For the Higher Tier, students are also required to use quantity of reactants in terms of moles and units for rate of reaction in mol/s.

Students should be able to:
- calculate the mean rate of a reaction from given information about the quantity of a reactant used or the quantity of a product formed and the time taken
- draw, and interpret, graphs showing the quantity of product formed or quantity of reactant used up against time
- draw tangents to the curves on these graphs and use the slope of the tangent as a measure of the rate of reaction
- **H** calculate the gradient of a tangent to the curve on these graphs as a measure of rate of reaction at a specific time.

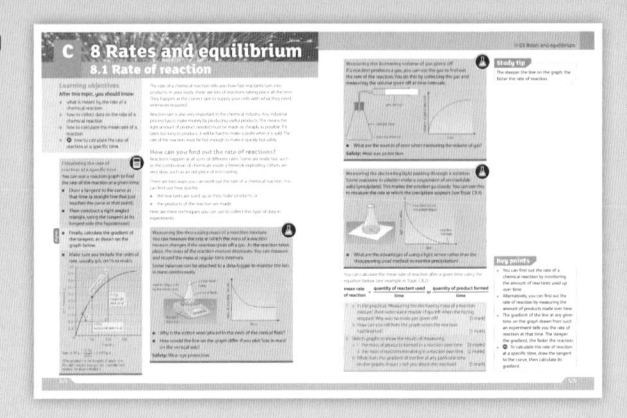

MS 1a, 1c, 1d, 4a, 4b, 4c, 4d, 4e

Aiming for	Outcome	Checkpoint	
		Question	Activity
Aiming for GRADE 4 ↓	Recall a definition for rate of reaction.		Starter 2
	Safely describe and follow a method to monitor rate of reaction.	1	Plenary 1, Main
	State the units for rate of reaction.		Starter 2
Aiming for GRADE 6 ↓	Explain how there can be different units for measuring rate of reaction.		Starter 2
	Calculate the mean rate of reaction.		Main
	Calculate the rate of reaction at a specific time.	End of chapter 3	Main
Aiming for GRADE 8 ↓	Plot and use a graph to calculate the gradient to measure the initial rate of reaction.	1, 2, End of chapter 1	Starter 1, Main
	Justify a chosen method for a given reaction to monitor the rate of reaction.		Plenary 1
	Explain why there is more than one unit for rate of reaction.		Starter 2

Maths
Students use their data to plot a graph with a line of best fit (4b), derive units from rate formulae, and design their own results table.

Literacy
Students discuss the results of their practical experiments then summarise all of the findings.

Practical

Title	Practical ambassador – measuring the decreasing mass of the reaction
Equipment	1 mol/dm^3 hydrochloric acid, marble chips, 250 cm^3 conical flask, 25 cm^3 measuring cylinder, top-pan balance that measures to 2 decimal places, cotton wool, stopwatch, eye protection
Overview of method	Use a measuring cylinder to transfer 25 cm^3 of hydrochloric acid into the conical flask. Zero/tare the balance and put the conical flask on the balance with the cotton wool in the neck. Note the mass. Add 1 g mass of marble chips and note the mass of the flask and contents every 30 seconds until the reaction has stopped.
Safety considerations	Hydrochloric acid is corrosive. Wear chemical splash-proof eye protection and wash hands after completing the practical.

C8 Rates and equilibrium

Title	Practical ambassador – measuring the increasing volume of gas given off
Equipment	0.5 mol/dm³ hydrochloric acid, marble chips, 250 cm³ conical flask, bung with an L-shaped delivery tube and a rubber connector on the end, gas syringe, clamp stand, 25 cm³ measuring cylinder, stopwatch, eye protection
Overview of method	Set up the gas syringe and ensure the plunger is on 0 cm³. Use a measuring cylinder to transfer 25 cm³ of hydrochloric acid into the conical flask. Add 1 g of marble chips and quickly put the bung in the neck of the conical flask and attach it to the gas syringe. Note the volume of gas in the gas syringe every 30 seconds until the reaction has stopped or the maximum volume has been collected.
Safety considerations	Hydrochloric acid is corrosive. Wear chemical splash-proof eye protection and wash hands after completing the practical.

Title	Practical ambassador – measuring the decreasing light passing through the solution
Equipment	0.1 mol/dm³ sodium thiosulfate, 2 mol/dm³ hydrochloric acid, 250 cm³ conical flask, paper with 'X' on it, 10 cm³ and 50 cm³ measuring cylinders, stopwatch, eye protection
Overview of method	Put the conical flask on the 'X'. Use a measuring cylinder to transfer 10 cm³ of sodium thiosulfate and 40 cm³ of water into the conical flask. Then measure 10 cm³ of acid and add to the mixture whilst simultaneously starting the stopwatch. Time until the cross is not visible.
Safety considerations	During this experiment sulfur dioxide (toxic) is produced which is toxic and can trigger an asthma attack. Carry out in a well-ventilated room, wearing eye protection, and wash hands after completing the practical. Hydrochloric acid is corrosive and chemical splash-proof eye protection should be warn throughout the practical.

Starter	Support/Extend	Resources
Predict (5 minutes) Ask students to sketch a graph of concentration against time, with lines of best fit to show how the concentration of the limiting reactant, reactant in excess, and product changes with time.	**Extend:** Ensure that students sketch on the same axes.	
Units of rate (10 minutes) Ask students what the rate of a reaction is. Supply students with the two rate formulae from the specification. Then give them different units for mass or volume and ask them to suggest the units that the rate would be measured in.	**Support:** Provide students with equation triangles for each expression.	**Interactive:** Units of rate

Main	Support/Extend	Resources
Practical ambassador (40 minutes) Split the class into three groups. Each group should complete one method from the practical list. All students should design their own results table, calculate the mean rate of reaction and, if appropriate, plot their results in a graph.	**Extend:** Ask students to calculate the rate of reaction at certain points on the graph.	**Practical:** Practical ambassador **Calculation sheet:** Calculating rates
Once the practical has been completed, provide students with some data for volume of gas produced every minute in a reaction between zinc and hydrochloric acid. Students plot a graph and calculate the mean rate of reaction at given times. A calculation sheet is available for further practice on calculating mean and initial rates from graphs.	**Extend:** Introducing using a tangent to a curve to calculate the rate of reaction.	

Plenary	Support/Extend	Resources
Rate (5 minutes) Ask students to list as many ways as they can think of for monitoring the rate of reaction for the reaction between magnesium and hydrochloric acid.	**Support:** Give the word equation for the reaction. **Extend:** Ask students to suggest and justify the best method of monitoring the reaction.	
Sharing methods (10 minutes) Arrange students in groups of three ensuring each person has completed a different practical from Main. Students share their experiences of each experiment and summarise their findings.		

Homework		
Refer students to a rate of reaction graph in the student book. Ask students to explain why data needs to be collected over a large range.	**Extend:** Students justify why rate of reaction values at certain times in the experiment could be more useful than mean rate of reaction.	

kerboodle

A Kerboodle highlight for this lesson is **Maths skills: Calculating rates**. Refer to the **Content map** on Kerboodle for a full list of resources and assessment.

C8.2 Collision theory and surface area

AQA spec Link: 6.1.2 Factors which affect the rates of chemical reactions include the surface area of solid reactants.

Students should be able to recall how changing these factors affects the rate of chemical reactions.

6.1.3 Collision theory explains how various factors affect rates of reactions. According to this theory, chemical reactions can occur only when reacting particles collide with each other and with sufficient energy. The minimum amount of energy that particles must have to react is called the activation energy.

Increasing the surface area of solid reactants increases the frequency of collisions and so increases the rate of reaction.

Students should be able to explain the effects on rates of reaction of:

- changes in the size of pieces of a reacting solid in terms of surface area to volume ratio
- use simple ideas about proportionality when using collision theory to explain the effect of a factor on the rate of a reaction.

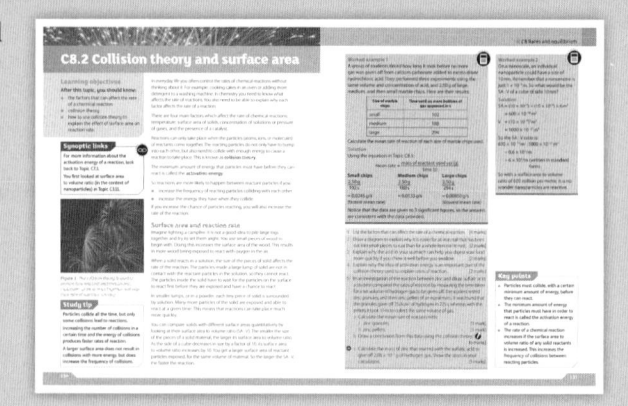

WS 1.2
MS 1a, 1b, 1c, 2a, 3a, 3c, 4a, 4c, 4e, 5c

Aiming for	Outcome	Checkpoint	
		Question	Activity
Aiming for GRADE 4	Describe how surface area of a solid can be increased.	2	Starter 1, Main, Plenary 2
	State that chemical reactions can only occur when a collision occurs with enough energy.		Main
	List the factors that can affect the rate of a chemical reaction.	1	Main
Aiming for GRADE 6	Describe how changing the surface area changes the rate of reaction.	2, 3	Starter 1, Main
	Describe what the activation energy of a reaction is.	4	Starter 2
	Calculate the surface area to volume ratio.		Plenary 2
Aiming for GRADE 8	Use collision theory to explain in detail how increasing surface area increases the rate of reaction.	3, 5	Main
	Use a graph to calculate the rate of reaction at specific times in a chemical reaction.		Main
	Explain why many collisions do not lead to a chemical reaction.	4	Main

Maths
Students calculate the surface area to volume ratio (1c), mean rate of reaction (1b), and rate of reaction at given times of a chemical reaction.

Key words
collision theory, activation energy

Practical

Title	Investigating the effect of surface area
Equipment	250 cm³ conical flask, 25 cm³ measuring cylinder, top-pan balance which measures to 2 decimal places, cotton wool, stopwatch, 1 mol/dm³ hydrochloric acid, at least two different grades of marble chips, eye protection
Overview of method	Use a measuring cylinder to transfer 25 cm³ of hydrochloric acid into the conical flask. Zero/tare the balance and put the conical flask on the balance with the cotton wool in the neck. Note the mass. Add 1 g mass of marble chips and note the mass of the flask and contents every 30 seconds until the reaction has stopped.
Safety considerations	Hydrochloric acid is corrosive. Wear chemical splash-proof eye protection and wash hands after completing the practical.

C8 Rates and equilibrium

Starter	Support/Extend	Resources
Surface area (5 minutes) Give students a sample of icing sugar, caster sugar, granulated sugar, and sugar lumps. Ask students to explain the difference between them and to predict which one would dissolve fastest into a cup of hot tea and why. **Collision theory and surface area** (10 minutes) Use the interactive to introduce collision theory and the effect of surface area on the rate of a reaction. Students choose the correct words to complete a paragraph that describes collision theory. They then put statements in order to describe how increasing the surface area of a solid increases the rate of the reaction.	**Extend:** Ask students to predict, with a balanced symbol equation, which type of sugar would combust the quickest. The chemical formula of sugar (sucrose) is $C_{12}H_{22}O_{11}$.	**Interactive:** Collision theory and surface area

Main	Support/Extend	Resources
Investigating the effect of surface area (40 minutes) Explain to students that calcium carbonate is a base and will react with hydrochloric acid to form a salt, water, and carbon dioxide. Ask students to write an equation to summarise this reaction and then to suggest how they could monitor the reaction. Explain or demonstrate how the rate of the reaction can be measured using a top-pan balance. Students should design their own results table to investigate high and low surface areas and make a prediction, which explains what they think will happen and why, using collision theory in their answer. Students then record the data every 10 seconds for one minute, repeating the experiment with the same mass of marble chips but of a different size. Students plot a graph with both lines of best fit on the same axis and compare the mean rate of reaction at a set time.	**Extend:** Go through how to use a tangent to a curve to calculate the rate of reaction. Ask students to calculate the rate of reaction initially and at 20, 40, and 60 seconds.	**Practical:** Investigating the effect of surface area

Plenary	Support/Extend	Resources
Exam questions (10 minutes) Give students a fictitious candidate answer of an exam question. Students should then look at the question and discuss in small groups which answers deserved credit. Then use question and answer to feed back to the whole class. Reveal the mark scheme and see how close the students' thoughts were to the actual marking. Alternatively, students answer an exam question and swap with a partner to mark their answer. **Surface area tweet** (5 minutes) Students write a tweet (142 characters) to summarise the content from the lesson/		

Homework		
Ask students why the investigation into the rate of reaction between marble chips and acid, detailed above, cannot be completed with sulfuric acid.	**Support:** Remind students that some metal salts like calcium sulfate are insoluble.	

kerboodle
A Kerboodle highlight for this lesson is **Calculation sheet: Calculating surace areas**. Refer to the **Content map** on Kerboodle for a full list of resources and assessment.

C8.3 The effect of temperature

AQA spec Link: 6.1.2 Factors which affect the rates of chemical reactions include the temperature.

Students should be able to recall how changing these factors affects the rate of chemical reactions.

6.1.3 Collision theory explains how various factors affect rates of reactions. According to this theory, chemical reactions can occur only when reacting particles collide with each other and with sufficient energy. The minimum amount of energy that particles must have to react is called the activation energy.

Increasing the temperature increases the frequency of collisions and makes the collisions more energetic, and so increases the rate of reaction.

Students should be able to:

- predict and explain using collision theory the effects of changing temperature on the rate of a reaction
- use simple ideas about proportionality when using collision theory to explain the effect of a factor on the rate of a reaction.

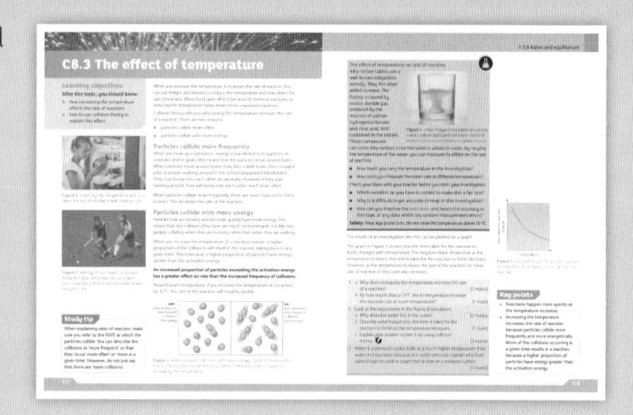

WS 1.2
MS 1b, 1c, 2a, 3b, 3c, 4a, 4c, 4e

Aiming for	Outcome	Checkpoint	
		Question	Activity
Aiming for GRADE 4 ↓	Describe how temperature affects the rate of reaction.	1	Main 1, Main 2, Plenary 2
	Safely complete an experiment on how temperature affects the rate of a reaction.	2	Starter 2, Main 1
Aiming for GRADE 6 ↓	Use collision theory to explain how changing temperature alters the rate of reaction.	1, 2, 3	Main 2, Plenary 1
	Calculate mean rates of reaction.	End of chapter 3	Main 1
Aiming for GRADE 8 ↓	Use a graph to calculate the rate of reaction at specific times in a chemical reaction.	End of chapter 1	Main 1, Plenary 2
	Calculate $\frac{1}{t}$ and plot a graph with a more meaningful line of best fit.		Main 1

Maths
Students calculate the mean rate of reaction (1b) and rate of reaction at given times of a chemical reaction.

Literacy
Students explain in detail how and why temperature affects rate of reaction.

Key words
precision

Practical

Title	The effect of temperature on rate of reaction
Equipment	indigestion tablets containing sodium hydrogencarbonate and citric acid, distilled water, conical flask with bung and delivery tube, water baths at different temperatures, ice bath, −10 to 110 °C thermometer, eye protection, stopwatch, measuring cylinder, water trough, clamp stand and boss
Overview of method	Fill the water trough with water, then fill the measuring cylinder with water, and clamp upside down in the water trough, making sure no water is lost. Set up the conical flask, bung, and delivery tube so that the exit of the delivery tube is under the measuring cylinder. Put 30 cm³ of distilled water into the conical flask and heat/cool to the required temperature. Add the indigestion tablet, quickly stoppering the conical flask. Use the stopwatch to measure how long it takes for a set volume of carbon dioxide to be produced.
Safety considerations	Complete in a well-ventilated room, wearing eye protection, and wash hands after completing the practical.

C8 Rates and equilibrium

Starter	Support/Extend	Resources
Language of measurement (5 minutes) Ask students to define variable, independent variable, dependent variable, control variable, valid. **Method outline** (10 minutes) Give students the equation for the reaction of sodium thiosulfate with hydrochloric acid, including state symbols. Ask students to suggest which method they could use to monitor the rate of this reaction. Ask students to write an outline method for this experiment.	**Support:** Remind students of the different methods that they have studied to monitor rate of reaction and that this reaction makes a mixture of products including insoluble sulfur.	**Interactive:** Language of measurement

Main	Support/Extend	Resources
The effect of temperature on rate of reaction (30 minutes) Ask students to design a suitable results table then run the practical. Encourage students to plot a graph of time taken for a set amount of carbon dioxide to be produced against temperature of reactants. Then draw conclusions consistent with results. Ask students to calculate the mean rate of reaction for each temperature.	**Support:** This practical can be completed as a class demonstration. **Extend:** Explain that rate is inversely proportional to time taken for the reaction to finish. Ask students to plot a graph of $\frac{1}{t}$ against temperature.	**Practical:** The effect of temperature on rate of reaction
Comparison poster (10 minutes) Give students an A5 light blue piece of paper to represent a colder temperature and an A5 light pink piece of paper to represent a warmer temperature. On each piece of paper they should draw a particle diagram and explain what the rate of reaction would be and why, using collision theory. The pieces of paper could be stuck together to make a double-sided poster.	**Extend:** Students add a real-life example of when you want to slow down a reaction by lowering the temperature and when you want to speed up a reaction by increasing temperature.	

Plenary	Support/Extend	Resources
Collision theory Pictionary (10 minutes) Split the class into groups of six. Assign each student in the group one of the following phrases: increase temperature, decrease temperature, collision theory, collision, activation energy, rate of reaction. In small groups, each student takes it in turn to try and draw their phrase with an image without words or symbols. The rest of the group have to guess the phrase.	**Support:** Complete this as a whole class exercise, looking for a volunteer to complete their work on the board whilst the rest of the class guess.	
Data handling (5 minutes) Hydrogen peroxide decomposes into oxygen and water. Ask students to write an equation for this reaction and identify the independent and dependent variables. Students sketch a graph which would allow them to calculate the mean rate of reaction and the rate of reaction at specific points.		

Homework		
Ask students to write an outline of a method to investigate how changing the temperature will affect the rate of reaction between magnesium ribbon and hydrochloric acid. Their method should include a results table and a sketched graph of their predicted results.		

C8.4 The effect of concentration or pressure

AQA spec Link: 6.1.2 Factors which affect the rates of chemical reactions include the concentrations of reactants in solution and the pressure of reacting gases.

Required practical: Investigate how changes in concentration affect the rates of reactions by a method involving measuring the volume of a gas produced and a method involving a change in colour or turbidity.

This should be an investigation involving developing a hypothesis.

6.1.3 Collision theory explains how various factors affect rates of reactions. According to this theory, chemical reactions can occur only when reacting particles collide with each other and with sufficient energy. The minimum amount of energy that particles must have to react is called the activation energy.

Increasing the concentration of reactants in solution and the pressure of reacting gases increases the frequency of collisions and so increases the rate of reaction.

Students should be able to:

- predict and explain using collision theory the effects of changing conditions of concentration and pressure on the rate of a reaction
- use simple ideas about proportionality when using collision theory to explain the effect of a factor on the rate of a reaction.

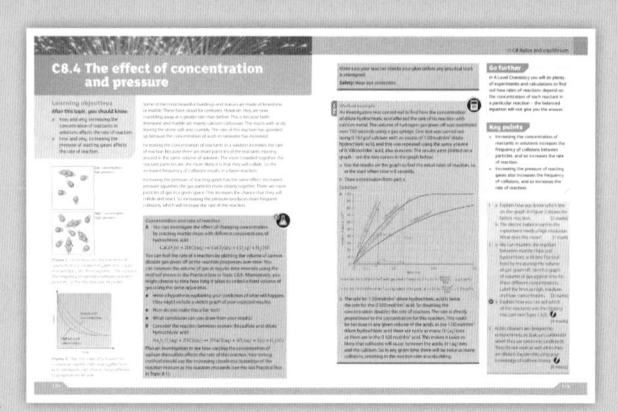

WS 1.2, 2.4, 2.6, 3.1, 3.2, 3.5
MS 1a, 1b, 1c, 2a, 2b, 3a, 3b, 3c, 4a, 4c, 4e

Aiming for	Outcome	Checkpoint	
		Question	Activity
Aiming for GRADE 4	Describe how changing concentration affects the rate of reaction.		Starter 2, Main, Plenary 2
↓	Describe how changing pressure affects the rate of gas phase reactions.		Plenary 2
Aiming for GRADE 6	Use collision theory to explain how changing concentration or pressure alters the rate of reaction.	3, 4, End of chapter 1	Starter 2, Main, Plenary 2
	Calculate mean rates of reaction.	End of chapter 3	Main
↓	Explain how to change gas pressure.		Starter 1, Plenary 1
Aiming for GRADE 8	Interpret a rate of reaction graph, including calculating the rate of reaction at specific times in a chemical reaction.	1, 2, End of chapter 1	Main
	Explain why changing pressure has no effect on the rate of reaction for some reactions.		Plenary 2
↓	Justify quantitative predictions and evaluate in detail their investigation into the effect of concentration on rate of reaction.		Main

Maths
Students calculate mean rate of reaction (2b) and rate of reaction at given times of a chemical reaction. They also design a results table and sketch a graph to predict results (4a).

Literacy
Students write a prediction and evaluate their investigations. They also explain their predictions in their homework.

Required practical

Title	The effect of concentration on rate of reaction
Equipment	**Measuring the production of a gas** eye protection, 100 cm³ conical flask, rubber bung and delivery tube to fit conical flask, water trough, clamp stand, boss and clamp, 100 cm³ measuring cylinder, stopwatch, marble chips, dilute hydrochloric acid at different concentrations (no higher than 2.0 mol/dm³)
	Measuring a colour change 0.1 mol/dm³ sodium thiosulfate, dilute hydrochloric acid at different concentrations (no higher than 2.0 mol/dm³), 100 cm³ conical flask, paper with 'X' on it, measuring cylinder, stopwatch, eye protection

C8 Rates and equilibrium

Overview of method	**Measuring the production of a gas** Fill the water trough with water, then fill the measuring cylinder with water, and clamp upside down in the water trough. Set up the conical flask, bung, and delivery tube so that the exit of the delivery tube is under the measuring cylinder. Add 50 cm^3 of hydrochloric acid into the conical flask. Add 1 g of marble chips into the conical flask, put the bung back into the flask as quickly as you can, and start the stopwatch. Record the volume of gas produced every 10 seconds for two minutes. Repeat the experiment with each of the concentrations of hydrochloric acid. **Measuring a colour change** Put the conical flask on the paper above the 'X'. Add 10 cm^3 of sodium thiosulfate and 20 cm^3 of hydrochloric acid into the conical flask, simultaneously starting the stopwatch. Time until the 'X' is no longer visible.
Safety considerations	Hydrochloric acid is corrosive. Ensure that the end of the syringe does not shoot out. Wear chemical splash-proof eye protection and wash hands after completing the practical. Sulfur dioxide is toxic. Take care with students who are asthmatic. Follow CLEAPSS advice for disposal procedures.

Starter	Support/Extend	Resources
Gas pressure (5 minutes) Demonstrate the egg in a conical flask trick. Hard boil an egg and take the shell off. Then light a splint and put it into a 250 cm^3 conical flask, quickly put the egg into the top of the flask so that it seals the aperture. Ask students to explain their observations. **Bringing ideas together** (10 minutes) Arrange students into small groups. Then ask them to make a visual summary to consolidate their knowledge of rate of reaction in terms of collision theory and changing conditions. Give students sticky notes and ask them to write key terms such as collision, collision theory, temperature, pressure, concentration, surface area, and rate of reaction. Students should then stick the notes on sugar paper and, using marker pens, add arrows and text on the arrows to generate sentences connecting pairs of key terms.	**Support:** Remind students that gas pressure is caused by particles hitting the sides of the container. **Support:** Arrange students into groups of mixed ability. **Extend:** Ask students to critique a different group's work and tackle common misconceptions.	

Main	Support/Extend	Resources
The effect of concentration on rate of reaction (40 minutes) Students investigate how concentration affects the rate of reaction. They should write a prediction which includes what they think will happen and explain their thoughts using collision theory. Students will need to carry out both experiments to complete the required practical. This will take two lessons. Ensure students have time to repeat tests so that you have a set of repeat data for each acid concentration to check precision and improve accuracy. Encourage students to comment on how the experiment was made a fair test and to draw conclusions consistent with their graphical results, including calculating the mean rate of reaction. Students should also discuss the quality of the data collected and explain improvements that could be made to their investigation.	**Support:** Give students a prose with missing words for them to complete to generate their prediction. **Extend:** Ask students to calculate the initial rate of reaction for each of the different concentrations to check quantitative predictions made.	**Required practical:** The effect of concentration on rate of reaction

Plenary	Support/Extend	Resources
Effect of concentration and pressure (10 minutes) Students identify whether particle diagrams show high concentration and pressure or low concentration and pressure. They then complete a paragraph to describe the effect of concentration and pressure on rate of reaction. **Oxidation** (5 minutes) Students write an equation to represent the reaction between iron and oxygen. Ask students to predict, including referring to collision theory, their observation of iron wool burning in air and then in a gas jar of oxygen.	**Extend:** Ask students to explain why the gas jar of oxygen was a higher concentration of oxygen but not higher pressure than air.	**Interactive:** Effect of concentration and pressure

Homework		
Students plan a results table to use if investigating how the concentration of hydrochloric acid affects the rate of reaction with magnesium ribbon. They then make a prediction in the form of a sketched graph of the results. This should then be justified with prose which references collision theory.		

kerboodle

A Kerboodle highlight for this lesson is **Bump up your grade: Changing the rate**. Refer to the **Content map** on Kerboodle for a full list of resources and assessment.

# C8.5 The effect of catalysts

AQA spec Link: 6.1.2 Factors which affect the rates of chemical reactions include the presence of catalysts.

Students should be able to recall how changing these factors affects the rate of chemical reactions.

6.1.3 Collision theory explains how various factors affect rates of reactions. According to this theory, chemical reactions can occur only when reacting particles collide with each other and with sufficient energy. The minimum amount of energy that particles must have to react is called the activation energy.

6.1.4 Catalysts change the rate of chemical reactions but are not used up during the reaction. Different reactions need different catalysts. Enzymes act as catalysts in biological systems.

Catalysts increase the rate of reaction by providing a different pathway for the reaction that has a lower activation energy.

A reaction profile for a catalysed reaction can be drawn in the following form:

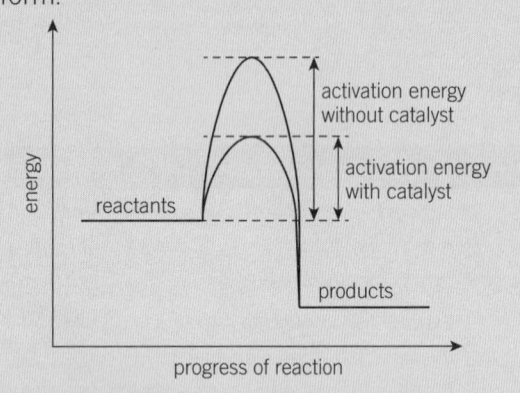

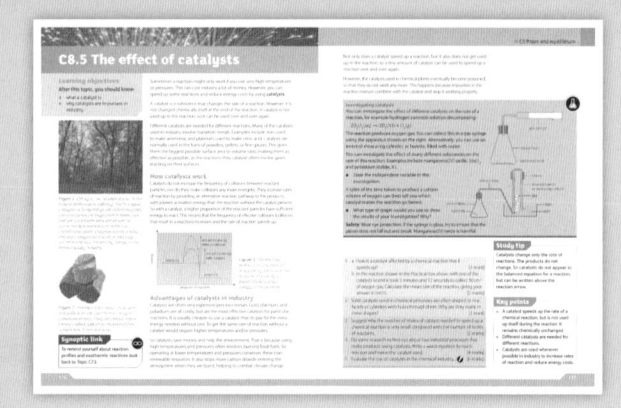

MS 1a, 2a, 2b, 4a, 4c, 4e

Aiming for	Outcome	Checkpoint	
		Question	Activity
Aiming for GRADE 4	Define a catalyst.	End of chapter 3	Starter 2, Main, Plenary 1
	Describe how adding a catalyst affects the rate of reaction.	1	Starter 2, Main, Plenary 1
	Describe and carry out a method to safely investigate which catalyst is best for a reaction.	End of chapter 3	Main
Aiming for GRADE 6	Use collision theory to explain how adding a catalyst alters the rate of reaction.		Main
	Explain, with an example, the industrial use of a catalyst.	2, 4, 5	Plenary 2
	Calculate the mean rate of reaction.	1, End of chapter 3	Main
Aiming for GRADE 8	Use a reaction profile diagram to explain in detail the effect of adding a catalyst.	3	Starter 2
	Justify the use of catalysts in industry and in household products.	5	Plenary 2
	Explain what an enzyme is and how it works.		Starter 2, Main

Maths
Students create a results table (2c) and draw their results onto a graph (4a).

Key words
catalysts, climate change

C8 Rates and equilibrium

Practical

Title	Investigating catalysis
Equipment	250 cm³ conical flask, bung with an L-shaped delivery tube and a rubber connector on the end, water trough, measuring cylinder, 25 cm³ measuring cylinder, stopwatch, eye protection, 10 volume hydrogen peroxide, manganese(IV) dioxide, potassium iodide, the enzyme catalase (found in raw liver, potatoes, and celery) top-pan balance, weighing boat, spatula
Overview of method	Set up the measuring cylinder upside down and full of water in the water trough. Use a measuring cylinder to transfer 25 cm³ of hydrogen peroxide into the conical flask. Use a top-pan balance to measure 1 g of the manganese(IV) dioxide catalyst into a weighing boat. Transfer the catalyst to the conical flask and quickly put the bung in the neck of the conical flask and feed the delivery tube under the inverted measuring cylinder to collect the gas. Note the volume of gas every 10 seconds until the reaction has stopped or the maximum volume has been collected. Repeat with all catalysts that are available.
Safety considerations	Hydrogen peroxide is an oxidising agent and an irritant. Manganese(IV) dioxide is harmful. Iodide is harmful. Follow CLEAPSS advice for disposal procedures. Wear eye protection and wash hands after completing the practical. If food stuffs are used, dispose of appropriately and sterilise surfaces after use.

Starter	Support/Extend	Resources
Reaction profiles (5 minutes) Draw an exothermic reaction profile diagram for a generic reaction. Then ask students to predict the shape of the reaction profile if a catalyst was added. Use question and answer to build up the correct diagram on the board by using volunteers to modify the diagram.	**Support:** Remind students of the key words that they should include on the diagram, for example, the axis labels.	
Factors that affect rates (10 minutes) Ask one student to give a reaction condition that affects the rate of a reaction. Ask another student to explain what effect this condition has. Go around the class, taking the time to check for, and correct, any misconceptions. Then ask students to explain the effect a catalyst has on a reaction. Then use the interactive to introduce catalysis and the effect catalysts have on the rate of a reaction.		**Interactive:** Factors that affect rates

Main	Support/Extend	Resources
Investigating catalysis (40 minutes) Students investigate how different catalysts affect the decomposition of hydrogen peroxide. Use the catalysts manganese(IV) dioxide, potassium iodide, and the enzyme catalase (found in raw liver, potatoes, and celery). Students record their results in a table, then display them on the same graph. Explain that catalysts provide an alternative reaction pathway that has a lower activation energy.	**Extend:** Ask students to calculate the rate of reaction for the different concentrations at different times to quantitatively compare results.	**Practical:** Investigating catalysis

Plenary	Support/Extend	Resources
Jeopardy (5 minutes) Provide each student with a key point from the lesson (more than one student can have the same key point). Students generate three questions that are answered by their key point.	**Support:** Allow students to work in small groups.	
Pros and cons (10 minutes) Explain to students that catalysts are often used in industry, for example, iron is used in the Haber process which is a key part in the production of fertilisers. Students then evaluate the use of catalysts in industrial processes.	**Extend:** Students justify using iron as a catalyst in the Haber process including ideas to increase the effectiveness of the catalyst.	

Homework		
Students complete the WebQuest where they research the advantages of using nanoparticles are catalysts. Alternatively, students create a presentation or script for a TV/radio interview to explain what a catalyst is, its function, and an example of how using a catalyst in the chemical industry impacts both on the productivity of the chemical companies involved and on the environment.		**WebQuest:** Catalytic nanoparticles

kerboodle

A Kerboodle highlight for this lesson is **Calculation sheet: Proportionality**. Refer to the **Content map** on Kerboodle for a full list of resources and assessment.

C8.6 Reversible reactions

AQA spec Link: 6.2.1 In some chemical reactions, the products of the reaction can react to produce the original reactants. Such reactions are called reversible reactions and are represented:

$A + B \rightleftharpoons C + D$

The direction of reversible reactions can be changed by changing the conditions.

For example:

ammonium chloride $\underset{\text{cool}}{\overset{\text{heat}}{\rightleftharpoons}}$ ammonia + hydrogen chloride

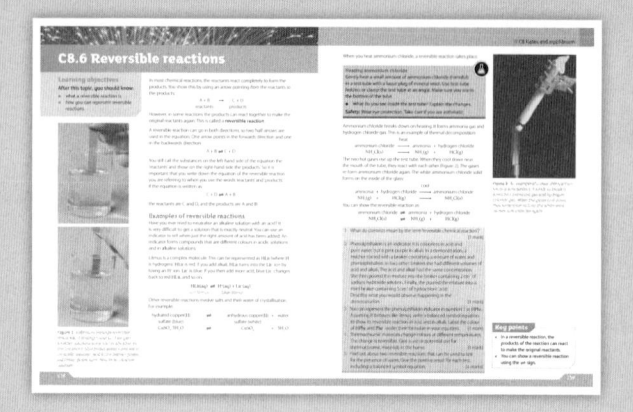

MS 1c

Aiming for	Outcome	Checkpoint	
		Question	Activity
Aiming for GRADE 4	Define a reversible reaction.	1	Main, Plenary 2
	Write a word equation for a familiar reversible reaction.		Main, Plenary 1
	State an example of a reversible reaction.		Main, Plenary 1, Plenary 2
Aiming for GRADE 6	Explain, using a familiar example, how a reaction can be reversible.		Main, Plenary 1
	Describe a familiar reversible reaction using a balanced symbol equation.	5	Starter 1, Main, Plenary 1
	Predict the observations of a familiar reversible reaction when the conditions are changed.	2	Main, Plenary 1, Plenary 2
Aiming for GRADE 8	Describe an unfamiliar reversible reaction, using a balanced symbol equation with state symbols.	3	Plenary 2
	Justify the use of reversible reactions in the lab and items available in the home.	4, 5	Plenary 1
	Justify the classification of a reaction as reversible.		Main

Literacy
Students create a card-matching exercise for the important words of the lesson and their definitions. They also give examples of reversible reactions that are used in real life, and explain why they are useful.

Key words
reversible reaction

Practical

Title	Heating ammonium chloride
Equipment	ammonium chloride powder, spatula, boiling tube, boiling-tube holder, Bunsen burner and safety equipment, mineral wool
Overview of method	Add about one spatula of ammonium chloride in the bottom of a boiling tube. Loosely fit a mineral wool plug in the top of the boiling tube. Using a boiling-tube holder, warm the bottom of the tube in the top of the blue gas cone when the Bunsen burner has the air hole open.
Safety considerations	Ammonium chloride is harmful, ammonia gas is produced which is toxic and hydrogen chloride gas is produced which is corrosive and toxic. Wear chemical splash-proof eye protection and complete the experiment in a well-ventilated room.

C8 Rates and equilibrium

Title	Blue bottle demonstration
Equipment	250 cm³ conical flask, 1 dm³ conical flask with stopper or bung, 8 g potassium hydroxide, 10 g glucose (dextrose), 0.05 g methylene blue, 50 cm³ ethanol, measuring cylinder, top-pan balance
Overview of method	In a 250 cm³ conical flask make a solution of methylene blue in ethanol. Add the potassium hydroxide into the 1 dm³ conical flask. Add 300 cm³ of water and the glucose. Gently swirl until the solids are dissolved. Add about 5 cm³ of the methylene blue solution, leave until colourless and then stopper the flask.
Safety considerations	Potassium hydroxide is corrosive, methylene blue is harmful, and ethanol is flammable and harmful. Wear chemical splash-proof eye protection when preparing the blue bottle and wash hands after preparation.

Starter	Support/Extend	Resources
Interpret (5 minutes) Show students the reversible reaction equation for the thermal decomposition of ammonium chloride. Ask students to suggest what the equation means, focusing on the arrows. Encourage students to name the type of reaction (thermal decomposition and neutralisation). **Reaction card sort** (10 minutes) In pairs, ask students to create a card-matching exercise for the important words for the lesson with their definitions, for example, reactants, products, reversible reaction, equilibrium. Then students should swap their card sort with another group and time how long it takes them to match the words with the definitions.	**Extend:** Ask students to write a balanced symbol equation for the reaction. **Support:** Supply the important words and the definitions.	**Interactive:** Interpret

Main	Support/Extend	Resources
Heating ammonium chloride (40 minutes) Ask students to complete the experiment. Students draw a labelled diagram of the experiment and annotate it to record the observations that they have noted. They then add equations to show the different reactions occurring in different parts of the boiling tube and the overall equation with the reversible/equilibrium arrows. Students explain why the reaction is considered to be a reversible reaction.	**Support:** Use question and answer to annotate the reaction on the board. **Extend:** Ensure students use balanced symbol equations, including state symbols, to illustrate the reactions.	**Practical:** Heating ammonium chloride

Plenary	Support/Extend	Resources
Reactions at home (5 minutes) Ask students to think of some examples of where a reversible reaction would be useful in everyday life (e.g., the hand warmers studied in Topic C7.2). Students explain why a reversible reaction is useful in the examples they give. **Blue bottle demonstration** (10 minutes) Prepare the blue bottle as detailed, then alternate between shaking the bottle and leaving it. Ask students to suggest what is happening. Use question and answer to ensure that students realise that a reversible reaction is occurring which is shown as a colour change using an indicator.	**Extend:** Explain to students that methylene blue is a redox indicator. The sugar solution is in alkaline conditions and the indicator is colourless. When shaken, oxygen is added and the indicator is oxidised into the blue form. Students could try to make a simplified symbol equation to illustrate the reaction of the indicator.	

Homework		
Explain to students that yellow crystals of iodine trichloride reversibly decompose at room temperature to form green chlorine gas and brown iodine monochloride liquid. Ask students to write an equation to illustrate this reaction and predict the observations that they would make if the iodine trichloride was in a sealed bottle.		

kerboodle

A Kerboodle highlight for this lesson is **Literacy skills: Reversible reactions**. Refer to the **Content map** on Kerboodle for a full list of resources and assessment.

139

C8.7 Energy and reversible reactions

AQA spec Link: 6.2.2 If a reversible reaction is exothermic in one direction, it is endothermic in the opposite direction. The same amount of energy is transferred in each case. For example:

hydrated copper sulfate (blue) $\underset{\text{exothermic}}{\overset{\text{endothermic}}{\rightleftharpoons}}$ anhydrous copper sulfate (white) + water

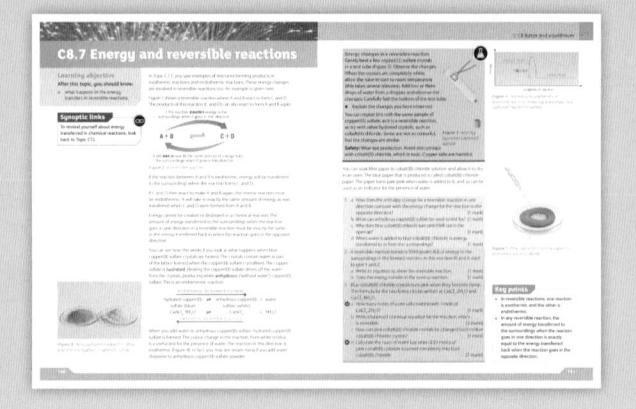

Aiming for	Outcome	Checkpoint	
		Question	Activity
Aiming for GRADE 4	State whether a reversible reaction is exothermic or endothermic in the reverse direction if the forward direction is stated.		Starter 2, Main, Plenary 1
↓	Write a word equation for the reversible reaction of dehydration/hydration of copper sulfate.		Main, Plenary 1
Aiming for GRADE 6	Explain why the energy change in a reversible reaction is exothermic in one direction and endothermic in the reverse direction.	1	Starter 2
	Generate balanced symbol equations for reversible reactions from information provided.	2, 3, End of chapter 4	Starter 1, Starter 2, Main, Plenary 1
↓	Make predictive observations of familiar reversible reactions when information is supplied.		Main, Plenary 2
Aiming for GRADE 8	Explain in detail the energy changes in an equilibrium system.	1, 2	Starter 2, Main
	Suggest and explain a simple laboratory test which could be completed using a reversible reaction.	1	Starter 1, Main, Plenary 1, Plenary 2
↓	Make predictive observations of unfamiliar reversible reactions when information is supplied.	3	Starter 1

Maths
Students draw reaction profile diagrams. They also write balanced equations.

Literacy
Students write a revision blog.

Key words
anhydrous, hydrated

Practical

Title	Energy changes in a reversible reaction
Equipment	anhydrous copper(II) sulfate, spatula, water, dropping pipette, Bunsen burner and safety equipment, boiling-tube holder, boiling tube, eye protection
Overview of method	Add about half a spatula of copper(II) sulfate crystals into a boiling tube. Using a boiling-tube holder, gently heat the blue powder in a Bunsen flame and observe the colour change to white. Allow the solid to cool completely then, using the dropping pipette, add a few drops of water and observe the colour change.
Safety considerations	Copper sulfate is harmful. If the water is added to a hot boiling tube the glass could fracture due to thermal shock. Be aware of burns due to using the Bunsen burner to heat the boiling tube. Wear chemical splash-proof eye protection and wash hands after completing the practical. Cobalt chloride is toxic and harmful. Handle with tongs and wash hands after use.

■ C8 Rates and equilibrium

Starter	Support/Extend	Resources
Cobalt chloride paper (5 minutes) Explain that cobalt chloride paper can be used as a test for the presence of water. Add a drop of water to the cobalt chloride paper from a dropping pipette, and then gently dry the paper next to a Bunsen flame or with a hair dryer. Ask students to write equations to illustrate this reaction, to annotate their work with the colours, and to explain how you can re-use the paper. **Reaction profile diagram** (10 minutes) Remind students of the reversible reaction for the thermal decomposition of ammonium chloride, studied in Topic C8.6. Ask students to draw a reaction profile diagram to show this reaction (endothermic). Then ask students to suggest what the reaction profile diagram for the neutralisation reaction between ammonia and hydrogen chloride gas would look like (exothermic and the reverse of the initial one).	**Extend:** Before the demonstration ask students to predict what they expect to see. **Support:** Show students the general reaction profile diagram for an endothermic reaction. **Extend:** Encourage students to see the connection between the activation energy of the forward and reverse reactions.	

Main	Support/Extend	Resources
Energy changes in a reversible reaction (40 minutes) Explain that the water of crystallisation can be removed from many ionic salts by gentle heating. This can be illustrated by gently heating hydrated copper sulfate to leave the anhydrous copper sulfate. Run the experiment as detailed in the practical box. Ask students to generate a pictorial flow chart to record their observations and write an equation to illustrate the changes. Their annotations should include the colour of each chemical, the energy change in each step, and what simple laboratory test this reversible reaction could be used for.	**Extend:** You may wish to calculate the moles of water of crystallisation. Measure the mass of the hydrated copper sulfate, and the mass of the anhydrous copper sulfate. The difference in mass is due to the mass of the water of crystallisation. Therefore, the empirical formula for this compound can be generated.	**Practical:** Energy changes in a reversible reaction

Plenary	Support/Extend	Resources
Finish the sentence (5 minutes) Students use the interactive to complete the following sentences. • A $\rightleftharpoons$ in an equation shows (a reversible reaction) • In a reversible reaction, reactants make products (and products make reactants under the same conditions) • In a reversible reaction, if the forward reaction is exothermic (the reverse reaction will be endothermic) • The hydration of copper sulfate is (a reversible chemical reaction that can be used as a test for water) **Desiccator** (10 minutes) Show students a desiccator. Explain that there is a drying agent such as silica gel below the mesh and chemicals are put in the sealed vessel to dry out or to remain in a dry environment. However, the gel is often impregnated with anhydrous copper sulfate. Ask students to suggest why this is so and how this could help a laboratory technician.	**Support:** Encourage students to work in pairs to generate the sentences. **Extend:** Ask students to explain why anhydrous copper sulfate could not be used to test if a liquid was safe to drink.	**Interactive:** Finish the sentence

Homework		
Ask students to imagine that a top publisher has commissioned them to create a GCSE blog. Show students a selection of GCSE-focused blogs and ask them to discuss in groups what they like and dislike about the material. Explain that they have 250 words and a maximum of three images to explain energy and reversible reactions. Students could work in small teams to complete this, allowing them to distribute the tasks as they desire. Ask students to discover other examples of energy changes in reversible reactions.	**Support:** Supply a writing frame to help students complete their blog. This should include what a reversible reaction is, an example of a reversible reaction, and its use. **Extend:** Students could include web links to useful sites which include videos and exam practice for this topic.	

kerboodle
A Kerboodle highlight for this lesson is **Extension sheet: Energy and reversible reactions**. Refer to the **Content map** on Kerboodle for a full list of resources and assessment.

C8.8 Dynamic equilibrium

AQA spec Link: 6.2.3 When a reversible reaction occurs in apparatus which prevents the escape of reactants and products, equilibrium is reached when the forward and reverse reactions occur at exactly the same rate.

6.2.4 **H** The relative amounts of all the reactants and products at equilibrium depend on the conditions of the reaction.

If a system is at equilibrium and a change is made to any of the conditions, then the system responds to counteract the change.

The effects of changing conditions on a system at equilibrium can be predicted using Le Chatelier's Principle.

Students should be able to make qualitative predictions about the effect of changes on systems at equilibrium when given appropriate information.

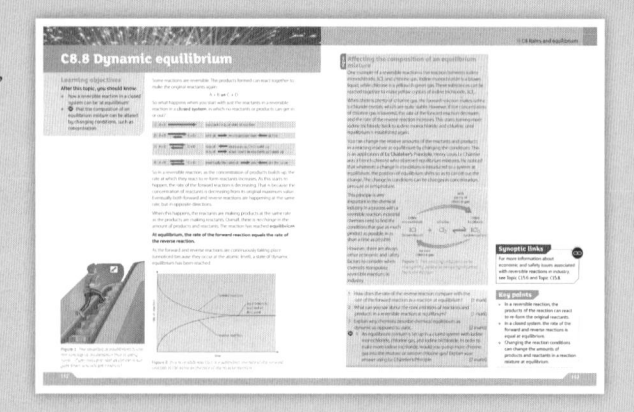

WS 1.2

Aiming for	Outcome	Checkpoint	
		Question	Activity
Aiming for GRADE 4 ↓	Define a dynamic equilibrium.	3	Starter 2, Main, Plenary 1
	Describe a closed system.		Starter 1
Aiming for GRADE 6 ↓	Describe how to achieve dynamic equilibrium.		Main, Plenary 2
	Describe how rate of the forward reaction compares to rate of the backward reaction in a dynamic equilibrium.	1	Main, Plenary 1, Plenary 2
	H Describe Le Chatelier's Principle.		Main
Aiming for GRADE 8 ↓	Explain dynamic equilibrium.	3	Main
	H Explain why the concentration of chemicals in a dynamic equilibrium remains constant.	2	Starter 2, Main
	H Predict the effect on the rate of forward and reverse reactions by applying the Le Chatelier's Principle when the conditions of a dynamic equilibrium are changed.	4	Main, Plenary 2

Literacy
Students use scientific terminology to explain how concentration affects a dynamic equilibrium.

Key words
closed system, equilibrium, Le Chatelier's Principle

142

C8 Rates and equilibrium

Starter	Support/Extend	Resources
Dynamic equilibrium (5 minutes) Interactive where students complete a paragraph to summarise reversible reactions and the energy changes involved.	**Extend:** Ask students to suggest what an isolated system would be.	**Interactive:** Dynamic equilibrium
Modelling (10 minutes) Split the class into groups of three, give each group a tray and 20 small similar objects (such as balls, pencils, rubbers). Ask students to put 10 objects in the tray and 10 objects on the table. One person from the group should take objects out of the tray, and the second person should put objects back. The third person should keep time, so that both people work at the same rate. Run the model for a short time. Then ask students to relate this model to a reversible reaction.	**Support:** Demonstrate the model at the front of the class with volunteers rather than small groups. **Extend:** Ask students to work at different rates for removing and adding the items and ask students to explain the outcome on the yields.	

Main	Support/Extend	Resources
Dynamic equilibrium and Le Chatelier's Principle (40 minutes) Describe to students the escalator model for dynamic equilibrium. Imagine that you are walking up an escalator that is going down. If your pace matches the movement of the escalator your relative position stays the same, even though both you and the escalator are moving. You may wish to refer students to Figure 1 of the student book. Then ask small groups of students to generate their own model to explain dynamic equilibrium and to illustrate the features of a dynamic equilibrium. If time, students could demonstrate their models. **H** Introduce Le Chatelier's Principle to students. They should then go through worked examples of several equilibrium systems for reversible reactions already met in the specification or in the lessons so far. They should use the worked examples to explain how changing the concentration of a reactant or product would affect the rates of each reaction and therefore the yield of the product.	**Extend:** Ask students to evaluate the models and then vote on the best model. **Extend: H** Ask students to predict how a change in pressure or temperature may affect the equilibrium reaction.	**Activity:** Dynamic equilibrium and Le Chatelier's Principle

Plenary	Support/Extend	Resources
Fizzy water (5 minutes) Show students a bottle of fizzy water and shake it. Ask students to explain how this is a dynamic equilibrium (carbon dioxide dissolves in and is released from the water). Carefully open the top over the sink. Ask students to explain their observations (the open system means that the carbon dioxide escapes into the atmosphere). **Think, pair, square on catalysts** (10 minutes) **H** Ask students to predict the effect on dynamic equilibrium of adding a catalyst. They then share their ideas in a pair and finally as a whole table. Encourage each table to feed back and use question and answer to guide the class so that they understand that a catalyst will increase both the forward and backward rate by the same amount and therefore will have no effect on equilibrium.	**Extend:** Ask students to write a balanced symbol equation for this reversible change.	

Homework			
Students produce a flow chart to explain how a dynamic equilibrium is achieved quickly from a reversible reaction. Students should use examples in their flow chart.			

kerboodle

A Kerboodle highlight for this lesson is **Extension sheet: Dynamic equilibrium**. Refer to the **Content map** on Kerboodle for a full list of resources and assessment.

Higher tier

C8.9 Altering conditions

AQA spec Link: 6.2.4 The relative amounts of all the reactants and products at equilibrium depend on the conditions of the reaction.

If a system is at equilibrium and a change is made to any of the conditions, then the system responds to counteract the change.

The effects of changing conditions on a system at equilibrium can be predicted using Le Chatelier's Principle.

Students should be able to make qualitative predictions about the effect of changes on systems at equilibrium when given appropriate information.

6.2.5 If the concentration of one of the reactants or products is changed, the system is no longer at equilibrium and the concentrations of all the substances will change until equilibrium is reached again.

If the concentration of a reactant is increased, more products will be formed until equilibrium is reached again.

If the concentration of a product is decreased, more reactants will react until equilibrium is reached again.

Students should be able to interpret appropriate given data to predict the effect of a change in concentration of a reactant or product on given reactions at equilibrium.

6.2.6 If the temperature of a system at equilibrium is increased:
- the relative amount of products at equilibrium increases for an endothermic reaction
- the relative amount of products at equilibrium decreases for an exothermic reaction.

If the temperature of a system at equilibrium is decreased:
- the relative amount of products at equilibrium decreases for an endothermic reaction
- the relative amount of products at equilibrium increases for an exothermic reaction.

Students should be able to interpret appropriate given data to predict the effect of a change in temperature on given reactions at equilibrium.

6.2.7 For gaseous reactions at equilibrium:
- an increase in pressure causes the equilibrium position to shift towards the side with the smaller number of molecules as shown by the symbol equation for that reaction
- a decrease in pressure causes the equilibrium position to shift towards the side with the larger number of molecules as shown by the symbol equation for that reaction.

Students should be able to interpret appropriate given data to predict the effect of pressure changes on given reactions at equilibrium.

WS 2.1
MS 1c

Aiming for	Outcome	Checkpoint	
		Question	Activity
Aiming for GRADE 6	Explain how changing conditions for a system at dynamic equilibrium affects the rate of the forward and reverse reactions.		Starter 2, Main 1, Main 2, Plenary 1
	Predict the effect on yield of changing temperature, concentration, or pressure in a given equilibrium system.	1, 2, 3, 4, End of chapter 4	Main 1, Main 2, Plenary 1
Aiming for GRADE 8	Explain why changing pressure has no effect on some systems.	4	Homework
	Justify, in detail, the compromise conditions chosen in given industrial processes.		Plenary 2

Maths
Students summarise Le Chatelier's Principle using mathematical language.

Literacy
Students justify industrial conditions.

■ C8 Rates and equilibrium

Practical

Title	Observing equilibrium
Equipment	three plastic syringes with septum caps filled with generated N_2O_4, ice bath, warm water bath (60–80 °C), white background
Overview of method	In each plastic syringe with a septum cap have an equilibrium mixture of NO_2 and N_2O_4 gases. Hold one syringe in front of a white background so that the students can easily see the colour. Put one syringe in an ice bath, keep one at ambient and the third in a warm water bath. Allow the syringes to get to their new temperature and then compare the colours. Using the ambient syringe, hold in front of a white background and push in the plunger to increase the pressure then pull the plunger slightly to reduce the pressure. Allow students to observe the colour changes.
Safety considerations	N_2O_4 is toxic. Make the gas in a fume cupboard and ensure that the syringes are sealed. Be aware that the water bath could cause scalding. Wear chemical splash-proof eye protection and wash hands after completing the practical.

Starter	Support/Extend	Resources
Equilibrium equation (5 minutes) Ask students to write an equilibrium equation for dinitrogen tetroxide turning into nitrogen dioxide. Make sure students use the equilibrium arrow ⇌.	**Extend:** For the forward reaction 58 kJ/mol of energy is transferred from the surroundings. Students suggest what this says about the forward and reverse reactions.	
Le Chatelier's tweet (10 minutes) Using the student book and notes from the previous lesson, students summarise Le Chatelier's Principle in a tweet (no more than 140 characters).		

Main	Support/Extend	Resources
Observing equilibrium (20 minutes) Explain to students that at room temperature and pressure, nitrogen dioxide is a brown gas and dinitrogen tetroxide is a colourless (pale yellow) gas. Ask students to write the equation for the reaction. Encourage students to predict the effect on the position of equilibrium when the temperature is lowered or increased. Demonstrate the effect and ask students to explain the observation of the colour change. Ask students to predict the effect of changing pressure, demonstrate this, and again ask students to explain their observations.	**Extend:** Ask students to predict how the demonstration would have been different, if at all, if a sealed syringe of dinitrogen tetroxide had been used.	**Practical:** Observing equilibrium
The Haber Process (20 minutes) Explain to students that ammonia is an important feedstock chemical for making fertilisers. It can be made by a reversible reaction between hydrogen and nitrogen gas. Ask students to write an equation for this reversible reaction. Then explain that the forward reaction is exothermic. Ask students to determine the energy change for the backward reaction. Label the high and low pressure sides of the equation. If necessary, briefly remind students of Le Chatelier's Principle. Then ask students to work in small groups to suggest the effect on the yield of ammonia of changing the temperature and the pressure.	**Support:** Use molymod to generate the balanced equation in terms of molecules.	

Plenary	Support/Extend	Resources
Yield up or down (5 minutes) Write the equation for an equilibrium system students have met and the energy change for the forward reaction. Shout out a change in condition and students predict if the yield of the forward reaction will decrease, increase, or there will be no change.	**Support:** Encourage students to work in small groups.	**Interactive:** Yield up or down
Conditions of the Haber process (10 minutes) Give students the balanced symbol equation for the Haber Process. Students predict conditions that would generate the highest yield (low temperatures and high pressures). Explain to students that a temperature of about 450 °C and a pressure of 200 atmospheres are used with an iron catalyst. Ask students to justify why these compromise conditions are used (see Topic 15.6).		

Homework			
Ask students to sketch a graph and annotate it to explain why changing pressure has no effect on the following reaction: $H_2(g) + I_2(g) \rightleftharpoons 2HI(g)$			

kerboodle

A Kerboodle highlight for this lesson is **Literacy sheet: Altering conditions**. Refer to the **Content map** on Kerboodle for a full list of resources and assessment.

C8 Rates and equilibrium

Overview of C8 Rates and equilibrium

In this chapter, students have learnt about the factors that affect the rate of a reaction, including temperature, surface area, concentration, and pressure. Students should be able to explain the effect of each factor on the rate of reaction using collision theory – understanding that each factor increases the *frequency* of effective collisions, **not** just the number of collisions. They should also be able to explain the effect of catalysts on the rate of a reaction in terms of providing an alternative reaction pathway with a lower activation energy.

Students have also learnt about reversible reactions and dynamic equilibrium. Students should apply their knowledge on endothermic and exothermic reactions to equilibrium reactions to be able to predict the effect of temperature changes on the reversible reactions and the position of the equilibrium. Higher-tier students should also be able to use Le Châtelier's principle to explain the effect of temperature and pressure on the position of equilibrium.

Required practical

All students are expected to have carried out the required practical:

Practical	Topic
Investigate how changes in concentration affect the rates of reactions by a method involving measuring the volume of a gas produced and a method involving a change in colour or turbidity.	C8.4
This should be an investigation involving developing a hypothesis.	

MyMaths

You can find additional support for the maths skills covered in this chapter on **MyMaths**, including calculating a mean, calculating surface area, and drawing tangents determining the gradient.

kerboodle

For this chapter, the following assessments are available on Kerboodle:

C8 Checkpoint quiz: Rates and equilibirum
C8 Progress quiz: Rates and equilibrium 1
C8 Progress quiz: Rates and equilibrium 2
C8 On your marks: Rates and equilibrium
C8 Exam-style questions and mark scheme: Rates and equilibrium

Checkpoint follow up lesson

A student's route through this lesson can be determined using the Checkpoint assessment. Percentage pass marks are supplied in the Checkpoint teacher notes.

For each successive route through it is assumed that the student can perform to their current route as well as previous routes. For example, students working at Aiming for 6 are assumed to be secure in Aiming for 4 knowledge and understanding and working towards achieving all the learning outcomes for Aiming for 6.

	Aiming for 4	Aiming for 6	Aiming for 8
Learning outcomes	Calculate a mean rate of reaction.	Calculate a rate of reaction at given times, using a graph of practical results.	
	Describe in simple terms how temperature and surface area affect the rate of a reaction.	Explain how collision theory can be used to explain the effect of temperature, surface area, pressure, and concentration on rate of reaction.	Use Le Châtelier's principle to explain how the composition of an equilibrium mixture can be altered.

Starter — **Modelling the rate of a reactions (10 minutes)**

Ask for two volunteers to come to the front of the classroom. Explain that they will compete against each other to make pictures using sticky notes. They will each have a minute to draw a flower and colour it on as many sticky notes as possible, before sticking it on the board in their own marked off areas. Ask another student to time the minute and another student to count the number of pictures produced.

Ask the class who won the competition, and how they could tell. Ask how this links to reactions. Draw out that the pen and post it notes were similar to the reactants, the completed picture similar to the products, the amount of pictures drawn is the amount of product, and the minute is the reaction time. Calculate each competitor's 'rate' and remind students of the equation for the mean rate of reactions.

Discuss how models are useful but also have their limitations, for example, the person drawing is not involved.

Differentiated checkpoint activity

The Aiming for 4 Checkpoint follow-up sheet provides highly-structured support for analysing experimental results to calculate the mean average rate. Aiming for 4 students will need to carry out some simple practical investigations:

- time how long it takes to dissolve a teaspoon of sugar in lukewarm water compared with hot water
- time the reaction between a strip of magnesium metal and powdered magnesium metal with dilute hydrochloric acid.

The purpose of these practicals is to observe the changes to rate caused by temperature change and surface are change. The substances required should already be prepared for students (e.g., in small weighing boats or test tubes), and it should be explained that the mass of magnesium is the same in the powdered sample as in the strip, and that the volumes of acid or water are all equal.

After completing the practical activities, students will complete a series of questions and tasks on the sheet. They will need calculators.

Students use the Aiming for 6 Checkpoint follow-up sheet to carry out a practical and plot a graph of their results to analyse their results. The sheet contains prompts but does not give detail. Aiming for 6 students will need to react a small strip of magnesium with dilute hydrochloric acid, and collect the hydrogen gas formed using an inverted measuring cylinder in a water bath. They use their results to plot a graph of volume of hydrogen gas against time. The sheet will guide them through the process and provide a series of questions and tasks to consolidate their understanding.

All practicals need to be fully planned and risk assessed before students carry them out.

Students use Aiming for 8 Checkpoint follow-up sheet to create a poster about equilibrium. The sheet provides minimal support for students and they should be aiming to work independently. Students could work in pairs if extra support is required. They will need poster materials.

Kerboodle resource C8 Checkpoint follow up: Aiming for 4, C8 Checkpoint follow up: Aiming for 6, C8 Checkpoint follow up: Aiming for 8

Plenary — **(10 minutes)**

Ask students to work in pairs to suggest how they could monitor the rate of a fuel (e.g., a candle or ethanol in a spirit burner) burning in oxygen.

Ask students to work in pairs – student 1 describes why changing a factor such as temperature affects the rate (without naming the factor). Student 2 has to guess the factor being described, and add one piece of information to the description. Aim to describe at least two factors.

| **Progression** | Provide students with experimental results showing the effect of pressure, for students to calculate the mean rate, draw a particle diagram, and write an explanation. Encourage students try without their notes first. | Students may need their notes for support but should attempt first without. | Students could apply their understanding to industrial processes and researching some examples where conditions used are a compromise. This looks forward to Chapter C15. |

147

C 9 Crude oil and fuels
9.1 Hydrocarbons

AQA spec Link: 7.1.1 Crude oil is a finite resource found in rocks. Crude oil is the remains of an ancient biomass consisting mainly of plankton that was buried in mud.

Crude oil is a mixture of a very large number of compounds. Most of the compounds in crude oil are hydrocarbons, which are molecules made up of hydrogen and carbon atoms only.

Most of the hydrocarbons in crude oil are hydrocarbons called alkanes. The general formula for the homologous series of alkanes is C_nH_{2n+2}.

The first four members of the alkanes are methane, ethane, propane, and butane.

Alkane molecules can be represented in the following forms:

C_2H_6 or H—C—C—H (with H atoms on each carbon)

Students should be able to recognise substances as alkanes given their formulae in these forms.

Students do not need to know the names of specific alkanes other than methane, ethane, propane, and butane.

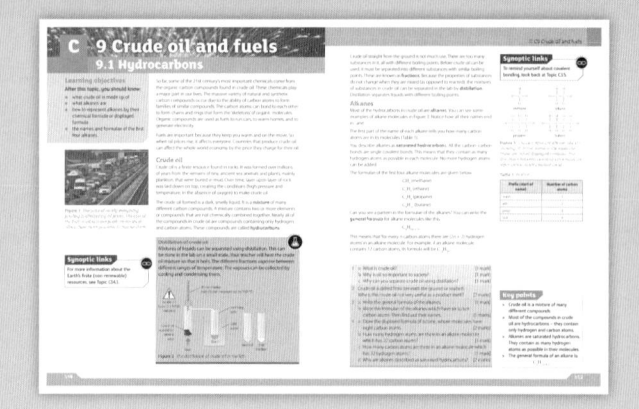

WS 1.2
MS 1a

Aiming for	Outcome	Checkpoint	
		Question	Activity
Aiming for GRADE 4	Describe the composition of crude oil.	1	Starter 2, Main, Plenary 2
	State a definition of a hydrocarbon.	End of chapter 2	Main, Plenary 1
	State a definition of an alkane.		Main, Plenary 2
Aiming for GRADE 6	Describe how to separate crude oil into fractions in a school laboratory.		Main
	Classify a hydrocarbon as an alkane.	4, End of chapter 2, 5	Main, Plenary 1
	State the names and describe the first four alkanes.	End of chapter 2	Main, Plenary 1
Aiming for GRADE 8	Explain why fractional distillation is used to separate crude oil into fractions.	1, 2	Main
	Apply a general formula to generate a molecular formula and a displayed formula for a straight-chain alkane.	3, 4, End of chapter 1	Main, Homework
	Classify and justify the classification of a chemical as an alkane.	4	Plenary 1

Maths
Students apply the general formula of the alkanes to generate specific formulae.

Literacy
Students describe how crude oil is formed. They also evaluate answers to a practice question.

Key words
mixture, hydrocarbons, fractions, distillation, alkanes, saturated hydrocarbons, general formula

Practical

Title	Distillation of crude oil
Equipment	boiling tube with side arm, bung with 0–360 °C thermometer through, five test tubes (as collecting tubes – ignition tubes can also be used to display small volumes of fractions), two beakers, ice/water mixture, mineral wool, synthetic crude oil, Bunsen burner and safety equipment, six watch glasses, taper, matches

148

C9 Crude oil and fuels

Overview of method	Soak the mineral wool in the synthetic crude oil and place in the boiling tube. Fix the bung and ensure that the bulb of the thermometer is adjacent to the side arm. Put a collecting tube into an ice bath, and the end of the delivery tube from the side arm into the top of it. Gently heat the boiling tube with a Bunsen flame, and notice when the temperature reading has stabilised (around 80 °C). When the temperature rises again, quickly change the current collecting tube for a new one. Repeat four times, collecting five fractions, and leaving a residue in the boiling tube. Each fraction can be collected about every 50 °C up to about 300 °C. The residue remains on the mineral wool, making the sixth fraction. These fractions can be ignited. Carefully pour them onto mineral wool held on a watch glass, then using a lighted taper, ignite the fractions.
Safety considerations	Wear eye protection and complete in a well-ventilated room.

Starter	Support/Extend	Resources
Diagram (5 minutes) Show students the molecular formulae and displayed formulae of the first four alkanes. Students classify them as molecular formulae or displayed formulae. **Crude oil and hydrocarbons** (10 minutes) Students use the interactive to put a series of statements that describe the formation of crude oil in the correct order. They then match the name, chemical formula, and structural formula for the first four alkanes.	**Extend:** Ask students to suggest the formulae of some alkanes with more than four carbon atoms and to find out their names.	**Interactive:** Crude oil and hydrocarbons

Main	Support/Extend	Resources
Distillation of crude oil (40 minutes) Give students a molecular modelling kit and explain which pieces represent carbon atoms, hydrogen atoms, and covalent bonds. Then give students the formulae of the first four alkanes and ask them to make the molecular models of these. Tell students the names of these alkanes and ask them to draw a table with three columns (name, molecular formula, displayed formula). Demonstrate the distillation of crude oil as detailed in the practical box. Use question and answer to ensure that students understand the processes involved. Highlight that each fraction is in fact a mixture of hydrocarbons rather than a pure substance. Students should then draw a diagram of the equipment used and annotate it to describe and explain how distillation separates crude oil.	**Support:** Give students the information for them to put in the table. **Extend:** Ask students to look at the molecular models and see if they can generate the general formula for the homologous series. **Extend:** Ask students to suggest a method to further separate each fraction into pure chemicals.	**Practical:** Distillation of crude oil

Plenary	Support/Extend	Resources
Sorting (5 minutes) Give students a list of names, and molecular and displayed formulae for organic chemicals. Students identify whether the organic chemicals are hydrocarbons and whether the hydrocarbons are alkanes. **Discussing questions** (10 minutes) Show students an exam-style practice question. Ask students to discuss the answer and then choose a few students to share with the whole class the points they would include in their answer. Then reveal the mark scheme and any relevant points from the examiner's report for that question. Encourage students to evaluate the answer they came up with.	**Extend:** Include organic compounds which do not fit either of the classifications (alcohols, ethers, carboxylic acids, etc.)	

Homework		
Give students the structural formula of butane. Ask them to list all the information that they can about this molecule. They should comment on bonding, structure, where it can be found, molecular formula, general formula, and which family of chemicals it belongs to.	**Extend:** Students draw the displayed formula of the branched alkane with the same molecular formula as butane (methylpropane).	

kerboodle
A Kerboodle highlight for this lesson is **Bump up your grade: All about alkanes**. Refer to the **Content map** on Kerboodle for a full list of resources and assessment.

C9.2 Fractional distillation of oil

AQA spec Link: 7.1.2 The many hydrocarbons in crude oil may be separated into fractions, each of which contains molecules with a similar number of carbon atoms, by evaporating the oil and allowing it to condense at different temperatures. This process is called fractional distillation.

The fractions can be processed to produce fuels and feedstock for the petrochemical industry.

Many of the fuels on which we depend for our modern lifestyle such as petrol, diesel oil, kerosene, heavy fuel oil, and liquefied petroleum gases, are produced from crude oil.

Many useful materials on which modern life depends are produced by the petrochemical industry, such as solvents, lubricants, polymers, detergents.

The vast array of natural and synthetic carbon compounds occurs due to the ability of carbon atoms to form families of similar compounds.

7.1.3 Some properties of hydrocarbons depend on the size of their molecules, including boiling point, viscosity, and flammability. These properties influence how hydrocarbons are used as fuels.

Students should be able to recall how boiling point, viscosity, and flammability change with increasing molecular size.

Knowledge of trends in properties of hydrocarbons is limited to:
- boiling points
- viscosity
- flammability.

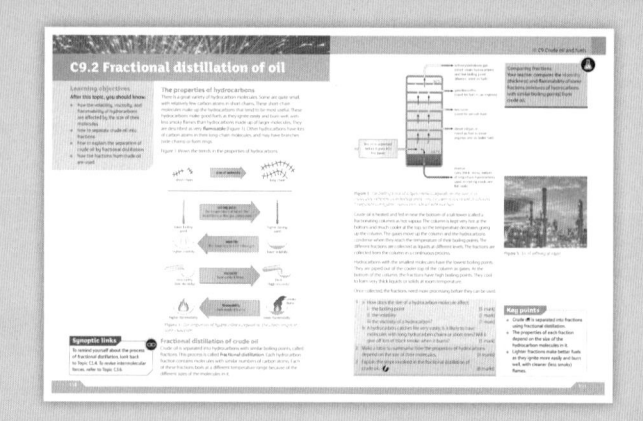

MS 1c, 2c

Aiming for	Outcome	Checkpoint	
		Question	Activity
Aiming for GRADE 4 ↓	Name the different fractions from crude oil.		Main
	State a use for each fraction from crude oil.		Plenary 1
Aiming for GRADE 6 ↓	Describe how the trend in colour, viscosity, flammability, and boiling point changes as the length of the hydrocarbon chain changes.	2, 3, End of chapter 1	Starter 1, Main, Plenary 2
	Describe how the properties of a fraction of crude oil make it appropriate for its use.		Plenary 1
Aiming for GRADE 8 ↓	Explain in detail how fractional distillation is used to separate crude oil into fractions.	3	Main
	Explain how chain length affects the properties of crude oil fractions.	1, 3, End of chapter 1	Main
	Make predictions about the properties of crude oil fractions from the fraction's hydrocarbon chain length.	1, 3, End of chapter 1	Starter 2, Plenary 1, Homework

Maths
Students draw a bar chart (2c).

Literacy
Students explain how fractional distillation of crude oil is carried out in the petrochemical industry.

Key words
flammable, fractional distillation, viscosity

Practical

Title	Comparing fractions – flammability
Equipment	three different samples of alkanes (e.g., butane, wax, paraffin) in sealed labelled sample bottles and in reagent bottles, three dropping pipettes, three watch glasses, mineral wool, heatproof mat, eye protection, taper, matches

■ C9 Crude oil and fuels

Overview of method	Give out the sealed samples for students to look at. Put a small piece of mineral wool on each watch glass. Using a dropping pipette add a sample of each alkane to separate watch glasses. Using a lighted taper ignite each sample of alkanes. Ensure that students compare the ease of lighting and the cleanness of the flame. If using wax, use a tea light and ignite the wick.
Safety considerations	Butane is flammable. Keep away from naked flames and sources of ignition. Wear eye protection and complete in a well-ventilated room.

Title	Comparing fractions – viscosity
Equipment	clamp, boss, and stand, sheet of acrylic, pens, samples of different chain-length straight-chain alkanes, dropping pipettes, stopwatch, eye protection
Overview of method	Put a piece of smooth acrylic sheet at a slight angle to make a slope. Use a white board pen to make two lines about 5 cm apart. Using a dropper put one drop of a fraction on the first line and time how long it takes for the liquid to run down the sheet to the second line. Repeat for some different alkanes.
Safety considerations	Wear eye protection and complete in a well-ventilated room.

Starter	Support/Extend	Resources
Distil the order (5 minutes) Ask students to put the following words in the correct order to describe fractional distillation: mixture, separate, boil, heat, condense. (mixture → heat → boil → condense → separate) **Drawing a bar chart** (10 minutes) Ask students to plot a bar chart for methane (M_r = 16, boiling point = −162 °C) ethane (M_r = 30, boiling point = −89 °C), propane (M_r = 44, boiling point −42 °C), and butane (M_r = 58, boiling point −1 °C). Ask students to state the trend in this data.	**Support:** Ask students to draw a table of the data. **Extend:** Ask students to draw a scatter graph and predict the boiling point for pentane, C_5H_{10}.	

Main	Support/Extend	Resources
Comparing fractions (40 minutes) Give students the molecular formula of an alkane from each fraction of crude oil. Demonstrate the flammability of each fraction as detailed in the first practical box and ask students to state the trend. Then ask students to predict which would have the highest and lowest viscosity based on the molecular formula of the alkanes to be tested. Run the demonstration as detailed in the second practical box to test their predictions. Students should summarise the trends by writing a list of the fractions and adding an annotated arrow alongside to describe each trend (similar to how reactivity is shown in the metal reactivity series). Students should use the student book to include the trends in colour.		**Practical:** Comparing fractions

Plenary	Support/Extend	Resources
Uses of fractions (10 minutes) Students match the names of the fractions with their uses, and explain which property of each fraction makes it appropriate for its uses. **Spotting patterns** (10 minutes) Students use the calculation sheet to analyse data and identify trends in the properties of hydrocarbons.		**Interactive:** Uses of fractions **Calculation sheet:** Spotting patterns

Homework		
Explain that there are two saturated non-branched hydrocarbons with six carbon atoms – hexane C_6H_{14} and cyclohexane C_6H_{12}. Ask students to draw the displayed formula for each chemical and then to suggest some properties.	**Extend:** Students explain why a cycloalkane does not follow the general formula, C_nH_{2n+2}.	

kerboodle

A Kerboodle highlight for this lesson is **Literacy sheet: Fractional distillation**. Refer to the **Content map** on Kerboodle for a full list of resources and assessment.

C9.3 Burning hydrocarbon fuels

AQA spec Link: 7.1.3 The combustion of hydrocarbon fuels releases energy. During combustion, the carbon and hydrogen in the fuels are oxidised. The complete combustion of a hydrocarbon produces carbon dioxide and water.

Students should be able to write balanced equations for the complete combustion of hydrocarbons with a given formula.

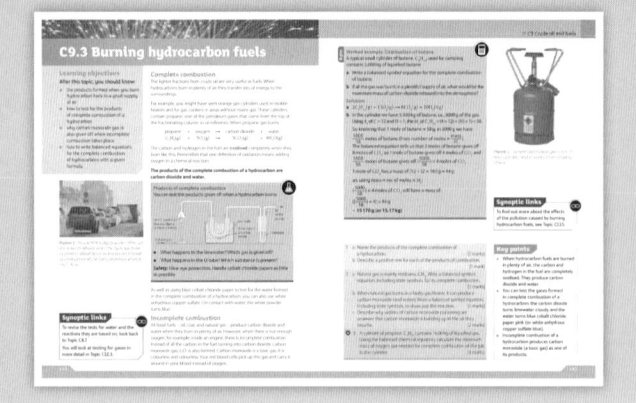

WS 1.4
MS 1c

Aiming for	Outcome	Checkpoint	
		Question	Activity
Aiming for GRADE 4	Define complete and incomplete combustion.	1	Starter 2, Plenary 1
	Write a word equation to describe the complete combustion of a hydrocarbon.	End of chapter 2, 4	Main 1, Homework
	Write a word equation to describe the incomplete combustion of a hydrocarbon.	End of chapter 2, 4	Main 1, Homework
Aiming for GRADE 6	Explain the differences between complete and incomplete combustion.		Starter 2, Plenary 1
	Write balanced symbol equations for the complete and incomplete combustion of hydrocarbons.	2, End of chapter 2, 4	Plenary 2, Homework
	Explain how to test for the products of complete combustion.	1, End of chapter 4	Starter 1, Main 1
Aiming for GRADE 8	(H) Justify the use of a given fuel over another.		Main 2
	Explain in detail how the production of carbon monoxide in incomplete combustion can be lethal.	2, End of chapter 2	Plenary 1
	(H) Use balanced symbol equations to calculate amounts of reactants or products in a combustion reaction.	3	Main 2

Maths
Higher-tier students calculate the moles of carbon dioxide produced on combustion.

Literacy
Students explain why domestic heating boilers must be serviced regularly.

Key words
oxidised

Practical

Title	Products of complete combustion
Equipment	Bunsen burner, heat-proof mat, eye protection, glass funnel, boiling tube, limewater, cobalt chloride paper, three delivery tubes, vacuum water pump, two bungs each with one hole in for the delivery tubes, one bung with two holes in, U-tube, ice, three stands, bosses and clamps
Overview of method	Put the Bunsen burner in the centre of a heat-proof mat, invert the glass funnel, and clamp into position about 2 cm above the top of the flame. Use a small piece of rubber tubing to connect the funnel to an n-shaped delivery tube, push the other end through a bung. Using a second stand, boss and clamp, mount a U-tube.

■ C9 Crude oil and fuels

	Put a piece of cobalt chloride paper into the bottom of the U-tube. Push the bung into one side of the U-tube. Using the third stand, boss and clamp, hold a boiling tube in position that is half-full with limewater. Connect the U-tube to the boiling tube using another n-shaped delivery tube, putting a single-holed bung into the other side of the U-tube. Put a two-holed bung in the top of the boiling tube and use an L-shaped delivery tube to connect to a vacuum water pump. Turn on the water pump to draw gases through the apparatus and then light the Bunsen burner.
Safety considerations	Limewater is an irritant and cobalt chloride paper is toxic. Wear eye protection, complete in a well-ventilated room and wash hands after the practical.

Starter	Support/Extend	Resources
Lab tests (5 minutes) Ask students to recall the simple laboratory test for: • oxygen (glowing splint re-lights) • carbon dioxide (limewater turns cloudy) • water (cobalt chloride paper turns from blue to pink). **Bunsen burner** (10 minutes) Set up a Bunsen burner on the safety flame. Ask students to name the fuel and give the molecular and displayed formulae. Demonstrate how the yellow flame is 'dirty' by holding some glassware in it to show the soot that coats it. Explain that this is incomplete combustion, producing carbon as one of the products. Open the air hole to show complete combustion and use question and answer to compare the flames.	**Support:** Ask students to match up the chemical with its test. **Extend:** Ask students to write a balanced equation for the combustion of methane to form water and carbon dioxide.	**Interactive:** Lab tests

Main	Support/Extend	Resources
Products of complete combustion (20 minutes) Explain to students that they are going to investigate the combustion of methane. Explain that this is a type of oxidising reaction and ask students to explain why. Encourage students to predict the products of the reaction and suggest simple laboratory tests that could be used to determine the identity of the products. Demonstrate the complete combustion of methane using a Bunsen burner. **Fuel for cars** (20 minutes) **H** Explain that cars can be fuelled on petrol (which contains a lot of decane) as well as natural gas (mainly methane). The complete combustion of petrol releases 6779 kJ/mol and methane 882 kJ/mol. Students use the worked example in the student book to generate balanced symbol equations and calculate the amount of carbon dioxide produced. Ask students to evaluate the use of each fuel thinking about the ease of ignition, storage, supply, energy density, and type of flame produced.	**Extend:** Ask students to explain why the experiment should be run again, without the Bunsen burner, just drawing air through the apparatus. **Support:** Split the class into small groups and ensure that each group focuses on only one way of comparing the fuels. **Extend:** Ask students to think about environmental, social, and economic arguments.	**Practical:** Products of complete combustion

Plenary	Support/Extend	Resources
The dangers of incomplete combustion (5 minutes) Explain to students that methane can be used in homes for central heating. Ask students to suggest why boilers should be serviced regularly to ensure that only complete combustion is happening. **Balancing equations** (10 minutes) Students use the maths skills interactive to practise balancing symbol equations for combustion reactions, including using fractions.		**Maths skills:** Balancing equations

Homework		
Students write the equations for the complete and incomplete combustion of the first four alkanes.	**Support:** Students only write word equations. **Extend:** Students write balanced symbol equations including state symbols.	

C9.4 Cracking hydrocarbons

AQA spec Link: 7.1.4 Hydrocarbons can be broken down (cracked) to produce smaller, more useful molecules.

Cracking can be done by various methods including catalytic cracking and steam cracking.

Students should be able to describe in general terms the conditions used for catalytic cracking and steam cracking.

The products of cracking include alkanes and another type of hydrocarbon called alkenes.

Alkenes are more reactive than alkanes and react with bromine water, which is used as a test for alkenes.

Students should be able to recall the colour change when bromine water reacts with an alkene.

There is a high demand for fuels with small molecules and so some of the products of cracking are useful as fuels.

Alkenes are used to produce polymers and as starting materials for the production of many other chemicals.

Students should be able to balance chemical equations as examples of cracking given the formulae of the reactants and products.

Students should be able to give examples to illustrate the usefulness of cracking. They should also be able to explain how modern life depends on the uses of hydrocarbons.

(For combined science students do not need to know the formulae or names of individual alkenes.)

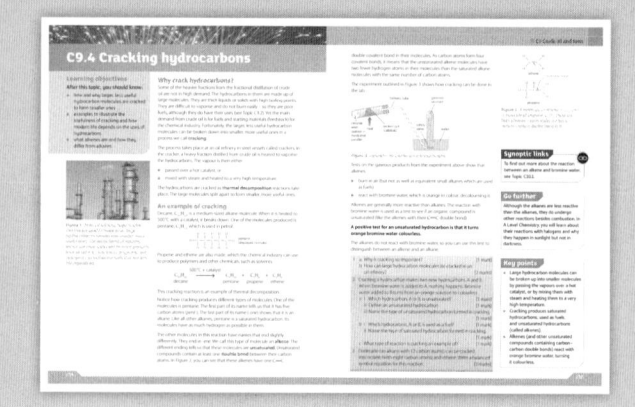

WS 2.4
MS 1c

Aiming for	Outcome	Checkpoint	
		Question	Activity
Aiming for GRADE 4	Define the process of cracking.	End of chapter 5	Main, Plenary 2, Homework
	Generate a word equation to describe cracking.	End of chapter 5	Main, Plenary 1, Homework
	Recognise and give examples of alkenes.	2, End of chapter 5	Starter 1, Main, Plenary 1, Plenary 2, Homework
Aiming for GRADE 6	Describe the process of cracking, including conditions.	1, 2, End of chapter 5	Main, Homework
	Generate a balanced symbol equation to describe cracking.	3	Main, Plenary 1, Homework
	Describe a chemical test to show an alkene is present.		Starter 2, Main
Aiming for GRADE 8	Use examples to explain the process of cracking and why it is so important to the petrochemical industry.	1, End of chapter 5	Main, Homework
	Explain the similarities and differences between alkanes and alkenes.		Starter 1, Plenary 2
	Explain, using balanced symbol equations, the reaction between bromine water and an alkene.		Main, Plenary 1, Homework

Maths
Students write balanced symbol equations.

Key words
cracking, thermal decomposition, alkene, unsaturated, double bond

154

■ C9 Crude oil and fuels

Practical

Title	Cracking
Equipment	eye protection, four test tubes with bungs, test-tube rack, boiling tube with one-holed bung, delivery tube fitted with a Bunsen valve, water bath, Bunsen burner and safety equipment, stand, boss and clamp, two dropping pipettes, wooden splint, medicinal (liquid) paraffin, 10 cm^3 measuring cylinder, mineral wool, broken pottery / aluminum oxide / pumice stone / zeolite catalyst, paraffin, 0.01 mol/dm^3 bromine water, matches and match box
Overview of method	Put a mineral wool plug in the bottom of the boiling tube. Add 2 cm^3 of paraffin. Clamp the boiling tube near its mouth so that it is slightly tilted upwards and place a heap of catalyst in centre of the tube. Fit the delivery tube. Half-fill the water bath and position the apparatus so that the end of the delivery tube with the Bunsen valve is immersed in water. Fill two test tubes with water and stand inverted in the trough. Strongly heat the catalyst for a few minutes then flick the flame to the mineral wool to vaporise some of the paraffin. Keep the catalyst hot. When there is a steady stream of bubbles, collect two test tubes of gas and put a bung in each tube under the water. Use a lighted splint to test the first tube of gas. Then add a few drops of bromine water to the second test tube, replace the bung, and shake until decolourised. Compare these tests with the original liquid paraffin used.
Safety considerations	Bromine water is harmful. Medicinal paraffin (liquid paraffin – a mixture of alkanes of chain length C_{20} and greater) is flammable and bromine water is harmful. Wear eye protection throughout and wash hands after completing the experiment. To prevent suck back, do not stop heating until the delivery tube is removed from the water bath. If suck-back looks likely to happen, lift the whole apparatus so that the delivery tube is removed from the water bath.

Starter	Support/Extend	Resources
Ethane and ethene (5 minutes) Students sort statements according to whether they describe ethane, ethene, or both. Students then complete equations to describe potential products formed in the cracking of decane. **Molecular model** (10 minutes) Give students a molecular modelling kit. Ask them to make a bromine molecule, and a hydrocarbon with the formula C_2H_4 (ethene). Then ask students to imagine that when these chemicals are mixed together they add to make one product. Ask students to make that product. Encourage students to attempt a balanced symbol equation for this reaction.	**Extend:** Ask students to suggest what would happen if ethane was mixed with bromine.	**Interactive:** Ethane and ethene

Main	Support/Extend	Resources
Cracking (40 minutes) Complete the practical as detailed. Ask students to draw a labelled diagram of the experiment and add annotations to explain how the reaction occurs. This should include the equation for the reaction, a definition of an alkene, a chemical test for alkenes, and an explanation why cracking is useful for industry.	**Support:** This practical requires a lot of dexterity and suck-back is a safety concern. Complete this experiment as a demonstration and give students pre-prepared tubes of an alkane and alkene to test with bromine water.	**Practical:** Cracking

Plenary	Support/Extend	Resources
Crack the equation (5 minutes) Ask students to write as many equations as they can for the cracking of decane, $C_{10}H_{12}$. **Comparing hydrocarbons** (10 minutes) Students produce a comparison table of the similarities and differences between alkanes and alkenes. Their tables should include interpretations of structural formulae.	**Support:** Give students incomplete word equations. **Extend:** Encourage students to attempt to name the compounds using naming conventions.	

Homework		
Students complete the WebQuest where they research what occurs during industrial cracking, and its importance.		**WebQuest:** Cracking

kerboodle

A Kerboodle highlight for this lesson is **Literacy skills: Cracking hydrocarbons**. Refer to the **Content map** on Kerboodle for a full list of resources and assessment.

C9 Crude oil and hydrocarbons

Overview of C9 Crude oil and hydrocarbons

In this chapter, students have learnt about hydrocarbons and been introduced to the alkanes. They should now be able to identify alkanes from their formulae, and be able to name and draw the displayed formula of the first four alkanes. Students have also learnt about some of the reactions of hydrocarbons, including combustion (both complete and incomplete) and cracking. All students should be able to write balanced symbol equations for the complete combustion of hydrocarbons and to describe the conditions of cracking. All students should be able to describe the test for alkenes (a product of cracking) but students studying *AQA GCSE Combined science: Trilogy* do not need to know the names of the alkenes produced.

Students have also learnt about crude oil as a source of hydrocarbons and the fractional distillation of crude oil. They should be able to describe how the size of the hydrocarbon molecule affects its properties, including viscosity, boiling point, and flammability.

MyMaths

You can find additional support for the maths skills covered in this chapter on **MyMaths**, including significant figures and representing 3D structures using 2D models.

kerboodle

For this chapter, the following assessments are available on Kerboodle:

C9 Checkpoint quiz: Crude oil and hydrocarbons
C9 Progress quiz: Crude oil and hydrocarbons 1
C9 Progress quiz: Crude oil and hydrocarbons 2
C9 On your marks: Crude oil and hydrocarbons
C9 Exam-style questions and mark scheme: Crude oil and hydrocarbons

Checkpoint follow up lesson

A student's route through this lesson can be determined using the Checkpoint assessment. Percentage pass marks are supplied in the Checkpoint teacher notes.

For each successive route through it is assumed that the student can perform to their current route as well as previous routes. For example, students working at Aiming for 6 are assumed to be secure in Aiming for 4 knowledge and understanding and working towards achieving all the learning outcomes for Aiming for 6.

	Aiming for 4	Aiming for 6	Aiming for 8
Learning outcomes	Describe how crude oil is formed.	Describe the difference between alkanes and alkenes in terms of bonding.	Describe in detail how fractional distillation and cracking are carried out on an industrial scale.
	Name and draw the first four alkanes.	Describe how fractional distillation takes place.	
	Describe how alkanes can be distinguished from alkenes.	Describe how cracking takes place and why it is an important industrial process.	
Starter	**Uses of crude oil (5 minutes)** Ask students to come up with a list of products or substances that they use in everyday life that originate from crude oil.		
	Hydrocarbon combustion (5 minutes) Reiterate that crude oil provides us with numerous substances, including fuels. Carry out a practical of burning a fuel in a spirit burner. Ask students what will happen if the gases formed are passed through limewater and an inverted U-tube containing cobalt chloride apaper or anhyrous cpopper sulfate. Discuss that when hydrocarbon fuels burn they produce water and carbon dioxide, unless they do not have enough oxygen to react with and they will produce carbon monoxide.		
Differentiated checkpoint activity	The Aiming for 4 Checkpoint follow-up sheet provides highly-structured questions that could be used as a cut and stick for producing a leaflet. You will need to demonstrate the test of an alkene with bromine water and compare the result with athe result for an alkane.	Students use the Aiming for 6 Checkpoint follow-up sheet to create a leaflet on hydrocarbons. The sheet contains a series of prompt questions to guide students with the content to include.	Students use Aiming for 8 Checkpoint follow-up sheet to create a leaflet on the industrial uses of cracking and fractional distillation. The sheet provides minimal support for students and they should be aiming to work independently. Aiming for 8 students will require access to the Internet or the library to carry out research.
	Kerboodle resource C9 Checkpoint follow up: Aiming for 4, C9 Checkpoint follow up: Aiming for 6, C9 Checkpoint follow up: Aiming for 8		
Plenary	**Leaflet review (5 minutes)** Ask students to lay their leaflets around the room. Students should then choose another person's leaflet to review. They should read the other person's leaflet and decide on two strong points about the leaflet and one point that could be improved on. Aiming for 4 students should peer assess each other's completed sheets, or mark their sheets against the correct answers if more appropriate for the ability level.		
	Key points (5 minutes) Ask students to decide as a pair three key learning points from the chapter. Review these as a class. Address any misconceptions that arise.		
Progression	To progress, provide students with a series of statements that describe cracking and fractional distillation and have them put them in order. Students could add further annotations to their statements.	To progress, students should make sure they include balanced symbol equations for all of the reactions. Students could carry out further research on industrial cracking to add more detail to their leaflet.	Students could research longer-chain alkanes and branched alkanes, extroplating their understanding of the trends in properties to these alkanes.

C 10 Organic reactions
10.1 Reactions of the alkenes

C GCSE Chemistry only

AQA spec Link: 7.2.1 Alkenes are hydrocarbons with a double carbon-carbon bond. The general formula for the homologous series of alkenes is C_nH_{2n}.

Alkene molecules are unsaturated because they contain two fewer hydrogen atoms than the alkane with the same number of carbon atoms.

The first four members of the homologous series of alkenes are ethene, propene, butane, and pentene.

Alkene molecules can be represented in the following forms:

C_3H_6 or

Students do not need to know the names of individual alkenes other than ethene, propene, butene, and pentene.

7.2.2 Alkenes are hydrocarbons with the functional group C=C. It is the generality of reactions of functional groups that determine the reactions of organic compounds.

Alkenes react with oxygen in combustion reactions in the same way as other hydrocarbons, but they tend to burn in air with smoky flames because of incomplete combustion.

Alkenes react with hydrogen, water, and the halogens, by the addition of atoms across the carbon-carbon double bond so that the double bond becomes a single carbon-carbon bond. Students should be able to:

- describe the reactions and conditions for the addition of hydrogen, water, and halogens to alkenes
- draw fully displayed structural formulae of the first four members of the alkenes and the products of their addition reactions with hydrogen, water, chlorine, bromine, and iodine.

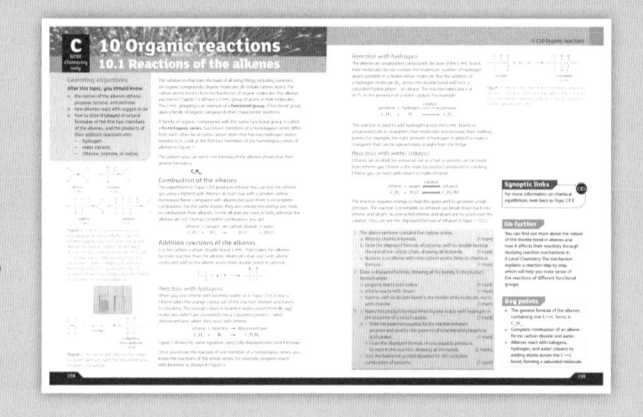

WS 1.2
MS 1c, 5b

Aiming for	Outcome	Checkpoint	
		Question	Activity
Aiming for GRADE 4 ↓	State a definition of an alkene.		Main, Plenary 2
	Name the first four alkenes.		Starter 1, Main
	State the product of a combustion and an addition reaction of an alkene.		Starter 1
Aiming for GRADE 6 ↓	Draw the displayed structural formulae for the first four alkenes.	1	Starter 2, Main
	Draw the displayed structural formulae for the products of the addition reactions between alkenes and hydrogen, water (steam), or a halogen.	2, 3, End of chapter 3	Main
	Predict the word and balanced symbol equations for the complete combustion of an alkene when the number of carbon atoms is given.	1, 3	Main
Aiming for GRADE 8 ↓	Predict the word and balanced symbol equations to describe reactions between alkenes and hydrogen, water (steam), or a halogen.	2, 3	Main, Homework
	Compare and contrast the reactivity of alkanes and alkenes.		Plenary 1
	Predict the general formula of an alkene.		Starter 1

■ C10 Organic reactions

Maths
Students apply the general formula of the alkenes to write the chemical formulae of unfamiliar alkenes. They also represent alkenes as 2D models (5b).

Literacy
Students explain the meaning of the terms functional group and homologous series.

Key words
functional group, homologous series

Starter	Support/Extend	Resources
Identifying alkenes (5 minutes) Show students the displayed formulae of the first four alkenes. Explain to students how to determine the name of a molecule. Then ask students to identify the names of the first four alkenes. Ask students to determine the molecular formula. Students then sort statements according to whether they describe alkenes or alkanes.	**Extend:** Include all the isomers of butene and pentene.	**Interactive:** Identifying alkenes
Molecular models (10 minutes) Give students the molecular formula for the first four alkenes. Ask students to use a molecular modelling kit to create the structures and then to draw the displayed formulae in their notes.	**Extend:** Ask students to determine the general formula. **Support:** Ask students to work in pairs and encourage them to start with the carbon chain and then add the hydrogen atoms. **Extend:** Asks students to also build the isomers of butene and pentene.	

Main	Support/Extend	Resources
Alkene profile (40 minutes) Ask students to characterise alkenes and create a profile to state their properties and reactions. Students should include a displayed formula, space filling model, and molecular formula as the pictures in the profile. Then give students four index cards – one for each of the first four alkenes. Ask them to make a top trumps style card that includes the formulae, homologous series, and the reactions of the alkenes in terms of observations and equations. Students could develop a scoring system for each category so that a game of top trumps could be played.	**Extend:** Additional cards can added for the first three alkanes and examples from other homologous series.	**Activity:** Alkene profile

Plenary	Support/Extend	Resources
Comparing (5 minutes) Ask students to draw a table to list the similarities and differences between alkanes and alkenes. The table should focus on the chemical reactivity as well as the difference in structure of the two classes of compounds. Students should then write a paragraph to conclude which is the most reactive and why.		
Reflection of learning (10 minutes) Ask students to look at the Learning objectives box in the student book. Ask them to rate how confident they feel about each learning objective – red being not at all confident, amber being a bit unsure, and green being very confident. Then ask some students to share their thoughts and use question and answer to ensure that the whole class has met the objectives set.	**Support:** Encourage students to review the key points and see if that helps them meet the objectives.	

Homework		
Ask students to write word equations to show how the first four alkenes react with oxygen, hydrogen, water (steam), chlorine, bromine, and iodine, showing the displayed formula of the product formed with water (steam) and with bromine.	**Extend:** Students write balanced symbol equations using structural formulae.	

kerboodle
A Kerboodle highlight for this lesson is **Bump up your grade: Cracking up: Alkenes**. Refer to the **Content map** on Kerboodle for a full list of resources and assessment.

GCSE Chemistry Only

C10.2 Structures of alcohols, carboxylic acids, and esters

AQA spec Link: 7.2.3 Alcohols contain the functional group –OH.

Methanol, ethanol, propanol, and butanol are the first four members of a homologous series of alcohols.

Alcohols can be represented in the following forms:

CH_3CH_2OH or

```
    H   H
    |   |
H — C — C — O — H
    |   |
    H   H
```

7.2.4 Carboxylic acids have the functional group –COOH.

The first four members of a homologous series of carboxylic acids are methanoic acid, ethanoic acid, propanoic acid, and butanoic acid.

The structures of carboxylic acids can be represented in the following forms:

CH_3COOH or

```
    H       O
    |      //
H — C — C
    |      \
    H       O — H
```

Students should be able to recognise carboxylic acids from their names or from given formulae.

Students do not need to know the names of individual carboxylic acids other than methanoic acid, ethanoic acid, propanoic acid, and butanoic acid.

Students do not need to know the names of esters other than ethyl ethanoate.

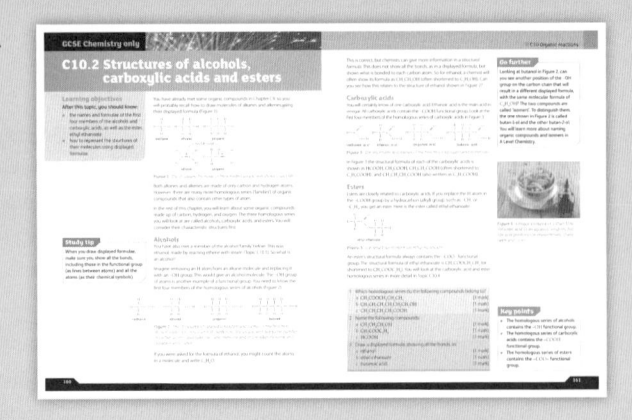

WS 1.2
MS 5b

Aiming for	Outcome	Checkpoint Question	Checkpoint Activity
Aiming for GRADE 4	Recognise the functional group in an alcohol and a carboxylic acid.	End of chapter 1	Starter 2, Main 1, Main 2, Plenary 2
	Name for the first four primary alcohols and the first four carboxylic acids.	2	Main 1, Main 2, Plenary 2, Homework
	Name ethyl ethanoate from its formula.	2, End of chapter 5	Main 1, Main 2, Plenary 2, Homework
Aiming for GRADE 6	Classify an organic compound as an alcohol, a carboxylic acid, or an ester.	1, End of chapter 1	Starter 2, Main 1, Main 2, Plenary 1, Plenary 2
	Draw the structural and displayed formulae for the first four primary alcohols and the first four carboxylic acids.	3, End of chapter 1, 4	Main 1, Homework
	Draw the structural and displayed formulae for ethyl ethanoate.	3	Main 1, Homework
Aiming for GRADE 8	Predict the structure for primary alcohols or carboxylic acids when the number of carbon atoms is given.		Main 2
	Suggest a general formula for a homologous series.		Main 1
	Suggest why an organic acid is not an alcohol even though it contains an –OH functional group.		Main 1

Maths
Students visualise alcohols and carboxylic acids in 2D models (5b).

Literacy
Students use their scientific understanding to create a key or flow chart to identify hydrocarbons.

C10 Organic reactions

Starter	Support/Extend	Resources
Smells (5 minutes) Dip cotton buds in methanol, ethanol, propanol, butanol, methanoic acid, ethanoic acid, propanoic acid, butanoic acid, and ethyl ethanoate. Allow students to safely smell the chemicals by wafting the evaporated smells into their noses. Ask students to describe the smells and suggest where they have experienced the smell before. **Sorting** (10 minutes) Show students the displayed formulae for methanol, ethanol, propanol, butanol, methanoic acid, ethanoic acid, propanoic acid, butanoic acid, and ethyl ethanoate. Ask students to sort the chemicals into groups and ask them to explain how they have grouped them.	**Extend:** Include all the isomers of propanol and butanol.	

Main	Support/Extend	Resources
Organic key (20 minutes) Students generate a key or flow chart to allow them to identify methanol, ethanol, propanol, butanol, methanoic acid, ethanoic acid, propanoic acid, butanoic acid, or ethyl ethanoate. Ensure students use structures, different types of formula, and reactions in their key.	**Extend:** Encourage students to suggest a general formula for each homologous series. **Extend:** Students should include the difference between an organic acid and an alcohol.	**Activity:** Organic key
Drawing and naming organic compounds (20 minutes) Students practise drawing full structural formulae and naming the first four alkenes, alcohols, and carboxylic acids, and drawing the products of common addition reactions of the alkenes.		**Calculation sheet:** Drawing and naming organic compounds

Plenary	Support/Extend	Resources
Classifying chemicals (5 minutes) Students sort chemical formulae according to whether they are alcohols, esters, or carboxylic acids. They then link each functional group they have studied so far (alkane, alkene, alcohol, carboxylic acid, and ester) with a description and an example.	**Extend:** Ask students to suggest the bonding in each compound.	**Interactive:** Classifying chemicals
Organic families (10 minutes) Ask students to make a comparison table comparing all the homologous series that they have studied (alkanes, alkenes, alcohols, and carboxylic acids). It should include the functional group, examples that are listed in the specification with names and displayed formulae, and the general formula.	**Support:** Split the class into four groups and give each group a different homologous series to complete. Each group can share their information on the board allowing the class to make a complete record.	

Homework		
Students complete the WebQuest where they research the use of organic molecules in perfumes. Alternatively, ask students to draw the displayed formulae, structural formulae, and molecular formulae for methanol, ethanol, propanol, butanol, methanoic acid, ethanoic acid, propanoic acid, butanoic acid, and ethyl ethanoate.	**Extend:** Ask students to find out how to name esters.	**WebQuest:** Smelly molecules

kerboodle

A Kerboodle highlight for this lesson is **Go further: Alcohol isomers**. Refer to the **Content map** on Kerboodle for a full list of resources and assessment.

GCSE Chemistry Only

C10.3 Reactions and uses of alcohols

AQA spec Link: 7.2.3 Students should be able to:

- describe what happens when any of the first four alcohols react with sodium, burn in air, are added to water, react with an oxidising agent
- recall the main uses of these alcohols.

Aqueous solutions of ethanol are produced when sugar solutions are fermented using yeast.

Students should know the conditions used for fermentation of sugar using yeast.

Students should be able to recognise alcohols from their names or from given formulae.

Students do not need to know the names of individual alcohols other than methanol, ethanol, propanol, and butanol.

Students are not expected to write balanced chemical equations for the reactions of alcohols other than for combustion reactions.

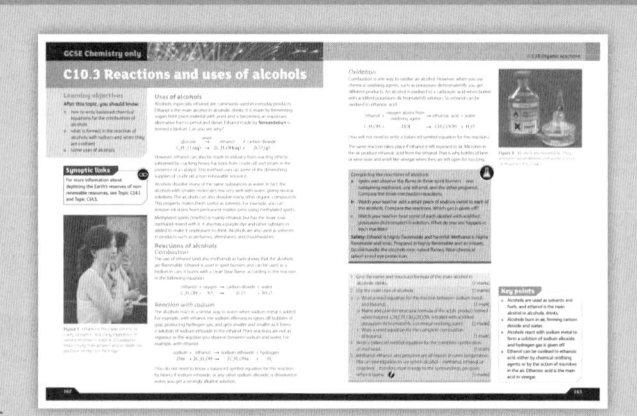

WS 2.4, 2.6, 3.1, 3.6
MS 1c

Aiming for	Outcome	Checkpoint	
		Question	Activity
Aiming for GRADE 4 ↓	State that fermentation can be used to make ethanol.		Starter 2, Plenary 1
	List some chemical properties of the first four alcohols.		Plenary 1, Homework
	Recognise the formula and structure of ethanol and state some of its uses.	1, 2	Starter 2
Aiming for GRADE 6 ↓	Describe fermentation to make aqueous solutions of ethanol, including a word equation.		Starter 2, Plenary 1
	Describe the reactions of alcohols, including using word equations.	3, End of chapter 2, 3	Starter 1, Main
	Explain the relationship between ethanol and ethanoic acid.		Main
Aiming for GRADE 8 ↓	Explain why solutions of ethanol have a pH of 7.	End of chapter 4	Main
	Describe complete combustion reactions of a range of alcohols using balanced symbol equations.	4, End of chapter 3	Starter 1, Main
	Plan an investigation to determine the relative energy transferred to the surroundings by the combustion of different alcohols.	5	Main

Maths
Students write balanced symbol equations.

Literacy
Students summarise their scientific knowledge to write a radio advert.

Key words
fermentation

Practical

Title	Comparing the reactions of alcohols
Equipment	Class practical: three spirit burners one with methanol, one with ethanol, and one with propanol, matches
	Demonstration: methanol, ethanol, and propanol, four dropping pipettes, three test tubes, test-tube rack, universal indicator, sodium metal, white tile, scalpel, three boiling tubes, boiling-tube holders, acidified potassium dichromate solution, Bunsen burner and safety equipment, eye protection

C10 Organic reactions

Overview of method	Class practical: Students light each spirit burner. They should consider how easily each spirit burner ignites, and observe the cleanness of the flame.
	Demonstration: Half fill separate test tubes with each alcohol. Add a few drops of universal indicator. Then add no more than 2 mm cube of sodium into each test tube and observe. Using a dropping pipette add about 3 cm^3 of acidified potassium dichromate to each boiling tube. Then use the other three dropping pipettes to add about 1 cm^3 of each alcohol to the separate boiling tubes. Using the boiling-tube holders, hold the boiling tubes in the blue Bunsen flame until the chemicals are boiling.
Safety considerations	Sodium is highly flammable and corrosive. Ethanol is highly flammable and harmful. Methanol is highly flammable and toxic. Propanol is highly flammable and irritant. Be very careful with the Bunsen burner flames – no naked flames near the stock bottles. Acidified potassium dichromate is toxic and oxidising. Wear chemical splash-proof eye protection. Use a fume cupboard.

Starter	Support/Extend	Resources
Alcohol equations (5 minutes) Explain to students that alcohols can be used as fuels. When alcohols are completely combusted, only carbon dioxide and water are made. Ask students to write equations for the combustion of methanol, ethanol, and propanol.	**Extend:** Ensure students write balanced symbol equations including state symbols.	
Ethanol (10 minutes) Ask students to draw the displayed formula, structural formula, and molecular formula of ethanol. Using the student book, they should find out the two methods of making ethanol industrially and note the conditions of each.	**Extend:** Ask students to write the equations to illustrate the two industrial methods for making ethanol.	

Main	Support/Extend	Resources
Comparing the reactions of alcohols (40 minutes) Ask students to design a suitable results table to note their observations. Run the class practical and the demonstration as detailed. Students should use their results to draw conclusions.	**Extend:** Students explain how the spirit burner experiment could be used to determine the relative energy released by combustion. They should predict which alcohol they think would transfer the most energy to the surroundings.	**Practical:** Comparing the reactions of alcohols

Plenary	Support/Extend	Resources
Producing ethanol (5 minutes) Provide students with statements that describe the process of fermentation to produce ethanol. Students put the statements in the correct order.		**Interactive:** Producing ethanol
They then do the same for the industrial process of producing ethanol.		
Alcohol question (10 minutes) Give students a fictitious student answer to an examination question about alcohol. Students should mark the work and add comments to explain where the candidate lost marks. Alternatively, have students answer the question then swap answers with a partner to mark and give feedback.	**Support:** Encourage students to include all the key points.	

Homework		
Students make a radio advert to sell the manufacture and use of alcohols.		

kerboodle

A Kerboodle highlight for this lesson is **Literacy skills: Uses of alcohols**. Refer to the **Content map** on Kerboodle for a full list of resources and assessment.

GCSE Chemistry Only

C10.4 Carboxylic acids and esters

AQA spec Link: 7.2.4 Students should be able to:

- describe what happens when any of the first four carboxylic acids reacts with carbonates, dissolves in water, reacts with alcohols
- **H** explain why carboxylic acids are weak acids in terms of ionisation and pH.

Students are not expected to write balanced chemical equations for the reactions of carboxylic acids.

Students do not need to know the names of esters other than ethyl ethanoate.

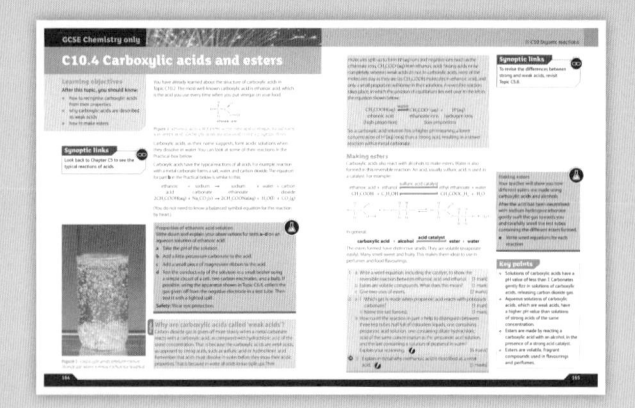

WS 2.4, 3.6
MS 1c

Aiming for	Outcome	Checkpoint	
		Question	Activity
Aiming for GRADE 4	Recognise a carboxylic acid from its name or formula.		Starter 1
	List some chemical properties of carboxylic acids.		Main 1
	Describe an ester and state some uses of this class of compounds.	1, End of chapter 5	Starter 1, Main 2
Aiming for GRADE 6	Describe why carboxylic acids are acidic.	End of chapter 7	Starter 2, Main 1, Plenary 1
	Use word equations to describe the reactions of carboxylic acids with metal carbonates and with alcohols.	End of chapter 4, 5	Main 1, Main 2
	Describe how to make an ester.	1	Main 2
Aiming for GRADE 8	Explain, using ionic equations, why carboxylic acids are weak acids.	3, End of chapter 7	Starter 2, Main 1, Plenary 1
	Predict the products of the reactions of a range of carboxylic acids with metal carbonates and with alcohols.	2, End of chapter 4, 6	Main 1
	Explain the term volatile in terms of molecular forces.	1, End of chapter 5	Plenary 2

Maths
Students calculate the percentage composition of oxygen in an ester (1c).

Literacy
Students use scientific terminology to explain experimental observations.

Practical

Title	Properties of ethanoic acid
Equipment	three test tubes, test-tube rack, 100 cm³ beaker, two graphite rods, two crocodile clips, three wires, low voltage power supply, lamp/ammeter/multimeter, eye protection, spatula, 1 cm length of magnesium ribbon, potassium carbonate powder, universal indicator solution/paper and colour chart, 0.1 mol/dm³ ethanoic acid solution
Overview of method	Half fill three test tubes with ethanoic acid solution. Add universal indicator to the first, half a spatula of potassium carbonate to the second, and one piece of magnesium ribbon to the third. Record any observations in a table. Half fill a beaker with ethanoic acid solution. Submerge the ends of the two graphite rods and then, using the wires and crocodile clips, make a series circuit with the power supply and the lamp or ammeter or multimeter. Ensure that the carbon rods do not touch, turn on the power supply, and observe to see if any current is flowing.
Safety considerations	Ethanoic acid is an irritant. Universal indicator solution and magnesium are flammable. Wear chemical splash-proof eye protection and wash hands after completing the practical.

■ C10 Organic reactions

Title	Making esters
Equipment	eye protection, test tube, dropping pipettes, 100 cm³ beaker, test tube, Bunsen burner, tripod, gauze, heatproof mat, tongs, ethanoic acid, concentrated sulfuric acid, ethanol, dilute sodium hydrogencarbonate
Overview of method	Half fill the beaker with water and place on the tripod and gauze over the Bunsen burner to make a warm water bath. In a test tube add two drops of sulfuric acid, 10 drops of ethanoic acid, and 10 drops of ethanol. Put the tube into the warm water bath, ensuring that it stands upright. Bring the water bath to the boil and allow the mixture to stand in the hot water for one minute with the flame removed. Use tongs to remove the reaction mixture if it begins to boil, and return to the hot water once cooled slightly. Use tongs to remove the tube and allow to cool. Pour the cooled mixture into a test tube half-full of sodium hydrogencarbonate solution. After effervescence has finished a layer of ester will separate and float on top of the aqueous layer.
Safety considerations	Ethanol is highly flammable and harmful. Keep ethanol away from the naked flame. Concentrated acids are corrosive and fumes are harmful. Wear chemical splash-proof eye protection.

Starter	Support/Extend	Resources
Formulae (5 minutes) Show students the displayed formulae of some carboxylic acids, alcohols, and esters. Ask them to suggest the molecular formula of each molecule and suggest the homologous series it belongs to. **Prediction** (10 minutes) Remind students that organic acids are weak acids (they partially ionise in aqueous solution). Ask students to predict their pH value and whether they would conduct electricity. They should explain their predictions.	**Extend:** Ask students to calculate the percentage composition of oxygen in each of the esters given.	

Main	Support/Extend	Resources
Properties of ethanoic acid (30 minutes) Students complete the practical as outlined. They then summarise their findings in a conclusion that explains the observations that they have made. Encourage students to write a word equation to illustrate each reaction. **Making esters** (20 minutes) Demonstrate how to make esters as detailed. This experiment will need to be carried out at the same time as students investigation into ethanoic acid. Allow students to carefully smell the products. Ask students to write a risk assessment for the experiment.	**Support:** To help students compare and contrast, demonstrate the experiment using a strong acid like hydrochloric acid before students complete their own investigation. **Extend:** Ask students to explain the role of the sulfuric acid.	**Practical:** Properties of ethanoic acid

Plenary	Support/Extend	Resources
Explaining pH (5 minutes) Ask students to explain why 10 cm³ of 0.1 mol/dm³ ethanoic acid will have a lower pH than the same volume and concentration of sulfuric acid. **Chemical tests** (10 minutes) Ask students to think about the functional groups of all the homologous series that they have studied and their classic chemical reactions. Students then sort chemical tests into which homologous series they can be used to test for.		**Interactive:** Chemical tests

Homework		
Students create a revision tool for the four homologous series they have studied – alkanes, alkenes, alcohols, and carboxylic acids		

kerboodle

A Kerboodle highlight for this lesson is **Literacy sheet: carboxylic acids and esters**. Refer to the **Content map** on Kerboodle for a full list of resources and assessment.

165

C10 Organic reactions

Overview of C10 Organic reactions

In this chapter, students have learnt about more organic functional groups – alkenes, alcohols, carboxylic acids, and esters. Students should be able to identify, name, and draw the structural formula of the first four alkenes, alcohols, and carboxylic acids, and should be able to identify, name, and draw the ester ethyl ethanoate.

Students have also learnt about the reactions of these four functional groups. They should be able to describe the reactions and conditions of alkenes (with halogens, water, and hydrogen), alcohols (combustion, oxidation, and reaction with sodium), and carboxylic acids (to make esters). Students should also be able to explain why carboxylic acids are called weak acids, referencing back to their understanding from *Chapter C5*.

MyMaths

You can find additional support for the maths skills covered in this chapter on **MyMaths**, including representing 3D structures using 2D models.

kerboodle

For this chapter, the following assessments are available on Kerboodle:

C10 Checkpoint quiz: Organic reactions
C10 Progress quiz: Organic reactions 1
C10 Progress quiz: Organic reactions 2
C10 On your marks: Organic reactions
C10 Exam-style questions and mark scheme: Organic reactions

Checkpoint follow up lesson

A student's route through this lesson can be determined using the Checkpoint assessment. Percentage pass marks are supplied in the Checkpoint teacher notes.

For each successive route through it is assumed that the student can perform to their current route as well as previous routes. For example, students working at Aiming for 6 are assumed to be secure in Aiming for 4 knowledge and understanding and working towards achieving all the learning outcomes for Aiming for 6.

	Target 4	Target 6	Target 8
Learning outcomes	Identify alcohol, alkene, carboxylic acid, and ester functional groups.	Name and draw examples of alcohols and carboxylic acids.	Describe the reactions and products of alkenes, alcohols, carboxylic acids.
	State the products of one reaction of an alcohol, alkene, and a carboxylic acid.	Name the general products of the reactions of alkenes, alcohols, and carboxylic acids.	
Starter	**Identify yourself (10 minutes)** Give each student a sticky note that say alkene, alcohol, carboxylic acid, or ester on them. Make sure students do not see the sticky note (e.g., stick onto foreheads or backs). Students then walk around the classroom and pose questions to each other to try and find out the homologous series they belong to. Explain they are only allowed to ask yes or no questions and they are not allowed to ask 'Am I an alkene?' etc. Once students have decided, they should stand in an area of the classroom that has been labelled with the name of each functional group. Ask each group to check their labels and see if they were correct. If not, move to the appropriate labelled area. Each group should work together to come up with a list of key facts that helped them identify the homologous series they belonged to. Display these lists, as they will be returned to in the plenary.		
Differentiated checkpoint activity	The Aiming for 4 Checkpoint follow-up sheet provides highly-structured questions that could be used as a cut and stick for producing a poster.	Students use the Aiming for 6 Checkpoint follow-up sheet to create a series of fact sheets on each functional group studied in the chapter. The sheet provides prompt questions to guide students with what should be included on their fact sheets.	Students use Aiming for 8 Checkpoint follow-up sheet to create a poster on the four functional groups studied in the chapter. Minimal support is provided and students should be working independently.
	Kerboodle resource C10 Checkpoint follow up: Aiming for 4, C10 Checkpoint follow up: Aiming for 6, C10 Checkpoint follow up: Aiming for 8		
Plenary	**List review (10 minutes)** Students return to their lists from the starter. They need to review the list and decide if their original ideas were correct, or how they should be corrected. Students should also add extra facts they have found out from the Checpoint activity. Discuss as a class, addressing any misconceptions or mistakes. Remove the lists and write on the board the four functional groups. Ask students to provide links between the words.		
Progression	Students should attempt to write word equations and conditions for the reactions they include.	Students write a brief method for carrying out each reaction they include on their fact sheet. They should also attempt to include any relevant balanced symbol equations.	Students write a detailed method for carrying out each reaction they include on their poster, including considerations of any safety precautions.

C 11 Polymers
11.1 Addition polymerisation

GCSE Chemistry only

AQA spec Link: 7.3.1 Alkenes can be used to make polymers such as poly(ethene) and poly(propene) by addition polymerisation.

In addition polymerisation reactions, many small molecules (monomers) join together to form very large molecules (polymers).

For example:

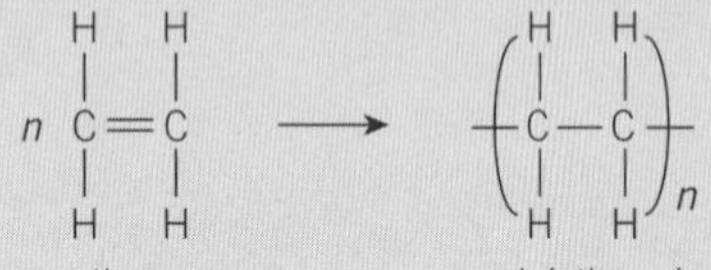

$$n \begin{array}{c} H \\ | \\ C= \\ | \\ H \end{array} \begin{array}{c} H \\ | \\ C \\ | \\ H \end{array} \longrightarrow \left(\begin{array}{cc} H & H \\ | & | \\ -C-C- \\ | & | \\ H & H \end{array} \right)_n$$

ethene → poly(ethene)

WS 1.2
MS 5b

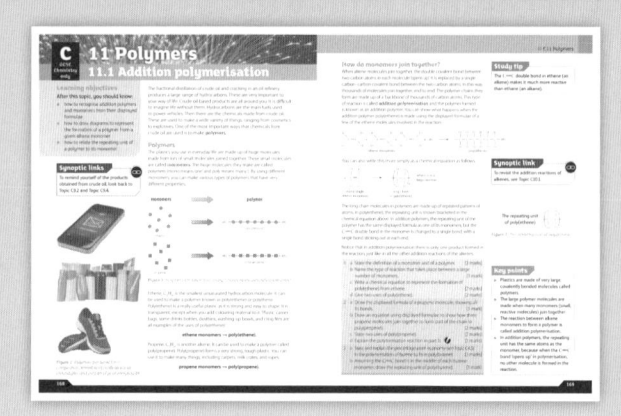

In addition polymers the repeating unit has the same atoms as the monomer because no other molecule is formed in the reaction.

Students should be able to:

- recognise addition polymers and monomers from diagrams in the forms shown and from the presence of the functional group C=C in the monomers
- draw diagrams to represent the formation of a polymer from a given alkene monomer
- relate the repeating unit to the monomer.

Aiming for	Outcome	Checkpoint	
		Question	Activity
Aiming for GRADE 4	Define a monomer and a polymer.	1	Main 1, Main 2
	State some uses of poly(ethene) and poly(propene).	1, 3	Main 2
	Write a word equation for the formation of poly(ethene) and poly(propene).	1, End of chapter 1	Main 1
Aiming for GRADE 6	Describe how monomers become polymers.	1, 3, End of chapter 1	Main 1
	Draw the monomer for an addition polymer when the structure of the polymer is given.	End of chapter 3	Main 2, Plenary 2
	Draw an addition polymer structure when the structure of the monomer is given.	End of chapter 5	Main 2, Plenary 2
Aiming for GRADE 8	Explain why monomers for addition polymers must be unsaturated.	2	Main 1
	Explain the process of addition polymerisation in detail, including using balanced symbol equations and the concept of atom economy.	1, 3, 4, End of chapter 2	Main 1, Main 2, Plenary 2
	Explain how the repeating unit of a polymer relates to the monomer.	4, End of chapter 3, 5	Main 2, Plenary 2

Maths
Students visualise 2D and 3D models to identify monomers and polymers (5b).

Literacy
Students explain how a polymer can be represented by a model.

Key words
monomers, polymers, addition polymerisation

■ C11 Polymers

Starter	Support/Extend	Resources
Alkenes (5 minutes) Ask students to draw the displayed structural formula of ethene and propene. **Paper clip polymers** (10 minutes) Explain that polymerisation is the chemical reaction where small molecules known as monomers become one long molecule known as a polymer. Ask students to use paperclips to model polymerisation. Circulate around the classroom giving hints and tips and then choose one group to demonstrate their model. Students should state that each paper clip is a monomer and then join them together to make a chain. The joining is polymerisation and the resulting chain is a polymer.	**Support:** Give students the molecular formula for these compounds.	

Main	Support/Extend	Resources
Modelling addition polymerisation (20 minutes) Ask each student to use a molecular modelling kit to make a molecule of ethene. Then explain that under high pressure and with a catalyst one bond from the C=C breaks open and two monomers join together. Get students to do this in pairs, then to join with others until the whole class has made one long model. Using question and answer, build up the structures of the monomer and polymer and make an equation. Then repeat the process with poly(propene).	**Extend:** Ask students to suggest and evaluate their own model of a polymer.	
Polymer table (20 minutes) Ask students to draw a table with five columns (monomer name, monomer structure, polymer name, polymer structure, uses). They then use the student book to complete the table for poly(ethene) and poly(propene).	**Extend:** Include other addition polymers such as PVC and PTFE.	**Activity:** Polymer table

Plenary	Support/Extend	Resources
Drawing addition polymers (10 minutes) Provide students with a series of alkene monomers and polymers. Ask students to draw the polymer or monomer that formed the polymer.	**Extend:** Ask students to write equations for the polymerisation of the monomers studied.	
Poly(tetrafluoroethene) (10 minutes) Show students a section of poly(tetrafluoroethene) made of at least three monomers. Students identify the structure of the monomer, the repeating unit of the polymer, and state the type of polymerisation used. Then show students but-2-ene and ask them to identify the polymer.	**Support:** Draw the structure of but-2-ene next to the structure of ethene and poly(ethene) to help students identify the similarities.	**Interactive:** Poly(tetrafluoroethene)

Homework		
Some scientists think that a necklace made of beads is a good model for a polymer. Ask students to explain how this can model a polymerisation reaction.	**Extend:** Ask students to evaluate this model.	

kerboodle

A Kerboodle highlight for this lesson is **Maths skills: Drawing addition polymers**. Refer to the **Content map** on Kerboodle for a full list of resources and assessment.

GCSE Chemistry Only — Higher tier

C11.2 Condensation polymerisation

AQA spec Link: 7.3.2 Condensation polymerisation involves monomers with two functional groups. When these types of monomers react they join together, usually losing small molecules such as water, and so the reactions are called condensation reactions.

The simplest polymers are produced from two different monomers with two of the same functional groups on each monomer.

For example: ethane diol

HO — CH$_2$ — CH$_2$ — OH

or   HO — ☐ — OH

and hexanedioic acid

HOOC — CH$_2$ — CH$_2$ — CH$_2$ — CH$_2$ — COOH

or   HOOC — ☐ — COOH

polymerise to produce a polyester:

n HO — ☐ — OH + n HOOC — ☐ — COOH → -(- ☐ — OOC — ☐ — COO -)-$_n$ + 2nH$_2$O

Students should be able to explain the basic principles of condensation polymerisation by reference to the functional groups in the monomers and the repeating units in the polymers.

WS 1.2
MS 5b

Aiming for	Outcome	Checkpoint	
		Question	Activity
Aiming for GRADE 6	Describe condensation polymerisation.		Main 1, Main 2
	Draw a simplified structure of the monomers for a condensation polymer when the structure of the polymer is given.	End of chapter 4	Main 1, Main 2
	Draw a simplified structure of a condensation polymer when the structure of the monomers are given.	End of chapter 4	Main 1, Main 2
Aiming for GRADE 8	Predict the products of condensation polymerisation.	4	Main 1
	Explain the process of condensation polymerisation in detail, including using equations.	2, 3, 4, End of chapter 4	Starter 1, Starter 2, Main 1, Main 2
	Compare and contrast in detail, giving appropriate examples, the two methods of polymerisation.	1	Plenary 1

Maths
Students visualise 2D models to identify monomers and polymers (5b).

Literacy
Students make a presentation about condensation polymers.

Practical

Title	Making nylon
Equipment	micro-beaker, plastic forceps, glass rod, 0.4 mol/dm^3 1,6-diaminohexane (labelled A), 0.15 mol/dm^3 decanedioyl dichloride solution dissolved in hexane (labelled B)
Overview of method	Carefully add about 1 cm depth of solution A to the micro-beaker. Very gently pour a similar depth of solution B into the beaker (it will float and make a two-phase liquid). Put the forceps tips to the bottom of the beaker and draw up slowly through the layers. At the interface, the nylon strand will form and can be pulled up out of the liquid. Drape the end of the strand over the glass rod and rotate the glass rod to continue to draw out the nylon.
Safety considerations	1,6-diaminohexane (solution A) and Decanedioyl dichloride (solution B) are corrosive and hexane (solutionb B) is highly flammable and harmful. Wear eye protection and nitrile gloves whilst completing the practical in a well-ventilated lab. Do not touch the nylon unless it has been washed well under cold running water.

C11 Polymers

Starter	Support/Extend	Resources
Esters (5 minutes) Students complete the interactive to describe what esters are and how they are made. then use the interactive to introduce condensation polymerisation. Students sort statements according to whether they describe addition polymerisation or condensation polymerisation.		**Interactive:** Esters
Interpreting formulae (10 minutes) Show students the structural formulae for hexanoic acid and ethane diol. Ask students to replace any hydrocarbon sections with a rectangle. Then ask them to classify which homologous series each molecule belongs to.	**Extend:** Ask students to suggest why this model is useful when considering polymerisation.	

Main	Support/Extend	Resources
Making nylon (25 minutes) After discussing the formation of polyester, as outlined in the student book, ask students to suggest what would happen if a basic $-NH_2$ group reacted with a carboxylic acid. Ask students to draw a simplified structure of diaminohexane and decanedioic acid. Demonstrate the nylon rope trick as detailed in the practical box. Ask students to then write an equation to describe the reaction they have observed.	**Extend:** Ask students to write a balanced symbol equation for the reaction.	**Practical:** Making nylon
Condensation polymers (15 minutes) Split the class into groups of four. Each group should make a three-minute presentation about condensation polymerisation. Ensure all students participate by assigning roles within the groups – one person should talk generally about the topic, one person about polyesters, a third person about polyamides, and one person concluding.		

Plenary	Support/Extend	Resources
Addition versus condensation (5 minutes) Ask students to draw a table which compares and contrasts addition and condensation polymerisation. Their table should include examples of each.	**Support:** Give students the types of information that they should include.	
Presentations (10 minutes) Choose a few groups to give their presentations from Main 2. Alternatively, pair up groups and have them present to each other.	**Extend:** Students give one piece of positive feedback and one improvement.	

Homework		
Students complete the WebQuest where they research a specific polymer and how it is produced. They use their research to produce an information leaflet for a materials company.		**WebQuest:** Polymers
Alternatively, ask students to draw a flow chart to explain how nylon can be made.		

kerboodle

A Kerboodle highlight for this lesson is **Bump up your grade: Condensation and addition polymers**. Refer to the **Content map** on Kerboodle for a full list of resources and assessment.

GCSE Chemistry Only

C11.3 Natural polymers

AQA spec Link: 7.3.3 (H) Amino acids have two different functional groups in a molecule. Amino acids react by condensation polymerisation to produce polypeptides.

For example, glycine is H_2NCH_2COOH and polymerises to produce the polypeptide $(-HNCH_2COO-)_n$ and nH_2O
Different amino acids can be combined in the same chain to produce proteins.

7.3.4 Other naturally occurring polymers important for life include proteins, starch, and cellulose.

Students should be able to name the types of monomers from which these naturally occurring polymers are made.

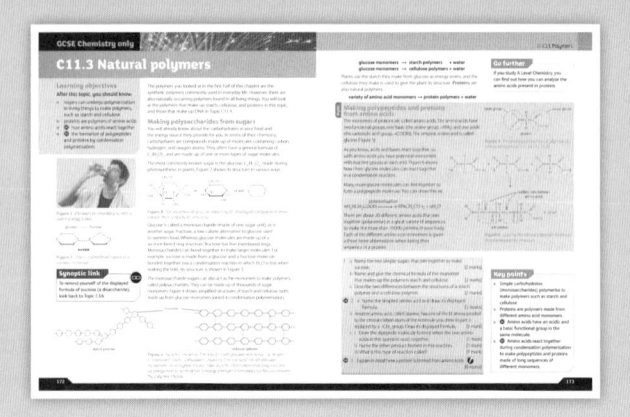

WS 1.4
MS 5b

Aiming for	Outcome	Checkpoint	
		Question	Activity
Aiming for GRADE 4	State an example of a natural polymer.		Starter 1, Main 1, Main 2
	Describe the relationship between sugar as a monomer and starch or cellulose as a polymer.	1	Starter 1, Main 1, Main 2
	Describe the relationship between amino acids as a monomer and protein as a polymer.		Plenary 1
Aiming for GRADE 6	Identify the monomer from the structural formula of a polymer.	2	Starter 2, Main 1, Main 2, Plenary 2
	(H) Describe the structure of an amino acid.		Main 1, Main 2
Aiming for GRADE 8	(H) Predict the products of condensation polymerisation using natural monomers.	2, End of chapter 6	Starter 2, Main 1, Main 2
	Explain in detail the process of condensation polymerisation with natural monomers, including using equations.	2, 3, End of chapter 6	Main 1
	(H) Explain how amino acids react together in an acid–base reaction.		Plenary 1

Maths
Students visualise 2D models to identify monomers and polymers (5b).

Literacy
Students write an article about natural condensation polymers.

Key word
proteins

C11 Polymers

Starter	Support/Extend	Resources
Starch and sugar (5 minutes) Give students a small piece of bread when they enter the classroom. Ask them to keep chewing for about three minutes and then describe the taste (becomes sweet as the amylase in the saliva breaks the starch down into sugars). Be aware of any students with allergies.	**Extend:** Ask students to write an equation to illustrate the reaction.	
Predicting (10 minutes) **H** Show students the structural formula of glycine. Ask them to circle the acidic group in red and the basic group in blue. Explain that this is a monomer for a condensation polymer. Ask students to suggest the structure of the polymer.	**Support:** Remind students of the peptide links that they discovered in their work on nylon.	

Main	Support/Extend	Resources
Polymer flick book (20 minutes) Students produce a flick book showing how separate molecules make a natural polymer. Students make a series of images on thin card about 10 cm². Each image should be slightly different. Stack the images and hold the top left-hand corner on the edge of a table. Flick through the book at the bottom right-hand corner and this should create an animation of the reaction. Foundation-tier students should focus on starch or cellulose. **H** Higher-tier students should show how two glycine molecules first react in an acid–base reaction to form a polypeptide, then how the polypeptide further reacts to form a polymer.	**Extend:** Some students may have advanced computing skills and be able to make a computer animation.	
Natural condensation polymers (20 minutes) Ask students to write a small feature article for a science magazine about the importance of natural condensation polymers. **H** Higher-tier students should discuss polypeptides, and include an equation to show how a polypeptide is formed.	**Support:** Give students a writing frame to help them form their article. Students should define the terms polymer, monomer, and polymerisation in their work, and describe with examples of a natural polymer.	**Activity:** Natural condensation polymers

Plenary	Support/Extend	Resources
Classifying polymers (5 minutes) Show students the structures of polypeptides, amino acids, monosaccharides, and polysaccharides. Ask students to classify them based on their structures. Then show students a series of polymers for them to identify the structure of the monomer(s). **LO diagram** (10 minutes) Ask students to copy each learning objective from the student book and then illustrate each one with a labelled diagram.	**Support:** Give students the functional group(s) that are required for each classification.	**Interactive:** Classifying polymers

Homework		
Ask students to write general equations to show how polysaccharides and proteins are formed. Students should highlight the functional group reacting and use colours to show how a small molecule is released when the polymerisation occurs.		

kerboodle

A Kerboodle highlight for this lesson is **Literacy sheet: Natural polymers**. Refer to the **Content map** on Kerboodle for a full list of resources and assessment.

173

GCSE Chemistry Only

C11.4 DNA

AQA spec Link: 7.3.4 DNA (deoxyribonucleic acid) is a large molecule essential for life. DNA encodes genetic instructions for the development and functioning of living organisms and viruses.

Most DNA molecules are two polymer chains, made from four different monomers called nucleotides, in the form of a double helix.

Students should be able to name the types of monomers from which these naturally occurring polymers are made.

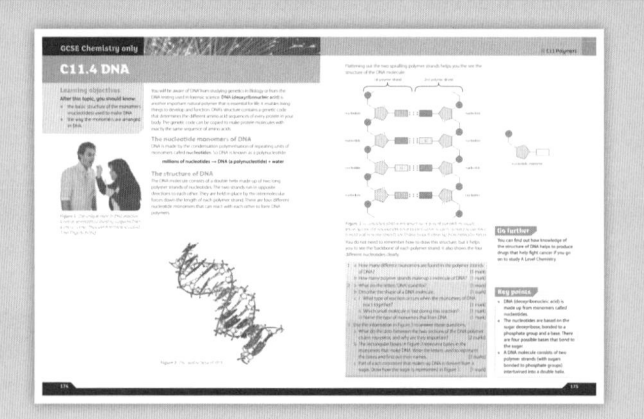

WS 1.2, 2.4
MS 1c

Aiming for	Outcome (Level)	Checkpoint	
		Question	Activity
Aiming for GRADE 4 ↓	State that DNA is an example of a natural polymer.		Starter 1
	State what DNA stands for.	2	Starter 1
	Name the type of monomers used to make DNA.	1, End of chapter 7	Starter 2
Aiming for GRADE 6 ↓	Describe the main structure of DNA.	1, 2, End of chapter 7	Starter 2, Main
	Describe the importance of DNA for living systems.		Plenary 1
	Sketch the shape of a DNA strand.		Starter 1, Starter 2, Main
Aiming for GRADE 8 ↓	Explain the shape of the DNA polymer.	3, End of chapter 7	Starter 2, Main
	Explain how nucleotides form DNA.	2, End of chapter 7	Main
	Explain the purpose of DNA.		Main

Maths
Students calculate the percentage composition of DNA in a kiwi fruit (1c).

Literacy
Students explain the sample from the practical.

Key words
DNA (deoxyribonucleic acid), nucleotides

Practical

Title	Extracting DNA from kiwifruit
Equipment	blender, kiwi fruit, sodium chloride, sieve, washing-up liquid, protease (e.g., meat tenderiser), water bath at 60 °C, test tube, ice bath, ice cold ethanol, glass rod, eye protection, 250 cm³ conical flask, tablespoon, paper towel
Overview of method	Peel a kiwi fruit and blend with a little sodium chloride and water until it is a viscous paste. Sieve and collect the liquid into a conical flask. Add two tablespoons of washing-up liquid and swirl to mix then leave for 10 minutes in the warm water bath. Half fill a test tube with the mixture and add the protease. Tilt your test tube to 45° and slowly pour in well-chilled ethanol so that a layer is formed on top of the mixture. The white clumps are DNA which can be collected using the glass rod and dried on a paper towel.
Safety considerations	Ethanol is highly flammable and harmful. Protease is harmful. Wear eye protection and wash hands after the practical.

174

C11 Polymers

Starter	Support/Extend	Resources
Model (5 minutes) Show students a model of DNA and ask them to suggest what they are studying in the lesson. Encourage students to share any information they already know about DNA. **Label DNA** (10 minutes) Ask students to use the student book to label a diagram of a DNA double helix with the key parts.	**Extend:** Ask students to describe each part of the diagram.	**Interactive:** Label DNA

Main	Support/Extend	Resources
Extracting DNA from kiwifruit (40 minutes) Ask students to extract the DNA from kiwifruit. Allow students to dry their sample and use sticky tape to fix it into their notes. They then write a paragraph to explain what the sample is made from. Students should the sketch the shape of the DNA molecule that they have extracted from the kiwifruit. They annotate to describe the structure and highlight the nucleotides and the two separate polymer chains.	**Extend:** Take the mass of the kiwifruit that is used and the mass of the DNA collected. Then an estimation of percentage composition can be calculated.	**Practical:** Extracting DNA from kiwifruit

Plenary	Support/Extend	Resources
Summarise and condense (5 minutes) Ask students to summarise the lesson in three sentences, then to reflect on them and to further summarise into one sentence, and finally into three words. **DNA exam** (10 minutes) Give students a 5-mark question about DNA. Allow them five minutes to tackle it, then reveal the mark scheme and ask students to mark their own work.	**Support:** Use a question from a foundation-tier paper. **Extend:** Add time pressure by giving students an 8-mark question but only five minutes to answer.	

Homework		
Ask students to define the term protease (link with Biology). Then ask them to predict the effect of protease on DNA. Students should then suggest why protease is needed to extract the DNA from the kiwi fruit.		

kerboodle
A Kerboodle highlight for this lesson is **Go further: Anti-cancer drugs**. Refer to the **Content map** on Kerboodle for a full list of resources and assessment.

C11 Polymers

Overview of C11 Polymers

In this chapter, students have learnt about different types of manufactured polymers, including addition polymers and condensation polymers. Students should be able to identify an addition polymer from polymer and monomer diagrams – drawing the monomer from the polymer and the polymer from the monomer. Students have been introduced explicitly to poly(ethene) but it is important that they can identify and draw other addition polymers and associated monomers. Higher-tier students should also be able to describe the basic principles of condensation polymerisation.

Students have also studied natural polymers, including polysaccharides, proteins, and DNA. Students should be able to identify the types of monomers that form these polymers, and be able to describe the basic structure of DNA. Higher-tier students should understand in greater detail how amino acids react together to form proteins.

With all polymers, students should understand the difference between the monomer and the repeating unit of the polymer.

MyMaths

You can find additional support for the maths skills covered in this chapter on **MyMaths**, including representing 3D structures using 2D models.

kerboodle

For this chapter, the following assessments are available on Kerboodle:

C11 Checkpoint quiz: Polymers
C11 Progress quiz: Polymers 1
C11 Progress quiz: Polymers 2
C11 On your marks: Polymers
C11 Exam-style questions and mark scheme: Polymers

Checkpoint follow up lesson

A student's route through this lesson can be determined using the Checkpoint assessment. Percentage pass marks are supplied in the Checkpoint teacher notes.

For each successive route through it is assumed that the student can perform to their current route as well as previous routes. For example, students working at Aiming for 6 are assumed to be secure in Aiming for 4 knowledge and understanding and working towards achieving all the learning outcomes for Aiming for 6.

	Aiming for 4	Aiming for 6	Aiming for 8
Learning outcomes	Describe how addition polymerisation occurs.	Describe in detail how addition polymerisation occurs.	Compare addition and condensation polymerisation.
	Identify a repeating unit within a polymer.	Identify repeating units and monomers for given polymers.	
Starter	**Identifying polymers (5 minutes)** Display images of products made from and containing polymers. Ask pupils if they know the polymers present. Come up with a list of polymer names and ask students if they can categorise them into natural or artificial polymers. **Defining key terms (5 minutes)** Ask students to work in pairs to define the following terms: • monomer • polymer • repeating unit • addition polymerisation. Ask pairs to provide their definitions, and tell students they will return to these at the end of the lesson.		
Differentiated checkpoint activity	Students use the Aiming for 4 Checkpoint follow-up sheet to model polymers. Students will need to be supported as they model addition polymerisation and each step will need to be discussed. You will need to ensure they carry each step out correctly. Students will need: • modelling clay in two colours • two different colours of pipe cleaners • two pieces of string • pair of scissors. Warn students that cut pipe cleaners can have sharp ends.	Students use the Aiming for 6 Checkpoint follow-up sheet to model polymers. They use their model to draw a series of diagrams to explain the addition polymerisation of ethene. Students will need to have enough space to carry out a role play.	Students use Aiming for 8 Checkpoint follow-up sheet to produce a detailed comparison of addition polymerisation and condensation polymerisation. This can be done as a prose or as a poster, in which case they will need to be provided with poster materials.
	Kerboodle resource C11 Checkpoint follow up: Aiming for 4, C11 Checkpoint follow up: Aiming for 6, C11 Checkpoint follow up: Aiming for 8		
Plenary	**Revisiting definitions (10 minutes)** Ask pairs to look at the displayed definitions they generated in the starter and decide if the definitions were correct or incorrect. For correct definitions they should add any further detail they can and for incorrect definitions, they should adapt them accordingly. Share the definitions as a group and address any misconceptions that have arisen.		
Progression	Students should attempt to write an equation to represent the polymerisation of ethene.	Provide students with other monomers and addition polymers, such as but-2-ene and poly(pent-3-ene). Students identify the polymer and monomer, and write an equation for the polymerisation.	Provide students with examples of addition and condensation polymers and have students identify which type, the monomer, and write an equation for the polymerisation without their notes.

4 Analysis and the Earth's resources

Specification links

Topic		Paper
2.2	How bonding and structure are related to the properties of substances	Paper 1
8.1	Purity, formulations, and chromatography	Paper 2
8.2	Identification of common gases	Paper 2
8.3	Identification of ions by chemical and spectroscopic means	Paper 2
9.1	The composition and evolution of the Earth's atmosphere	Paper 2
9.2	Carbon dioxide and methane s greenhouse gases	Paper 2
9.3	Common atmospheric pollutants and their sources	Paper 2
10.1	Using the Earth's resources and obtaining potable water	Paper 2
10.2	Life cycle assessment and recycling	Paper 2
10.3	Using materials	Paper 2
10.4	The Haber process and the use of NPK fertilisers	Paper 2

Required practicals

Practical	skills	Topic
Investigate how paper chromatography can be used to separate and tell the difference between coloured substances. Students should calculate R_f values.	AT 1 – use of appropriate apparatus to make and record a range of measurements accurately. AT 4 – safe use of a range of equipment to purify and/or separate chemical mixtures including chromatography.	C12.2
Use of chemical tests to identify the ions in unknown single ionic compounds.	AT 1 – safe use of a Bunsen burner. AT 8 – use of appropriate qualitative reagents and techniques to analyse and identify unknown samples or products including gas tests, flame tests, precipitation reactions.	C12.5
Analysis and purification of water samples from different sources, including pH, dissolved solids, and distillation.	AT 2 – safe use of appropriate heating devices and techniques including use of a Bunsen burner and a water bath or electric heater. AT 3 – use of appropriate apparatus and techniques for the measurement of pH in different situations. AT 4 – safe use of a range of equipment to purify and/or separate chemical mixtures including evaporation, distillation.	C14.2

Maths skills

Skill		Topic
1a	Recognise and use expressions in decimal form.	C12.2, C14.5, C15.2, C15.5, C15.6
1b	Recognise and use expressions in standard form.	C14.1
1c	Use ratios, fractions and percentages.	C12.1, C12.2, C12.5, C13.2, C14.4, C14.5, C15.2, C15.5, C15.6, C15.7
1d	Make estimates of the results of simple calculations.	C12.2, C14.5
2a	Use an appropriate number of significant figures.	C12.2, C14.5
2b	Find arithmetic means.	C14.5
2c	Construct and interpret frequency tables and diagrams, bar charts and histograms.	C13.1, C13.2, C14.1, C14.2
2h	Make order of magnitude calculations.	C14.1
3a	Understand and use the symbols: $=, <, \ll, \gg, >, \propto, \sim$.	C12.1
3c	Substitute numerical values into algebraic equations using appropriate units for physical quantities.	C12.1
4a	Translate information between graphical and numeric form.	C13.2, C14.1, C14.5
4c	Plot two variables from experimental or other data.	C13.2

C4 Analysis and the Earth's resources

KS3 concept	GCSE topic	Checkpoint	Revision
Pure substances have only one type of particle present, mixtures have more than one substance chemically joined together.	C12.1 Pure substances and mixtures	Ask students to explain why distilled water is pure but tap water is not.	Provide students with a selection of particle model diagrams and they sort them into pure and impure.
A single spot on a chromatogram represents one chemical. Identical chromatograms are formed by the same chemical. The solvent chosen must dissolve the mixture.	C12.2 Analysing chromatograms	Give students a chromatogram and ask them to list all the information that they can gain from it.	Allow students to complete simple paper chromatography of three pens – two are the same. Discuss what can be concluded from the chromatogram.
Recall the simple laboratory gas tests for hydrogen, carbon dioxide and oxygen.	C12.3 Testing for gases	Ask students to make an index card with the outline method for testing the three gases.	Give students a matching exercise. They should match the outline method, labelled diagram, name of gas and formula of gas together.
State the main gases in dry air and suggest the percentage composition of these gases in dry air.	C13.1 History of our atmosphere	Students should write their own crossword to cover the composition of dry air.	Give students data in a table for the composition of dry air. Ask them to display this information as a pie chart, bar chart and convert between ppm, decimal and percentage composition.
Describe the carbon cycle on Earth.	C13.3 Greenhouse gases	Ask students to create a poster about the carbon cycle.	Give students an outline of the carbon cycle and a list of the processes for them to add to the diagram.
Explain how the production of carbon dioxide by humans is having an effect on climate change.	C13.4 Global climate change	Ask students write a Tweet to summarise where carbon dioxide is coming from and the effect it has on climate change.	Give students an article about climate change. Ask them to read it and summarise it in no more than 50 words.
Describe the difference between finite and renewable resources and give an example of each.	C14.1 Finite and renewable resources	Students should define finite and renewable resources and give an example of each.	Give students a selection of resources and the definition for finite and renewable resources. Students should then draw a table sorting out the information into types of resources.
Recall the general properties of polymers.	C15.3 Properties of polymers.	Ask students to look around the classroom and list three uses of polymers and which properties make them suitable for the function.	Give students a prose with a selection of missing words. Students should complete the prose which then states the properties of polymers.

C 12 Chemical analysis
12.1 Pure substances and mixtures

AQA spec Link: 8.1.1 In chemistry, a pure substance is a single element or compound, not mixed with any other substance.

Pure elements and compounds melt and boil at specific temperatures. Melting point and boiling point data can be used to distinguish pure substances from mixtures.

In everyday language, a pure substance can mean a substance that has had nothing added to it, so it is unadulterated and in its natural state, for example, pure milk.

Students should be able to use melting point and boiling point data to distinguish pure from impure substances.

8.1.2 A formulation is a mixture that has been designed as a useful product. Many products are complex mixtures in which each chemical has a particular purpose. Formulations are made by mixing the components in carefully measured quantities to ensure that the product has the required properties. Formulations include fuels, cleaning agents, paints, medicines, alloys, fertilisers, and foods.

Students should be able to identify formulations given appropriate information.

Students do not need to know the names of components in proprietary products.

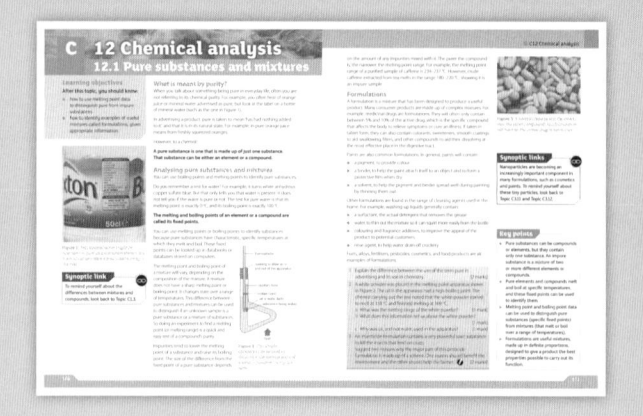

WS 1.4, 2.2, 4.1
MS 1c, 3a, 3c

Aiming for	Outcome	Checkpoint	
		Question	Activity
Aiming for GRADE 4	State what a pure substance is.	1	Starter 2
	Describe how melting point and boiling point data can be used to identify pure substances.	2	Main, Plenary 1, Plenary 2
	State what a formulation is.	End of chapter 1	Starter 2, Main, Plenary 2
Aiming for GRADE 6	Describe the difference between pure substances, impure substances, and formulations.	1	Starter 1, Starter 2, Main, Plenary 2
	Explain how melting point and boiling point data can be used to determine the purity of a substance.	2	Main, Plenary 1
	State uses of formulations.		Main, Homework
Aiming for GRADE 8	Justify the classification of pure substances, impure substances, and formulations when data is supplied.		Starter 1
	Explain in detail the use of formulations.	3, End of chapter 1	Main, Homework
	Calculate percentage composition of components in a range of formulations.	End of chapter 1	Plenary 1

Maths
Students calculate the percentage composition of components in a formulation (1c) and use a data book to identify a chemical from its melting point and boiling point data.

Literacy
Students define the key terms from this lesson.

180

C12 Chemical analysis

Starter	Support/Extend	Resources
Pure or impure (5 minutes) Give students sealed samples of chemicals and ask them to sort them into groups of pure and impure.	**Extend:** Ask students to sort the impure chemicals into a subgroup of formulations.	
Mixture definitions (10 minutes) Ask students to use the student book to define the following terms: pure, impure, formulation, melting point, and boiling point.	**Support:** Give students the definitions and the key words so that they can match them.	**Interactive:** Mixture definitions

Main	Support/Extend	Resources
Aspirin (40 minutes) Explain to students that pure aspirin can be synthesised in the lab and has a melting point of 136 °C but over-the-counter pain killer medication containing aspirin is a formulation. Ask students to suggest and justify the components in the tablet, for example, binding agents to stick the tablet together, flavours to make it taste nicer, colours to make it distinctive, and bulking agents so that it is big enough to take easily. Then ask students to suggest how the melting point of an aspirin tablet would compare to the pure compound and why. Show students a data book of melting point and boiling point data. Give students some melting point and boiling point data and ask them to identify each chemical.	**Extend:** Show students how to use melting point apparatus and allow them to take the melting point of a crushed aspirin tablet. **Support:** Give students a table containing data for only five chemicals. **Extend:** Give students larger ranges and ask them to suggest if the chemical is pure or impure and to justify their conclusion.	**Activity:** Aspirin

Plenary	Support/Extend	Resources
Percentage composition of aspirin (5 minutes) Give students some empty packets of aspirin. Ask them to work out the percentage of aspirin in a tablet and in a dose. **A pure visual summary** (10 minutes) Students make a visual summary to show how pure substances, impure substances, and formulations are related.	**Support:** Allow students to work in pairs. **Extend:** Ask students to include all the information from the key points.	

Homework		
Ask students to find an example of a formulation in their home. They should look at the contents and suggest which are the active parts and identify any additives that they recognise.		

C12.2 Analysing chromatograms

AQA spec Link: 8.1.3 Chromatography can be used to separate mixtures and can give information to help identify substances. Chromatography involves a stationary phase and a mobile phase. Separation depends on the distribution of substances between the phases.

The ratio of the distance moved by a compound (centre of spot from origin) to the distance moved by the solvent can be expressed as its R_f value:

$$R_f = \frac{\text{distance moved by substance}}{\text{distance moved by solvent}}$$

Different compounds have different R_f values in different solvents, which can be used to help identify the compounds. The compounds in a mixture may separate into different spots depending on the solvent but a pure compound will produce a single spot in all solvents.

Students should be able to:
- explain how paper chromatography separates mixtures
- suggest how chromatographic methods can be used for distinguishing pure substances from impure substances
- interpret chromatograms and determine R_f values from chromatograms.
- provide answers to an appropriate number of significant figures.

Required practical: Investigate how paper chromatography can be used to separate and tell the difference between coloured substances. Students should calculate R_f values.

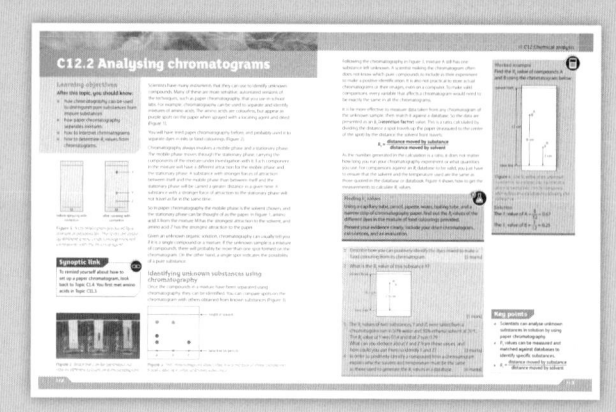

WS 2.2, 3.1, 2, 3
MS 1a, 1c, 1d, 2a

Aiming for	Outcome	Checkpoint	
		Question	Activity
Aiming for GRADE 4 ↓	Describe and safely carry out a method to make a paper chromatogram.	1	Starter 2, Main, Plenary 1
	Describe how to calculate R_f values.	2	Main, Plenary 2
	Describe a use of chromatography.		Starter 1
Aiming for GRADE 6 ↓	Explain how chromatography separates solutes.		Main
	Calculate R_f values from given data.	3	Main, Plenary 2
	Use a chromatogram to determine if a sample is pure or impure.		Main, Plenary 2
Aiming for GRADE 8 ↓	Explain why different substances and different conditions will have different R_f values.	3, 4, End of chapter 6	Main
	Calculate R_f values from a chromatogram, using an appropriate number of significant figures.	End of chapter 6	Main, Plenary 2, Homework
	Interpret a chromatogram to identify unknown substances.	End of chapter 6	Main, Plenary 2

Maths
Students calculate R_f values (1c, 2a).

Literacy
Students describe how to produce a chromatogram and explain the process of chromatography.

Key words
R_f (retention factor), pipette

■ C12 Chemical analysis

Required practical

Title	Calculating R_f values
Equipment	food colourings, capillary tube (one per food colouring), pencil, pipette, water, boiling tube, narrow strip of chromatography paper, ruler, boiling-tube rack
Overview of method	Place the chromatography paper in a portrait arrangement and using a pencil and ruler, draw a line 1.5 cm from the bottom of the paper. Using the capillary tube, put a small dot of the food colouring on the pencil line and, using the pencil, write the colour under the sample. Add about a 1 cm depth of water to a boiling tube and put in a boiling-tube rack. Carefully lower the paper into the boiling tube, taking care to keep the pencil line above the water level. Allow the chromatogram to develop until the water line (solvent front) is beyond the last colour spot. Make a pencil mark at the final level of the solvent front and allow the chromatogram to dry. Measure from the base line to the centre of each spot of the chromatogram and from the base line to the solvent front. Now calculate the R_f values.
Safety considerations	Some students may be allergic to food colouring. Be careful not to break the capillary tubes as they are made of thin glass.

Starter	Support/Extend	Resources
Thinking about chromatography (5 minutes) Use question and answer to remind students of the main principles of chromatography. Ask students to then suggest some uses for chromatography. **Chromatography** (10 minutes) Ask students to think back to their work on separating mixtures in Topic C1.4. They then complete a crossword to revise what they already know about chromatography.	**Support:** Show students some images of chromatography in action.	**Interactive:** Chromatography

Main	Support/Extend	Resources
Calculating R_f values (40 minutes) Ask students to draw a suitable results table and then run the practical as outlined in the practical box. Ensure that students calculate the R_f values for each chemical.	**Extend:** Explain that the stationary phase of thin layer chromatography (TLC) gives a more repeatable result. Allow students to form a chromatogram using this method and ask students to compare the R_f values between different paper chromatography and TLC and suggest why they are different.	**Required practical:** Calculating R_f values

Plenary	Support/Extend	Resources
Label a chromatogram (5 minutes) Show students a diagram from the compulsory practical. Ask then to label the solvent, base line, solvent front, stationary phase, and mobile phase. **R_f** (10 minutes) Students use the calculation sheet for further practice on calculating R_f values.	**Extend:** Students annotate their diagram to explain how to calculate R_f for a chemical. **Extend:** Give students an image of a 'two-way' chromatogram and ask them to interpret it.	**Calculation sheet:** R_f

Homework		
Students complete the WebQuest where they research how chromatography can be used to check the purity of a substance. They use their research to produce a laboratory guide for the procedure. Alternatively, ask students to evaluate the results of their chromatogram experiment. Students could complete a table with three columns: What went wrong? How could this be prevented? How could this be improved? This helps students to critically consider each step of the method. They should also compare their results with a teacher's chromatogram, to discuss accuracy, and other groups, to discuss reproducibility.		**WebQuest:** Paper chromatography

kerboodle

A Kerboodle highlight for this lesson is **Maths skills: Calculating an R_f value**. Refer to the **Content map** on Kerboodle for a full list of resources and assessment.

C12.3 Testing for gases

AQA spec Link: 8.2.1 The test for hydrogen uses a burning splint held at the open end of a test tube of the gas. Hydrogen burns rapidly with a pop sound.

8.2.2 The test for oxygen uses a glowing splint inserted into a test tube of the gas. The splint relights in oxygen.

8.2.3 The test for carbon dioxide uses an aqueous solution of calcium hydroxide (limewater). When carbon dioxide is shaken with or bubbled through limewater the limewater turns milky (cloudy).

8.2.4 The test for chlorine uses litmus paper. When damp litmus paper is put into chlorine gas the litmus paper is bleached and turns white.

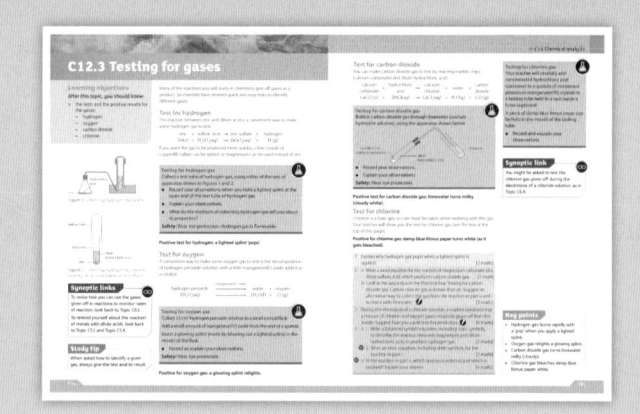

WS 1.2, 1.6, 2.2, 3.5

Aiming for	Outcome	Checkpoint	
		Question	Activity
Aiming for GRADE 4 ↓	Safely carry out the laboratory test for hydrogen, oxygen, carbon dioxide, and chlorine.	2	Main, Plenary 2
	Describe how to safely carry out the laboratory test for chlorine gas.	2	Main, Plenary 2
	Identify hydrogen, carbon dioxide, and oxygen from a laboratory test.		Main, Plenary 2
Aiming for GRADE 6 ↓	Explain why limewater turns milky when it reacts with carbon dioxide.		Main, Plenary 2
	Interpret results to identify a gas that is present.	3, 5	Plenary 2
	Explain why hydrogen 'pops' near a naked flame.	1	Main, Plenary 2
Aiming for GRADE 8 ↓	Write balanced symbol equations, including state symbols, for the reactions of limewater with carbon dioxide and hydrogen with oxygen.	2, 4	Starter 1, Plenary 2, Homework
	Explain why a glowing splint re-ignites in oxygen.		Main, Plenary 2
	Explain why chlorine gas turns damp indicator paper colourless.		Main, Plenary 2

Maths
Students balance symbol equations.

Literacy
Students write procedures.

Practical

Title	Making and testing gases
Equipment	Testing for hydrogen: zinc granules, spatula, 2 mol/dm³ or less hydrochloric acid, 250 cm³ conical flask, bung with a hole in the top with an upwards delivery tube, test tube, bung, water trough, splint, Bunsen burner and safety equipment, eye protection Testing for oxygen: 10 vol hydrogen peroxide solution, manganese dioxide powder, spatula, 100 cm³ conical flask, Bunsen burner and safety equipment, eye protection Testing for carbon dioxide: calcium carbonate (marble chips), spatula, 2 mol/dm³ or less hydrochloric acid, 250 cm³ conical flask, bung with a hole in the top with n-shaped delivery tube, test tube, limewater, test-tube rack, eye protection
Overview of method	Testing for hydrogen: Fill the water trough and test tube with water. Submerge the test tube in the trough, still full of water. Add about 100 cm³ of hydrochloric acid into the conical flask and add a spatula of zinc granules. Put the bung in the conical flask and put the end of the delivery tube into the water bath. Wait about a minute to ensure the air has been removed from the system. Then collect the gas in the test tube by delivery over water. Put a bung on the test tube whilst the lip is still under the water. Test the gas by removing the bung and holding a lighted splint at the neck of the test tube.

C12 Chemical analysis

	Testing for oxygen: Add about 25 cm³ hydrogen peroxide to the conical flask with one spatula of manganese dioxide. Light a splint and gently blow or tap it so that it is only glowing. Hold the glowing splint in the neck of the conical flask and observe. Testing for carbon dioxide: Half fill the test tube with limewater and place in the test-tube rack. Put the end of the delivery tube into the liquid. Add about 25 cm³ of hydrochloric acid to the conical flask and add a few marble chips. Quickly put the bung on the conical flask and observe the limewater.
Safety considerations	Zinc is flammable and hydrochloric acid is an irritant. Wear eye protection and wash hands after completing the practical. Hydrogen peroxide is an oxidiser and an irritant. Manganese dioxide is harmful. Wear eye protection and wash hands after completing the practical. Hydrochloric acid and limewater are irritants. Wear eye protection and wash hands after completing the practical.

Title	Testing for chlorine
Equipment	concentrated hydrochloric acid, spatula, moistened potassium manganate(VII) crystals, boiling tube, boiling-tube rack, blue litmus paper, eye protection, dropping pipette, water in a wash bottle
Overview of method	Add half a spatula of damp potassium manganate(VII) crystals into a boiling tube help in a boiling-tube rack. Add about 2 cm³ of concentrated hydrochloric acid into the boiling tube. Then hold damp litmus paper over the mouth of the boiling tube and observe.
Safety considerations	Concentrated hydrochloric acid is corrosive, potassium manganate(VII) is harmful, and chlorine gas is toxic. Complete the procedure in a fume cupboard. Wear eye protection and wash hands after completing the practical.

Starter	Support/Extend	Resources
Complete (5 minutes) Ask students to complete the following word equations: • metal + hydrochloric acid → • metal carbonate + hydrochloric acid → • hydrogen peroxide → **Testing for gases** (10 minutes) Ask students to draw the dot and cross diagrams for hydrogen, oxygen, carbon dioxide, and chlorine molecules. Then use the interactive to introduce the chemical test for each substance. Students match the substance with its chemical test.	**Support:** Give students the formulae for each substance. **Extend:** Ask students to draw displayed structural formulae as well.	**Interactive:** Testing for gases

Main	Support/Extend	Resources
Making and testing gases (40 minutes) Split the class into three groups. Give each group one gas – hydrogen, oxygen, or carbon dioxide – to make and test as detailed. Allow each group to make and test their gas. Then students watch a demonstration of the test for chlorine gas. Students make a small presentation to explain what they have done.		**Practical:** Making and testing gases

Plenary	Support/Extend	Resources
Explain (5 minutes) Ask students to explain why a lighted splint going out is not a conclusive test for carbon dioxide gas. **Procedure** (10 minutes) Explain to students that to allow results to be compared between laboratories, it is important that agreed procedures are followed. Ask students to write a set of procedures to identify the gas produced in an experiment when a solid effervesces when added to a liquid.	**Support:** Demonstrate that a lighted splint goes out in a sample of carbon dioxide or in a sample of chlorine gas. **Extend:** Ask students to include equations to explain the observations for each test.	

Homework		
Ask students to write equations for the reactions of: zinc and hydrochloric acid, calcium carbonate and hydrochloric acid, hydrogen and oxygen, catalytic decomposition hydrogen peroxide.	**Extend:** Ask students to write balanced symbol equations with state symbols.	

kerboodle

A Kerboodle highlight for this lesson is **Literacy skills: Detecting gases**. Refer to the **Content map** on Kerboodle for a full list of resources and assessment.

GCSE Chemistry Only

C12.4 Tests for positive ions

AQA spec Link: 8.3.1 Flame tests can be used to identify some metal ions (cations). Lithium, sodium, potassium, calcium, and copper compounds produce distinctive colours in flame tests:

- lithium compounds result in a crimson flame
- sodium compounds result in a yellow flame
- potassium compounds result in a lilac flame
- calcium compounds result in a red flame
- copper compounds result in a green flame.

If a sample containing a mixture of ions is used some flame colours can be masked.

Students should be able to identify species from the results of the tests in 8.3.1 to 8.3.5.

Flame colours of other metal ions are not required knowledge.

8.3.2 Sodium hydroxide solution can be used to identify some metal ions (cations).

Solutions of aluminium, calcium, and magnesium ions form white precipitates when sodium hydroxide solution is added but only the aluminium hydroxide precipitate dissolves in excess sodium hydroxide solution.

Solutions of copper(II), iron(II), and iron(III) ions form coloured precipitates when sodium hydroxide solution is added.

Copper(II) forms a blue precipitate, iron(II) a green precipitate, and iron(III) a brown precipitate.

Students should be able to write balanced equations for the reactions to produce the insoluble hydroxides.

Students are not expected to write equations for the production of sodium aluminate.

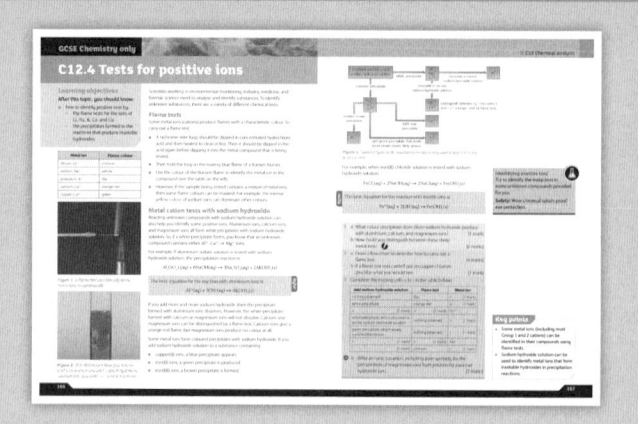

WS 2.2

Aiming for	Outcome	Checkpoint	
		Question	Activity
Aiming for GRADE 4	Safely carry out a flame test.	2	Starter 1, Main 2
	Safely carry out testing for metal ions using sodium hydroxide.		Main 1
	Write a word equation for the reaction between sodium hydroxide and a specified metal salt solution.		Main 1
Aiming for GRADE 6	Identify a metal ion from the colour of a flame or the colour of the hydroxide precipitate.	1, 2, 3, End of chapter 2, 3, 4	Main 1, Plenary 1
	Write balanced symbol equations, including state symbols, for the production of an insoluble metal hydroxide.		Main 1
	Explain why a flame test cannot be used to identify a mixture of metal solutions.		Main 2
Aiming for GRADE 8	Evaluate flame tests as a method for identifying of positive metal ions.		Main 2
	(H) Write balanced ionic equations, including state symbols for the production of an insoluble metal hydroxide.	5	Starter 2, Main 1
	Explain why iron(II) hydroxide solution often changes colour when it stands in air.		Plenary 2

■ C12 Chemical analysis

Maths		Literacy
Students write balanced symbol and ionic equations.		Students write an evaluation of flame tests.

Practical

Title	Identifying positive ions
Equipment	solutions to be tested (e.g., copper(II) chloride, iron(II) chloride and iron(III) chloride), dropping pipettes, dilute sodium hydroxide solution, a dimple dish (spotting tray), eye protection
Overview of method	Add two drops of the solution to be tested into a dimple. Then add two drops of sodium hydroxide solution. (Use a different dropping pipette for each solution.) Note the colour of any precipitate formed.
Safety considerations	Some metal ion solutions are irritants or harmful so choose the solutions with the lowest risk. Sodium hydroxide solution is corrosive. Wear chemical splash-proof eye protection and wash hands after completing the practical.

Starter	Support/Extend	Resources
Sorting the flame test method (5 minutes) Show students the procedure for completing a flame test as separate sentences as in the student book. Ask students to sort them into the correct order.		
Equations (10 minutes) Explain to students that when aluminium carbonate, magnesium carbonate, or calcium carbonate reacts with sodium hydroxide solution a white precipitate of the metal hydroxide is formed along with aqueous sodium carbonate. Ask students to write balanced symbol equations for these reactions.	**Support:** Write the formulae so that only the balancing is required. **Extend:** Ask students to write the ionic equations for the reactions.	

Main	Support/Extend	Resources
Identifying positive ions (25 minutes) Ask students to draw a suitable results table and then allow them to complete the practical outlined. They then conclude which metal ions are present.	**Extend:** Students should justify why only chlorides were used.	**Practical:** Identifying positive ions
Flame tests (15 minutes) Students look at the main principles for flame tests, and evaluate the technique, considering why it cannot be used to identify solutions with more than one metal ion or differentiate between lithium and calcium compounds.	**Extend:** 🄷 Ask students to investigate whether the colour depends on the metal ion or the negative ion.	

Plenary	Support/Extend	Resources
Testing for positive ions (5 minutes) Show students five flame test results and ask them to write down the metal ion present. They then sort cations according to whether they form a coloured or a white precipitate when sodium hydroxide is added to them.	**Support:** Encourage students to use the table in the student book to refer to.	**Interactive:** Testing for positive ions
Explain (10 minutes) Ask students to work in small groups to explain why iron(II) hydroxide turns from a green precipitate to a brown precipitate when it is left in an open test tube.	**Support:** Give the formula of iron(II) ions and ask what other stable ion it can form and what process this involves (oxidation).	

Homework		
Ask students to write a procedure for identifying iron(II), iron(III), copper(II), and aluminium ions using test tubes.	**Support:** Refer students to the flame test procedure in the student book and ask them to copy this style.	

kerboodle

A Kerboodle highlight for this lesson is **Bum up your grade: What compound is it?**. Refer to the **Content map** on Kerboodle for a full list of resources and assessment.

GCSE Chemistry Only

C12.5 Tests for negative ions

AQA spec Link: 8.3.3 Carbonates react with dilute acids to form carbon dioxide gas. Carbon dioxide can be identified with limewater.

8.3.4 Halide ions in solution produce precipitates with silver nitrate solution in the presence of dilute nitric acid. Silver chloride is white, silver bromide is cream, and silver iodide is yellow.

8.3.5 Sulfate ions in solution produce a white precipitate with barium chloride solution in the presence of dilute hydrochloric acid.

Required practical: Use of chemical tests to identify the ions in unknown single ionic compounds covering the ions from sections 8.3.1 to 8.3.5.

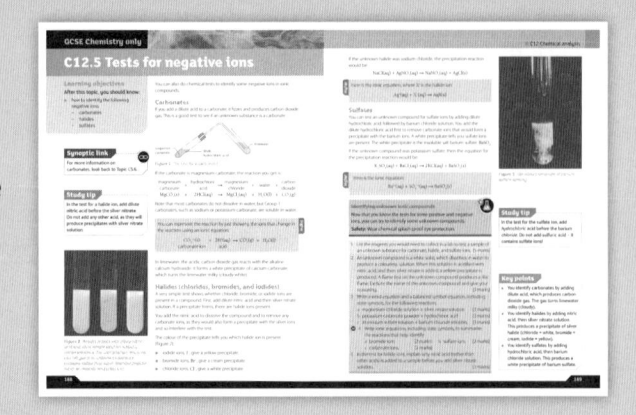

WS 3.5, 3.6
MS 1c

Aiming for	Outcome	Checkpoint	
		Question	Activity
Aiming for GRADE 4	Safely carry out testing for carbonates, halides, and sulfate ions.	1	Main, Plenary 1
	Write a word equation for the reaction when a specific carbonate, halide, or sulfate is being tested with support.	3	Main
Aiming for GRADE 6	Identify the presence of carbonate, a specific halide, or sulfate ions from simple laboratory tests.	End of chapter 2	Starter 2, Main, Plenary 1
	Write balanced symbol equations, including state symbols for the reactions in the simple laboratory tests for carbonate, halide, or sulfate ions.	3	Main
	Explain why it can be difficult to identify halides using this method.		Main
Aiming for GRADE 8	Evaluate the halide ion test.	5	Main, Plenary 1
	Write balanced ionic equations, including state symbols, for simple laboratory tests for carbonate, halide, or sulfate ions.	4	Main
	Explain in detail how to identify a compound from the results of simple laboratory tests.	2, End of chapter 2 3, 4	Main, Plenary 1, Plenary 2, Homework

Maths
Students balance symbol and ionic equations.

Literacy
Students write a summary table of the different chemical tests.

Required practical

Title	Identifying unknown ionic compounds – precipitation test
Equipment	metal ion solutions, dimple dish (spotting tile), lots of dropping pipettes, dilute sodium hydroxide, eye protection
Overview of method	Add two drops of the solution to be tested into a dimple. Then add two drops of sodium hydroxide solution and note the colour of any precipitate formed.
Safety considerations	Some metal ion solutions are irritants or harmful so choose the solutions with the lowest risk. Sodium hydroxide solution is corrosive. Wear eye protection and wash hands after completing the practical.

Title	Identifying unknown ionic compounds – carbonate tests
Equipment	metal ion solutions, two test tubes, dilute hydrochloric acid, bung with n-shaped delivery tube, test-tube rack, stand, boss and clamp, limewater

C12 Chemical analysis

Overview of method	Half fill a test tube with limewater and put in a test-tube rack. Half fill a second test tube with the solution to be tested, mount at a 45° angle using the stand, boss and clamp. Add about 2 cm^3 of dilute hydrochloric acid and quickly insert the bung and delivery tube end so that any gas that is made is bubbled through the limewater. Observe to see if the limewater goes cloudy.
Safety considerations	Some metal ion solutions are irritants or harmful so choose the solutions with the lowest risk. Hydrochloric acid is an irritant. Wear chemical splash-proof eye protection and wash hands after completing the practical.

Title	Identifying unknown ionic compounds – halide test
Equipment	metal ion solutions, dimple tray, dilute nitric acid, silver nitrate solution, dropping pipettes
Overview of method	Add two drops of the solution to be tested into a dimple. Then add two drops of nitric acid solution and two drops of silver nitrate solution. Note the colour of any precipitate formed.
Safety considerations	Some metal ion solutions are irritants or harmful so choose the solutions with the lowest risk. Nitric acid is an irritant. Wear chemical splash-proof eye protection and wash hands after completing the practical.

Title	Identifying unknown ionic compounds – sulfate test
Equipment	metal ion solutions, dimple tray, dilute hydrochloric acid, barium chloride solution, dropping pipettes
Overview of method	Add two drops of the solution to be tested into a dimple. Then add two drops of hydrochloric acid solution and two drops of barium chloride solution. Note the colour of any precipitate formed.
Safety considerations	Some metal ion solutions are irritants or harmful so choose the solutions with the lowest risk. Barium chloride is toxic, and nitric acid is an irritant. Wear chemical splash-proof eye protection and wash hands after completing the practical.

Starter	Support/Extend	Resources
Ion formula (5 minutes) Students write the formula for the sulfate ion, carbonate ion, and all the halide ions. **Test for ions table** (10 minutes) Ask students to write a comparison table with three columns (test, outline, expected result) to summarise the simple laboratory tests for ions from Topic C12.4.	**Support:** Complete the table on the board giving ownership for each test to different groups of students. When they have found the information they can fill it in on the board.	

Main	Support/Extend	Resources
Identifying unknown ionic compounds (40 minutes) Show students some compounds labelled with letters. Then ask them to use simple laboratory tests for carbonates, sulfates, and halides to identify the chemicals. They should record their results in a suitable results table and justify their conclusion.	**Extend:** Ask students to write equations to illustrate the chemical reactions in the positive tests. **Support:** Ask students to identify only one chemical and to complete each test on that chemical.	**Required practical:** Identifying unknown ionic compounds

Plenary	Support/Extend	Resources
Discover the chemical (5 minutes) Give students examples of simple laboratory tests, from this and Topic C12.4, and ask students to identify the chemical. For example, this chemical produces an yellow flame test and produces a white precipitate with barium chloride. The chemical is (sodium sulfate). **Secret identity** (10 minutes) Ask students to identify the mystery chemicals, for example, what chemical produces a green flame test and a blue precipitate when mixed with sodium hydroxide solution but a white precipitate when mixed with dilute nitric acid and silver nitrate solution? (copper(II) chloride)	**Extend:** Add information from other tests with negative results, for example, does not effervesce when dilute acid is added.	**Interactive:** Discover the chemical

Homework		
Students explain how simple laboratory tests can be used to differentiate between lithium chloride and calcium bromide.		

kerboodle

A Kerboodle highlight for this lesson is **WebQuest: Identifying chemicals**. Refer to the **Content map** on Kerboodle for a full list of resources and assessment.

GCSE Chemistry Only

C12.6 Instrumental analysis

AQA spec Link: 8.3.6 Elements and compounds can be detected and identified using instrumental methods. Instrumental methods are accurate, sensitive, and rapid.

8.3.7 Flame emission spectroscopy is an example of an instrumental method used to analyse metal ions in solutions.

The sample is put into a flame and the light given out is passed through a spectroscope. The output is a line spectrum that can be analysed to identify the metal ions in the solution and measure their concentrations.

Students should be able to interpret an instrumental result given appropriate data in chart or tabular form, when accompanied by a reference set in the same form, limited to flame emission spectroscopy.

WS 1.3, 1.4, 1.6

Aiming for	Outcome	Checkpoint	
		Question	Activity
Aiming for GRADE 4 ↓	List some of the advantages and disadvantages of instrumental techniques.	End of chapter 7	Main
	State an example of an instrumental technique.	End of chapter 7	Main, Plenary 1, Homework
	State a use for flame emission spectroscopy.	End of chapter 7	Plenary 2, Homework
Aiming for GRADE 6 ↓	Compare and contrast instrumental techniques with simple laboratory tests.	1	Starter 2
	Describe the main processes of flame emission spectroscopy.		Plenary 2, Homework
	Explain how flame emission spectroscopy is an improvement on flame tests.		Plenary 2, Homework
Aiming for GRADE 8 ↓	Evaluate the use of instrumental techniques.		Main, Plenary 2
	Explain how metal ions emit light when in a flame.	2	Plenary 2, Homework
	Interpret results from flame emission spectroscopy when data is given.	3	Plenary 2

Maths
Students interpret results from flame emissions spectroscopy.

Literacy
Students use scientific knowledge to create a persuasive argument for or against the use of instrumental analysis.

■ C12 Chemical analysis

Starter	Support/Extend	Resources
Laboratory history (5 minutes) Show students an image of a lab from different stages in history, up to the most high-tech labs available today. Ask students to suggest how and why the lab environments have changed. **Thinking about techniques** (10 minutes) Ask students to reflect on the simple laboratory techniques they have learnt to test for gases and ions. In groups, they should list the advantages and disadvantages of these techniques.	**Support:** Focus students by showing only a current image of a lab and one for the early 1900s. **Support:** Use question and answer to support the whole class in creating a list of advantages and disadvantages.	

Main	Support/Extend	Resources
Debating instrumental analysis (40 minutes) Explain that instrumental analysis allows quantitative data to be collected, which is very important when providing evidence in a Court of Law, such as in a pollution control case. Then review the advantages and disadvantages of these techniques. Split the class into two groups, one for and one against the motion 'Instrumental analysis should not be used to analyse substances in samples taken by the Environment Agency'. Students should prepare their arguments to try and persuade. Ask students to have a free vote for or against the motion. Then chair the debate and re-vote. Ask a few students to share their ideas why they have or have not changed their mind.	**Extend:** You may wish to add a touch of drama by imagining you are debating a motion in the House of Commons to reduce the policing budget and instrumental analysis is set to be cut from the budget due to the higher cost.	**Activity:** Debating instrumental analysis

Plenary	Support/Extend	Resources
Montage (5 minutes) Many popular crime scene dramas have montages of analytical techniques. Show a clip of this and ask students to note how many different analytical techniques they saw. Reveal the answer and replay the clip pointing out the different techniques. **Flame emission spectroscopy** (10 minutes) Explain that the distinctive colours in a flame test only give qualitative information but this instrumental method can be used to give quantitative data such as concentration.	**Extend:** Encourage students to name any of the techniques.	

Homework		
Ask students to create a flow chart to describe and explain the main features of flame emission spectroscopy. Students should include information about how to interpret line spectra and the industrial use of flame emission spectrometers.		

kerboodle

A Kerboodle highlight for this lesson is **Literacy sheet: Instrumental analysis**. Refer to the **Content map** on Kerboodle for a full list of resources and assessment.

C12 Chemical analysis

Overview of C12 Chemical analysis

In this chapter, students have learnt about various techniques for analysing substances. All students should now understand the difference between a pure substance, a mixture, and a formulation, and what is meant by purity. Students should also have built upon their understanding of chromatography experiments from *Chapter C1* and be able to analyse a chromatogram, both qualitatively and quantitatively using R_f values. Students should also be able to describe the different experimental tests for gases, including both the procedure and positive result.

Students studying *AQA GCSE Chemistry* should also be able to describe experimental tests for positive and negative ions, and be able to write balanced symbol equations for them. They should be able to apply their knowledge of all of the tests they have learnt to be able to plan and investigation to identify positive and negative ions. Students have also studied flame emission spectroscopy, and should be able to interpret instrumental results.

Required practical

All students are expected to have carried out the required practicals:

Practical	Topic
Investigate how paper chromatography can be used to separate and tell the difference between coloured substances. Students should calculate R_f values.	C12.2

All students studying *AQA GCSE Chemistry* are also expected to have carried out the required practical:

Practical	Topic
Use of chemical tests to identify the ions in unknown single ionic compounds.	C12.5

Students studying *AQA GCSE Combined science: Trilogy* do not need to carry out this required practical.

MyMaths

You can find additional support for the maths skills covered in this chapter on **MyMaths**, including using ratios.

kerboodle

For this chapter, the following assessments are available on Kerboodle:

C12 Checkpoint quiz: Chemical analysis
C12 Progress quiz: Chemical analysis 1
C12 Progress quiz: Chemical analysis 2
C12 On your marks: Chemical analysis
C12 Exam-style questions and mark scheme: Chemical analysis

Checkpoint follow up lesson

A student's route through this lesson can be determined using the Checkpoint assessment. Percentage pass marks are supplied in the Checkpoint teacher notes.

For each successive route through it is assumed that the student can perform to their current route as well as previous routes. For example, students working at Aiming for 6 are assumed to be secure in Aiming for 4 knowledge and understanding and working towards achieving all the learning outcomes for Aiming for 6.

	Aiming for 4	**Aiming for 6**	**Aiming for 8**
Learning outcomes	Describe how to test for common gases.	Describe how to test for common positive ions.	Evaluate the different analytical techniques.
	Describe how paper chromatography is carried out.	Describe how to test for common negative ions.	
	Identify tests for positive and negative ions.	Describe how flame emission spectroscopy is carried out.	
Starter	**Why do we need to identify substances? (10 minutes)** Ask students to come up with three reasons/ situations where it is important to be able to identify substances. Discuss the list of situations they come up with. Then ask students to consider why it is important for tests to be quick and fairly straightforward, as opposed to involving expensive equipment. Draw up a list of substances they recall that can be identified using simple chemical tests.		
Differentiated checkpoint activity	The Aiming for 4 Checkpoint follow-up sheet guides students through the simple tests for the gases oxygen, hydrogen, carbon dioxide, and chlorine, and a paper chromatography experiment. Aiming for 4 students will need to be provided with the appropriate apparatus for these experiments and support with carrying out the tests. They should work in small groups and work their way through each process in a circus type activity. Students studying *AQA GCSE Chemistry* will finish with a matching exercise for the tests for positive and negative ions. Students then cut and stick the different tasks from their sheet to create a poster summarising the key tests from the chapter. The Aiming for 6 checkpoint follow-up sheet provides guidance for students to create a booklet that gives instructions on how to carry out each test studied in this chapter. Students use the Aiming for 8 Checkpoint follow-up sheet to evaluate all of the tests they have studied in this chapter, creating a poster that summarises the advantages and disadvantages of the techniques studied. They should include instrumental analysis as well as the experimental techniques. **Kerboodle resource** C12 Checkpoint follow up: Aiming for 4, C12 Checkpoint follow up: Aiming for 6, C12 Checkpoint follow up: Aiming for 8		
Plenary	**Work review (5 minutes)** Ask students to lay their work around the room. Students should then choose another student's poster of booklet to review. They should read the other student's work and decide on two strong points about the work and one point that could be improved on. **Key points (5 minutes)** Ask students to work in pairs to decide three key learning points from the chapter. Review these as a class. Check that the list drawn up in the starter was not missing any key tests. Address any misconceptions should they arise.		
Progression	Students create a flow-chart that someone could follow to identify an unknown substance, combining all of the tests that it is appropriate for them to know.	Provide students with a series of metal ions that need to be identified for different reasons. Students identify the most appropriate way to identify the ion. Encourage students to think about costs when considering which test to use.	Students could then be provided with Internet access to research Gas chromatography–mass spectrometry and its use in crime scene analysis. Students will need guidance with this research.

C 13 The Earth's atmosphere
13.1 History of our atmosphere

AQA spec Link: 9.1.2 Theories about what was in the Earth's early atmosphere and how the atmosphere was formed have changed and developed over time. Evidence for the early atmosphere is limited because of the time scale of 4.6 billion years.

One theory suggests that during the first billion years of the Earth's existence there was intense volcanic activity that released gases that formed the early atmosphere and water vapour that condensed to form the oceans. At the start of this period the Earth's atmosphere may have been like the atmospheres of Mars and Venus today, consisting of mainly carbon dioxide with little or no oxygen gas.

Volcanoes also produced nitrogen which gradually built up in the atmosphere and there may have been small proportions of methane and ammonia.

When the oceans formed carbon dioxide dissolved in the water and carbonates were precipitated producing sediments, reducing the amount of carbon dioxide in the atmosphere. No knowledge of other theories is required.

Students should be able to, given appropriate information, interpret evidence and evaluate different theories about the Earth's early atmosphere.

9.1.3 Algae and plants produced the oxygen that is now in the atmosphere by photosynthesis, which can be represented by the equation:

$$6CO_2 + 6H_2O \rightarrow C_6H_{12}O_6 + 6O_2$$

carbon dioxide + water → glucose + oxygen

Algae first produced oxygen about 2.7 billion years ago and soon after this oxygen appeared in the atmosphere. Over the next billion years plants evolved and the percentage of oxygen gradually increased to a level that enabled animals to evolve.

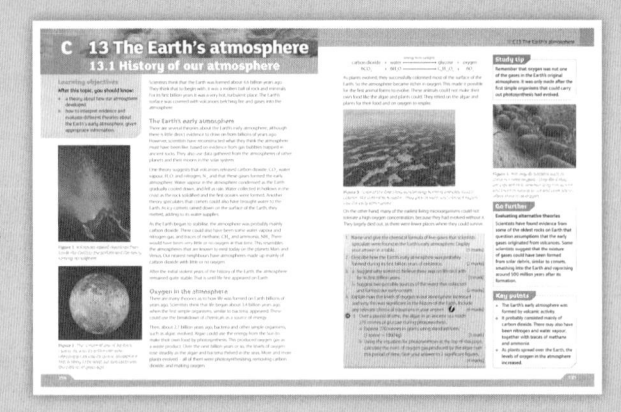

WS 1.1, 1.2, 1.3, 3.5, 3.6, 4.1
MS 2c

Aiming for	Outcome	Checkpoint	
		Question	Activity
Aiming for **GRADE 4** ↓	Describe the Earth's early atmosphere.	1	Main, Plenary 1
	Describe how oxygen was formed in the development of the atmosphere.	4	Main, Plenary 1
Aiming for **GRADE 6** ↓	State the composition, including formulae, of the Earth's early atmosphere.	1	Main, Plenary 1
	Describe a theory for the development of the Earth's atmosphere.	2, End of chapter 1	Main, Plenary 1, Plenary 2
	Explain, using word equations, how gases were formed in the atmosphere and how oceans were formed.	3, 4, End of chapter 1	Main
Aiming for **GRADE 8** ↓	Use a theory to explain in detail how the atmosphere developed.	3, End of chapter 1	Main, Plenary 2
	Explain the limits of the theory for the development of the Earth's atmosphere and why it has changed.		Main, Homework
	Use balanced symbol equations to explain how gases were formed in the atmosphere and explain how oceans were formed.	3, 4, End of chapter 1	Main

Maths
Students calculate the volume of oxygen released during photosynthesis.

Literacy
Students write a prediction.

C13 The Earth's atmosphere

Practical

Title	Gases in the atmosphere
Equipment	250 cm^3 beaker, glass funnel, strand of *Elodea* (Canadian pondweed), aerated water, test tube, spill, limewater, lamp, rubber bung that tightly fits the test tube, eye protection
Overview of method	Put the *Elodea* in the bottom of the beaker, then add about 200 cm^3 of water. Trap the elodea under the upturned funnel. Fill a test tube with water and then put on the top of the spout of the funnel, ensuring that the lip of the test tube is below the water level. This allows any gas to be collected by displacement of water. Leave this apparatus on a sunny windowsill and then next to a lit lamp overnight. Carefully remove the test tube from the beaker. Stopper it with a tightly fitting rubber bung before turning it over. Then repeat to get a second testtubes. Test one with limewater and the other with a glowing splint.
Safety considerations	Limewater is an irritant. Wear eye protection and wash hands after completing the practical.

Starter	Support/Extend	Resources
Photosynthesis (5 minutes) Ask students to write an equation for photosynthesis and explain the importance of this chemical reaction to life on Earth. **Photosynthesis and the atmosphere** (10 minutes) Students choose the correct words to complete the word and balanced symbol equations for photosynthesis. They then put the different stages in the development of the atmosphere in the correct order.	**Extend:** Encourage students to write the balanced symbol equation.	**Interactive:** Photosynthesis and the atmosphere

Main	Support/Extend	Resources
Gases in the atmosphere (40 minutes) Ask students to set up the equipment as outlined in the practical box. Students should write a prediction about what they think will happen, why, and what they think the results of the gas test will be. Then ask students to make a timeline to describe the key stages in the development of the Earth's atmosphere. Students could have access to text books and the Internet for research. You may need to revisit the practical in another lesson.	**Support:** Use question and answer to help students understand how the atmosphere developed. **Support:** Remind students of the gas tests in Topic C12.3. **Extend:** Ask students to write balanced symbol equations for the production of oxygen and the reaction of carbon dioxide with limewater.	**Practical:** Gases in the atmosphere

Plenary	Support/Extend	Resources
Atmosphere ordering (5 minutes) Show an artist's impressions of the Earth and its atmosphere in each of the key stages of the theory outlined in the student book. Students order the images. **Atmosphere marks** (10 minutes) Show students an exam question with candidate-style answers. Ask students to annotate the script with examiner-style comments. Then reveal the actual marks awarded and comment on any misconceptions and examination technique. Alternatively, students answer the exam question, swap answers, and mark each other's, using the mark scheme.	**Extend:** Ask students to explain what each image is showing.	

Homework		
Students complete the WebQuest where they research the early atmosphere and the modern atmosphere and find out about theories on how the different gas levels have changed.		**WebQuest:** The history of the atmosphere

kerboodle
A Kerboodle highlight for this lesson is **Bump up your grade: How did the atmosphere get to be like this?**. Refer to the **Content map** on Kerboodle for a full list of resources and assessment.

C13.2 Our evolving atmosphere

AQA spec Link: 9.1.1 For 200 million years, the proportions of different gases in the atmosphere have been much the same as they are today:
- about four-fifths (approximately 80%) nitrogen
- about one-fifth (approximately 20%) oxygen
- small proportions of various other gases, including carbon dioxide, water vapour, and noble gases.

9.1.2 Volcanoes also produced nitrogen which gradually built up in the atmosphere and there may have been small proportions of methane and ammonia.

9.1.4 Algae and plants decreased the percentage of carbon dioxide in the atmosphere by photosynthesis.

Carbon dioxide was also decreased by the formation of sedimentary rocks and fossil fuels that contain carbon.

Students should be able to:
- describe the main changes in the atmosphere over time and some of the likely causes of these changes
- describe and explain the formation of deposits of limestone, coal, crude oil, and natural gas.

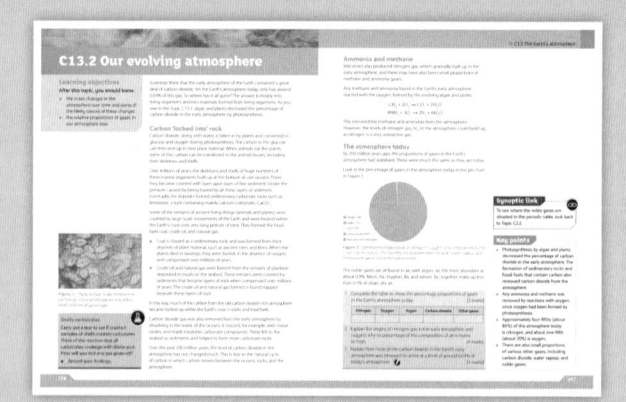

WS 1.2, 4.1
MS 1c, 2c, 4a, 4c

Aiming for	Outcome	Checkpoint	
		Question	Activity
Aiming for GRADE 4	State that the levels of carbon dioxide have decreased in the atmosphere.		Plenary 2
	List the names and symbols of the gases in dry air.		Main 2
	State where methane and ammonia in the atmosphere may have come from.		Plenary 2
Aiming for GRADE 6	Describe how the proportion of carbon dioxide in the early atmosphere was reduced.	3	Starter 1, Main 1, Plenary 2
	State the composition of dry air.	1	Starter 2, Main 2
	Use word equations to show how carbon dioxide can form sedimentary rocks.	End of chapter 1	Main 1, Plenary 2, Homework
Aiming for GRADE 8	Use a theory to explain in detail how the early atmosphere developed to form the atmosphere today.	2, 3	Main 1, Plenary 2
	Explain why the composition of the Earth's atmosphere has not changed much for 200 million years.		Homework
	Use balanced symbol equations to explain how carbon dioxide forms sedimentary rock and how methane and ammonia were removed from the atmosphere.	End of chapter 1	Main 1, Main 2, Plenary 2

Maths
Students calculate the percentage of oxygen in the air (1c). Students also present data as a percentage, fraction, decimal, and pie chart (2c).

Literacy
Students summarise how the amount of carbon dioxide in the atmosphere has changed over time.

C13 The Earth's atmosphere

Practical

Title	Shelly carbonates
Equipment	two test tubes, dilute hydrochloric acid, bung with L-shaped delivery tube, test-tube rack, stand, boss and clamp, eye protection, limewater, samples of crushed chalk, marble, and limestone (all calcium carbonates) and pumice (aluminosilicate)
Overview of method	Half fill a test tube with limewater and put in a test-tube rack. Half fill a second test tube with the solution to be tested, mount at a 45° angle using the stand, boss and clamp. Add about 2 cm³ of dilute hydrochloric acid and quickly insert the bung and delivery tube end so that any gas that is made is bubbled through the limewater. Observe to see if the limewater goes cloudy.
Safety considerations	Limewater is an irritant. Hydrochloric acid is an irritant. Wear eye protection and wash hands after completing the practical.

Starter	Support/Extend	Resources
What is the connection? (5 minutes) Split the class into small groups of around three students. Show (or give) each group small samples of chalk, limestone, marble, and a bottle of calcium carbonate. Ask students to suggest the connection. **Gases in dry air** (10 minutes) Students match atmospheric gases with the percentage they make up of the atmosphere. They then complete a crossword to summarise what they know already about the atmosphere.		**Interactive:** Gases in dry air

Main	Support/Extend	Resources
Shelly carbonates (30 minutes) Explain to students that carbon in fossilised bones and shells can be trapped in sedimentary rocks in the form of the chemical calcium carbonate. Ask students to suggest a simple chemical test that they could use to show that a rock is a carbonate. Then allow students to complete the practical as outlined in the practical box to test samples of rocks to determine which contain carbonates. **Composition of air** (10 minutes) Give students the spec link 9.1.1 as detailed. Ask students to write this data in a table, as a percentage, a fraction, and a decimal. Then ask students to draw a pie chart of the data.	**Extend:** Ask students to look up the accurate percentages of dry air and plot them as a bar chart.	**Practical:** Shelly carbonates

Plenary	Support/Extend	Resources
Atmosphere gas taboo (10 minutes) Assign each student a gas that has, at some point, been found in the Earth's atmosphere. Give students one minute to produce a list of three words that can be used to describe it. Then split students into small groups and students take it in turns to describe their gas without using the words they have produced. The other students try to guess the gas. **Gas flow chart** (10 minutes) Ask students to make two flow charts which show how carbon dioxide and nitrogen were made in the early atmosphere and any processes which have occurred that have changed their composition in the atmosphere. Students should include equations and percentage compositions.	**Extend:** Students have to produce five words that cannot be used. **Extend:** Ask students to draw the dot and cross diagrams of the gases. **Extend:** Ask students to link the flow charts and add additional branches to explain how the current composition of dry air has been made.	

Homework		
Summarise in no more than 50 words how carbon dioxide was formed in the atmosphere and how the levels have been relatively stable for the last 20 million years.		

C13.3 Greenhouse gases

AQA spec Link: 9.2.1 Greenhouse gases in the atmosphere maintain temperatures on Earth high enough to support life. Water vapour, carbon dioxide, and methane are greenhouse gases.

Students should be able to describe the greenhouse effect in terms of the interaction of short and long wavelength radiation with matter.

9.2.2 Some human activities increase the amounts of greenhouse gases in the atmosphere. These include:

- carbon dioxide
- methane.

Students should be able to recall two human activities that increase the amounts of each of the greenhouse gases carbon dioxide and methane.

Based on peer-reviewed evidence, many scientists believe that human activities will cause the temperature of the Earth's atmosphere to increase at the surface and that this will result in global climate change.

However, it is difficult to model such complex systems as global climate change. This leads to simplified models, speculation, and opinions presented in the media that may be based on only parts of the evidence and which may be biased.

Students should be able to:

- evaluate the quality of evidence in a report about global climate change given appropriate information
- describe uncertainties in the evidence base
- recognise the importance of peer review of results and of communicating results to a wide range of audiences.

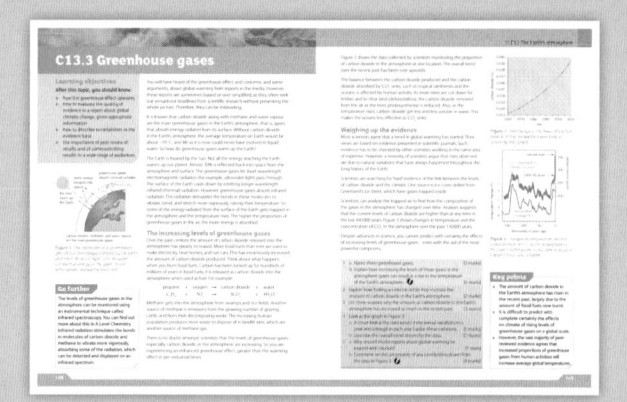

WS1.2, 1.3, 1.6

Aiming for	Outcome	Checkpoint	
		Question	Activity
Aiming for GRADE 4	Describe the greenhouse effect.	1	Main 2, Plenary 1, Plenary 2
	Name three greenhouse gases.	1, End of chapter 3	Starter 1, Main 2, Plenary 1, Plenary 2
	State some human activities that affect the proportion of greenhouse gases in the atmosphere.	3	Main 1, Main 2, Plenary 2
Aiming for GRADE 6	Explain the greenhouse effect.	1	Main 2, Plenary 2
	Explain how greenhouse gases increase the temperature of the atmosphere.	1	Main 1, Main 2, Plenary 2
	Explain how human activity can change the proportion of greenhouse gases in the atmosphere.	2, 3, End of chapter 3	Main 1, Main 2
Aiming for GRADE 8	Justify why scientists, as well as the public, disagree about the cause of climate change.	5, End of chapter 3	Main 1
	Explain the difference between global warming and the greenhouse effect.		Main 1, Main 2
	Evaluate evidence to suggest if global warming is man-made or natural.	4, End of chapter 4	Main 1, Main 2

Maths
Students measure temperature and display their data in an appropriate way.

Literacy
Students use their scientific knowledge to draw and write a conclusion.

198

C13 The Earth's atmosphere

Practical

Title	Greenhouse gases
Equipment	200 cm^3 water, two conical flasks, two bungs with a hole for a thermometer or temperature probe, source of methane, heat lamp, two thermometers or two data loggers with temperature probes.
Overview of method	Add 100 cm^3 of water to each conical flask. Fill one conical flask with air and the other with methane. Put a tight-fitting bung into each flask with a thermometer through the centre into the water. Put the set-up under a heat lamp.
Safety considerations	Methane is flammable. Keep away from sources of ignition and flames.

Starter	Support/Extend	Resources
Climate change (5 minutes) Show students a dot and cross diagram of water, a ball and stick diagram of methane, and the molecular formula of carbon dioxide. Ask students to identify the compounds and suggest the topic of the lesson. Students then sort statements on global warming and climate change according to whether they are true or false. **Greenhouse gases** (10 minutes) Set up the experiment to consider the effect of greenhouse gases. Ask students to predict what will happen to the temperature of each flask and to suggest why they think this.	**Extend:** Ask students to draw the ball and stick diagram, dot and cross diagram, and molecular formula of these three greenhouse gases. **Support:** Use a data logger with a temperature probe and project the graph of the live data. **Extend:** Take the temperature of the flasks every five minutes and get students to plot a line graph of the results.	**Interactive:** Climate change

Main	Support/Extend	Resources
Climate change? (30 minutes) Scientists at the University of East Anglia's Climate Research Unit have provided data to show that climate change can be linked to human activity. However, other researchers feel that climate change may not be due to human activity. Ask students to write their conclusion which is backed up by their research. If the Internet is available students should research arguments for and against climate change affected by human activity. **Compare and contrast** (10 minutes) Give students an A4 sheet of paper and ask them to fold it in half to have two A5 sections. One should be marked Greenhouse effect (natural) and the second Global warming or enhanced greenhouse effect (man-made). Ask students to draw a labelled diagram to explain each phenomenon.	**Support:** Ask students to write a bullet point list of the information they have found. **Extend:** You may wish to show students the black body radiation curve of the Earth and show which regions are absorbed by different gases in the atmosphere.	**Activity:** Climate change?

Plenary	Support/Extend	Resources
Greenhouse gases (5 minutes) Look at the experiment and note that both flasks have had an increase in temperature of the water due to the heat lamp. However, the methane-filled flask has heated up more quickly. Please note, if you are measuring how long it takes to reach a specific temperature, you will need to use a data logger. However, if you are expecting the methane flask to be hotter, then you just need a thermometer. **What is happening to Earth?** (10 minutes) Read out statements and ask students to put their thumbs up for true statements and thumbs down for false statements. Students could also label the key features of the greenhouse effect in a diagram.		**Interactive:** What is happening to Earth?

Homework		
Ask students to draw the dot and cross diagrams of the main greenhouse gases in the air – methane, carbon dioxide, and water.		

kerboodle

A Kerboodle highlight for this lesson is **Literacy skills: Greenhouse gases**. Refer to the **Content map** on Kerboodle for a full list of resources and assessment.

C13.4 Global climate change

AQA spec Link: 9.2.3 An increase in average global temperature is a major cause of climate change.

Students should be able to:

- describe briefly four potential effects of global climate change
- discuss the scale, risk, and environmental implications of global climate change.

9.2.4 The carbon footprint is the total amount of carbon dioxide and other greenhouse gases emitted over the full life cycle of a product, service or event.

The carbon footprint can be reduced by reducing emissions of carbon dioxide and methane.

Students should be able to:

- describe actions to reduce emissions of carbon dioxide and methane
- give reasons why actions may be limited.

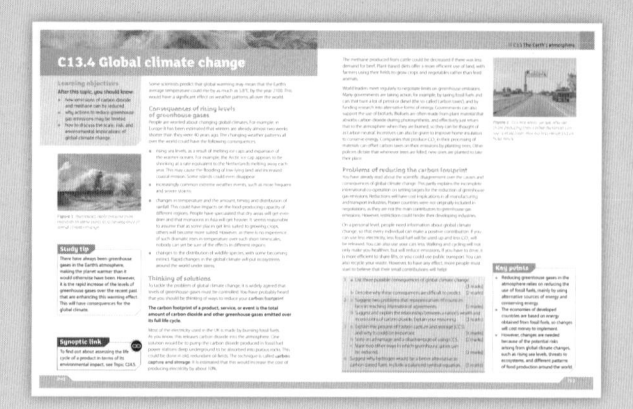

WS 1.3, 1.5

Aiming for	Outcome	Checkpoint	
		Question	Activity
Aiming for GRADE 4	List some of the possible outcomes of climate change.	1	Starter 1, Starter 2, Main, Plenary 1, Plenary 2
	State a definition for carbon footprint.		Main
	List some ways to reduce a carbon footprint.	End of chapter 3	Main, Plenary 2, Homework
Aiming for GRADE 6	Explain the possible effects of global climate change and why they are difficult to predict.	1	Starter 2, Main
	Explain possible methods to reduce greenhouse gas emissions.	2, 3	Starter 2, Main, Plenary 2
	Explain some of the problems in trying to reduce greenhouse gas emissions.	2	Main
Aiming for GRADE 8	Evaluate the scale, risk, and environmental impact of global climate change.	2	Starter 2, Main
	Justify why reducing greenhouse gas emissions can be difficult to achieve.	3	Main
	Evaluate the use of products, services, or events in terms of their carbon footprint.	4	Main

Literacy
Students use their scientific knowledge to write a conclusion.

Key words
carbon footprint, carbon capture and storage

200

■ C13 The Earth's atmosphere

Starter	Support/Extend	Resources
Polar ice (5 minutes) Show an image of the extent of the polar ice caps in 1800, 1900, 2000, and the present day. Ask students to speculate what the images show. Ensure students can distinguish between the enhanced greenhouse effect and depletion of the ozone layer by CFCs. **Climate change** (10 minutes) Use question and answer to find out what students already know about climate change. Ask students to list the impact of climate change.	**Extend:** Ask students to sort the impacts into environmental, social, and economic.	

Main	Support/Extend	Resources
Discussing climate change (40 minutes) Students should look back at the conclusion they wrote in the previous lesson. They then add to this conclusion what the potential effects of global climate change are, what actions are being taken to try to reduce the effects of global climate change, and what are the problems faced. Students then make a list of all their daily routines that may contribute to their carbon footprint. Ask students to make a bullet-point list of three ways that they could reduce their carbon footprint and the steps they can take to achieve this. Students could use an online calculator to calculate their carbon footprint.	**Support:** Ask students to write a bullet-point list of the information they have found. **Extend:** You may wish to show students the black body radiation curve of the Earth and show which regions are absorbed by different gases in the atmosphere.	**Activity:** Discussing climate change

Plenary	Support/Extend	Resources
Consequences list (5 minutes) Students look at statements describing consequences of global warming. They sort them according to whether they are economic, environmental, or social. **Radio advert** (10 minutes) Ask students to write a brief radio advert (no more than one minute) about the possibility of climate change, its impact, and how you could change your lifestyle to reduce the effect.	**Extend:** Ask for volunteers to read their advert out.	**Interactive:** Consequences list

Homework		
Ask students to make a flow chart to describe the process of carbon capture and storage.		

kerboodle
A Kerboodle highlight for this lesson is **WebQuest: Capturing carbon**. Refer to the **Content map** on Kerboodle for a full list of resources and assessment.

C13.5 Atmospheric pollutants

AQA spec Link: 9.3.1 The combustion of fuels is a major source of atmospheric pollutants.

Most fuels, including coal, contain carbon and/or hydrogen and may also contain some sulfur.

The gases released into the atmosphere when a fuel is burnt may include carbon dioxide, water vapour, carbon monoxide, sulfur dioxide, and oxides of nitrogen. Solid particles and unburnt hydrocarbons may also be released that form particulates in the atmosphere.

Students should be able to:

- describe how carbon monoxide, soot (carbon particles), sulfur dioxide, and oxides of nitrogen are produced by burning fuels
- predict the products of combustion of a fuel given appropriate information about the composition of the fuel and the conditions in which it is used.

9.3.2 Carbon monoxide is a toxic gas. It is colourless and odourless and so is not easily detected.

Sulfur dioxide and oxides of nitrogen cause respiratory problems in humans and cause acid rain.

Particulates cause global dimming and health problems for humans.

Students should be able to describe and explain the problems caused by increased amounts of these pollutants in the air.

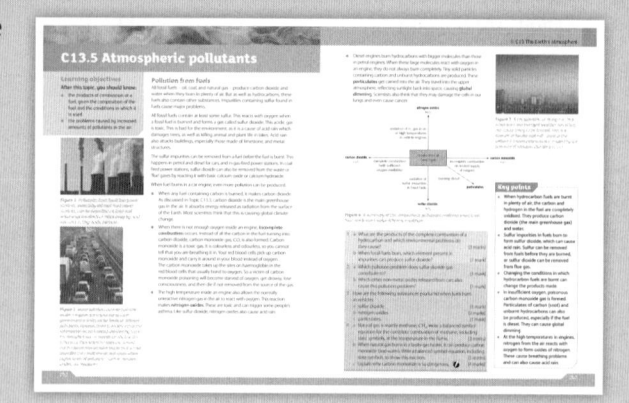

WS 1.4

Aiming for	Outcome	Checkpoint	
		Question	Activity
Aiming for GRADE 4	List some atmospheric pollutants.	1, 2	Starter 2, Main, Plenary 1
	Describe how carbon monoxide and soot (carbon) can be made from the incomplete combustion of fossil fuels.	3	Main
	Complete word equations to describe how atmospheric pollutants can be made.	3	Starter 2, Plenary 2
Aiming for GRADE 6	Explain how sulfur dioxide and nitrogen oxides are made when fossil fuels are combusted.	1, 3	Main
	Describe the health impacts of atmospheric pollutants.	1, 4	Main
	Use balanced symbol equations to show how atmospheric pollutants are formed.	4	Starter 2, Main, Plenary 2
Aiming for GRADE 8	Predict the products of combustion of a fuel given appropriate information about the composition of the fuel and the conditions in which it is used.	4	Main
	Evaluate the negative social, economic, and environmental consequences of atmospheric pollution.	1, 2, End of chapter Q 2	Plenary 1
	Suggest and explain methods to reduce atmospheric pollution.	End of chapter Q 2	Main

Maths
Students write balanced symbol equations.

Key words
incomplete combustion, nitrogen oxides, particulates, global dimming

C13 The Earth's atmosphere

Practical

Title	Burning sulfur
Equipment	gas jar of oxygen with about 5 cm depth of water at the bottom with universal indicator added, Bunsen burner, heat proof mat, eye protection, deflagrating spoon, sulfur flowers, spatula
Overview of method	Set up a Bunsen burner. Fill the deflagrating spoon with sulfur flowers. Heat the sulfur until it catches fire and quickly put into the gas jar of oxygen. Swirl gas jar and observe any colour changes in the universal indicator.
Safety considerations	oxygen is oxidising. Sulfur burns to produce toxic sulfur dioxide gas. This practical should ideally be carried out in a fume cupboard but could be completed in a well-ventilated room if the gas jar is quickly removed to the fume cupboard after combustion. Take care with any students with breathing problems. Wear chemical splash-proof eye protection.

Title	Using fuels
Equipment	Bunsen burner, flame proof mat, two evaporating dishes, tongs, eye protection
Overview of method	Set up a Bunsen burner. Using the tongs, hold the evaporating dish in the blue flame for about 10 seconds. Repeat with the second evaporating dish held in the yellow flame.
Safety considerations	Thermal burns can be caused.

Starter	Support/Extend	Resources
Burning sulfur (5 minutes) Demonstrate the combustion of sulfur. Ask students to suggest what the solution formed at the bottom of the gas jar indicates about the product of the reaction and then use this evidence to predict the effect on the atmosphere. **Equations** (10 minutes) Ask students to write the combustion equations for nitrogen forming nitrogen monoxide, nitrogen forming nitrogen dioxide, a hydrocarbon forming carbon dioxide and water, a hydrocarbon forming carbon, carbon monoxide, and water, and finally sulfur forming sulfur dioxide.	**Extend:** Ask students to write a symbol equation for the production of sulfur dioxide and sulfuric and sulfurous acids. **Support:** Ask students to write only word equations. Work as a class and build up the equations on the board through question and answer.	

Main	Support/Extend	Resources
Using fuels (40 minutes) Introduce students to what a fossil fuel is, how fossil fuels are made, and the environmental consequences of using them. Students then complete the practical as detailed. Ask students what they notice as they use the flames. Students should focus on each flame separately, writing an equation to illustrate the reaction, and then annotate the products to explain their environmental impact as atmospheric pollutants. Then explain that fossil fuels often contain sulfur impurities, which are now removed from petrol. Ask students to write a combustion equation for this reaction when sulfur impurities are not removed, and again to annotate the equation to explain the effects of the product as an atmospheric pollutant. Ask students to generate a visual summary of fossil fuels, encouraging them to use equations in their work.	**Extend:** Explain to students that hydrocarbon gases in the form of autogas can be used in car engines. Ask students to write an equation for the production of NO_x in a car engine and again annotate the products to explain their impact as atmospheric pollutants.	**Practical:** Using fuels

Plenary	Support/Extend	Resources
Pollutant match (5 minutes) Ask students to match the pollutant with the effect. **Pollutant equations** (10 minutes) Ask students to write a list of the key points of the lesson. They then write an equation to illustrate each key point.	**Extend:** Ask students to match the pollutant with the balanced equation to show its formation as well as the effect.	**Interactive:** Pollutant match

Homework		
Ask students to draw a labelled diagram to describe how acid rain is formed in industry and from car engines.	**Extend:** Ask students to include and explain the effects of acid rain.	

kerboodle

A Kerboodle highlight for this lesson is **Literacy sheet: Atmospheric pollution**. Refer to the **Content map** on Kerboodle for a full list of resources and assessment.

C13 The Earth's atmosphere

Overview of C13 The Earth's atmosphere

In this chapter, students have learnt about the Earth's atmosphere. Students only need to be able to describe the volcanic activity theory of the origin of the atmosphere, but they should be able to interpret evidence concerning other theories, and be able to evaluate them. To describe the history of the atmosphere students will need to have a sense of the timescales involved.

Along with an understanding of the origins of the atmosphere, students should also understand how it has evolved over time. This includes both how the general composition of the atmosphere has changed and how the atmosphere is currently being affect by human activity. Students should be able to describe the human activities that are thought to cause global warming, and be able to explain some of the effects this has on the climate of the Earth. Students should also be able to explain the effect of other pollutants on the Earth, including carbon monoxide, sulfur dioxide, nitrogen oxides, and particulates.

Throughout this chapter, students have had many opportunities to develop their working scientifically skills, including evaluating models and interpreting and evaluating evidence for scientific theories.

MyMaths

You can find additional support for the maths skills covered in this chapter on **MyMaths**, including standard form and using large numbers, interpreting data, and pie charts.

kerboodle

For this chapter, the following assessments are available on Kerboodle:

C13 Checkpoint quiz: The Earth's atmosphere
C13 Progress quiz: The Earth's atmosphere 1
C13 Progress quiz: The Earth's atmosphere 2
C13 On your marks: The Earth's atmosphere
C13 Exam-style questions and mark scheme: The Earth's atmosphere

Checkpoint follow up lesson

A student's route through this lesson can be determined using the Checkpoint assessment. Percentage pass marks are supplied in the Checkpoint teacher notes.

For each successive route through it is assumed that the student can perform to their current route as well as previous routes. For example, students working at Aiming for 6 are assumed to be secure in Aiming for 4 knowledge and understanding and working towards achieving all the learning outcomes for Aiming for 6.

	Aiming for 4	**Aiming for 6**	**Aiming for 8**
Learning outcomes	State how the atmosphere has changed from its early origins to the modern day.	Describe how the atmosphere has changed from its early origins to the modern day.	Outline how the Earth's atmosphere continually changes over time.
		Describe how the atmosphere and climate may be affected by increased levels of greenhouse gases.	Explain how human influence may have led to changes in the Earth's atmosphere and climate.
Starter	**Revising the atmosphere (10 minutes)** Ask students to draw up a list of the common greenhouse gases and where they come from. Then ask students to draw up a list of possible consequences of global warming and climate change. Recap that the atmosphere has evolved over many millions of years and the level of carbon dioxide has been much higher in the past, during the early atmosphere. Ask students to state one way (either during the stages of the early atmosphere or the modern atmosphere) that carbon dioxide (and hence carbon) can be removed from the atmosphere.		
Differentiated checkpoint activity	The Aiming for 4 Checkpoint follow-up sheet supports students with creating a timeline for the Earth's atmosphere. They are provided with prompt sentences to complete, which are in the correct order, and are encouraged to draw diagrams for each stage.	The Aiming for 6 Checkpoint follow-up sheet supports students with creating an annotated timeline for the Earth's atmosphere. They are given prompt statements to help them identify the key stages to include in their timeline.	Students use the Aiming for 8 Checkpoint follow-up sheet to write a letter to people living at the beginning of the Industrial revolution. The purpose of their letter is to explain how human activity affects the atmosphere and the climate, and to encourage them to take sensible steps to help reduce the issues faced currently.
	Kerboodle resource C13 Checkpoint follow up: Aiming for 4, C13 Checkpoint follow up: Aiming for 6, C13 Checkpoint follow up: Aiming for 8		
Plenary	**Work review (5 minutes)** Ask students to lay their timelines/letters around the room. Students should then choose another student's work to review. They should read the other student's work and decide on two strong points about it and one point that could be improved on. **Key points (5 minutes)** Ask students to decide as a pair three key learning points from the chapter. Review these as a class. Address any misconceptions should they arise.		
Progression	Encourage students to include word equations for any relevant processes. Students could be encouraged to include symbol equations as well.	Students include the evidence that supports the different parts of their timeline, and include an evaluation of the evidence.	Students research alternative theories about the history of the earth's atmosphere and evaluate the evidence presented for them.

C 14 The Earth's resources
14.1 Finite and renewable resources

AQA spec Link: 10.1.1 Humans use the Earth's resources to provide warmth, shelter, food, and transport.

Natural resources, supplemented by agriculture, provide food, timber, clothing, and fuels.

Finite resources from the Earth, oceans, and atmosphere are processed to provide energy and materials.

Chemistry plays an important role in improving agricultural and industrial processes to provide new products, and in sustainable development, which is development that meets the needs of current generations without compromising the ability of future generations to meet their own needs.

Students should be able to:

- state examples of natural products that are supplemented or replaced by agricultural and synthetic products
- distinguish between finite and renewable resources given appropriate information
- extract and interpret information about resources from charts, graphs, and tables
- use orders of magnitude to evaluate the significance of data.

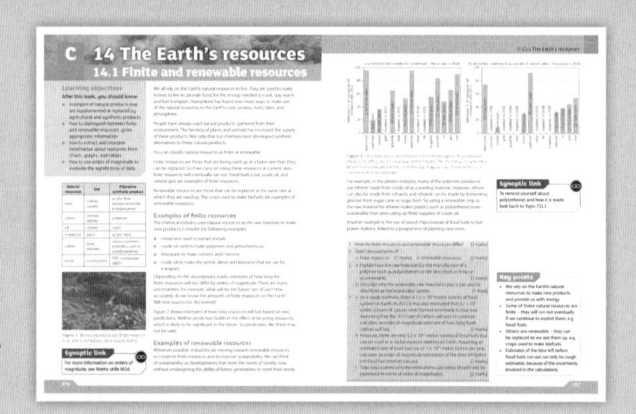

WS 3.2
MS 1b, 2c, 2h, 4a

Aiming for	Outcome	Checkpoint	
		Question	Activity
Aiming for GRADE 4	List some human uses of the Earth's resources.		Main
	Give examples of a finite and a renewable resource.	2	Starter 2
	State an example of a natural product that is supplemented or replaced by agricultural or synthetic products.		Starter 1, Main
Aiming for GRADE 6	Describe and classify a resource as finite or renewable when information is given.	1, 3	Starter 2, Plenary 2
	Explain the use of natural, sustainable, and finite resources.	3	Main
	Interpret information from different formats including graphs, charts, tables, and prose.		Main
Aiming for GRADE 8	Understand data and interpret information using orders of magnitude to compare.	4	Main, Plenary 1
	Explain the role of chemistry in improving agricultural and industrial processes.		Main
	Draw conclusions consistent with information provided from graphs, charts, tables, and prose and evaluate the validity of the data.	4	Main

Maths
Students express numbers in standard form (1b) and make estimates using orders of magnitude (2h).

Literacy
Students research how the uses of crude oil have changed over time, and materials that have been / are being developed to replace it. They use this information to create a timeline of crude oil.

C14 The Earth's resources

Starter	Support/Extend	Resources
What's the connection (5 minutes) Show students a sheep skin top, a woolly jumper, and a polyester jumper. Ask students to suggest the connection and what they will be studying this lesson.		
Sorting resources (10 minutes) Students use the interactive to sort a list of resources according to whether they are finite or renewable.	**Support:** Define the two terms before beginning the activity.	**Interactive:** Sorting resources
Then provide students with information about resources in prose format. Students have to interpret the information to identify finite and renewable resources.	**Extend:** Ask students to justify their groupings.	

Main	Support/Extend	Resources
Crude oil timeline (40 minutes) Explain to students that in some parts of the world crude oil pools on the surface. In the early 1900s this was set on fire, and then the tar-like substance was removed and used as a fuel. The process became industrialised using fractional distillation to separate the crude oil into fractions and now the fractions undergo further processing to make polymers that have replaced natural fibres in fabrics.	**Extend:** Encourage students to think about the uses of crude oil across the Earth, and not just in the UK.	**Activity:** Crude oil timeline
Ask students to research the development of the exploitation of crude oil and how chemists have developed techniques to allow products of crude oil to replace natural renewable resources. Students should make a timeline showing the development, including information about finite, renewable, natural, and synthetic resources.		
Their timeline should also include how the uses of crude oil have changed over time.		

Plenary	Support/Extend	Resources
Orders of magnitude (5 minutes) Ask students to express the following numbers in standard form: 6 billion, 1800, 805, 100 million.	**Extend:** Ask students to use the Maths Skills section of the student book to suggest the number of significant figures each number is expressed to.	
Fossil fuels (10 minutes) Ask students to look at the graphs in Figure 2 of Topic C14.1 of the student book and explain what they show. Students should evaluate the usefulness of this data and suggest limits to the predictions.		

Homework		
Ask students to explain why polymers made from corn starch, such as biodegradable composting bags, are sustainable.		

kerboodle

A Kerboodle highlight for this lesson is **Calculation sheet: Orders of magnitude**. Refer to the **Content map** on Kerboodle for a full list of resources and assessment.

C14.2 Water safe to drink

AQA spec Link: 10.1.2 Water of appropriate quality is essential for life. For humans, drinking water should have sufficiently low levels of dissolved salts and microbes. Water that is safe to drink is called potable water. Potable water is not pure water in the chemical sense because it contains dissolved substances.
The methods used to produce potable water depend on available supplies of water and local conditions.
In the United Kingdom (UK), rain provides water with low levels of dissolved substances (fresh water) that collects in the ground and in lakes and rivers, and most potable water is produced by:
- choosing an appropriate source of fresh water
- passing the water through filter beds
- sterilising

Sterilising agents used for potable water include chlorine, ozone, or ultraviolet light.
If supplies of fresh water are limited, desalination of salty water or sea water may be required. Desalination can be done by distillation or by processes that use membranes such as reverse osmosis. These processes require large amounts of energy.
Students should be able to:
- distinguish between potable water and pure water
- describe the differences in treatment of ground water and salty water.

Required practical: Analysis and purification of water samples from different sources, including pH, dissolved solids, and distillation.

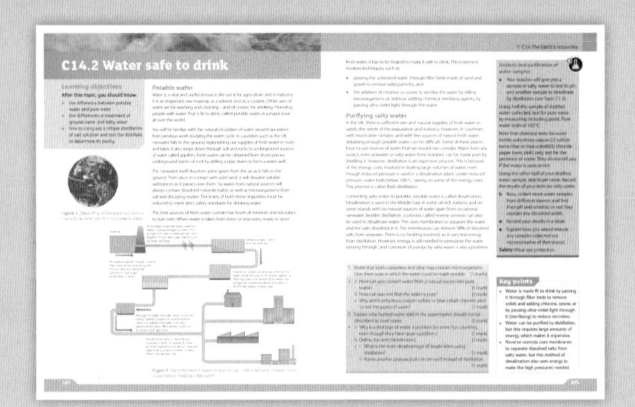

WS 1.3, 1.4, 1.5, 2.2, 2.3
MS 2c

Aiming for	Outcome	Checkpoint	
		Question	Activity
Aiming for GRADE 4	Describe why potable water is important.		Starter 2
	List the key processes to make drinking water.	1, 2	Main, Plenary 1
	Safely distil salty water.		Main
Aiming for GRADE 6	Explain why the method of obtaining potable water depends on the local conditions.		Main
	Explain reasons for filtration and sterilisation in water treatment.		Plenary 1, Plenary 2
	Describe and explain in detail how to safely distil salty water.		Main, Plenary 1, Plenary 2
Aiming for GRADE 8	Explain the difference between pure water and potable water.	2, 3	Starter 2, Main
	Justify the choice of potable water supply in a given scenario.	4, End of chapter 1	Main
	Explain in detail why desalination is not often used to generate safe clean drinking water and justify when it is used.	4	Homework

Maths
Students decide the best way to record their results for the practical.
H Higher-tier students also determine the original concentration of the salt solution. Students also draw a pie chart from given data.

Literacy
Students write their own method for the practical.

208

■ C14 The Earth's resources

Required practical

Title	Analysis and purification of water samples
Equipment	300 cm³ and 100 cm³ round-bottom flasks, Bunsen burner, gauze, tripod, heatproof mat, anti-bumping granules, thermometer −10 to 110 °C, quick-fit thermometer holder, condenser, quick-fit clips, saline, electric balance, measuring cylinder, pH meter, clamp and stand
Overview of method	Set up a simple distillation apparatus. Half fill the larger round-bottom flask with saline and add a few anti-bumping granules. Connect to the condenser and use the Bunsen burner to boil the mixture. Collect the distillate in the smaller round-bottom flask. Once distillation is complete, test the purity of the sample. Take half of the sample and measure the boiling point (pure water will boil at 100 °C). Take the other half of the sample and measure the pH.
Safety considerations	Thermal burns can occur and any imperfections in the glassware could cause cracking when they are heated. Wear eye protection.

Starter	Support/Extend	Resources
Water purification (10 minutes) Show students a diagram of a simple distillation set-up. Ask students to label the equipment. Then introduce the four methods of water purification from the specification. Students match each method with its description.	**Extend:** Ask students to suggest why anti-bumping granules should be added to the mixture.	**Interactive:** Water purification
Pie chart (10 minutes) Explain to students that 97% of the water on Earth is in the oceans and seas, with the remaining 3% being fresh water. Ask students to use this data to draw a pie chart. Then ask students to consider how drinking water could be made from the water supplies.	**Extend:** Ask students to suggest where the fresh water would be found (e.g., lakes and glaciers). **Support:** Remind students that water from the oceans and seas is not suitable for drinking.	

Main	Support/Extend	Resources
Analysis and purification of water samples (40 minutes) Ask students to write an outline method of how to use distillation to make pure water from salt water. Then allow students to complete the practical. **H** Higher-tier students should devise and carry out a method to determine the concentration of the original salt solution.	**Extend:** Ask students to suggest how they could determine if there were any other solutes other than NaCl in the sample. **Support:** Get small groups to research one technique and then put the information on a table on the board for everyone to copy into their notes.	**Required practical:** Analysis and purification of water samples

Plenary	Support/Extend	Resources
Making drinking water (5 minutes) Show students a pictorial flow chart of how drinking water is made in the UK. Ask students to label the key parts of the procedure. **Compare and contrast** (10 minutes) Ask students to complete a three-column table with the following headings: | Process | How it works | Potable? | The table allows students to compare and contrast distillation, desalination, filtering, and sterilising.	**Extend:** Ask students to explain why filtration and chlorination or ozonation are part of the process.	

Homework		
Students complete the WebQuest where they research potable water.		**WebQuest:** Potable water

kerboodle

A Kerboodle highlight for this lesson is **Literacy skills: Water safe to drink**. Refer to the **Content map** on Kerboodle for a full list of resources and assessment.

C14.3 Treating waste water

AQA spec Link: 10.1.3 Urban lifestyles and industrial processes produce large amounts of waste water that require treatment before being released into the environment. Sewage and agricultural waste water require removal of organic matter and harmful microbes. Industrial waste water may require removal of organic matter and harmful chemicals.

Sewage treatment includes:
- screening and grit removal
- sedimentation to produce sewage sludge and effluent
- anaerobic digestion of sewage sludge
- aerobic biological treatment of effluent.

Students should be able to comment on the relative ease of obtaining potable water from waste, ground, and salt water.

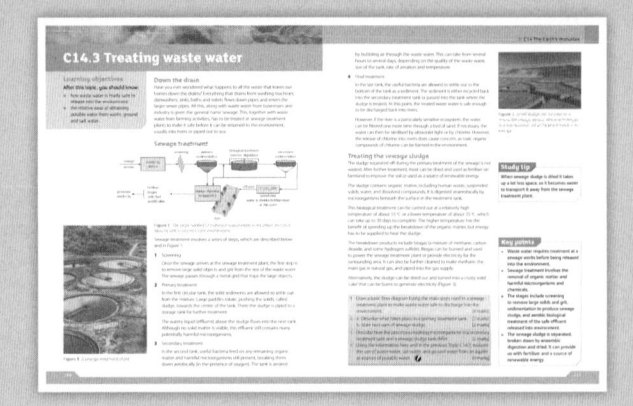

WS 1.2

Aiming for	Outcome	Checkpoint	
		Question	Activity
Aiming for GRADE 4 ↓	List what is removed from waste water before it can be released.		Starter 1, Main, Plenary 1
	State the main processes in sewage treatment.	1	Main
	State uses of sewage slurry.	2	Main
Aiming for GRADE 6 ↓	Explain why waste water should be treated before it is released into the environment.		Starter 1, Main
	Describe the main processes in sewage treatment.	1, 2	Main, Plenary 1
	Explain uses of sewage slurry.		Main
Aiming for GRADE 8 ↓	Evaluate the ease of obtaining potable water from waste, ground, or salt water.	4	Homework
	Explain in detail how and why waste water is processed before it is released into the environment.	3	Main
	Evaluate the use of sewage slurry.		Main

Maths
Students make estimations of water usage.

Literacy
Students create a flow chart of the stages of waste water treatment.

210

C14 The Earth's resources

Starter	Support/Extend	Resources
Waste water (5 minutes) Students order sentences to describe the process of water treatment. They then identify what the water may contain that means it needs to be treated before it can be released into the environment. **How much water do you use?** (10 minutes) Use an online water calculator to calculate how much water each student uses on average.	**Support:** Show students some images of industry and domestic life that produce waste water. **Extend:** Make a tally chart to display the class data.	**Interactive:** Waste water

Main	Support/Extend	Resources
Sewage treatment (40 minutes) Model water treatment by using 'pond water' made of water, flour, sand, stones, and pond weed. Filter the water, collecting the filtrate, and show how it is still cloudy. Leave the filtrate to stand, then syphon off the water from the top. Treat this water with a water purification tablet. Use question and answer as well as the diagram in the student book to explain the processes in water treatment. Then ask students to create a flow chart to explain how waste water is treated. They should include uses of sewage slurry and explain its usefulness.	**Support:** If the school is near a treatment plant, you may be able to organise a visit.	**Activity:** Sewage treatment

Plenary	Support/Extend	Resources
Finish the sentences (5 minutes) Ask students to complete the following sentences: • Waste industrial water contains… • Sedimentation produces… • Anerobic digestion is used… **Questions** (10 minutes) Ask students to write two questions about sewage treatment in the UK, using the student book and specification excerpt to guide them. Then ask students to swap the questions with a partner who should answer them as fully as possible.	**Support:** Show students the ends of the sentences so they can match them with the start. **Support:** Give students a list of AQA command words and encourage them to use these in their questions. **Extend:** Ask students to ramp the questions.	

Homework		
Ask students to evaluate the use of ground water, salt water, and waste water as sources for potable water.	**Support:** Ask students to list the advantages and disadvantages of each source of water for processing into potable water. **Extend:** Give students different scenarios and they should justify their chosen source of water to make potable water.	

Higher tier

C14.4 Extracting metals from ores

AQA spec Link: 10.1.4 The Earth's resources of metal ores are limited.

Copper ores are becoming scarce and new ways of extracting copper from low-grade ores include phytomining, and bioleaching. These methods avoid traditional mining methods of digging, moving, and disposing of large amounts of rock. Phytomining uses plants to absorb metal compounds. The plants are harvested and then burnt to produce ash that contains the metal compounds.

Bioleaching uses bacteria to produce leachate solutions that contain metal compounds.

The metal compounds can be processed to obtain the metal. For example, copper can be obtained from solutions of copper compounds by displacement using scrap iron or by electrolysis. Students should be able to evaluate alternative biological methods of metal extraction, given appropriate information.

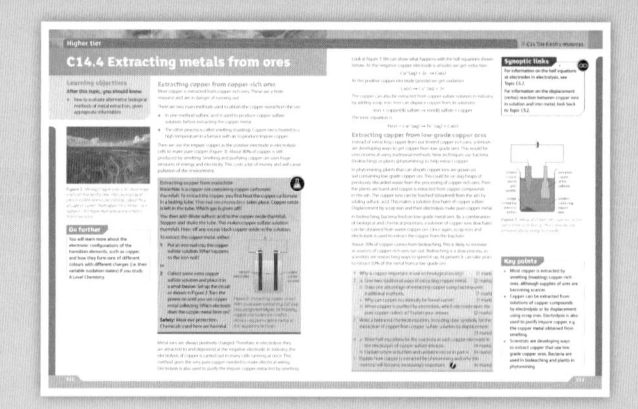

MS 1c

Aiming for	Outcome	Checkpoint	
		Question	Activity
Aiming for GRADE 6	Describe the processes of phytomining and bioleaching.	End of chapter Q2	Main, Plenary 1
	Write balanced symbol equations to explain metal extraction techniques.	3	Main, Plenary 2, Homework
	Explain the need for new ways of extracting metals (in particular copper).	1, 2	Main
Aiming for GRADE 8	Explain in detail how phytomining and bioleaching extract metals.	End of chapter Q3	Main
	Write ionic equations to explain metal extraction techniques and identify the species being oxidised or reduced.	4, End of chapter Q2	Main
	Evaluate biological methods of metal extraction.	5	Plenary 2

Maths
Students calculate the percentage copper in copper ore (1c).

Literacy
Students use scientific terminology to write a summary of how to extract copper from its ore.

Key words
thermal decomposition, bioleaching

Practical

Title	Extracting copper from malachite
Equipment	Bunsen burner, flameproof mat, spatula, copper carbonate powder, 2 mol/dm³ or less sulfuric acid, dropping pipette, boiling tube, boiling-tube holder, boiling-tube rack, filter funnel, filter paper, 100 cm³ conical flask, eye protection, iron nail, 100 cm³ beaker, three wires, two crocodile clips, low voltage power supply, two carbon electrodes
Overview of method	Put about three spatulas of copper carbonate into a boiling tube. Using the boiling-tube holder, heat strongly at a 45° angle in the blue Bunsen flame. When all of the powder has changed colour from green to black, remove from the heat and allow to cool in the boiling-tube rack. Using a dropping pipette, half fill the boiling tube with dilute sulfuric acid. Mix well and leave for a minute for the reaction to complete. Filter the contents of the boiling tube into the conical flask and keep the filtrate. To collect the copper add an iron nail to the solution and a displacement reaction will occur on the surface of the nail to produce copper. Alternatively, transfer the blue filtrate into the beaker and set up a simple electrolysis cell. When the current flows, copper will collect on the cathode.
Safety considerations	Copper carbonate, copper oxide, and copper sulfate are harmful. Dilute sulfuric acid is corrosive. Wear chemical splash-proof eye protection throughout and wash hands after completing the practical.

C14 The Earth's resources

Starter	Support/Extend	Resources
Copper (5 minutes) Show students images of copper being used, for example, cooking pans, electrical wires, and plumbing supplies. Ask students to suggest the properties of copper.	**Extend:** Ask students to justify each specific use of copper in terms of the properties, including explanations based on its structure and bonding.	
Malachite (10 minutes) Allow students to look and feel samples of real malachite. Explain that the main compound in this mineral is copper(II) carbonate and ask students to write the formula for this compound. Explain that typically for metal carbonates it can undergo thermal decomposition. You may wish to show students a simulation of this and then ask students to write an equation for this reaction.	**Extend:** Ask students to suggest how to obtain the copper from the copper oxide produced in the thermal decomposition reaction.	

Main	Support/Extend	Resources
Extracting copper from malachite (40 minutes) Split the class in half. Ask one group to extract the copper from malachite using the displacement method and the other group to extract it using the electrolysis method. Whilst the boiling tube is cooling and then the displacement reaction is occurring, students should summarise the extraction process and for each stage they should write an equation.	**Support:** Only use the displacement method and demonstrate the electrolysis method. **Extend:** Students should measure the mass of malachite at the beginning and the mass of copper collected at the end and use these values to estimate the percentage copper content of the ore.	**Practical:** Extracting copper from malachite

Plenary	Support/Extend	Resources
Extracting metals (10 minutes) Students choose the correct words to complete a paragraph on the extraction of copper. They then sort statements according to whether they describe bioleaching or phytomining.		**Interactive:** Extracting metals
Ambassador for extraction (10 minutes) Ask students to work in pairs, where each student has used a different method for extraction of copper from malachite. Each student should explain the method they used, whilst the other student takes notes.	**Extend:** Students should evaluate the two different methods and conclude which is the better method.	

Homework		
Students complete the WebQuest where they research phytomining, its effectiveness, and why an alternative to traditional extraction is needed. Alternatively, ask students to explain how smelting with carbon could be used to extract copper from its ore. Students should use equations in their answer.	**Extend:** Students should include notes on reduction and oxidation in the extraction process in terms of electron transfer.	**WebQuest:** Phytomining

kerboodle

A Kerboodle highlight for this lesson is **Go further: Transition elements and variable oxidation states**. Refer to the **Content map** on Kerboodle for a full list of resources and assessment.

C14.5 Life Cycle Assessments

AQA spec Link: 10.2.1 Life Cycle Assessments (LCAs) are carried out to assess the environmental impact of products in each of these stages:
- extracting and processing raw materials
- manufacturing and packaging
- use and operation during its lifetime
- disposal at the end of its useful life, including transport and distribution at each stage.

Use of water, resources, energy sources, and production of some wastes can be fairly easily quantified. Allocating numerical values to pollutant effects is less straightforward and requires value judgements, so LCA is not a purely objective process. Selective or abbreviated LCAs can be devised to evaluate a product but these can be misused to reach pre-determined conclusions, e.g. in support of claims for advertising purposes. Students should be able to carry out simple comparative LCAs for shopping bags made from plastic and paper.

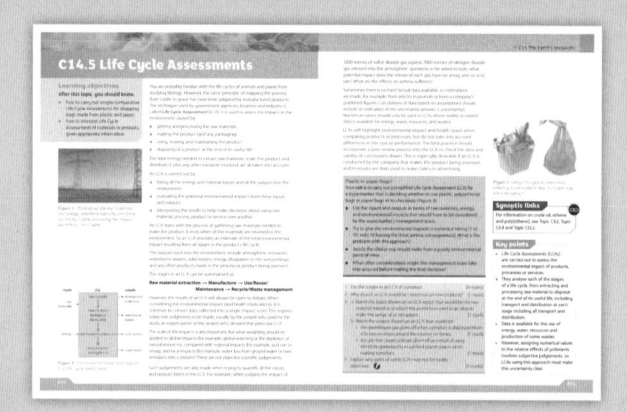

WS 1.3, 4, 5
MS 1a, 1c, 1d, 2a, 2b, 4a

Aiming for	Outcome	Checkpoint	
		Question	Activity
Aiming for GRADE 4 ↓	State the different stages of an LCA in the correct order.	1	Starter 1, Main
	Carry out an LCA for shopping bags made from plastic or paper with support.		Main, Plenary 1
Aiming for GRADE 6 ↓	Explain the importance of LCA and how it can be misused.	2	Main, Plenary 2
	Carry out LCAs for different products when data is supplied.	3	Main, Homework
Aiming for GRADE 8 ↓	Explain the limits of LCAs.	4, End of chapter 5	Plenary 2
	Evaluate products in detail using LCAs.	End of chapter 5	Main, Homework

Maths
Students calculate the LCA and generate a mean (2b).

Literacy
Students write an instruction sheet about LCA.

Key words
Life Cycle Assessment (LCA)

214

C14 The Earth's resources

Starter	Support/Extend	Resources
Life Cycle Assessment (5 minutes) Show students the stages of the Life Cycle Assessment and ask them to put them in the correct order.		**Interactive:** Life Cycle Assessment
Evaluating shopping bags (10 minutes) Give each table a selection of shopping bags – different sizes, long-life, reuseable, paper, card, plastic, biodegradable plastic, and so on. Ask each student to choose their favourite bag and justify why. Using question and answer, write a list of things to consider when choosing a shopping bag (e.g., price, size, durability, aesthetics, environmental impact).	**Support:** Focus students by asking them to consider the use of the bag, how they feel when they use it, and the cost.	

Main	Support/Extend	Resources
Paper or plastic? (40 minutes) Show students a plastic shopping bag and a paper shopping bag. Students complete a simple LCA for each product. Initially, they can list the inputs and outputs in terms of raw materials, energy, and environmental impacts. Then they should give each factor a subjective rating on a scale of 1 to 10. Students then conclude which is the best bag.	**Support:** Allow students to work in small groups. **Extend:** Ask students to evaluate the validity of this method for comparing products.	**Activity:** Paper or plastic?
Then show students a patient information leaflet from a packet of drugs. Focus on the key sections: what it is, how to take it, expected outcomes, and possible side effects. Ask students to use this as inspiration to make an instruction sheet to explain what an LCA is, how to perform one, and the expected outcomes, and drawbacks to this system of evaluating products.	**Extend:** Ask students to use their instruction sheet to evaluate single use and rechargeable batteries.	

Plenary	Support/Extend	Resources
Voting for shopping bags (5 minutes) Collect data from the class to show the LCA values for each bag. Ask students to calculate the mean from the data and decide which bag the class thinks is best.	**Extend:** Students discuss the range of the LCA values and the reasons for this.	
Evaluating the LCA (10 minutes) Ask students to evaluate this as a method of determining whether a product should be brought to market. Suggest some ways that the system could be made more robust.		

Homework		
Ask students to choose a pair of products that have the same function but are made of different material. They then complete an LCA for each product to determine which has the lower environmental impact.		

kerboodle

A Kerboodle highlight for this lesson is **WebQuest: Life Cycle Assessment**. Refer to the **Content map** on Kerboodle for a full list of resources and assessment.

215

C14.6 Reduce, reuse, and recycle

AQA spec Link: 10.2.2 The reduction in use, reuse, and recycling of materials by end users reduces the use of limited resources, use of energy sources, waste, and environmental impacts.

Metals, glass, building materials, clay ceramics, and most plastics are produced from limited raw materials. Much of the energy for the processes comes from limited resources. Obtaining raw materials from the Earth by quarrying and mining causes environmental impacts.

Some products, such as glass bottles, can be reused. Glass bottles can be crushed and melted to make different glass products. Other products cannot be reused and so are recycled for a different use.

Metals can be recycled by melting and recasting or reforming into different products. The amount of separation required for recycling depends on the material and the properties required of the final product. For example, some scrap steel can be added to iron from a blast furnace to reduce the amount of iron that needs to be extracted from iron ore.

Students should be able to evaluate ways of reducing the use of limited resources, given appropriate information.

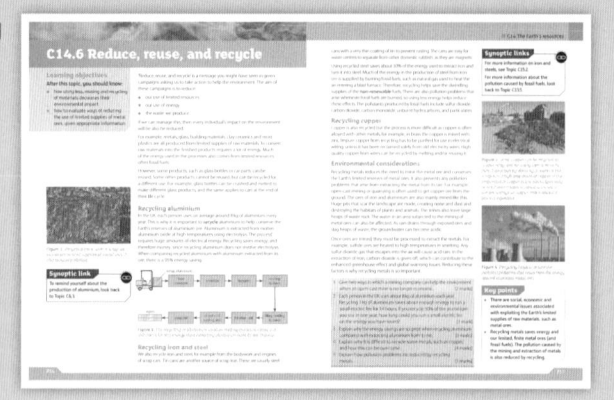

Aiming for	Outcome	Checkpoint Question	Checkpoint Activity
Aiming for GRADE 4	List some products that can be reused or recycled.		Starter 1, Main, Plenary 1
	Describe how metal can be reused and recycled.		Plenary 1
	Describe how glass can be reused and recycled.		Plenary 1
Aiming for GRADE 6	Explain the importance of reusing and recycling products.		Main, Plenary 1, Plenary 2
	Explain why some recycling can be difficult.	4	Main, Plenary 2
	Evaluate ways of reducing the use of limited resources when information is given.	3, End of chapter 4	Main, Plenary 2
Aiming for GRADE 8	Evaluate the environmental, economic, and social impacts of reusing and recycling products.	2, 5	Main, Plenary 1, Plenary 2
	Evaluate ways of reducing the use of limited resources.		Starter 1, Main, Plenary 2
	Suggest ways of minimising the environmental impact of exploiting raw materials.	5	Main, Plenary 2

Maths
Students manipulate data to evaluate the reusing and recycling of products.

Literacy
Students prepare a debate.

Key words
recycle, non-renewable, blast furnace

C14 The Earth's resources

Starter	Support/Extend	Resources
Bottled water (5 minutes) Students use the interactive to identify the definitions of used, reused, and recycle, and then match these key terms to an example relating to bottled water. They then match a piece of packaging with the material it is made of and a common use.		**Interactive:** Bottled water
Where does it come from? (10 minutes) Ask students to make a list of materials that are used on most days of our lives in the UK. Then ask students to briefly state where these materials have come from, for example, wood from trees, copper extracted from ores and purified, glass from sand and recycled.	**Extend:** Ask students to classify the materials as sustainable or non-renewable.	

Main	Support/Extend	Resources
Recycling metals (40 minutes) Ask students to consider the recycling of aluminium drinks cans. Split the class into two groups to prepare for a debate on the motion: 'Aluminium drinks cans should not be recycled'. Each group of students could have an 'expert' with viewpoints that they could question in the debate. Students should develop an expert character such as a research chemist to be used as an expert in the debate to sway the arguments. Give each group a profile of the expert and an overview of their thoughts. Then run the debate.	**Support:** Encourage students to make a list of the advantages and disadvantages of recycling. **Extend:** Ask students to play the parts of the 'experts'.	**Activity:** Recycling metals

Plenary	Support/Extend	Resources
Use, reuse, and recycle (10 minutes) Show students a selection of objects made of different materials, such as a metal drinks can, plastic milk bottle, glass milk bottle, bottle of water, and a can of beans. Using sticky notes, students work in small groups to state what type of material is mainly in the product, which raw materials are needed to make it, and how to reuse/recycle it.	**Extend:** Ask students to evaluate if it would be best to reuse, recycle, or just put the product in landfill.	
What do you think? (10 minutes) Ask students to summarise their thoughts on aluminium recycling, justifying their opinion and stating whether they have changed their mind.		

Homework		
Ask students to compare and contrast the recycling of iron and glass. Ask students to consider the statement: scrap iron is to pig iron as glass cutlet is to new glass.		
Students should understand that scrap iron is put into the blast furnace as well as iron ore to make new iron. Cutlet is broken used glass, which is added to the melt when new glass is made.		

kerboodle

A Kerboodle highlight for this lesson is **Bump up your grade: Using polymers**. Refer to the **Content map** on Kerboodle for a full list of resources and assessment.

C14 The Earth's resources

Overview of C14 The Earth's resources

In this chapter, students have learnt about the difference between finite and renewable resources. It is important that students understand that renewable resources are not an infinite supply, but are replaceable at a rate similar to the rate they are used up, whereas finite resources are used up faster than they can be replenished. Students understanding of finite and renewable resources should be applied to the need to reuse and recycle, and they should be able to describe and evaluate ways of reducing the use of finite resources, and carry out life cycle assessments on products.

Students then looked at specific resources that we use, including water and metals (in particular copper). Students should be able to describe the different ways that water is treated, both to create potable water and to remove waste products so it is safe to release into the environment. Students have already met metal-ore extraction and electrolysis, and higher-tier students should have applied that knowledge to the extraction of copper, as well as understanding alternative biological methods used to extract copper.

Required practical

All students are expected to have carried out the required practicals:

Practical	Topic
Analysis and purification of water samples from different sources, including pH, dissolved solids, and distillation.	C14.2

MyMaths

You can find additional support for the maths skills covered in this chapter on **MyMaths**, including drawing graphs, using standarf orm, orders of magnitude, using ratios, and using percentages.

kerboodle

For this chapter, the following assessments are available on Kerboodle:

C14 Checkpoint quiz: The Earth's resources
C14 Progress quiz: The Earth's resources 1
C14 Progress quiz: The Earth's resources 2
C14 On your marks: The Earth's resources
C14 Exam-style questions and mark scheme: The Earth's resources

Checkpoint follow up lesson

A student's route through this lesson can be determined using the Checkpoint assessment. Percentage pass marks are supplied in the Checkpoint teacher notes.

For each successive route through it is assumed that the student can perform to their current route as well as previous routes. For example, students working at Aiming for 6 are assumed to be secure in Aiming for 4 knowledge and understanding and working towards achieving all the learning outcomes for Aiming for 6.

	Aiming for 4	Aiming for 6	Aiming for 8
Learning outcomes	Describe how potable water can be obtained using distillation.	Explain how distillation purifies water and can be used to desalinate water.	Describe and explain the different methods for extracting copper.
	Describe how potable water can be obtained by passing freshwater through filter beds.	Describe how desalination can occur using reverse osmosis/ membranes.	Discuss the issues surrounding the sustainability and effectiveness of the methods discussed.
Starter	**Finite or renewable? (5 minutes)** Recap the differences between finite resources and renewable resources. Ask students to give names of resources that fall into each category. Produce a list on the board. Ask students to justify their choices for each resource they name. **Using the Earth's resources (5 minutes)** Ask students to discuss in pairs the meaning of the phrase 'reduce, reuse, recycle'. Discuss as a class the meanings of each word and why we need to use the Earth's resources carefully. Explain that they will be working on an activity that relates to using the Earth's resources responsibly.		
Differentiated checkpoint activity	**(40 minutes)** Explain to students that they will be using their Checkpoint follow-up sheet to produce a script for a television programme about obtaining resources. Aiming for 4 and Aiming for 6 students will focus on potable water and Aiming for 8 students on copper metal. They will need to work as a group (if appropriate) to come up with a five minute script. They will also need to develop any resources they need for their mini-programme, for example, posters showing key equations or diagrams of equipment. Students should be asked to present their programmes, following the script they have written. This could take place in a separate lesson if needs be, and could even be filmed to make the experience more authentic. The process of distillation (e.g., of salty or inky water) should be demonstrated to Aiming for 4 and Aiming for 6 students. You may wish to provide Internet access or additional printed resources (as well as the student book) to students so that they can find additional information, diagrams, and so on for their script **Kerboodle resource** C14 Checkpoint follow up: Aiming for 4, C14 Checkpoint follow up: Aiming for 6, C14 Checkpoint follow up: Aiming for 8		
Plenary	**Watching and reviewing (10 minutes)** Each group should perform their script. After having watched the group, the 'audience' should evaluate their script by considering how well do they now understand the process explained. They should come up with two strong points about the script and one way the script could have been improved.		
Progression	Students could evaluate Aiming for 6 scripts.	Students could evaluate Aiming for 8 scripts.	Students evaluate the advantages and disadvantages of each extraction method in their script.

C GCSE Chemistry only
15 Using our resources
15.1 Rusting

AQA spec Link: 10.3.1 Corrosion is the destruction of materials by chemical reactions with substances in the environment. Rusting is an example of corrosion. Both air and water are necessary for iron to rust.

Corrosion can be prevented by applying a coating that acts as a barrier, such as greasing, painting, or electroplating. Aluminium has an oxide coating that protects the metal from further corrosion.

Some coatings are reactive and contain a more reactive metal to provide sacrificial protection, e.g., zinc is used to galvanise iron.

Students should be able to:
- describe experiments and interpret results to show that both air and water are necessary for rusting
- explain sacrificial protection in terms of relative reactivity.

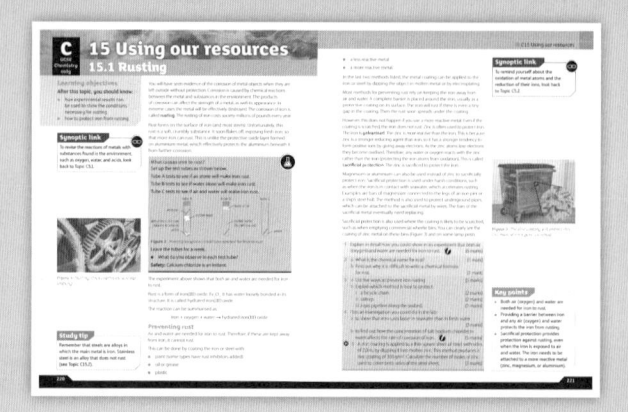

WS 2.2, 3.5

Aiming for	Outcome	Checkpoint	
		Question	Activity
Aiming for GRADE 4	Define the term corrosion.		Starter 1
	State what is required for iron to rust.		Starter 1, Main
	List some ways to prevent rusting.	3	Main, Plenary 1
Aiming for GRADE 6	Describe an experiment to investigate the conditions required for rusting to occur.	1, 4, End of chapter 1	Main
	With the help of equations, describe the process of rusting.	2	Main
	Explain how different corrosion prevention techniques work.	End of chapter 1	Main, Plenary 1, Plenary 2
Aiming for GRADE 8	Explain in detail why corrosion is a problem.	End of chapter 1	Starter 1
	Write balanced equations to describe rusting and identify species that are oxidised and reduced.		Main
	Evaluate rust prevention techniques and suggest which is best for a specific purpose.	3	Plenary 2

Maths
Students balance redox equations.

Literacy
Students create a leaflet for homework to explain what rusting is and how it can be prevented.

Key words
rusting, galvanising, sacrificial protection

Practical

Title	What causes iron to rust?
Equipment	three test tubes, two bungs, boiled water, oil, drying agent-anhydrous calcium chloride (or calcium oxide powder), cotton wool, spatula, three iron nails, test-tube rack, three dropping pipettes, water, eye protection
Overview of method	Label the test tubes A, B, and C, and place in a test-tube rack. In test tube A, put half a spatula of the drying agent. Suspend an iron nail on loosely packed cotton wool above the drying agent and seal the tube with a bung. Put an iron nail in test tubes B and C. Half fill test tube B with boiled water and add a small layer of oil then seal with a bung. Place a little water in test tube C and leave open to the air. Leave the set-up for one week and then observe the nails.
Safety considerations	Calcium oxide is corrosive and calcium chloride is an irritant. Wear Chemical splash-proof eye protection. Wash hands after completing the practical.

C15 Using our resources

Starter	Support/Extend	Resources
What's gone wrong? (5 minutes) Show students some images of rusted vehicles and buildings. Ask students to suggest what has happened and why it is a problem. Briefly describe the process of rusting and encourage students to write a word equation for the corrosion of iron.		
Reactivity (10 minutes) Ask students to think about the two metals, iron and zinc. Students write word equations for the reaction of these metals with oxygen. Then ask students to suggest which metal would react first and to explain why.	**Support:** Direct students to the reactivity series in Topic C5.3 to help them.	

Main	Support/Extend	Resources
What causes iron to rust? (40 minutes) This practical will need to be revisited in another lesson. Set up the experiment as detailed. If possible arrange for students to take a photograph of their experiment at the same time each day. Students can then compare the images to draw conclusions consistent with their results. Encourage students to write a word equation for the reaction and explain why it is considered to be a redox reaction. Discuss the difficulty in writing the balanced symbol equation but encourage higher-tier students to write a half equation focusing on the reaction of iron.	**Extend:** Students should also investigate rusting using brine. **Extend:** Ask students to investigate galvanised nails and to observe and explain what happens if the coating is scratched off in places.	**Practical:** What causes iron to rust?

Plenary	Support/Extend	Resources
Classifying rust prevention (5 minutes) Students match the terms oxidation, corrosion, and rusting with their definitions. They then sort methods of rust prevention according to whether they are a barrier method or a sacrificial method.	**Support:** Discuss the different methods of rust prevention and what they are mainly used for.	**Interactive:** Classifying rust prevention
Rust prevention (10 minutes) Show students different scenarios of using iron, for example, cooking pans, cars, bikes, bridges, buildings. Ask students to work in pairs to suggest which method of rust prevention would be best in each case and to explain why.		

Homework		
Students design a leaflet to explain what rust is and how it can be prevented.	**Extend:** Students include examples of appropriate situations to use each method of preventing rust. **Extend:** Students' leaflets should contain balanced symbol equations.	

kerboodle

A Kerboodle highlight for this lesson is **Literacy sheet: Rusting**. Refer to the **Content map** on Kerboodle for a full list of resources and assessment.

GCSE Chemistry Only

C15.2 Useful alloys

AQA spec Link: 10.3.2 Most metals in everyday use are alloys. Bronze is an alloy of copper and tin. Brass is an alloy of copper and zinc.

Gold used as jewellery is usually an alloy with silver, copper, and zinc. The proportion of gold in the alloy is measured in carats. 24 carat being 100% (pure gold), and 18 carat being 75% gold.

Steels are alloys of iron that contain specific amounts of carbon and other metals. High carbon steel is strong but brittle. Low carbon steel is softer and more easily shaped. Steels containing chromium and nickel (stainless steels) are hard and resistant to corrosion.

Aluminium alloys are low density.

Students should be able to:

- recall a use of each of the alloys specified
- interpret and evaluate the composition and uses of alloys other than those specified given appropriate information.

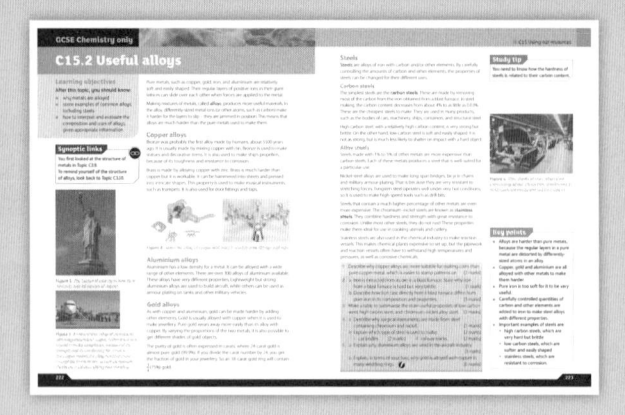

MS 1a, 1c

Aiming for	Outcome	Checkpoint	
		Question	Activity
Aiming for GRADE 4 ↓	State the difference between a metal before and after being alloyed.	1	Main
	State the elements in steel and bronze.		Main, Plenary 1
	List some common examples of alloys and their uses.		Starter 1, Main
Aiming for GRADE 6 ↓	Explain in detail why pure metals are often alloyed before they are used.	1	Starter, 1 Main
	Describe how different amounts of carbon affect the properties of iron.	2, 3	Plenary 1
	Identify an appropriate purpose for an alloy when given data on its properties.	4	Plenary 1
Aiming for GRADE 8 ↓	Explain the term carat.	5	Starter 1
	Use data on the properties of unfamiliar alloys to explain a suitable alloy for a given purpose.		Plenary 1
	Evaluate an alloy in terms of its properties and uses.	4, 5	Plenary 2

Maths
Students calculate the percentage of gold in different carats (1c). They also interpret data provided to identify appropriate uses of alloys.

Literacy
Students use observations from a model to write and draw conclusions on alloys.

Key words
alloys, steels, carbon steels, stainless steel

Practical

Title	Modelling alloys – pure and impure metals
Equipment	bottom of a Petri-dish, detergent solution, Pasteur pipette
Overview of method	Half fill the Petri-dish bottom with detergent solution. Use the Pasteur pipette to generate a raft of equal-sized bubbles. Push on a row of bubbles and notice how they slip easily, modelling the ductility of a pure metal crystal. Then add five extra-large bubbles, push on a row of bubbles and compare the effect.
Safety considerations	Detergent solution is an irritant. Wash hands after use.

222

■ C15 Using our resources

Title	Modelling alloys – steel
Equipment	modelling clay, sand
Overview of method	Split the modelling clay into five samples. The sand represents the carbon. Add 2 g of sand to one sample, 4 g to the next sample, 8 g to the next sample, and 16 g to the fourth sample. Leave one sample without sand (this models iron). Work the sand into the modelling clay so that it is mixed thoroughly. Make each sample into a cylinder and pull to compare the ductility of the material.
Safety considerations	Modelling clay can be made with peanut oil and this can be an allergy risk for some students.

Starter	Support/Extend	Resources
Gold (5 minutes) Show students images of different gold jewellery, including the hallmarks. Ask students to suggest what the hallmarks mean and why gold is often alloyed. Briefly introduce carats and ask students to calculate the percentage of gold in 18 and 9 carat gold. **Remember metals** (10 minutes) Students have already studied metallic bonding, metal extraction, and metal reactivity. However, it can be useful to remind students about their previous learning. Therefore, ask students to recall the reactivity series. Students should relate this to methods of metal extraction. You may wish to ask them to answer some true or false statements about metal extraction and go on to consider steel as an alloy rather than a pure metal.	**Support:** Ask students to recall the reactivity series in Topic C5.3 and metal extraction in Topic C5.3 and Topic C6.3 to help them.	

Main	Support/Extend	Resources
Modelling alloys (40 minutes) Ask students to recall the model for metallic bonding. Then complete the Modelling alloys – pure and impure metals practical as outlined to show the effect of alloying a pure metal. Students should record their conclusions by drawing a labelled diagram of the experiment. Explain to students that they are going to model the effect of having carbon in iron to make steel. Ask students to predict what they think the effect will be and why, based on the metallic bonding model. Then complete the Modelling alloys – steel practical as outlined. Ask students to write a conclusion from their experiment.	**Extend:** Ask students to illustrate the model with an alloy that they need to study. **Extend:** Ask students to research the carbon contents of different steels and how this relates to their use.	**Practical:** Modelling alloys

Plenary	Support/Extend	Resources
Identifying alloys (5 minutes) Students match steel alloys with different compositions of carbon to their properties and uses. Then provide students with the composition and property data on a selection of unfamiliar alloys not on the specification. Students use the information given to match each alloy to its use. **Expressing values and percentages** (10 minutes) Students work through the calculation sheet to evaluate the composition and uses of alloys.		**Interactive:** Identifying alloys **Calculation sheet:** Expressing values and percentages

Homework		
Students suggest what material they would use to make a nail, a car hub cap, and a bike frame. They should choose from the alloys studied and explain their choices.		

kerboodle

A Kerboodle highlight for this lesson is **Literacy skills: Useful alloys**. Refer to the **Content map** on Kerboodle for a full list of resources and assessment.

GCSE Chemistry Only

C15.3 The properties of polymers

AQA spec Link: 2.2.5 Polymers have very large molecules. The atoms in the polymer molecules are linked to other atoms by strong covalent bonds. The intermolecular forces between polymer molecules are relatively strong and so these substances are solids at room temperature.

Students should be able to recognise polymers from diagrams showing their bonding and structure.

10.3.3 The properties of polymers depend on what monomers they are made from and the conditions under which they are made. For example, low density (LD) and high density (HD) poly(ethene) are produced from ethene.

Thermosoftening polymers melt when they are heated. Thermosetting polymers do not melt when they are heated.

Students should be able to:

- explain how low density and high density poly(ethene) are both produced from ethene
- explain the difference between thermosoftening and thermosetting polymers in terms of their structures.

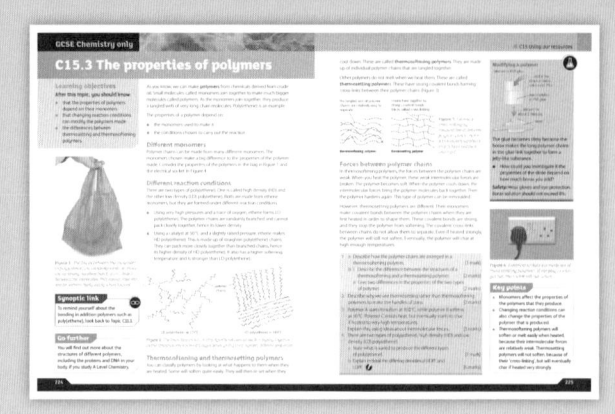

Aiming for	Outcome	Checkpoint	
		Question	Activity
Aiming for GRADE 4	Describe the properties of a thermosetting plastic.	End of chapter 4	Starter 1, Main 2
	Describe the properties of a thermosoftening plastic.	1, End of chapter 4	Starter, 1 Main 2
	Describe the difference between LD and HD poly(ethene).	1, End of chapter 4	Main 1, Plenary 1
Aiming for GRADE 6	Explain how thermosetting plastics and thermosoftening plastics are different in terms of structure and bonding.	1, 3, End of chapter 4	Main 2
	Describe the different conditions used to make poly(ethene).	4	Plenary 1
	Explain how the structure of poly(ethene) affects its properties and therefore its uses.	4	Starter 1
Aiming for GRADE 8	Explain in detail, giving examples, how the properties of plastics can be changed.		Starter 2
	When data about the properties of plastics is given, suggest a suitable plastic for a given purpose.		Homework
	Evaluate a plastic in terms of its properties and uses.	2	Plenary 2

Maths
Students design a results table and draw a graph with line of best fit from their results as part of the main lesson activity.

Literacy
Students explain the use of thermosoftening and thermosetting plastics.

Key words
polymers, thermosoftening polymers, thermosetting polymers

Practical

Title	Modifying a polymer
Equipment	100 cm³ measuring cylinder, two 250 cm³ beakers, dropping pipettes, hot plate, stirring rod, 4 g PVA glue, 4 g borax, eye protection, food colouring, coin, stopwatch
Overview of method	Before the lesson, make up the solution of borax with 100 cm³ of water in the beaker. You may wish to warm the water to encourage dissolving. During the lesson, in a separate beaker, gently warm 100 cm³ of water and stir in the PVA glue until it has dissolved, taking care not to boil the liquid. You may wish to add food colouring. Then remove from the heat and add a few drops of borax solution, stir, and observe how the texture changes.
Safety considerations	Borax solution is an irritant, wear eye protection throughout, and wear gloves when touching the 'slime'. Do not allow students to take the slime out of the laboratory.

■ C15 Using our resources

Title	Heating plastics
Equipment	samples of a thermosoftening plastic and a thermosetting plastic, tin lid, tripod, gauze, Bunsen burner and safety equipment, gas rod, eye protection, fume cupboard
Overview of method	Set up the Bunsen burner in the fume cupboard. Put a sample of each plastic on the same tin lid and position over the Bunsen burner on the tripod and gauze. Heat gently, and observe any changes. You may wish to touch the heated plastic with the end of the glass rod to show how it has softened and becomes pliable. On heating more strongly, the thermosetting plastic will char and may catch fire if temperature is high enough.
Safety considerations	Toxic fumes will be released and this experiment must be carried out in a fume cupboard.

Starter	Support/Extend	Resources
Poly(ethene) (5 minutes) Give students a sample of HD poly(ethene) (e.g., plastic drinks bottle) and LD poly(ethene) (e.g., shopping bag). Ask students to note the similarities and differences between the materials. Then reveal that they are the same chemical but made in different ways, which affects the properties and hence the use. **Modelling a polymer** (10 minutes) Show students a necklace made out of beads. Explain that each bead represents a monomer and the necklace represents a polymer. Model a thermosoftening plastic, showing how the material is pliable and the chains easily move. Then using super glue (wear gloves), stick parts of the chain together (modelling cross-links). Ask students to suggest how this changed the properties and explain that this models thermosetting plastics.	**Support:** Have a list of adjectives/properties on the board for students to choose from. **Extend:** Focus students on the attractions between the polymer chains and how in thermosoftening there are intermolecular forces of attraction between polymer chains but in thermosetting there are covalent bonds. Relate this to work on structure and bonding.	

Main	Support/Extend	Resources
Modifying a polymer (25 minutes) Ask students to investigate how the amount of borax solution added affects the viscosity of a polymer. Students should design an appropriate results table and test the viscosity by timing how long it takes a coin to fall to the bottom of a sample of a plastic. **Heating plastics** (15 minutes) Demonstrate to students the practical as detailed in the second practical box. Students explain their observations with two labelled particle diagrams and explain, in terms of forces between the polymer chains, the differences in thermosetting and thermosoftening plastics in terms of their properties.	**Extend:** Students should draw a line graph with a line of best fit to display their results. **Support:** Complete this as a demonstration and use question and answer to illicit the key observations.	**Practical:** Modifying a polymer

Plenary	Support/Extend	Resources
LDPE and HDPE (5 minutes) Students use the interactive to sort statements on the polymerisation and properties according to whether they describe the LDPE or HDPE. **Compare copper and PTFE** (10 minutes) Show students a sample of a copper water pipe and a plastic water pipe. Ask students to list the advantages and disadvantages of each material for the purpose. Students then justify which they would choose for a domestic use and why.		**Interactive:** LDPE and HDPE

Homework
Students explain why thermosetting plastics should be used to make ovenproof ready-meal dishes whereas thermosoftening plastics can be used to make yoghurt pots.

kerboodle

A Kerboodle highlight for this lesson is **Go further: The structure of poymers**. Refer to the **Content map** on Kerboodle for a full list of resources and assessment.

225

GCSE Chemistry Only

C15.4 Glass, ceramics, and composites

AQA spec Link: 10.3.3 Most of the glass we use is soda-lime glass, made by heating a mixture of sand, sodium carbonate, and limestone. Borosilicate glass, made from sand and boron trioxide, melts at higher temperatures than soda-lime glass.

Clay ceramics, including pottery and bricks, are made by shaping wet clay and then heating in a furnace.

Most composites are made of two materials, a matrix or binder surrounding and binding together fibres or fragments of the other material, which is called the reinforcement.

Students should be able to recall some examples of composites.

Students should be able to, given appropriate information:

- compare quantitatively the physical properties of glass and clay ceramics, polymers, composites, and metals
- explain how the properties of materials are related to their uses and select appropriate materials.

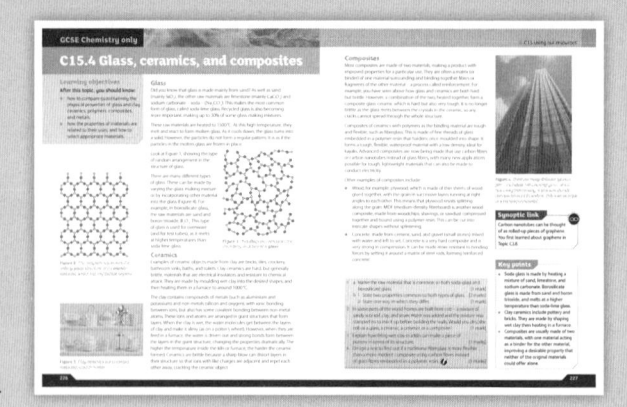

WS 1.4, 3.5, 3.8

Aiming for	Outcome	Checkpoint	
		Question	Activity
Aiming for GRADE 4 ↓	Describe how to make soda-lime glass and borosilicate glass.	1	Plenary 1
	Describe how to make clay ceramics.		Plenary 1
	State examples of clay ceramics and composites.		Starter 1
Aiming for GRADE 6 ↓	Describe what a composite is.		Starter 1, Plenary 2
	Explain the difference between a composite and an advanced composite.		Plenary 1
	Compare quantitatively the physical properties of glass and clay ceramics, polymers, composites, and metals.	1, 4	Starter 2, Main
Aiming for GRADE 8 ↓	Explain the properties of ceramics and composites in terms of structure and bonding.	3	Plenary 1
	When data about the properties of a material is provided, classify it and suggest a suitable material for a given purpose.	2	Main
	Evaluate materials in terms of their properties and uses.		Main

Maths
In the main part of the lesson students take measurements using a protractor, calculate means, and plot their results on a graph with a line of best fit.
They also interpret data to suggest appropriate uses for materials.

Literacy
Students have ample opportunities to explain how the properties of materials are linked to their uses, including making a poster for homework to explain how the materials used to make sports equipment have changed over time.

C15 Using our resources

Practical

Title	Properties of materials
Equipment	materials to test (all the same size), G-clamp, clamp and stand, 200 g slotted mass on hook, tray to catch masses, ruler, stopwatch, tube, 100 g slotted masses, ball bearings, vice, suspended hammer, protractor, eye protection
Overview of method	**Testing flexibility** Clamp the material to the end of the desk and clamp a ruler vertically so that the material is level with 0 cm on the ruler. Hang a 200 g mass on the free end of the material and measure how far the free end has bent after 30 seconds. **Testing hardness** Put the ball bearing on top of the sample and place the tube over the ball bearing. Drop a 1 kg mass down the tube so that it hits the ball bearing. Measure the diameter of the dint left in the material with a ruler. **Testing toughness** Put the sample of material in a vice and, lifting the suspended hammer to the same height each time, let it fall and hit the material. Repeat five times then measure the angle that the sample has been bent to. Repeat for other samples of the same material and calculate an average.
Safety considerations	Be careful not to drop masses on feet. Wear eye protection. Do not test Pyrex or glass as they will shatter in some of the tests. Wear eye protection.

Starter	Support/Extend	Resources
Group materials (5 minutes) Give students a selection of materials such as pyrex, soda-lime glass, wet clay, pottery, plywood, and reinforced concrete. Ask students to group the material and classify them as ceramic, glass, or composite. These should be the materials students will study in the main part of the lesson. **Sports equipment** (10 minutes) Show students examples of solid wood tennis rackets, laminated wood tennis rackets, and modern carbon-fibre tennis rackets. Ask students to suggest why there has been a change in the design.	**Support:** Define each class of material and then get students to sort the samples. **Extend:** Explain to students that glass is a subclass of ceramics.	

Main	Support/Extend	Resources
Properties of materials (40 minutes) Allow students to investigate the properties of the materials that they grouped in the first starter activity. Then ask them to suggest general properties for each group of materials and how these relate to the functions that they are given.	**Extend:** Students should draw a line graph with a line of best fit to display their quantitative results.	**Practical:** Properties of materials

Plenary	Support/Extend	Resources
Finish the sentences (5 minutes) Students use the interactive to finish off the sentences: • A clay ceramic is… • A glass is… • A composite is… • An advanced composite is… **Thought experiment** (10 minutes) Ask students to predict which would be stronger, a block of ice made from pure water or a block of ice made from pure water with cotton wool in the mould. Students explain how they would test the strength, and use science to qualify their prediction.	**Extend:** Ask three students to read out their sentence and then pass comment on which is the most scientific, has best grammar, and so on.	**Interactive:** Finish the sentences

Homework		
Students make a poster explaining, in terms of properties, why the materials used to make sports equipment have changed over time, using an example.	**Support:** Remind students of the points raised in Starter 2 and ask students to use tennis rackets as their example.	

GCSE Chemistry Only

C15.5 Making ammonia – the Haber process

AQA spec Link: 10.4.1 The Haber process is used to manufacture ammonia, which can be used to produce nitrogen-based fertilisers.

The raw materials for the Haber process are nitrogen and hydrogen.

Students should be able to recall a source for the nitrogen and a source for the hydrogen used in the Haber process.

The purified gases are passed over a catalyst of iron at a high temperature (about 450 °C) and a high pressure (about 200 atmospheres). Some of the hydrogen and nitrogen reacts to form ammonia. The reaction is reversible so some of the ammonia produced breaks down into nitrogen and hydrogen:

nitrogen + hydrogen ⇌ ammonia

On cooling, the ammonia liquefies and is removed. The remaining hydrogen and nitrogen are recycled.

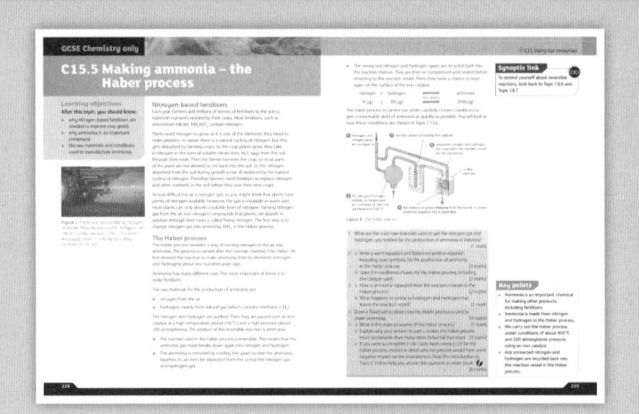

MS 1a, 1c

Aiming for	Outcome	Checkpoint	
		Question	Activity
Aiming for GRADE 4	State the purpose of the Haber process.		Starter 2, Main
	State the conditions for the Haber process.	2, 4	Main, Plenary 1
	Write a word equation to describe the Haber process.	2	Starter 1, Main
Aiming for GRADE 6	Describe how the raw materials are turned into the reactants for the Haber process.	1, 4	Main
	Describe how the Haber process is a reversible reaction.	4	Main, Plenary 1
	Describe the Haber process with the help of a balanced symbol equation including state symbols.	2, 3, 4, End of chapter 4	Starter 1, Main
Aiming for GRADE 8	Evaluate the Haber process using atom economy and LCA to determine its environmental impact.	5	Main
	Explain how costs are kept to a minimum in the Haber process.	4	Main, Plenary 1
	Explain, with the use of balanced symbol equations, where the reactants come from for the Haber process.	4	Main

Maths
Students balance symbol equations and calculate atom economy and LCA for the Haber process.

Literacy
Students create a summary flow chart of the Haber process for homework.

■ C15 Using our resources

Starter	Support/Extend	Resources
Ammonia equations (5 minutes) Students write a word equation and a balanced symbol equation for the reversible reaction between hydrogen and nitrogen to make ammonia. **The importance of ammonia** (10 minutes) Briefly introduce that the Haber process is used to turn nitrogen in the air into ammonia. Give a few uses for ammonia (e.g., as a fertiliser) and ask students to explain why the Haber process is important to the farming industry.	**Extend:** Ask students to balance the equation and add state symbols with the student book closed. **Extend:** Encourage students to make the connection that as the Haber process is important to the farming industry, it is also important to them as the farming industry produces their food.	

Main	Support/Extend	Resources
The Haber process (40 minutes) Talk through the Haber process, building up a schematic flow chart of the stages of the process. Use question and answer to make links to other areas of the specification such as percentage composition of dry air and particle diagrams to show the condensation of ammonia to separate it. Then ask students to create a poster that illustrates the Haber process. Their poster should include information about the atom economy, LCA, and environmental impact.	**Extend:** Ask students to explain how the Haber process could achieve an atom economy of 100%.	**Activity:** The Haber process

Plenary	Support/Extend	Resources
The Haber process (5 minutes) Students use the interactive to decide if statements about the Haber process are true or false. Students then complete a paragraph on the conditions of the Haber process. **Reaction profile diagram** (10 minutes) Explain to students that the energy change in the forward direction is an exothermic change transferring 92 kJ/mol to the surroundings. Students should use this information to draw an energy level diagram of the reaction.	**Extend:** Students should correct the false statements. **Support:** Show students the outline of the reaction profile diagram for an exothermic reaction. Students copy this and annotate it. **Extend:** Ask students to include the activation energy with an iron catalyst and without an iron catalyst.	**Interactive:** The Haber process

Homework		
Students create a flow chart which explains where the raw materials are obtained for the Haber process, how they are turned into the reactants, the conditions for the Haber process, and why the unreacted gases are recycled. Students should include equations to illustrate any reactions, including the phase change of the ammonia to allow it to be tapped off.	**Support:** Give students important statements that they must include and an outline for the flow chart.	

kerboodle

A Kerboodle highlight for this lesson is **Bump up your grade: Making ammonia**. Refer to the **Content map** on Kerboodle for a full list of resources and assessment.

The economics of the Haber process

AQA spec Link: 10.4.1 Students should be able to:

- interpret graphs of reaction conditions versus rate
- apply the principles of dynamic equilibrium to the Haber process
- explain the trade-off between rate of production and position of equilibrium
- explain how the commercially used conditions for the Haber process are related to the availability and cost of raw materials and energy supplies, control of equilibrium position, and rate.

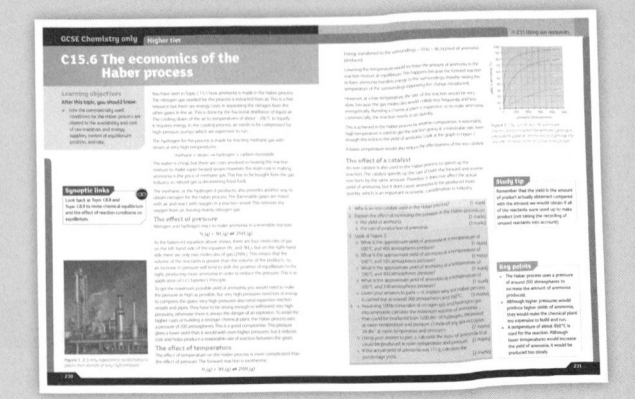

WS 3.5, 3.8
MS 1a, 1c

Aiming for	Outcome	Checkpoint	
		Question	Activity
Aiming for GRADE 6 ↓	Explain the effect of changing temperature on the yield of the Haber process.	1	Main, Plenary 1
	Explain the effect of changing pressure on the yield of the Haber process.	2	Main, Plenary 1
	Explain why the conditions used in the Haber process are a compromise.	End of chapter 5	Main, Plenary 1
Aiming for GRADE 8 ↓	Justify why the conditions used in the Haber process are a compromise.	3, End of chapter 3	Main, Plenary 1
	Explain the effect of an iron catalyst on the rate and position of equilibrium in the Haber process.	2, End of chapter 3, 4	Main, Plenary 1
	Use data to predict and explain the effect on the equilibrium and rate of reaction of changing conditions in the Haber process.	3, End of chapter 3	Plenary 1

Maths
Students interpret a graph to draw conclusions on the best conditions for the Haber process.

Literacy
Students consolidate what they have learnt about the Haber process to produce a pitch, justifying the conditions used in industry. Students also vote for their favourite pitch.

■ C15 Using our resources

Starter	Support/Extend	Resources
Annotating the Haber process (5 minutes) Ask students to write a balanced symbol equation for the Haber process with the energy change for the reaction. Ask students to colour in the equilibrium arrow in red to show the exothermic reaction and in blue to show the endothermic reaction, and use green to annotate the high and low pressure sides of the reaction.	**Extend:** Ask students to suggest the effect of adding a catalyst to the reaction.	
Revising the Haber process (10 minutes) Students complete a paragraph to describe where the raw materials for the Haber process come from, the conditions of the Haber process, and why unreacted gases are recycled.	**Support:** Students could use their flow chart of the Haber process that they made for homework from the previous lesson.	**Interactive:** Revising the Haber process

Main	Support/Extend	Resources
Pitching the Haber process (40 minutes) Ask students to imagine they are pitching for investment to an industrial plant which is set to make ammonia. In small groups, they should develop their three-minute pitch explaining the choice of conditions for the factory. Students then deliver their pitch to the rest of the class.	**Extend:** Ask students to choose and justify a geographical location for the plant.	**Activity:** Pitching the Haber process

Plenary	Support/Extend	Resources
Interpreting graphs (10 minutes) Ask students to look at the graph in Figure 2 in Topic 15.5 of the student book and list all the information they can obtain from it (dependent variable and unit, independent variable and unit). Then ask students to draw conclusions consistent with the data (as temperature increases the yield of ammonia decreases, as pressure increases yield of ammonia increases).		
Pitch perfect? (10 minutes) Use the plenary time to deliver more of the students' pitches. After all the pitches have been given, each team can vote for which one they would invest in (they cannot vote for themselves).	**Support:** Give students some key features that they must look out for in the pitch, for example, stating the conditions and explaining why they have been chosen.	

Homework		
Students complete the WebQuest where they find data on the Haber process and describe the optimum conditions for this. Alternatively, ask students to sketch graphs to show the effect on yield of reducing pressure and reducing temperature. Students should add annotations to their graphs to explain the effects shown.		**WebQuest:** The Haber process

kerboodle
A Kerboodle highlight for this lesson is **Calculation sheet: Interpreting graphs**. Refer to the **Content map** on Kerboodle for a full list of resources and assessment.

GCSE Chemistry Only

C15.7 Making fertilisers in the lab

AQA spec Link: 10.4.2 Compounds of nitrogen, phosphorus, and potassium are used as fertilisers to improve agricultural productivity. NPK fertilisers contain compounds of all three elements.

Industrial production of NPK fertilisers can be achieved using a variety of raw materials in several integrated processes. NPK fertilisers are formulations of various salts containing appropriate percentages of the elements.

Ammonia can be used to manufacture ammonium salts and nitric acid.

Phosphoric acid is neutralised with ammonia to produce ammonium phosphate.

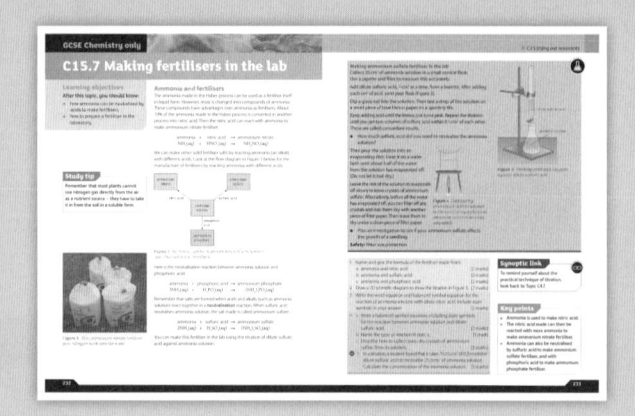

MS 1c

Aiming for	Outcome	Checkpoint	
		Question	Activity
Aiming for GRADE 4 ↓	State what a fertiliser is.		Starter 1, Plenary 1
	Identify the fertiliser produced from a reaction.	1	Main 2
	Write a word equation for the formation of the chemicals in NPK fertilisers.	3	Main 2
Aiming for GRADE 6 ↓	Explain the importance of fertilisers for agriculture.		Main 1, Plenary 1
	Describe in detail how fertilisers are produced in the laboratory.	4	Main 2
	Write balanced symbol equations for the reactions to make components of NPK fertilisers.	3, 4	Main 1, Main 2
Aiming for GRADE 8 ↓	Evaluate different processes to make NPK fertilisers.		Main 2
	Write ionic equations for reactions to make fertilisers.		Main 1
	Calculate the concentration of an ammonia solution from the results of a titration.	5	

Maths
Students calculate the percentage composition of different elements in fertilisers (1c).

Literacy
Students write questions and detail an acceptable range of answers.

Practical

Title	Making ammonium sulfate fertiliser in the lab
Equipment	dilute ammonia solution, 25 cm³ pipette and filler, 250 cm³ conical flask, 250 cm³ beaker, burette, funnel, dilute sulfuric acid, glass rod, blue litmus paper, evaporating dish, hot water bath, heatproof mat, eye protection
Overview of method	Fill a clean, dry burette with dilute sulfuric acid. Half fill the beaker with ammonia solution. Use the pipette and filler to accurately transfer 25 cm³ of ammonia solution in a small conical flask. Add dilute sulfuric acid, 1 cm³ at a time, from a burette and swirl the conical flask. Dip a glass rod into the solution and test the acidity using blue litmus paper. Keep adding the acid until the litmus just turns pink and note the titre. Repeat the titration until you get two concordant results. Pour the solution into an evaporating dish. Heat it on a water bath until about half of the water from the solution has evaporated off. Leave the rest of the solution to evaporate off slowly to leave crystals of ammonium sulfate.
Safety considerations	Ammonia and dilute sulfuric acid are corrosive. Wear eye protection and wash hands after the practical. Do not boil to dryness and keep the room well ventilated. Warn asthmatics not to breath in ammonia fumes.

■ C15 Using our resources

Starter	Support/Extend	Resources
Importance of fertilisers (5 minutes) Show students an image of a fertilised field of wheat and an unfertilised field of wheat. Ask students to define a fertiliser and to suggest its importance in agriculture. **Titration outline** (10 minutes) Ask students to write an outline method for completing a titration.	**Support:** Refer students back to Topic C4.7. **Support:** Give students separate cards each with one sentence for them to correctly order a titration method.	

Main	Support/Extend	Resources
Making ammonium sulfate fertiliser in the lab (30 minutes) Ask students to complete the practical as outlined in the practical box. Students should write a suitable results table to record their titres and write an equation to illustrate the neutralisation reaction. **Flow chart** (10 minutes) Ask students to make a flow chart to explain the processes involved in making ammonium nitrate fertiliser. Students should classify the reactions and add equations where possible.	**Extend:** Give students the concentration of the ammonia solution and ask them to work out the concentration of the sulfuric acid used.	**Practical:** Making ammonium sulfate fertiliser in the lab

Plenary	Support/Extend	Resources
What makes a good fertiliser? (5 minutes) Ask students to imagine that they are a farmer. They need to choose a suitable 'all round' fertiliser. Students should set themselves a list of questions that they would ask the sales representative and the range of suitable answers. **Percentage composition** (10 minutes) Ask students to calculate the percentage composition of nitrogen in different ammonium salts, for example, NH_4NO_3, NH_4Cl.	**Support:** Ask students to think about the elements the fertiliser should contain, whether they want it to dissolve in water, and in what state they would like the fertiliser. **Extend:** Ask students to calculate the percentage of nitrogen in $(NH_4)_2SO_4$.	**Interactive:** Percentage composition

Homework		
Students explain why ammonia is not a very good agricultural fertiliser.		

GCSE Chemistry Only

C15.8 Making fertilisers in industry

AQA spec Link: 10.4.2 Compounds of nitrogen, phosphorus, and potassium are used as fertilisers to improve agricultural productivity. NPK fertilisers contain compounds of all three elements.

Industrial production of NPK fertilisers can be achieved using a variety of raw materials in several integrated processes. NPK fertilisers are formulations of various salts containing appropriate percentages of the elements.

Ammonia can be used to manufacture ammonium salts and nitric acid.

Potassium chloride, potassium sulfate, and phosphate rock are obtained by mining, but phosphate rock cannot be used directly as a fertiliser.

Phosphate rock is treated with nitric acid or sulfuric acid to produce soluble salts that can be used as fertilisers.

Students should be able to:

- recall the names of the salts produced when phosphate rock is treated with nitric acid, sulfuric acid, and phosphoric acid
- compare the industrial production of fertilisers with laboratory preparations of the same compounds, given appropriate information.

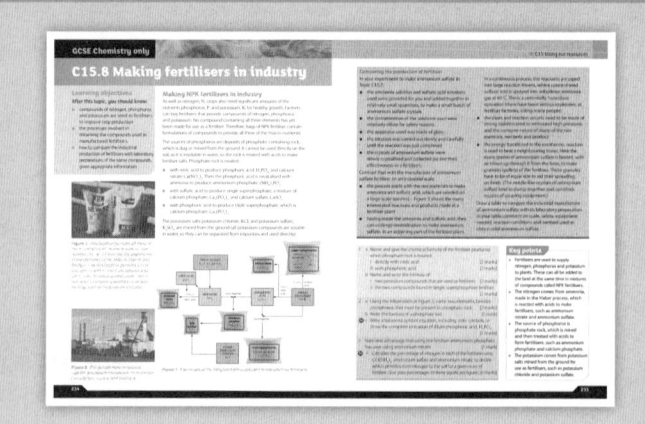

Aiming for	Outcome	Checkpoint	
		Question	Activity
Aiming for GRADE 4 ↓	Name the elements in NPK fertilisers.		Starter 1, Plenary 1
	Describe where the raw materials for NPK fertilisers come from.	2	Main
	Name and give the formulae of the chemicals in NPK fertilisers.	1	Main
Aiming for GRADE 6 ↓	Describe production of fertilisers in industry.		Main
	Compare and contrast the industrial and laboratory production of fertilisers.		Main, Plenary 1
	Write balanced symbol equations for the reactions to make components of NPK fertilisers.		Main, Homework
Aiming for GRADE 8 ↓	Evaluate the composition of fertilisers.	4	Main
	Evaluate different processes to make NPK fertilisers.	3	Main
	Write ionic equations to illustrate the reactions to make NPK fertilisers.		Starter 2, Main

Maths
Students write balanced symbol equations.

Literacy
Students compare different methods of production of fertilisers.

C15 Using our resources

Starter	Support/Extend	Resources
Plant nutrition (5 minutes) Ask students to explain why plants need the three primary macro-nutrients: nitrogen (to make amino acids and proteins), phosphorus (to make DNA and RNA), and potassium (needed for healthy growth). **Fertiliser equations** (10 minutes) Ask students to write equations for the reactions between ammonia and nitric acid, phosphoric acid, and sulfuric acid.	**Extend:** Ask students to find out about the secondary macro-nutrients and micro-nutrients needed by plants. **Support:** Ask students to write word equations.	

Main	Support/Extend	Resources
Compaing the production of fertilisers (40 minutes) Students use the student book to design and draw a table to compare the industrial manufacture of ammonium sulfate with its laboratory preparation. The table should contain information about scale, safety, equipment needed, reaction conditions, and method used to obtain solid ammonium sulfate. It should also include any relevant word and balanced symbol equations.	**Extend:** Provide students with other text books and, if available, the Internet to do further research on the industrial production of other fertilisers.	**Activity:** Comparing the production of fertilisers

Plenary	Support/Extend	Resources
Ammonia as a fertiliser (5 minutes) Students explain why ammonia is not a very good agricultural fertiliser and needs to be converted into other chemicals. **Examination question** (10 minutes) Give students an examination question and ask them to tackle it as best they can. After one minute they should swap their answer with a partner. They then have two minutes to review their partner's answer and add anything they think is missing. Repeat a second time giving three minutes. Reveal the mark scheme and ask students to assess their original answer, together with the points added subsequently.	**Extend:** Give students a question from a higher-tier paper. **Support:** Give students a question from a foundation-tier paper.	**Interactive:** Ammonia as a fertiliser

Homework		
Students make a visual summary to show how the ammonia-based fertilisers can be made. Their visual summary should include balanced symbol equations to show each stage of the production.	**Extend:** Higher-tier students should also write ionic equations.	

kerboodle
A Kerboodle highlight for this lesson is **Extension sheet: Fertilisers**. Refer to the **Content map** on Kerboodle for a full list of resources and assessment.

C15 Using our resources

Overview of C15 Using our resources

In this chapter, students have developed their understanding of rusting from KS3 to understand how both water and air are required for iron to corrode. They should be able to explain how the two methods for preventing rusting – barrier methods and sacrificial methods – disrupt the oxidation of iron and prevent corrosion.

Students have also studied a series of different material types – alloys, polymers, ceramics, glass, and composites. Students have previously met alloys and polymers in *Chapter C3* and *Chapter C11* respectively and students should have built upon this understanding. For each material, students should be able to identify key properties and link these to their common uses.

Students also studied the Haber process and how it is carried out economically on an industrial scale. This builds extensively upon knowledge of equilibrium conditions in *Chapter C8* and students should be able to explain why the industrial conditions for the Haber process are described as a compromise. Students should also be able to recognise the importance of the Haber process in the production of ammonia, being able to explain how ammonia is an important feedstock in the production of fertilisers, both in the laboratory and industrially alongside potassium and phosphorus fertilisers.

MyMaths

You can find additional support for the maths skills covered in this chapter on **MyMaths**, including using percentages, interpreting data, drawing graphs and calculating means.

kerboodle

For this chapter, the following assessments are available on Kerboodle:

C15 Checkpoint quiz: Using our resources
C15 Progress quiz: Using our resources 1
C15 Progress quiz: Using our resources 2
C15 On your marks: Using our resources
C15 Exam-style questions and mark scheme: Using our resources

Checkpoint follow up lesson

A student's route through this lesson can be determined using the Checkpoint assessment. Percentage pass marks are supplied in the Checkpoint teacher notes.

For each successive route through it is assumed that the student can perform to their current route as well as previous routes. For example, students working at Aiming for 6 are assumed to be secure in Aiming for 4 knowledge and understanding and working towards achieving all the learning outcomes for Aiming for 6.

	Aiming for 4	**Aiming for 6**	**Aiming for 8**
Learning outcomes	Describe what rust is and how it forms.	Describe what an alloy is.	Explain why the Haber process is economically important.
	Describe ways to prevent iron from rusting.	Describe different alloys.	Explain how conditions for the Haber process need to be chosen to give acceptable yields whilst maintaining acceptable rates.
		Describe how varying the composition of alloys affects their properties.	
Starter	**Definitions (10 minutes)** Display the key words corrosion, rust, alloy, polymer, glass, composite, and ceramic on the board. Ask students to work on their own to come up with a definition for each word and an example of each. Ask students to compare their answers with a partner, and then as a group of four. They should work together to come up with a final definition and at least two examples of each. Ask several groups to give their answers to the whole class. Discuss any misunderstandings that become apparent.		
Differentiated checkpoint activity	The Aiming for 4 Checkpoint follow-up sheet provides structured tasks to help students collate the key information on rusting. They then use these tasks to create a poster for a DIY store.	Students use the Aiming for 6 Checkpoint follow-up sheet to create a profile for the alloys brass, bronze, carbon steels, and stainless steel. The purpose of the profile is to support people with choosing the most appropriate alloy for their purpose. A template is provided on the sheet, which gives brief prompts of what to include in their profile. Students could be given access to the Internet or other appropriate text books to aid them.	Students use the Aiming for 8 Checkpoint follow-up sheet to produce a poster on the Haber process and the conditions used industrially. The sheet contains minimal guidance for students on what to include in their poster. You may wish to give students access to the Internet.
	Kerboodle resource C15 Checkpoint follow up: Aiming for 4, C15 Checkpoint follow up: Aiming for 6, C15 Checkpoint follow up: Aiming for 8		
Plenary	**Reviewing work (5 minutes)** Ask students to lay their work around the room. Students should then choose another student's poster to review. They should read the other student's poster and decide on two strong points about the work and one point that could be improved on. **Key points (5 minutes)** Ask students to decide as a pair three key learning points from the chapter. Review these as a class. Address any misconceptions should they arise.		
Progression	Encourage students to include word equations. Some students could be encouraged to attempt symbol equations for the reactions. Students could evaluate Aiming for 6 profiles.	Give students example scenarios and ask them to use their profiles to identify the best alloy to use. Students could evaluate Aiming for 8 posters.	Encourage students to incorporate understanding from other parts of the course. For example, they should consider the effect the surface area of the catalyst will have on the reaction rate. Very able students could be briefly introduced to the equilibrium constant.

Answers

C1.1
1a metals: Ba, V, Hg, K, U [1]; non-metals: P, Kr [1]
b non-metal, e.g., does not conduct electricity [1]
2 mixture: atoms not chemically bonded, [1] compound: atoms chemically bonded [1]
3 element: all atoms same type, [1] compound: more than one type of atom chemically combined [1]
4 tiny central nucleus [1] surrounded by orbiting electrons [1]
5a natrium [1] **b** aurum [1] **c** plumbum [1] **d** alium [1]
6 twice as many oxygen atoms as carbon atoms / carbon and oxygen atoms in carbon dioxide bond to each other in the ratio 1 : 2 (carbon : oxygen) [2]

C1.2
1a No atoms are created or destroyed in a chemical reaction [1] so equal numbers of each type of atom must appear on both sides of the equation. [1]
b $H_2 + Cl_2 \rightarrow 2HCl$ [1]
2a 17.6 g [1]
b $MgCO_3(s) \rightarrow MgO(s) + CO_2(g)$ [1]
3a $2KNO_3 \rightarrow 2KNO_2 + O_2$ [1]
b $4Li + O_2 \rightarrow 2Li_2O$ [1]
c $4Fe + 3O_2 \rightarrow 2Fe_2O_3$ [1]
d $Fe_2O_3 + 3CO \rightarrow 2Fe + 3CO_2$ [1]
4 $2Na(s) + 2H_2O(l) \rightarrow 2NaOH(aq) + H_2(g)$ [2]

C1.3
1 two or more substances (elements or compounds) [1] not chemically combined [1]
2 In a mixture relative proportions not in fixed ratio but in a compound they are. [1] Mixtures of H_2 and O_2 can contain any amount of each. [1] However, their compound H_2O always has two H connected to each O. [1]
3 Heat water in flask attached to condenser. [1] Steam moves into condenser. [1] Pure water condenses and is collected in beaker. [1] Solid impurities left in flask. [1]
4 Method A – any three from: add water to mixture, [1] stir and filter, [1] S insoluble in water so left as residue on filter paper, [1] wash S with distilled water to remove impurities then leave to dry, [1] evaporate $NaNO_3$ solution [1] by heating on water bath until point of crystallisation, [1] leave to dry, crystallising $NaNO_3$ [1] Method B – any three from: add xylene to mixture, [1] stir and filter, [1] $NaNO_3$ insoluble in xylene so left as residue on filter paper, [1] wash $NaNO_3$ with xylene and leave to dry, [1] evaporate xylene from filtrate of S solution [1] by warming on water bath (electrically heated / no naked flame [1]) in fume cupboard to crystallise S [1]

C1.4
1a see C1.4, Figure 1 [2]
b fractional distillation [1]
2 at about 80 °C (boiling point of ethanol) most water vapour condenses in fractionating column so ethanol is purer, [1] simple distillation: ethanol still boils, condensing in condenser and collected, [1] but as water vapour is not removed [1] more water collects in beaker with ethanol [1]

3a Dab a spot of ink [1] on near bottom of chromatography paper, [1] place in solvent, [1] allow solvent to soak up the paper, past ink, to separate dyes. [1]
b B is more soluble in propanone than A. [1]
4 produces highest percentage purity with ethanol, although contaminated with some propanol and water, [1] ineffective at separating water and propanol [1] because boiling points too close so evaporate and condense at same time / temperature [1]

C1.5
1a C [1]
b soda, lime [2]
2a electron [1]
b cloud of positive charge, [1] with tiny negatively charged electrons spread throughout [1]
3 positive charge concentrated into very small volume at centre of atom (nucleus), [1] electrons orbit nucleus [1]
4 Energy emitted from electron transitions can only have certain fixed energies, [1] so he refined the 'orbiting electrons' in Rutherford's nuclear model to 'orbiting electrons in energy levels (or shells) at fixed distances from the nucleus'. [1]

C1.6
1

Particle	Location	Relative charge	Relative mass
proton	in nucleus	+1	1
neutron	in nucleus	0	1
electron	orbiting nucleus	−1	negligible

[3]

2 cobalt, Co, atomic number 27, mass number 59 [1]
3 equal numbers of protons (+1) and electrons (−1) [1] so charges cancel out [1]
4a 7 p, 7 e, 7 n [1] **b** 17 p, 17 e, 18 n [1]
c 47 p, 47 e, 61 n [1] **d** 92 p, 92 e, 143 n [1]

C1.7
1a 5 p, 6 n, 5 e [1] **b** 7 p, 7 n, 7 e [1]
c 12 p, 12 n, 12 e [1] **d** 17 p, 20 n, 17 e [1]
e 53 p, 74 n, 53 e [1] **f** 9 p, 10 n, 10 e [1]
g 15 p, 16 n, 18 e [1] **h** 19 p, 20 n, 18 e [1]
i 13 p, 14 n, 10 e [1]
2a atoms of same element / number of protons with different numbers of neutrons / mass numbers [1]
b carbon-12
3a 0.09 nm [1] **b** 9×10^{-6} nm [1]
4a density [1]
b same electronic structures so same number of electrons in highest energy level / outermost shell [1]

C1.8
1a first / innermost [1]
b first = 2, second = 8 [1]
2a 2: circle with 2 crosses [1]
b 2, 2: 2 concentric circles, 2 crosses in each [1]
c 2, 8, 7: 3 concentric circles, 2 crosses in central, 8 in middle, 7 in outer shell [1]
d 2, 8, 8: see Figure 2 p. 16 [1]

3a 2, 8, 8, 1 [1]   **b** 1 [1]
4 phosphorus, P [1]
5a all have 1 electron (the same number of electrons) in outermost shell [1]
b lithium + oxygen → lithium oxide, sodium + oxygen → sodium oxide, potassium + oxygen → potassium oxide [3]
c 2Li + Cl$_2$ → 2LiCl [1]   2Na + Cl$_2$ → 2NaCl [1]

C2.1
1 Pattern broke down because of undiscovered elements, so not all octaves had similar properties. [1]
2a tellurium (Te), [1] iodine (I) [1]
b at certain places pattern of similar elements recurring at regular intervals was broken [1] until order of atomic weights reversed, [1] no good reason for reversing order so other scientists doubted validity of periodic table, [1] discovery of internal structure of atoms → chemists found atomic number was important in ordering elements, not atomic mass, [1] using number of protons in atoms to order elements toworked perfectly, anomalies explained by existence of isotopes with different numbers of neutrons [1]
3 gaps [1] for undiscovered elements and predicted their properties, [1] when elements were discovered predictions were remarkably accurate [1]

C2.2
1a repeated at regular intervals [1]
b i vertical column [1]
ii horizontal row [1]
2a many more metals. 75%–80% [1]
b lose one or more electrons (to form stable electronic structure) [1]
3a 2 [1] **b** 3 [1] **c** 1 [1] **d** 2 [1] **e** 8 [1] **f** 2 [1] **g** 8 [1] **h** 7 [1]
4 same number of electrons in highest energy level / outermost shell [1]
5 very stable electron arrangements [1]

C2.3
1 to avoid reactions with air / O$_2$ and H$_2$O [1]
2 melting point decreases [1]
3 all have one electron in outermost shell, [1] lose this to form ions [1] producing ions with stable electronic structure [1]
4a 2Cs(s) + I$_2$(g) → 2CsI(s) white solid [1]
b 2Cs(s) + Br$_2$(g) → 2CsBr(s) white solid [1]
5 explodes [1] on contact as H$_2$ is liberated very quickly, [1] alkali metals more reactive going down group so Cs, near bottom, extremely reactive, [1] U.I. turns purple [1] as strongly alkaline CsOH(aq) formed in reaction [1] 2Cs(s) + 2H$_2$O(l) → 2CsOH(aq) + H$_2$(g) [1]

C2.4
1a melting points increase [1]
b reactivity decreases [1]
2a gas: F, Cl; liquid: Br; solid: I, At [2]
b halogens [1]
3a Li$^+$ = 2 [1] F$^-$ = 2, 8 [1]
b share a pair of electrons (one from each atom) [1]
4a 2Na(s) + I$_2$(g) → 2NaI(s) [1]
b Cl$_2$(aq) + 2NaI(aq) → 2NaCl(aq) + I$_2$(aq) [1]
5 colourless solution of NaI [1] turns red/brown as bromine added, [1] bromine displaces iodide ions from solution, [1] forming (colourless) aqueous bromide ions and leaving red / brown iodine molecules in solution [1] as bromine more reactive than iodine [1] Br$_2$(aq) + 2NaI(aq) → 2NaBr(aq) + I$_2$(aq) [1]

C2.5
1 helium, [1] although smallest positive charge on He nucleus, [1] outer electrons nearest to nucleus, [1] no inner shells of electrons shielding nuclear charge [1]
2 electron in outermost shell less strongly attracted to nucleus than in Li, [1] greater distance between outer electron and nucleus → attraction in K weaker, [1] more inner shells shield outer electron in K, [1] so K loses outer electron more easily [1]
3 going down group, outermost shell further from attractive force of nucleus [1] so harder for Br atom to gain electron, [1] outer shell in Br shielded by more inner shells, [1] reducing attraction between electron and nucleus so Br less reactive than F [1]
4a Ca more reactive than Mg, [1] Group 2 elements more reactive going down group, [1] atoms react by losing two outer shell electrons, [1] easier to lose because greater distance between nucleus and outer electrons, [1] greater shielding effect in Ca compared with Mg [1]
b O more reactive than S, [1] Group 6 non-metals less reactive going down group, [1] atoms react by gaining two electrons, [1] harder for S atoms than O atoms, as in sulfur outer shell further from attractive force of nucleus, [1] shielded by more electron shells [1]

C2.6
1a electric conductors, [1] thermal conductors, [1] hard and strong, [1] high densities, [1] high melting points [1]
b lower melting point [1]
2a iron(II) chloride [1]   **b** chromium(III) oxide [1]
c manganese(II) bromide [1]   **d** nickel(II) carbonate [1]
3 copper(I) oxide, Cu$_2$O [1] copper(II) oxide, CuO [1]
4 vanadium(V) oxide, V$_2$O$_5$ [1] catalyst in oxidation of SO$_2$ to SO$_3$ [1] vanadium changes the charge on its ion / oxidation state, [1] in this case from 5+ to 4+ (forming vanadium(IV) oxide) when SO$_2$ is converted to SO$_3$, [1] then changes back to 5+ by reacting with oxygen to reform V$_2$O$_5$ catalyst [1]

C3.1
1

	General properties	Average distance between particles	Arrangement of particles	Movement of particles
solid	fixed shape, incompressible	touching	regular pattern	vibrate on the spot
liquid	no fixed shape, flow, very difficult to compress	most particles touching	irregular, random	slip and slide over and around each other
gas	no fixed shape, spreads out to fill container, easily compressed	large distances	irregular, random	can move very quickly, in a random manner, between collisions

[6]

239

Answers

2 any six from: as particles cool, average speed decreases [1] particles become much closer together at condensation point, [1] form liquid where particles move randomly, slipping over and around each other, [1] as liquid cools average speed of particles decreases [1] at freezing point particles remain in fixed positions, [1] vibrating, [1] vibrations decrease as solid cools [1]

3 any six from: as temperature increases, particles gain energy and average speed increases, [1] if pressure remains constant particles take up more space, [1] density decreases [1] as same mass of gas occupies larger volume, [1] if gas compressed, pressure increases as particles collide with walls of container more frequently, [1] so same mass of gas occupies smaller volume [1] and density of gas increases [1]

4 strength of attractive forces between particles varies in different substances, [1] stronger forces of attraction → higher melting points [1]

5 Fair test varying one factor, [1] e.g., temperature of water or surface area of paper towel, keeping all other variables constant, [1] monitor rate of evaporation by measuring mass of wet paper towel [1] on electric balance [1] at regular time intervals [1]

C3.2

1a covalent [1] **b** ionic [1]

2a 2,8 Al^{3+} [1] 3 lost [1]

b 2,8 F^- [1] 1 gained [1]

c 2,8,8 K^+ [1] 1 lost [1]

d 2,8 O^{2-} [1] 2 gained [1]

3 atoms of Group 1 lose the single electron from outermost shell, [1] transferring it to a Group 7 atom, [1] which has 7 electrons in its outermost shell, [1] both atoms become ions with the stable electronic arrangements of a noble gas [1]

C3.3

1

Atomic number	Atom	Electronic structure of atom	Ion	Electronic structure of ion
9	F	2,7	F^-	2,8
3	Li	2,1	Li^+	2
16	S	2,8,6	S^{2-}	2,8,8
20	Ca	2,8,8,2	Ca^{2+}	2,8,8

[4]

2a Groups 1, 2, and 3, charge = (group number)+ [1]

b Groups 5, 6, and 7, charge = (8 − group number)− [1]

3a two sets of 3 concentric circles both labelled K^+ with crosses as for Ca^{2+} in C3.3 Figure 2, [2] one set of 2 concentric circles labelled O^{2-} as in C3.3 Figure 1 [1]

b one set of 3 concentric circles both labelled Al^{3+} with crosses as for Ca^{2+} in C3.3 Figure 2, [1] three sets of 3 concentric circles all labelled Cl^- with crosses as in C3.3 Figure 2 [3]

4a no overall charge on an ionic compound, [1] in KBr the 1− charge on Br^- ion is cancelled by 1+ charge on K^+ ion, [1] in K_2O two K^+ ions needed to cancel 2− charge on O^{2-} ion [1]

b In MgO the 2− charge on O^{2-} ion cancels 2+ charge on Mg^{2+} ion [1] whereas two Cl^- ions are needed to cancel out the 2+ charge on an Mg^{2+} ion [1] in $MgCl_2$. [1]

5 Any three from: metal atoms have fewer electrons in outer shell [1] so lose electrons to form ions, [1] with stable electronic structure of noble gas, [1] ions contain more protons than electrons, giving positive ions. [1] Non-metal atoms with 5, 6 or 7 electrons in outer shells, [1] gain electrons to form ions [1] with electronic structure of noble gas, [1] ions have more electrons than protons, resulting in negative ions [1]

C3.4

1 higher concentration of ions from dissolved salts in seawater than in freshwater [1]

2 positive: chloride, bromide, oxide, iodide [2]
negative: lithium, calcium, sodium, zinc, barium [2]

3 strong electrostatic forces of attraction [1] between oppositely charged ions in giant lattice, [1] in all directions, [1] so a lot of energy required to separate ions in melting [1]

4 ions in solid fixed in position [1] only free to move (and carry their charge to electrodes) when molten or dissolved in water [1]

5 aluminium oxide, [1] Al^{3+} ions have higher charge than Na^+ ions, [1] so stronger electrostatic forces of attraction [1] between Al^{3+}, and O^{2-} ions [1] than between Na^+ ions, with single positive charge, and O^{2-} ions [1] (smaller size of Al^{3+} ions also contributes towards this effect)

C3.5

1 hydrogen iodide, sulfur dioxide, and nitrogen(III) chloride [1] because these contain only non-metallic elements. [1]

2a see C3.5, top of Figure 2 [2]

b similar to C3.5, top of Figure 3 but with two Cl atoms [2]

c similar to C3.5, top of Figure 3 but with F instead of Cl [3]

3a similar to C3.5, lower of Figure 4 but with P instead of N [3]

b similar to C3.5, top of Figure 4 but with C instead of O and two O instead of H [3]

4 hydrogen → helium [1] chlorine → argon [1]

5 Electrostatic attraction between electrons and positive nuclei [1] on either side of the pair of electrons [1] holds atoms together. [1]

C3.6

1a forces of attraction between molecules [1]

b $C_{12}H_{22}O_{11}$ [1]

2a giant covalent structure [1] with strong covalent bonds holding atoms strongly into regular giant lattices [1]

b very strong triple covalent bond between atoms in each N_2 molecule but very weak forces of attraction between N_2 molecules / weak intermolecular forces between N_2 molecules, [1] so molecules easily separated from each other [1]

3 good electrical insulator, [1] no overall charge on its molecules [1]

4 Only weak intermolecular forces of attraction between individual HCl molecules, [1] but very strong ionic bonds [1] which form strong electrostatic forces of attraction in all directions [1] in giant ionic lattice of sodium chloride. [1]

C3.7

1a diamond, graphite [1]

b allotropes [1]

2 very high melting and boiling points, hard, [1] insoluble in water, electrical insulator [1]

3 layers of hexagonally arranged carbon atoms, [1] arrows from negative to positive charge [1]

4 weak forces between layers of graphite atoms [1] so slip and slide over each other to act as a lubricant [1]

240

Answers

5 graphite: hexagons of C atoms arranged in layers, [1] each C atom forming three strong covalent bonds to its nearest neighbours, [1] as C atoms have 4 electrons in outer shell, this leaves one free outer electron on each, [1] free electrons drift freely along layers, enabling graphite to conduct electricity, [1] diamond: all outer shell electrons involved in covalent bonding, [1] no free electrons carry electrical charge [1]

C3.8

1a delivering drugs to parts of body where needed [1]

b shape of molecule similar to building designed by the architect Buckminster Fuller, [1] ('bucky-ball' from his first name and 'fullerenes' from his surname).

c C_{60} [1]

2 flexibility, [1] strength [1]

3a C atoms in each layer of graphene arranged in hexagons, [1] each C atom only forms three strong covalent bonds, [1] leaving one spare outer electron on each C atom [1] free to move along layer of C atoms, [1] these mobile delocalised electrons can drift along the layer conducting electricity [1]

b graphene: flexible, [1] strong, [1] graphite: brittle, [1] soft / easily flakes [1] When graphene used on supports they can bend without cracking or breaking any electrical circuits. [1] Graphene also better electrical conductor than graphite so more efficient when in use. [1]

C3.9

1 arranged in regular patterns [1]

2a because metal atoms lose outer shell electrons [1] into a 'sea' of (delocalised) electrons, [1] more protons (+) than electrons (−) [1]

b free-moving electrons within structure, [1] not associated with a particular atom [1]

3 2 electrons in magnesium outer shell, [1] donated into 'sea' of free-moving delocalised electrons, [1] electrostatic attraction [1] of negatively charged delocalised electrons for Mg^{2+} ions bonds ions in giant metallic lattice [1]

4 'glue' model → positively charged metal ions stuck in position in giant lattice, [1] as glue becomes solid when it sets [1] this is not helpful in visualising the fluid movement of delocalised electrons throughout structure [1]

C3.10

1a layers of atoms (positively charged ions) slide over each other easily [1]

b i malleable [1]
  ii ductile [1]

2 differently sized atoms inserted [1] regular arrangement of metal atoms (positively charged ions) disrupted, [1] more difficult for layers to move [1]

3 electricity: 'sea' of delocalised electrons drifting through metal's giant structure [1] because electrons free-moving, [1] thermal energy: mobile delocalised electrons gain energy when heated, [1] move around more quickly within the metal [1] transferring energy through metal quickly [1]

4 Each aluminium donates 3 electrons into 'sea' of mobile, delocalised electrons, [1] forming Al^{3+} ions, [1] compared to one electron in lattice of Na^+ ions. [1] Electrostatic forces of attraction in metallic bonding stronger in aluminium [1] because of higher charge on Al^{3+} ions [1] and more electrons involved in metallic bonding. [1]

C3.11

1 study of particles between 1 and 100 nm in size [1]

2a 5.0×10^{-8} m (= 50×10^{-9} nm) [1]

b 5.0×10^{-2} µm (= 50×10^{-3} µm) [1]

3a SA : V = 0.06 cm^2 : 0.001 cm^3 = 60/cm [1] which is $10 \times$ greater than the cube of side 1 cm [1]

b SA : V 10 m = 1000 cm so 6 000 000 (6×10^6) cm^2 : 1 000 000 000 (1×10^9) cm^3 = 0.006 (or 6×10^{-3})/cm [1] which is $10 \times$ less than cube of side 100 cm [1]

4 normal materials: most atoms, molecules or ions exist within body of material – not exposed at surface of material, [1] material has normal bulk properties of that particular material as determined by its structure and bonding, [1] nanoparticles: proportion of particles at surface is massively increased [1] for same mass of material, [1] so properties different, e.g., chemical reactivity much greater than bulk material [1]

C3.12

1 any two, e.g., antibactericide in fridges [1] sprays in operating theatres, [1] wound dressings [1] on clothes [1]

2a large surface area to volume ratio [1]

b explosions caused by sparks, [1] health problems if breathed in [1] if nanoparticles escape into air / environment [1]

3a e.g., in sun-screens [1] to block ultra-violet light, [1] in face creams [1] to deliver active ingredients deeper beneath surface of skin [1]

b delivering drugs to tumour, [1] absorbed by tumours and then absorb energy from lasers to damage tumour by affecting its proteins. [1]

4 balanced argument [1] expressing two concerns, [2] two advantages [1] plus evaluation of Drexler's assertion of reproducing nanoparticles. [1]

C4.1

1 The mean (average) relative mass of an atom of an element, taking into account the proportions of different isotopes naturally occurring in that element, [1] using the scale carbon-12 = 12. [1]

2a 62 [1] **b** 180 [1]

3a 0.005 moles [1]

b i 0.3 moles [1] **ii** 500 000 moles [1]

4a 5000 g or 5 kg [1] **b** 0.1 g [1] **c** 74.4 g [1]

5 due to averaging relative masses of different isotopes in a naturally occurring sample [1]

C4.2

1 2 molecules of HCl or 2 moles of HCl molecules [1]

2 4.0 g [2]

3a $2H_2O_2(aq) \rightarrow 2H_2O(l) + O_2(g)$ [1]

b 3.4 g [2]

4a $Ca(s) + 2H_2O(l) \rightarrow Ca(OH)_2(aq) + H_2(g)$ [1]

b 2.0 g [2]

C4.3

1 reactant used up first in a reaction [1]

2a 0.1 mol Cu [1] 0.05 mol O_2 [1] 0.1 mol CuO [1]

b Cu : O_2 : CuO (0.1 : 0.05 : 0.0) = 2 : 1 : 2 [1] 2 moles of Cu react with 1 mole of O_2 → 2 moles of CuO, so balanced equation is $2Cu + O_2 \rightarrow 2CuO$ [1]

3a $Fe_2O_3 + 2Al \rightarrow Al_2O_3 + 2Fe$ [1]

241

Answers

b $Fe_2O_3 = 32.0/160 = 0.2$ mol (reacts completely with $(0.2 \times 2) = 0.4$ mol of Al) [1] Al: $16.2/27 = 0.6$ mol so Al in excess and Fe_2O_3 is limiting reactant [1]

c 0.2 mol $Fe_2O_3 \rightarrow 0.2$ mol Al_2O_3 [1] mass 0.2 mol $Al_2O_3 = 10^2 \times 0.2 = 20.4$ g [1]

C4.4

1. conserve Earth's resources, [1] reduce waste and pollution [1]
2. reaction reversible, [1] some reactants give unexpected products, [1] some product lost in handling or left in apparatus, [1] reactants impure, [1] losses in separating target product [1]
3. 21% (21.2%) [3]
4. **a** $2NaHCO_3 \rightarrow Na_2CO_3 + H_2O + CO_2$ [1]
   b 86.8% [3]

C4.5

1. % atom economy = relative formula mass of desired product × 100% [1]
2. $CaCO_3 \rightarrow CaO + CO_2$ [1] atom economy = $(56/100) \times 100\% = 56\%$ [1]
3. **a** $[64.5/(46 + 36.5)] \times 100\% = 78.2\%$ [2]
   b Reaction 1: atom economy = 100% [1] no waste products to find alternative uses for, to dispose of, or treat before disposal (better for environment and saves money) [1]
   c any two from: if starting materials renewable (e.g., C_2H_5OH from fermentation of sugar cane or sugar beet is renewable whereas C_2H_4 from crude oil is non-renewable), [1] reaction conditions (e.g., if high temperatures or pressures are needed these usually require fossil fuels, causing pollution, and diminishing supplies of crude oil), [1] whether reactions are reversible (e.g., reactions that are not give higher percentage yield of product) [1]

C4.6

1. **a** 20 g/dm³ [1]   **b** 2.1 g/dm³ [1]
2. 70 g/dm³ [1]
3. greater mass of solute in a certain volume of water → more concentrated solution, [1] greater volume of water for a certain mass of solute → less concentrated solution [1]
4. 2.3 g [1]

C4.7

1. **a** meniscus [1]
   b i pipette [1] burette [1]
     ii bottom of meniscus [1] eye level with that point [1]
2. **a** measure known volume of sodium hydroxide solution into conical flask using pipette, [1] add a few drops of indicator, [1] pour dilute nitric acid into burette, recording burette reading, [1] slowly add acid into flask, swirling to mix two solutions, [1] continue until indicator changes colour, [1] repeat titration until two results concordant, then average [1]
   b $NaOH(aq) + HNO_3(aq) \rightarrow NaNO_3(aq) + H_2O(l)$ [1]
3. **a** for example, methyl orange, [1] phenolphthalein [1]
   b different colours in acidic and alkaline conditions to make end point clear [1]
   c repeat titration [1] until get two results / titres within 0.1 cm³ of each other [1]

C4.8

1. 0.002 moles [1]
2. $KOH(aq) + HNO_3(aq) \rightarrow KNO_3(aq) + H_2O(l)$ [1]

3. 0.0040 (4.0×10^{-3}) moles [1]
4. 0.0040 (4.0×10^{-3}) moles [1]
5. 0.32 mol/dm³ [1]
6. 20 g/dm³ to 2 sig. fig. / 20.2 g/dm³ to 3 sig. fig. [1]

C4.9

1. volume of gas occupied by 1 mole of gas at room temperature and pressure [1]
2. **a i** 1.5 mol [1] **ii** 417 mol [1]
   b i 216 dm³ (or 216 000 cm³) [2]
     ii 7.2 dm³ (or 7200 cm³) [2]
   c 0.064 g [2]
3. 300 dm³ (or 300 000 cm³) [1]
4. 0.048 dm³ (or 48 cm³) [3]

C5.1

1. **a** lithium + water → lithium hydroxide + hydrogen [1]
   $2Li(s) + 2H_2O(l) \rightarrow 2LiOH(aq) + H_2(g)$ [2]
   b zinc + hydrochloric acid → zinc chloride + hydrogen [1]
   $Zn(s) + 2HCl(aq) \rightarrow ZnCl_2(aq) + H_2(g)$ [2]
2. **a** gas given off / fizzing, magnesium gets smaller then disappears [1], thermal energy released / surroundings get warmer / solution and test tube gets hot [1]
   b metal + acid → salt + hydrogen [1]
   c magnesium + sulfuric acid → magnesium sulfate + hydrogen [1]
   $Mg(s) + H_2SO_4(aq) \rightarrow MgSO_4(aq) + H_2(g)$ [2]
3. **a** gold, silver, and platinum are very unreactive [1] will not tarnish not react with oxygen in the air so will stay bright for a long time [1]
   b react with water vapour (and oxygen) in the air [1] oil keeps oxygen and water vapour away from the metals [1]
   c zinc reacts with acidic foods at room temperature [1] tin does not [1]
4. Aluminium is protected by a tough / impervious layer of aluminium oxide. [1]
5. 4.00 g [3]

C5.2

1. **a** no reaction [1]
   b zinc + copper(II) sulfate → zinc sulfate + copper [1]
   $Zn + CuSO_4 \rightarrow ZnSO_4 + Cu$ [1]
   c magnesium + iron(II) chloride → magnesium chloride + iron [1]
   $Mg + FeCl_2 \rightarrow MgCl_2 + Fe$ [1]
2. Carbon is more reactive than zinc but less reactive than magnesium, [1] so displaces zinc but not magnesium. [1]
3. **a** below hydrogen in reactivity series [1]
   b $WO_3 + 3H_2 \rightarrow W + 3H_2O$ [1]
4. **a** $Zn(s) + Fe^{2+}(aq) \rightarrow Zn^{2+}(aq) + Fe(s)$ [1]
   b zinc atoms lose 2 electrons to form zinc(II) ions, [1] zinc atoms oxidised, as lose electrons, [1] iron(II) ions reduced, [1] as gain 2 electrons from zinc [1]
   c 0.05 mol zinc, [1] 0.025 mol iron(II) sulfate, [1] so as they react 1 mol : 1 mol, iron(II) sulfate is limiting reactant and zinc is in excess [1]

C5.3

1. A metal ore is a rock that contains enough of a metal or metal compound [1] to make it worth extracting the metal. [1]
2. very unreactive [1]

242

3 very low reactivity, [1] used for jewellery / electrodes in electrolysis [1]

4a zinc oxide + carbon → zinc + carbon monoxide [1]

b ZnO(s) + C(s) → Zn(l) + CO(g) [2]

C5.4

1 acid + metal → salt + hydrogen [1]

2a copper metal does not react with dilute acid / copper not reactive enough to displace hydrogen from acid [1]

b potassium metal explodes in dilute acid [1]

3a Fe(s) + H_2SO_4(aq) → $FeSO_4$(aq) + H_2(g) [2]

b Zn(s) + 2HCl(aq) → $ZnCl_2$(aq) + H_2(g) [2]

4a Zn(s) + $2H^+$(aq) → Zn^{2+}(aq) + H_2(g) [2]

b Zn → Zn^{2+} + $2e^-$ [1] $2H^+$ + $2e^-$ → H_2 [1]

c each zinc atom loses two electrons, [1] to two hydrogen ions, [1] to form hydrogen gas, [1] zinc atoms oxidised as lose electrons, [1] hydrogen ions reduced as gain electrons [1]

C5.5

1 acid + base → salt + water [1]

2 zinc oxide + hydrochloric acid → zinc chloride + water [1]
ZnO(s) + 2HCl(aq) → $ZnCl_2$(aq) + H_2O(l) [2]

3a NaBr [1] b MgF_2 [1] c KNO_3 [1] d $Al_2(SO_4)_3$ [1]

4 Heat copper sulfate solution in evaporating dish on a water bath, [1] some water evaporates from copper sulfate solution until point of crystallisation when crystals appear at the edge of the solution, [1] solution then left at room temperature for the remaining water to evaporate slowly, [1] leaving crystals in the dish. If small volume of solution remains on the crystalsdry by gently dabbing between two pieces of filter paper. [1]

5a Li_2O(s) + H_2SO_4(aq) → Li_2SO_4(aq) + H_2O(l) [2]

b 3.3 g [3]

C5.6

1a acid + alkali → salt + water [1]

b H^+ + OH^- → H_2O [1]

c acid + carbonate → salt + water + carbon dioxide [1]

2 LiOH(aq) + HCl(aq) → LiCl(aq) + H_2O(l) [2] any four from: add indicator to measured volume of lithium hydroxide solution, [1] add dilute hydrochloric acid until indicator just changes colour noting volume of acid needed, [1] repeat until results concordant then calculate mean, [1] repeat using this mean volume of acid without indicator, [1] evaporate water from LiCl solution by heating until point of crystallisation, [1] leave at room temperature for rest of water to evaporate; if necessary, dry off any remaining solution with filter paper [1]

3a $BaCO_3$(s) + $2HNO_3$(aq) → $Ba(NO_3)_2$(aq) + H_2O(l) + CO_2(g) [2]

b $2H^+$(aq) + CO_3^{2-}(s) → H_2O(l) + CO_2(g) [2]

C5.7

1a alkali dissolves in water [1]

b produce hydroxide ions in water [1]

c KOH(s) ⟶ K^+(aq) + OH^-(aq) [2]

2a H^+(aq) [1]

b HBr(aq)/(g) ⟶ H^+(aq) + Br^-(aq) [2]

3 distilled water pH = 7, [2] sodium hydroxide solution pH > 7, e.g., 14; [2] ethanoic acid pH < 7, e.g., 4 [2]

4 starts high and remains almost constant [1] until all alkali neutralised then falls very rapidly to low value, [1] continues almost level as excess acid added [1]

5 any three from: pH sensor and data-logger more accurate, [1] matching colours against pH chart by eye is subjective and difficult to judge, [1] pH sensor gives more repeatable measurements over narrower range, giving more precise data than U.I. paper, [1] also useful for monitoring changes in pH continuously over time, [1] if you only need a rough estimate of pH, [1] U.I. paper is quicker and easier to use [1]

C5.8

1 fizzing / rate gas is given off is slower with ethanoic acid than nitric acid [1]

2a pH = 5.0 [1]

b 0.000 000 01 mol/dm^3 [1] 1×10^{-7} mol/dm^3 [1]

3 Propanoic acid does not ionise completely when added to water, [1] reaction is reversible, [1] majority of molecules remain intact, [1] only a small fraction form H^+(aq) ions [1] (and propanoate (negative) ions). Therefore, propanoic acid does not produce as high a concentration of H^+(aq) ions as a strong acid of equal concentration. [1] Nitric acid is a strong acid, because its molecules ionise completely in water. [1]

4 pH depends on concentration of H^+(aq) ions, [1] so although weak acid does not ionise completely, [1] it could have a higher concentration of H^+(aq) ions if amount of strong acid per dm^3 is very, very small. [1] Strong acid ionises completely, [1] but in very dilute solution may produce fewer H^+(aq) ions in a given volume of solution than a concentrated solution of the weak acid. [1]

C6.1

1a breakdown of a compound by electricity [1]

b electrolyte [1] c ionic [1]

2

	Cathode (−)	Anode (+)	
a	zinc	iodine	[1]
b	lithium	bromine	[1]
c	iron	fluorine	[1]
d	sodium	oxygen	[1]
e	potassium	chlorine	[1]

3 2NaCl(l) → 2Na(l) + Cl_2(g) [2]

4a $CuCl_2$(aq) [1] $AgNO_3$(aq) [1]

b Copper and silver are below hydrogen in the reactivity series. [1]

5 solid: ions in fixed positions in giant lattice [1] molten / aqueous solution: ions free to move within liquid [1] and carry charge to oppositely charged electrode [1]

C6.2

1

	Cathode	Anode	
a	lithium	oxygen	[1]
b	copper	chlorine	[1]
c	hydrogen	oxygen	[1]

2a i lose electrons [1]

ii oxidation [1]

b i gain electrons [1]

ii reduction [1]

3a $2Cl^-$ → Cl_2 + $2e^-$ [1]

b $2Br^-$ → Br_2 + $2e^-$ [1]

c Mg^{2+} + $2e^-$ → Mg [1]

d Al^{3+} + $3e^-$ → Al [1]

Answers

  e $K^+ + e^- \rightarrow K$ [1]
  f $2H^+ + 2e^- \rightarrow H_2$ [1]
  g $2O^{2-} \rightarrow O_2 + 4e^-$ [1]
  h $4OH^- \rightarrow O_2 + 2H_2O + 4e^-$ [1]

C6.3

1a in solid, ions fixed in position in the giant lattice, [1] if molten, free to move so can move to electrodes [1]
  b To lower melting point, [1] save / conserve / reduce cost of energy [1]
2 Oxygen produced at the hot carbon anodes [1] reacts with the carbon to produce carbon dioxide, burning away anodes. [1]
3a cathode: $Al^{3+} + 3e^- \rightarrow Al$ [1] anode: $2O^{2-} \rightarrow O_2 + 4e^-$ [1]
  b O^{2-} ions lose electrons, oxidised, [1] Al^{3+} ions gain electrons, reduced [1]
4a heating aluminium oxide to decompose aluminium hydroxide formed in the process, [1] melting aluminium oxide / cryolite mixture, [1] electrical energy in electrolysis [1]
  b Aluminium ore is bonded to other elements in compounds difficult to break down. [1] Aluminium could be extracted until electrical cells used to pass electricity [1] through one of its molten compounds by electrolysis. [1]
  c 13.5 tonnes [3]

C6.4

1a chlorine, [1] hydrogen, [1] sodium hydroxide solution [1]
2 Cl_2: bleaches damp blue litmus paper [1] H_2: lighted splint burns with 'pop' [1]
3a anode: $2Cl^-(aq) \rightarrow Cl_2(g) + 2e^-$ [2]
  b cathode: $2H^+(aq) + 2e^- \rightarrow H_2(g)$ [2]
4a molten sodium chloride → sodium metal + chlorine [1] sodium chloride solution → chlorine + hydrogen + sodium hydroxide solution [1]
  b Difference at cathode due to $H^+(aq)$ ions [1] from ionisation of water, [1] so hydrogen produced instead of sodium. [1] Solution formed from excess sodium ions and hydroxide ions when $H^+(aq)$ ions and chloride ions discharged. [1]
  c 92.0 tonnes [1]

C7.1

1a exothermic [1]
  b endothermic [1]
  c i any two from: oxidation, [1] combustion, [1] neutralisation, [1] respiration [1]
    ii any two from: any thermal decomposition, [1] citric acid and sodium hydrogencarbonate, [1] photosynthesis [1]
2 beaker feels cold [1] dissolving process absorbs energy from surroundings, which includes beaker and hand holding it, [1] energy transferred into reaction mixture [1]
3 energy stored in reactants greater than in products, [1] difference transferred to surroundings as energy, [1] raising temperature of surroundings [1]
4a $MgCO_3(s) \rightarrow MgO(s) + CO_2(g)$ [2]
  b 117kJ taken in from surroundings [2]

C7.2

1a treat injuries with cold packs. [1] chill drinks in cans [1]
  b dissolving ammonium nitrate in water [1]

  c i NH_4NO_3 [1]
    ii to treat injuries with cold packs / to chill drinks in cans [1]
2a calcium oxide [1]
  b $CaO(s) + H_2O(l) \rightarrow Ca(OH)_2(aq)$ [2]
  c It would form a harmful alkaline solution. [1]
3a hand warmer uses energy transferred to surroundings [1] in oxidation of iron, [1] forming hydrated iron(III) oxide in exothermic reaction, [1] NaCl catalyst [1]
  b Supersaturated solution [1] made to crystallise by pressing a small metal disc. [1] Crystals spread throughout solution, transferring energy to surroundings. [1] Crystals are redissolved in hot water, ready to use again. [1]
  c disposable – advantage: lasts longer when activated, disadvantage: can only be used once. [1] reusable: opposite applies [1]
  d self-heating cans [1]

C7.3

1a reactants $H_2(g) + Cl_2(g)$ above products $HCl(g)$, [1] arrow points from reactants to products / down, [1] arrow labelled '184kJ/mol of energy released' [1]
  b reactants $H_2(g) + I_2(g)$ below products $2HI(g)$, [1] arrow points from reactants to products / up, [1] arrow labelled '26.5kJ/mol of energy absorbed' [1]
2 Compare energy required to break bonds with energy transferred to surroundings when new bonds form to get overall energy change. [1] If energy transferred breaking bonds greater, then endothermic, [1] if energy transferred to surroundings when new bonds are made greater then exothermic. [1]
3a Energy transferred from the surroundings to break bonds in [1] to overcome attraction between atoms, [1] so separated atoms have more energy stored than original molecule. [1]
  b structural diagram of methane and oxygen, showing C–H bonds being broken and carbon dioxide and water formed [2]
  c bonds broken: 4 C–H; 2 O=O [2]   bonds made: 2 C=O; 4 O–H [2]

C7.4

1 endothermic [1]
2 energy required to break a specific bond [1]
3 1.49kJ (to 3 sig. fig.) [2]
4a $H_2 + Cl_2 \rightarrow 2HCl$ [1] energy transferred to surroundings = 185kJ [5]
  b $2H_2 + O_2 \rightarrow 2H_2O$ [1] energy transferred to surroundings = 486kJ [5]

C7.5

1 must be difference in reactivity between two different metals to produce voltage [1]
2a diagram similar to C7.5, Figure 2 but with iron instead of copper [3]
  b iron [1]
  c zinc, more reactive than iron, [1] greater tendency to lose electrons and form positive ions, [1] zinc atoms → Zn^{2+} ions at negative terminal, donating 2 electrons to iron(II) ions [1] $Zn \rightarrow Zn^{2+} + 2e^-$ [1] Fe^{2+} ions → iron atoms at positive terminal [1] $Fe^{2+}(aq) + 2e^- \rightarrow Fe(s)$ [1]
3 dry cell: once one reactant is used up, [1] cell stops working and must be discarded as it cannot be recharged, [1] prone to leakage [1] if zinc casing is used up (as it changes to zinc ions) and dissolves releasing inner paste from outer casing [1]

C7.6

Answers

1a hydrogen and oxygen / air [1]

b water [1]

c hydrogen + oxygen → water [1]

2 2H$_2$(g) + 4OH$^-$(aq) → H$_2$O(l) + 4e$^-$ [2] O$_2$(g) + 2H$_2$O(l) + 4e$^-$ → 4OH$^-$(aq) [2]

3 Electricity to recharge cells from the mains might be produced by burning / combustion [1] of fossil fuel [1]. However, if electricity from renewable source, [1] such as wind power or solar cells, [1] no carbon dioxide produced. [1]

C8.1

1a all acid used up in reaction [1]

b line horizontal [1]

2a i similar to C8.1, mass of reacting mixture vs time graph [2]

ii similar to C8.1, volume of gas vs time graph [2]

b gradient → rate of reaction at that particular time [1]

C8.2

1 any five from: temperature, [1] concentration, [1] surface area, [1] pressure (if gas), [1] catalyst, [1] light [1]

2 iron nail and second iron nail cut into pieces [1] labelled 'greater surface area' [1]

3 well-chewed food in smaller pieces so greater surface area : volume ratio, [1] more food molecules exposed to attack at any given time by acid particles in stomach than unchewed food [1]

4 'activation energy' = minimum energy needed for reactant particles to react as only those colliding particles with activation energy will react, [1] so any collisions with insufficient energy will not react, so no effect on rate of reaction [1]

5a i 0.111 cm^3/s [1]

ii 0.219 cm^3/s [1]

b Zinc pellets had faster mean reaction [1] so larger surface area (surface area : volume) than zinc granules, [1] more zinc atoms exposed to attack by H$^+$(aq) ions from the acid, [1] increasing frequency of collisions. [1] In this case, data suggests pellets have twice as many zinc atoms exposed (twice surface area : volume) as zinc pellets, [1] as mean rate for pellets was ≈ twice that of zinc granules. [1]

c 0.1352 g [3]

C8.3

1a frequency of collisions increases, [1] more particles collide with energy greater than the activation energy in any given time [1]

b doubles [1]

2a sodium hydrogencarbonate and citric acid react together once water is present, [1] giving off carbon dioxide [1]

b decreases [1]

c hydrogencarbonate ions and H$^+$(aq) ions move more quickly at higher temperature, [1] so collide more often, [1] more collisions in a given time have energy > activation energy [1]

3 Chemical reactions occur more quickly in cooking process [1] as water under pressure can be heated to higher than 100 °C. [1]

C8.4

1a green line = highest concentration [1] because steepest [1]

b responds to small changes in mass [1]

2a similar to C8.4, graph of volume vs time showing high / medium / low concentration all reaching same maximum volume [3]

b calcium carbonate/marble chips = limiting reactant, [1] because all three acids give same volume of gas, [1] acid solutions each have different amount of acid, [1] so produce different final volumes of gas, [1] calcium carbonate was in excess [1]

3 many more collisions between acid particles (H$^+$(aq) ions) in undiluted cleaner and limescale (calcium carbonate) in a given time [1] resulting in faster reaction, [1] because number of acid particles (H$^+$(aq) ions) in a given volume is far higher in undiluted cleaner, [1] causing more frequent collisions with particles of limescale [1]

C8.5

1a remains chemically unchanged [1]

b 50 cm^3/(3.2 × 60) = 0.26 cm^3/s [2]

2 to make as effective as possible by maximising surface area : V ratio [1]

3 reactants used up as they turn into products but catalysts remain chemically unchanged at end of reaction, [1] catalysts can catalyse further conversion of reactants to products [1]

4 Haber process: nitrogen + hydrogen ⇌ ammonia, iron catalyst, [1] sulfuric acid/Contact process: sulfur dioxide + oxygen ⇌ sulfur trioxide, vanadium(V) oxide catalyst, [1] nitric acid: ammonia + oxygen ⇌ nitrogen(II) oxide (nitrogen monoxide) + water, platinum/rhodium catalyst, [1] margarine: unsaturated oil + hydrogen → hydrogenated fat, nickel catalyst [1]

5 speed up production process → more economical, [1] conserve energy resources because activation energy is lowered, [1] which reduces costs, [1] added benefit of reducing pollution from , [1] and saving our limited resources of, fossil fuels, [1] so catalysts make industrial processes more sustainable [1]

C8.6

1 reactants form products but products also react to re-form the reactants [1]

2 mixture of water and phenolphthalein colourless at start, turns pink–purple in alkaline sodium hydroxide solution, then turns back to colourless in excess acid [1]

3 HPhe ⇌ H$^+$(aq) + Phe$^-$(aq)
   colourless   pink–purple [1]

4 any one from: toothbrushes, [1] mugs, [1] strip thermometers [1]

5 white anhydrous copper sulfate powder turns blue in presence of water [1]:
CuSO$_4$ + 5H$_2$O ⇌ CuSO$_4$·5H$_2$O [1]
white   blue
blue cobalt chloride paper turns pink in presence of water [1]:
CoCl$_2$·2H$_2$O + 4H$_2$O ⇌ CoCl$_2$·6H$_2$O [1]
   blue   pink

C8.7

1a size / magnitude same but opposite signs [1]

b water [1]

c reacts with water vapour in air [1]

d Energy transferred to surroundings [1]

2a W + X ⇌ Y + Z [1]

b 50 kJ transferred into chemicals from surroundings [1]

3a 4 moles [1]

b CoCl$_2$·2H$_2$O + 4H$_2$O ⇌ CoCl$_2$·6H$_2$O [1]

c Warm / heat them up [1]

d 36 g [2]

245

Answers

C8.8

1. rate of reverse reaction = rate of forward reaction [1]
2. remain constant [1]
3. Although concentrations of reactants and products unchanged overall in reaction mixture, [1] forward and reverse reactions still taking place but at the same rate. [1]
4. Pump more chlorine gas into mixture to increase rate of forward reaction so more iodine trichloride produced, [1] removing extra chlorine introduced into equilibrium mixture. [1]

C8.9

1. decreases products [1]
2. increases amount of hydrogen gas formed [1]
3. **a** As pressure increases, colour of mixture lightens [1] as the forward reaction producing more N_2O_4 results in fewer gas molecules. [1]
   b colour of mixture darkens [1] as reverse reaction producing more NO_2 is endothermic [1]
4. no effect: number of gas molecules same on both sides of balanced equation [1]

C9.1

1. **a** mixture of hydrocarbons [1]
   b fuels, plastics, and many other products [1]
   c because it is a mixture of different substances with different boiling points [1]
2. crude oil mixture contains a wide range of hydrocarbons, [1] components have different properties so better to separate into fractions with different specific uses [1]
3. **a** $C_nH_{(2n+2)}$ [1]
   b hexane, C_6H_{14} [1] heptane, C_7H_{16} [1] octane, C_8H_{18} [1] nonane, C_9H_{20} [1] decane, $C_{10}H_{22}$ [1]
4. **a** similar to C9.1, Figure 3 with 8 C and 18 H
   b 46 [1]
   c 15 [1]
   d compounds of H and C only [1] with maximum number of H atoms possible in their molecules / contain only single covalent C–C bonds [1]

C9.2

1. **a i** larger hydrocarbon → higher boiling point [1]
   ii larger hydrocarbon → lower volatility [1]
   iii larger hydrocarbon → higher viscosity [1]
   b short-chain: it will burn with a clean flame / not smoky [1]
2. table which effectively shows patterns in boiling points (gets higher), [1] volatility (gets lower), [1] viscosity (gets more viscous), [1] and flammability (gets less flammable) as size of hydrocarbon molecules increases [1]
3. crude oil heated and enters fractionating column near bottom as vapour, [1] temperature decreases going up column, [1] gases condense when they reach their boiling points [1] so different fractions collected as liquids at different levels in a continuous process, [1] hydrocarbons with smallest molecules have lowest boiling points and are collected as gases from top of the column where temperature is lower, [1] fractions with higher boiling points collected nearer the bottom [1]

C9.3

1. **a** carbon dioxide [1] water [1]
   b carbon dioxide: turns limewater cloudy / milky, [1] water: turns blue cobalt chloride paper pink / white anhydrous copper sulphate blue [1]
2. **a** $CH_4(g) + 2O_2(g) \rightarrow CO_2(g) + 2H_2O(l)$ [2]
   b $2CH_4(g) + 3O_2(g) \rightarrow 2CO(g) + 4H_2O(l)$ or $CH_4(g) + 1\frac{1}{2}O_2(g) \rightarrow CO(g) + 2H_2O(l)$ [2]
   c difficult to detect because colourless [1] odourless gas [1]
3. 43 640 dm^3 (to 4 sig. fig.) [4]

C9.4

1. **a** to meet demands for fuels (petrol and diesel) from crude oil [1]
   b hydrocarbon vapours passed over a hot catalyst / mixed with steam at very high temperatures [2]
2. **a i** B [1]
   ii hydrocarbon containing at least one C=C double bond [1]
   iii alkene [1]
   b i A [1]
   ii alkane [1]
   c thermal decomposition [1]
3. $C_{12}H_{26} \rightarrow C_8H_{18} + 2C_2H_4$ [1]

C10.1

1. **a** C_5H_{10} [1]
   b see C10.1, Figure 1 [1]
   c C_9H_{18} [1]
2. **a** similar to C10.1, Figure 3 with 2 I instead of 2 Br [1]
   b see C10.2, Figure 2 [1]
   c similar to C10.1, Figure 3 with 4 C, 8 H and 2 Cl in the top centre [1]
3. **a** butane [1]
   b i $C_3H_6 + H_2O \rightleftharpoons C_3H_7OH$ or C_3H_8O [1]
   ii see C10.2, Figure 2, with OH in centre, not end [2]
   c $2C_5H_{10} + 15O_2 \rightarrow 10CO_2 + 10H_2O$ or $C_5H_{10} + 7\frac{1}{2}O_2 \rightarrow 5CO_2 + 5H_2O$ [1]

C10.2

1. **a** esters [1]
   b alcohols [1]
   c carboxylic acids [1]
2. **a** propanol / propan-1-ol [1]
   b ethyl ethanoate [1]
   c methanoic acid [1]
3. **a** see C10.2, Figure 2 [1]
   b see C10.2, Figure 3 [1]
   c see C10.2, Figure 5 [1]

C10.3

1. ethanol, CH_3CH_2OH (or C_2H_5OH) [2]
2. fuels, [1] solvents, [1] ethanol in alcoholic drinks [1]
3. **a** sodium + butanol → sodium butoxide + hydrogen [1]
   b butanoic acid, $CH_2CH_2CH_2COOH$ [2]
   c butanol + oxygen → carbon dioxide + water [1]
4. $2CH_3OH + 3O_2 \rightarrow 2CO_2 + 4H_2O$ [1]
5. Place methanol, ethanol and propanol in separate spirit burners, [1] weigh accurately, [1] use each burner separately to heat known volume of water for set time and record rise in temperature of water, [1] re-weigh spirit burners with remaining alcohols, [1] calculate rise in temperature produced if one gram of each alcohol burned / alcohol with largest temperature rise per gram releases most energy when it burns [1]

C10.4

1a ethanoic acid + ethanol $\xrightleftharpoons{\text{sulfuric acid catalyst}}$ ethyl ethanoate + water [1]

b evaporate / give off vapour easily [1]

c any two from flavourings [1] perfumes [1] polyester fabrics [1]

2a i carbon dioxide [1]

ii potassium propanoate [1]

b add a spatula of sodium carbonate / potassium carbonate to each test tube, [1] propanol in water forms neutral solution so no gas given off, [1] other two tubes give off gas, [1] but the one releasing gas more slowly is propanoic acid, [1] as weak acid with lower concentration of H⁺(aq) ions does not ionise completely in aqueous solution, [1] last tube has faster rate of reaction as dilute hydrochloric acid ionises completely, forming solution with higher concentration of H⁺(aq) ions [1]

3 methanoic acid is weak acid, does not ionise completely when added to water, [1] majority of its molecules remain intact, [1] only a fraction form H⁺(aq) ions and methanoate (negative) ions, [1] so methanoic acid produces lower concentration of H⁺(aq) ions in solution, [1] than a solution of strong acid of equal concentration which ionises completely in water. [1]

C11.1

1a monomer = small reactive molecule that joins with other monomers → polymer, [1] polymer = very large molecule made up of many repeating units [1]

b polymerisation [1]

c see C11.1 [2]

d any two e.g., carrier bags, [1] dustbins, [1] cling film, [1] bottles, [1] washing-up bowls [1]

2a see C10.1, Figure 1 [1]

b similar to C11.1 [2]

c any two e.g., carpet, [1] milk crate, [1] ropes [1]

d C=C double bond 'opens up' in neighbouring propene molecules, [1] forms single bonds, [1] joining monomers together in a long chain [1]

3a 100% atom economy, [1] because as C=C bond in butene 'opens up' during its polymerisation, [1] no other molecule formed / poly(butene) is only product [1]

b similar to C10.1 Figure 1 but with double bond in centre

C11.2

1 condensation polymerisation: small molecule given off as polymer forms, [1] addition polymerisation: polymer is the only product [1]

2 Usually two different monomers, [1] with two of the same reactive functional groups on each monomer, [1] react, monomers join end to end in a long polymer chain, [1] with a small molecule given off [1] as each link between the monomers forms. [1]

3 $n(\text{HO-CH}_2\text{-CH}_2\text{-OH}) + n\text{HOOC-CH}_2\text{-CH}_2\text{-CH}_2\text{-CH}_2\text{-COOH}$ [2]

4a $(\text{CH}_2\text{-CH}_2\text{-OOC-CH}_2\text{-CH}_2\text{-CH}_2\text{-CH}_2\text{-COO})_n + 2n\text{H}_2\text{O}$ [2]

b $(\text{CH}_2\text{-CH}_2\text{-OOC-CH}_2\text{-CH}_2\text{-CH}_2\text{-CH}_2\text{-COO})_n$ [1]

C11.3

1a glucose, [1] fructose [1]

b glucose, $C_6H_{12}O_6$ [2]

c starch polymer is branched / shorter / fewer monomers bonded together [1] weaker intermolecular forces than cellulose polymer [1]

2a glycine [1] C11.3, Figure 5 [1]

b similar to C11.3, Figure 5 with H → CH_3 [1]

c i similar to C11.3, Figure 6 with 2 peptides, not 3 [1]

ii water [1]

iii condensation reaction [1]

3 amino acids are monomers that form polymers called proteins, [1] react via condensation polymerisation, [1] amino acids can react with each other to form long chains because they have two functional groups, one basic (the amine group, –NH₂) and one acidic (the carboxylic acid group, –COOH), [1] so acid end of one amino acid reacts with basic end of next amino acid to join polymer chain, [1] giving off a water molecule in the process, [1] continues until protein is formed from a sequence of many different amino acid combinations [1]

C11.4

1a 4 [1]

b 2 [1]

2a deoxyribonucleic acid [1]

b double helix [1]

c i condensation (polymerisation) [1]

ii H_2O [1]

iii nucleotides [1]

3a intermolecular forces / hydrogen bonds, [1] hold two polymer strands / chains next to each other in double helix shape [1]

b A = adenine, [1] T = thymine, [1] C = cytosine, G = guanine [1]

c pentagon with O atom at one apex [1]

C12.1

1 advertising: 'nothing added' / unadulterated [1] chemistry: single substance [1]

2a 158 °C–169 °C / 11 °C [1]

b mixture / made up of more than one substance / contains impurities [1]

c white powder melts above 100 °C > maximum temperature in water bath [1]

3 solvent dilutes toxic agent, [1] → less harmful to larger animals / wildlife, [1] also makes pesticide thinner (less viscous), [1] → it will not block nozzles / can be sprayed more easily / [1] covers larger area of crops [1] / reduces cost as toxic agent is probably most expensive component in the formulation [1]

C12.2

1 allow paper to dry, [1] measure distance from pencil line to solvent front [1] and to each dye left on paper, [1] divide distance each dye moves by distance of solvent front to get Rf values, [1] match values against tables of data to identify dyes [1]

2 0.77 [1]

3 solubility of Z in solvent > solubility of Y in same solvent, [1] match Rf values against values of known substances in 50–50 water ethanol solvent at 20 °C to identify Y and Z [1] in a database / databook [1]

4 changing solvent [1] and temperature [1] both affect attraction of compound to solvent (mobile phase) paper (stationary phase) / solubility in solvent / distribution between mobile phase and stationary phase, [1] so distance spot travels along paper differs under different conditions, resulting in different Rf values [1]

C12.3

Answers

1 hydrogen reacts with oxygen in air to form steam / water, [1] transferring energy to surroundings in exothermic reaction, warming them up and making popping sound [1]

2a magnesium carbonate + hydrochloric acid → magnesium chloride + water + carbon dioxide [1]

b *Either*: remove bung and delivery tube, place mouths of the two angled tubes together, [1] wait a while, giving time for carbon dioxide to build up in reaction tube before spilling over and sinking down into tube with limewater, [1] stopper tube and shake the limewater, [1] or: remove bung and delivery tube, place a dropping pipette into reaction tube above acid, [1] withdraw carbon dioxide building up in tube, [1] squirt into limewater, repeat [1]

3 Collect gas given off above anode into small test tube, [1] insert glowing splint to see if it relights. [1] If relights, oxygen given off. [1] Hold damp piece of blue litmus paper above solution near anode / in test tube of gas collected, [1] if it turns white / is bleached, [1] chlorine given off. [1]

4a i $Mg(s) + H_2SO_4(aq) \rightarrow MgSO_4(aq) + H_2(g)$ [2]
   ii $Mg(s) + 2H^+(aq) \rightarrow Mg^{2+}(aq) + H_2(g)$ [2]

b magnesium oxidised, [1] atoms each lose 2 electrons, [1] hydrogen ions reduced, [1] each receive an electron [1]

5 E.g., use zinc / magnesium + dilute acid [1] obtain different proportions of hydrogen and air [1] collecting gas over water with inverted test tube full of water to collect 100% hydrogen (allow first bubbles to escape to remove displaced air from apparatus), stopper tube and label it 100%, [1] then vary proportions of water in collection test tube, [1] invert test tube each time, measure volume of water in full tube using measuring cylinder then measure and mark different proportions of that total volume on side of 4 more different tubes to give rough proportion of hydrogen in mixture, [1] then test each tube in turn with lighted splint positioned at set distance from a sound meter, record maximum sound level for each mixture [1]

C12.4

1a white [1]

b add sodium hydroxide solution, [1] forms white precipitate, [1] AlOH precipitate dissolves in excess sodium hydroxide solution (to identify Al^{3+}), [1] take original magnesium and calcium compounds → flame test, [1] calcium → (brick) red flame, [1] magnesium → no colour [1]

2a wire loop in conc. hydrochloric acid and heat to clean it → dip loop into conc. acid again before dipping in metal compound to be tested → hold loop in edge of a roaring Bunsen flame → match colour of flame to identify metal ions [4]

b green / blue-green flame [1]

3a brown precipitate [1]

b nothing observed (no change) [1]

c nothing observed (no change) [1]

d nothing observed (no change) [1]

e yellow [1]

f K+ [1]

g Ca^{2+} [1]

h Al^{3+} [1]

i Fe^{2+} [1]

j Li+ [1]

4 $Mg^{2+}(aq) + 2OH^-(aq) \rightarrow Mg(OH)_2(s)$ [2]

C12.5

1 dilute hydrochloric acid, [1] limewater, [1] dilute nitric acid, [1] silver nitrate solution, [1] barium chloride solution [1]

2 potassium iodide, [1] potassium ions → lilac flame, [1] silver iodide → pale yellow precipitate formed with silver nitrate solution [1]

3a magnesium chloride + silver nitrate → magnesium nitrate + silver chloride [1]
$MgCl_2(aq) + 2AgNO_3(aq) \rightarrow Mg(NO_3)_2(aq) + 2AgCl(s)$ [2]

b potassium carbonate + hydrochloric acid → potassium chloride + water + carbon dioxide [1]
$K_2CO_3(s)$ [or (aq)] $+ 2HCl(aq) \rightarrow 2KCl(aq) + H_2O(l) + CO_2(g)$ [2]

c aluminium sulfate + barium chloride → aluminium chloride + barium sulfate [1]
$Al_2(SO_4)_3(aq) + 3BaCl_2(aq) \rightarrow 2AlCl_3(aq) + 3BaSO_4(s)$ [2]

4a $Ag^+(aq) + Br^-(aq) \rightarrow AgBr(s)$ [2]

b $Ba^{2+}(aq) + SO_4^{2-}(aq) \rightarrow BaSO_4(s)$ [2]

c $2H^+(aq) + CO_3^{2-}(s) \rightarrow CO_2(g) + H_2O(l)$ [2]

5 dissolve compound and remove any carbonate ions [1] as these also form precipitate with silver ions interfering with test, [1] any other acids added produce precipitates with silver nitrate solution [1]

C12.6

1 advantages: highly accurate and sensitive, [1] quicker and identify minute traces of samples, [1] disadvantages: may be expensive, [1] require special training, [1] produce results often interpreted only by comparison with data from known substances filed in a database [1]

2 heating increases electron stored energy, [1] electrons move into higher energy levels, [1] as they return to lower energy levels, [1] difference in energy between two levels emitted as light, forming line spectrum, [1] unique for each element / ion, [1] so match against known spectra in database to identify samples [1]

3a 5.0×10^{-12} mol [2]

b Hg^{2+} [1]

c 2.5×10^{-10} mol/dm³ [3]

C13.1

1 carbon dioxide, CO_2, [1] water vapour, H_2O, [1] nitrogen, N_2, [1] methane, CH_4, [1] ammonia, NH_3 [1]

2 from volcanic activity / eruptions [1]

3a e.g., no liquid water because temperature too hot (above 100 °C) / too hot for organisms to survive [1]

b condensed water vapour from volcanoes, [1] melting icy comets [1]

4 The first organisms / algae (bacteria) to photosynthesise, [1] using carbon dioxide and water made the first oxygen gas as by-product of producing glucose for energy. [1] carbon dioxide + water → glucose + oxygen or $6CO_2 + 6H_2O \rightarrow C_6H_{12}O_6 + 6O_2$ [1] these evolved into first marine plants and then land plants, rising numbers of organisms involved in photosynthesis further increased levels of oxygen in

atmosphere, [1] eventually sufficient oxygen to support living organisms not directly relying on photosynthesis for energy. [1] These animals fed on algae and plants and could release energy stored in them by using oxygen gas in process of respiration. [1]

5a 2.7×10^8 g [1]

b 2.4×10^7 g [4]

C13.2

1

Nitrogen	Oxygen	Argon	Carbon dioxide	Other gases
78%	21%	0.9%	0.04%	0.06%

[3]

2 nitrogen gas / N_2 in mixture of volcanic gases in volatile early atmosphere, [1] along with traces of ammonia gas / NH_3, [1] ammonia reacted with oxygen to form more nitrogen gas, [1] levels of nitrogen gas remain high because very unreactive [1]

3 Once algae and plants had evolved, [1] they decreased percentage of carbon dioxide in early atmosphere through process of photosynthesis. [1] Levels of carbon dioxide also decreased by formation of sedimentary carbonate rocks such as limestone, [1] and fossil fuels containing carbon / hydrocarbons. [1]

C13.3

1a any three, e.g., carbon dioxide, [1] methane, [1] water vapour [1]

b When Earth heated by Sun, [1] greenhouse gases in atmosphere let short wavelength electromagnetic radiation pass through. [1] At night, surface of Earth cools down [1] by emitting longer wavelength radiation. [1] Greenhouse gases absorb this radiation, [1] so some energy radiated from surface of Earth gets trapped in atmosphere / cannot be dissipated out of atmosphere and temperature rises. [1]

2 If electricity used to boil kettle is generated in fossil fuel power station, [1] fuel burned gives off carbon dioxide as one of products. [1]

3 any three, e.g., massive increase in combustion of fossil fuels [1] increasing deforestation [1] warming of oceans [1]

4a small troughs caused by greater rate of photosynthesis [1] in summer when more sunlight / warmer temperatures / more plants in leaf, [1] reducing levels of carbon dioxide, [1] conversely, in winter rate of photosynthesis decreases, [1] resulting in slightly higher level of carbon dioxide [1]

b since 1960, carbon dioxide level increasing [1] at accelerating rate [1]

5a biased, only reporting on certain parts of scientific article [1]

b data show link between Earth's temperature and levels of carbon dioxide in atmosphere, [1] assumes gases trapped in ice core are accurate record of ancient air samples, [1] does not say whether increase in temperature of Earth caused by some other factor that then caused increase in carbon dioxide levels, [1] or whether increased level of carbon dioxide caused rise in temperatures [1]

C13.4

1a any three from: sea-level rise, [1] flooding, [1] increased coastal erosion, [1] more frequent and severe storms, [1] changes in amount, timing, and distribution of rainfall, [1] temperature and water stress for humans and wildlife, [1] changes in food-producing capacity of some regions, [1] changes to distributions of wildlife species [1]

b variables affecting climate too complex to model over long term, [1] no records of such rapid changes in levels of greenhouse gases or average global temperatures to base predictions on [1]

2a any two, e.g., dilemmas developing manufacturing industries and limiting greenhouse gases (and hence creating wealth), [1] disagreements about size or timing of targets set for reducing emissions in different countries, [1] how monitoring against targets is carried out [2]

b wealthier country → more industry / vehicles / power requirements, [1] so more carbon dioxide emitted from fossil fuel combustion [1]

3a carbon dioxide gas produced in industrial processes can be pumped underground [1] to be stored in porous rock, [1] not emitted into atmosphere [1] to increase level of greenhouse gases and cause greater risk of global climate change [1]

b advantage: helps halt increase in levels of carbon dioxide in atmosphere [1] disadvantage: costs more money than just releasing carbon dioxide into air, so consumers will pay more for electricity or products made in a process [1]

c any two from: generate electricity using alternative energy sources, [1] use biofuels in vehicles, [1] conserve energy [1]

4 when hydrogen burns (or is oxidised), [1] only waste product is water, [1] $2H_2(g) + O_2(g) \rightarrow 2H_2O(g)$ or (l), [1] carbon dioxide (and other pollutants) released in combustion of carbon-based fuels [1]

C13.5

1a carbon dioxide [1] and water [1] cause global climate change [1]

b sulfur [1]

2a acid rain [1]

b nitrogen oxides / NO and NO_2 [1]

3a oxidation / reaction of oxygen with sulfur impurities present [1]

b high temperatures inside engines, [1] making it possible for nitrogen in air to react with oxygen [1]

c incomplete combustion when oxygen insufficient to completely oxidise fuel [1]

4a $CH_4(g) + 2O_2(g) \rightarrow CO_2(g) + 2H_2O(g)$ [2]

b $2CH_4(g) + 3O_2(g) \rightarrow 2CO(g) + 4H_2O(g)$ / $CH_4(g) + 1.5O_2(g) \rightarrow CO(g) + 2H_2O(g)$ [2]

c cannot detect when breathing in toxic [1] gas, as colourless, [1] and odourless, [1] will react with haemoglobin in red blood cells, [1] reducing their capacity to carry oxygen gas around body which can result in death [1]

C14.1

1 finite resources used up at faster rate than replaced / running out, [1] renewable resources can be replaced at rate to match rate of consumption [1]

2a any two, e.g., (named) metal ores, [1] crude oil, [1] natural gas, [1] coal, [1] fossil fuels, [1] sulfur, [1] sodium chloride [1]

b any two, e.g., sugar beet, [1] sugar cane, [1] trees, [1] animal waste [1]

3a finite if ethene from crude oil, [1] renewable if ethene made using glucose from sugar cane / sugar beet [1]

b by using a crop (renewable resource), obtain ethanol needed to make starting material (ethane) without using up finite supplies of crude oil, so extending time crude oil is available in future [1]

249

Answers

4a 1×10^6 / a million years [1]
b 1×10^2 / a hundred years [1]
c any two, e.g., uncertainty estimating amount of 'usable' fossil fuels left on Earth, [1] rate of future consumption, [1] possibility of discovering new deposits, [1] new technologies to burn remaining fossil fuels more efficiently [1]

C14.2

1 sterilise using chlorine, [1] ozone, [1] passing ultra-violet light through it [1]
2a distillation [1]
b test boiling point = 100 °C [1]
c only test for presence of water, so all aqueous solutions test positive [1]
3 dissolved minerals / salts / carbon dioxide / gas in it [1]
4a seawater not potable [1]
b removal of salts from salty water [1]
c high energy costs [1]
d reverse osmosis [1]

C14.3

1 screening [1] → primary treatment / sedimentation [1] → secondary treatment / aerobic breakdown [1] → final treatment / sedimentation / filtering / sterilisation [1]
2a solid sediments allowed to settle out, [1] rotating paddles push the solids / sludge towards centre of tank where piped to storage tank [1]
b fertiliser [1] source of renewable energy / biogas / biomethane / to generate electricity [1]
3 secondary tank: digestion / breakdown of organic substances aerobic, [1] sludge tank: process anaerobic [1]
4 any six from: ground water from aquifer: easiest to make potable as already passed through layers of sand / gravel / rock so filtered, [1] just needs sterilising by adding chlorine or ozone, or passing ultra-violet light through it to reduce number of microbes, [1] process uses less energy than desalination of salt water by distillation or by reverse osmosis, [1] but takes longer; [1] waste water: needs screening, primary treatment / sedimentation, secondary treatment / aerobic breakdown, final treatment, followed by sedimentation (and filtering) to remove useful microorganisms and sterilisation, [1] starts with many more harmful substances and microorganisms → potential health hazard compared with salt water; [1] salt water: costs of setting up and running distillation plant (under reduced pressure) or reverse osmosis plant > those treating waste water so depends on circumstances when deciding between waste water or salt water as a source of potable water, but ground water is the best source [1]

C14.4

1 used in electrical wiring to deliver electricity needed to run appliances [1]
2a smelting of copper ores, [1] electrolysis of solutions containing copper ions [1]
b extracted from lower-grade ores than economical by traditional methods [1]
c very unreactive / low in reactivity series [1]
d negative electrode / cathode, [1] because copper ions positively charged [1]
3 $Fe(s) + CuSO_4(aq) \rightarrow FeSO_4(aq) + Cu(s)$ [2]
4a negative electrode: $Cu^{2+} + 2e^- \rightarrow Cu$ [1] positive electrode: $Cu \rightarrow Cu^{2+} + 2e^-$ [1]
b reduction at negative electrode, [1] Cu^{2+} ions gain electrons to become Cu atoms; [1] oxidation at positive electrode, [1] Cu atoms lose electrons to become Cu^{2+} ions [1]
5 plants absorb Cu^{2+} ions from low-grade copper ore as they grow, [1] then plants burnt, [1] Cu metal extracted from compounds found in ash by leaching Cu^{2+} ions in solution [1] by adding sulfuric acid, [1] then displacement by scrap iron [1] and electrolysis to extract pure Cu, [1] method more important as copper-rich deposits become scarcer [1]

C14.5

1 obtaining and processing raw materials, [1] manufacturing product (and packaging), [1] using, re-using, and maintaining product, [1] recycling or disposal of product [1]
2 so full environmental impact of product can be used in decision-making [1]
3a bauxite / aluminium oxide [1]
b i carbon dioxide [1]
  ii sulfur dioxide [1]
4 When quantifying relative seriousness of pollution effects made by subjective decisions, [1] or when lack of consensus on actual amounts of pollutants released, [1] always uncertainty in data represented. [1] Hence validity of conclusions drawn do not have status of truly objective conclusions arrived at through scientific approach. [1]

C14.6

1 e.g., fill with water to create recreational resource for fishing, sailing, wildlife reserve, etc., [1] / replace topsoil and replant vegetation [1]
2 56 hours [1]
3 aluminium oxide must be molten [1] and then electrolysed, [1] using large amounts of energy compared with energy required in recycling [1]
4 copper is found in variety of alloys with varying amounts of different metals, [1] making recycling of pure copper more difficult so making new alloys is one solution, [1] or improving percentage of copper in recycled mixture by adding pure copper [1] then electrolysing to complete purification process [1]
5 e.g., less scarring of landscape from open-cast mining [1] less pollution of water running through waste heaps [1] less fossil fuel burnt during extraction, reducing atmospheric pollution [1]

C15.1

1 three test tubes: 1: iron object in contact with just water, [1] boil water to remove dissolved air then cover surface with oil so no more air can re-dissolve into water, and stopper test tube, [1] 2: just air, [1] put calcium chloride in test tube to absorb any water vapour from air, stopper, make sure nail not in contact with calcium chloride, [1] 3: both air and water, [1] nail partly in

Answers

water and partly in air / cover nail in unboiled water and leave test tube unstoppered [1]

2a hydrated iron(III) oxide [1]

b composition varies depending on conditions so no one formula for all rust [1]

3a coat in paint, [1] oil or grease, [1] plastic, [1] a less reactive metal, [1] more reactive metal [1]

b i oil / grease [1] chain constantly rubs against cogs when bicycle is moving, so coatings such as paint wear off quickly / lubricates moving parts [1]

ii paint, [1] cheap / grease messy when people brush against railings [1]

iii sacrificial protection, [1] e.g., attaching blocks of zinc / magnesium / aluminium to pipe: expensive, but easier to maintain in inaccessible locations and more effective than other methods where constant contact with seawater [1]

4a Set up test tubes containing a nail with: sodium chloride solution, [1] water, [1] Use same volumes and control conditions to make fair test, judge amount of rust formed / change in dry mass of nail after a week in each test tube. [1]

b series of test tubes with nail in each in increasingly concentrated solutions of sodium chloride, [1] e.g., no sodium chloride in first test tube and regularly increasing masses of sodium chloride in same volume of water in each successive tube, [1] shake to dissolve, until salt solution saturated in final tube, [1] leave tubes in test tube rack for a week [1] then judge degree of rusting / change in dry mass of nail in each [1]

5 37 mol to 2 sig. fig. / 40 mol to 1 sig. fig. / 36.9 mol to 3 sig. fig. [3]

C15.2

1 harder, [1] not worn away so quickly [1]

2a contains too much carbon [1]

b contains about 4% carbon, [1] so cast iron very hard and brittle [1] pure iron, relatively soft and malleable [1]

3

Type of steel	Main useful properties
Low carbon steel	Relatively soft and malleable
High carbon steel	Hard / strong
Chromium–nickel steel	Corrosion resistant

[3]

4a do not rust, [1] easier to keep sterile and stay sharp [1]

b i low carbon steel, [1] can be stamped into shapes [1]

ii high carbon steel, [1] very strong and hard [1]

5a 'light-weight' alloys due to the density of aluminium, [1] so more passengers and / or cargo can be carried on aircraft, [1] alloying makes stronger to withstand high stresses on aeroplane in flight [1]

b makes gold more hard-wearing, [1] in alloy, regular layers of gold ions / atoms [1] in giant metallic structure / lattice [1] have different-sized ions / atoms of copper randomly introduced, [1] distorting layers, [1] more difficult for layers to slide over each other compared to pure gold with same-sized ions / atoms [1]

C15.3

1a in a tangled mess / random jumble of chains [1]

b i thermosoftening: relatively weak intermolecular forces hold chains in place, [1] thermosetting: strong covalent bonds / cross-links between chains [1]

ii thermosoftening: soften when heated and tend to be flexible, [1] thermosetting: heat-resistant (charring at high temperatures) and rigid [1]

2 handles would soften if thermosoftening polymers used, [1] thermal energy conducted through metal pan to its handle [1]

3 A and B: relatively weak intermolecular forces, [1] A has stronger intermolecular forces than B so needs higher temperature to soften it, [1] C: strong covalent bonds hold chains in position, so will not soften on heating [1]

4a reaction conditions different e.g., temperature, pressure, catalyst [1]

b HDPE: straighter chains, [1] pack more closely together, [1] little space between chains, so higher density, [1] LDPE: randomly branched chains, [1] chains cannot pack regularly / neatly together, [1] more space in its structure and lower density [1]

C15.4

1a sand [1]

b i any two from: transparent, [1] brittle, [1] electrical insulator, [1] hard [1]

ii borosilicate glass melts at higher temperature than soda-lime glass [1]

2 composite [1]

3 water between giant layers of atoms / ions in wet clay, [1] when clay heated water driven out, [1] strong bonds form between adjacent layers, [1] making clay a ceramic

4 e.g., test fibre glass and carbon fibre composite pieces of same size / dimensions, [1] suspending increasing mass [1] from pieces of horizontal material fixed at one end over edge of bench, [1] measure size of deflection from end of each composite to its original position with each additional mass, [1] plot graph of deflection against mass, with one line for each composite / use table of results to compare their flexibility [1]

C15.5

1 nitrogen gas from air, [1] hydrogen gas from natural gas [1]

2a nitrogen + hydrogen $\rightleftharpoons$ ammonia [1] $N_2(g) + 3H_2(g) \rightleftharpoons 2NH_3(g)$ [2]

b 450 °C, [1] 200 atmospheres, [1] iron catalyst [1]

3a cooled, condensed [1] collected as liquid [1]

b recycled to reaction mixture [1]

4 purify nitrogen and hydrogen, [1] pass over iron catalyst [1] at high temperature (450 °C) and pressure (200 atmos), [1] reversible reaction, producing ammonia [1]

5a 100% [1]

b 100% atom economy so no waste by-products formed in reaction, [1] no pollution from by-products, [1] no energy required for their disposal [1]

c any six from: although main reaction has 100% atom economy, [1] pollution and depletion of natural resources associated with Haber process, [1] e.g., natural gas often used as raw material for hydrogen, [1] using up this finite resource / fossil fuel, [1] energy and fuel also needed to extract nitrogen from air, [1] energy also required to maintain 200 atmospheres of pressure and 450 °C temperature needed for reaction, [1] using fossil fuels and giving

Answers

off carbon dioxide, a greenhouse gas → climate change, [1] and other possible pollutants e.g., toxic carbon monoxide, [1] also take into account energy from transport and distribution of raw materials [1]

C15.6

1. to increase rate of production of ammonia [1]
2. **a** increases yield of ammonia, [1] fewer molecules of gas on right-hand side of equation so increasing pressure favours forward reaction [1]
   b increase rate of production of ammonia, [1] higher pressure → more gas molecules in same volume, [1] collisions more frequent → reaction rate faster [1]
3. **a** 31% [1] **b** 10% [1]
   c 94% [1] **d** 82% [1]
   e conditions are a compromise, [1] yield of ammonia lower than ideal, [1] but rate of reaction reasonable at this temperature and pressure (with iron catalyst) [1]
4. **a** 800 dm³ [2]
   b 570 g (to 2 sig. fig.) or 567 g (to 3 sig. fig.) [3]
   c 20% (to 2 sig. fig.) or 19.8% / 19.9% (to 3 sig. fig.) (depends on answer to b) [2]

C15.7

1. **a** ammonium nitrate, [1] NH_4NO_3 [1]
   b ammonium sulfate, [1] $(NH_4)_2SO_4$ [1]
   c ammonium phosphate, [1] $(NH_4)_3PO_4$ [1]
2. see C15.7, Figure 3
3. ammonia + nitric acid → ammonium nitrate [1] $NH_3 + HNO_3 →$ NH_4NO_3 [1]
4. **a** ammonia + sulfuric acid → ammonium sulphate [1]
   $2NH_3(aq) + H_2SO_4(aq) → (NH_4)_2SO_4(aq)$ [1]
   b neutralisation [1]
   c any three from: heat on water bath [1] until half water evaporated / to point of crystallisation / until solution saturated, [1] leave to evaporate slowly forming crystals of ammonium sulfate, [1] alternatively, before all water evaporates, filter off any crystals [1], dab dry with filter paper, [1] leave to dry under clean filter paper [1]
5. 0.24 mol/dm³ to 2 sig. fig. [4]

C15.8

1. **a i** calcium nitrate, [1] $Ca(NO_3)_2$ [1]
   ii calcium phosphate / triple superphosphate, [1] $Ca_3(PO_4)_2$ [1]
   b i potassium chloride, KCl [1] potassium sulphate, K_2SO_4 [1]
   ii calcium phosphate, $Ca_3(PO_4)_2$ [1] calcium sulfate, $CaSO_4$ [1]
2. **a** calcium [1] oxygen [1]
   b PO_4^{3-} [1]
   c $H_3PO_4(aq) → 3H^+(aq) + PO_4^{3-}(aq)$ [2]
3. Ammonium phosphate supplies two essential plant nutrients: nitrogen and phosphorus, [1] ammonium nitrate only provides nitrogen. [1]
4. urea = 46.7% [2] ammonium nitrate = 35.0% [2] ammonium sulfate = 21.2% [2] urea supplies most nitrogen

MS1

1. 213 g [1]
2. **a** $3.8 × 10^{-5}$ mol/dm³ [1]
   b 32 years [1]
3. **a** 1 : 3 [1]
   b 180 tonnes [1]
   c $\frac{4}{5}$ [1]

MS2

1. **a** 2 [1] **b** 1 [1] **c** 2 [1] **d** 4 [1]
   e 3 [1] **f** 1 [1] **g** 4 [1] **h** 3 [1]
2. **a** 194 s (to 3 sig. fig.) [1]
   b discard 1st 'rough' titre then take mean of two results (within 0.1 cm³ of each other), so mean titre is (20.40 + 20.30) cm³/2 = 20.35 cm³ [1]
3. **a** qualitative [1]
   b

Metal oxide	Time taken to collect 10 cm³ of gas in s
A	18
B	27
C	12
D	35

[1]

   c bar chart with x-axis labelled 'Metal oxide' and y-axis labelled 'Time (to collect 10 cm³ of gas) in s'; bars correct height; gaps between bars; graph occupies over half area of grid, with sensible, even scale chosen [1]
4. **a** 1 [1]
   b divide total reserves by annual rate of usage, estimate using $7.5 × 10^{10}$ tonnes / $1.6 × 10^8$ tonnes/year by subtracting powers of 10 (10 − 8 = 2) so answer in order of 10^2 years (actual answer ≈ 470 years) [1]

MS3

1. **a** The pH of an acid is less than 7. [1]
   b Rate of reaction is proportional to the concentration of reactant A. [1]
   c 22 dm³ is approximately / roughly / about equal to 24 dm³. [1]
2. **a** $\frac{\text{percentage atom economy} × \text{sum of rel. formula mass of all the reactants}}{100}$
   = rel. formula mass of desired product [1]
   b $\frac{\text{Relative formula mass of the desired product} × 10}{1 \text{ percentage atom economy}}$
   = sum of rel. formula mass of reactants [1]
3. **a** $5.8 × 10^{-8}$ m [1]
   b $2.56 × 10^4$ cm³ [1]

MS4

1. **a** graph of positive, constant gradient passing through (0, 0), with vertical axis labelled y and horizontal axis labelled x [1]
   b graph of negative curve getting more shallow with vertical axis labelled y and horizontal axis labelled x [1]
2. **a** $y = mx + c$ [1]
   b m = gradient; c = intercept on y-axis [1]
   c $y = mx$ [1]
3. 1.14 cm³/s (+ or − 10%) [1]

MS5

1. Both models show central C atom bonded to 4 H atoms, but 2D model does not show bond angles whereas actual bond angles represented in 3D model (= 109.5°) [1]
2. **a** 20 nm × 20 nm × 6 = 2400 nm² [1]
   b 20 nm × 20 nm × 20 nm = 8000 nm³ [1]
   c 2400 nm² ÷ 8000 nm³ = 0.3 /nm [1]

Index

accuracy 266–267
acid rain 202–203
acids 74–77, 85, 90–99, 164–165
activation energy 117, 130, 136
active drugs 181
addition polymers 169
addition reactions 158–159
advanced composites 227
alcohols 159–163, 170–171
alkali metals 26–27, 30–31
alkalis 74–77, 92, 94, 96–97, 163
alkanes 149, 160
alkenes 154–155, 158–159, 168
alloys 54–55, 222–223
aluminium 106–107, 216, 222
amino acids 173
ammonia 119, 197, 228–231
ammonium chloride 139
ammonium sulfate 232–233
anaerobic digestion 210–211
analysis 180–193, 267–270
anhydrous 140
anodes 102, 104–108
anomalies 267, 270
aqueous solutions 6, 99, 104–105, 108–109
atmosphere 194–205
    ammonia 197
    carbon dioxide 194–196, 198–201
    composition 197
    early Earth 194
    evolution 196–197
    greenhouse gases 198–201
    methane 194, 197, 198, 201
    oxygen 194–195, 197
    photosynthesis 194–195
    pollutants 202–203
atom economy 70–71
atomic numbers 14, 16
atomic structure 4–21
atoms 4–5, 12–19
Avogadro constant 62–63

balanced equations 6–7, 64–67
ball and stick models 42, 46
bar charts 268
bases 92–93, 96–97, 163
batteries 120–121
bauxite 106–107, 206

biofuels 201
biogas 211
bioleaching 213
Bohr, Neils 13
boiling points 36–37, 47
    alkali metals 26
    halogens 28
    hydrocarbons 150–151
    purity analysis 180–181
bond energy 117–119
borosilicate glass 226
breaking bonds 117–119
brine 108–109
bromides, tests 189–190
bromine test 155, 158
bronze 222
burettes 74–75

cadmium 191
calcium carbonate 134, 196
calcium hydroxide 185
carats 222
carbon 49–51, 86, 88–89, 196, 223
carbonates 95, 188, 196
carbon capture and storage 200–201
carbon dioxide 185, 194–196, 198–202
carbon footprints 200–201
carbon monoxide 202–203
carboxylic acids 161, 163–165, 170–171
cars 202–203
catalysts 136–137, 159, 231
categoric variables 264
cathodes 102, 104–108
cation tests 186–187, 190–191
cells
    chemical 120–121
    fuel 122–123
cellulose 172–173
ceramics 226
Chadwick, James 13
changes in equilibria 143
changes of state 36–37
charge
    ions 16, 38–43
    sub-atomic particles 14
chemical analysis 180–193
    chromatograms 182–183
    gases 184–185

instrumental 190–191
    purity 180–181
chemical calculations 62–81
chemical cells 120–121
chemical changes 84–101
chemical equations 6–7
chemical symbols 4–5
chloride ions 108
chlorides 90, 189–190
chlorine 102, 109, 185
chromatograms 182–183
chromatography 10–11, 182–183
chromium-nickel steels 223
clay ceramics 226
climate change 199–202
coal, formation 196
coatings of nanoparticles 58
cobalt(II) chloride 141
collision theory 130–135
coloured ions 33
coloured precipitates 186–187
combustion 152–153, 158, 162–163, 202–203
complete combustion 152
composites 227
composition of atmosphere 197
compounds 5, 8
concentration 72–77, 134–135
conclusions 268–269
concrete 227
condensation 9–10
condensation polymers 170–171
conduction 42–43, 47, 49–51, 53, 55
conservation of mass 6
continuous variables 264
control groups 266
cooling 36–37, 115
copper 212–213, 217, 222
copper salts 93
copper(II) sulfate 140–141
corrosion 220–221
covalent bonds 38, 44–51, 149, 154–155, 224–225
cracking 154–155
crude oil 148–157, 196
crystallisation 8–9
crystals 52–55

Index

Dalton, John 12, 22–23
data 264–270
decreases in mass 128
decreasing light transmission 129
delocalised electrons 49–51, 53
deoxyribonucleic acid (DNA) 174–175
dependent variables 265
desalination 209
diamond 48–49
dilute acids 85
disaccharides 172
disappearing cross method 129
displacement reactions 29, 31, 86–89, 120–121
displayed formulae 149, 158–161, 164–165
distillation 9–10, 148–151, 209
DNA (deoxyribonucleic acid) 174–175
dot and cross diagrams 39, 44–45
double bonds 154–155, 158–159
double helix 174–175
drinking water 208–209
dynamic equilibrium 142–143

economics of Haber process 230–231
effluent 210–211
electricity
 cells 120–123
 conduction 42–43, 47, 49–51, 53, 55
electrodes 104–108, 120–121, 123
electrolysis 102–111
 aqueous solutions 103, 104–105, 108–109
 brine 108–109
 metal extraction 89, 106–107, 212–213
electrolytes 102
electronic structures 12–14, 18–19, 24–25, 30–31
electrons 5
 charge 14
 chemical cells 120–121
 delocalised 49–51, 53
 discovery 12–13
 electrolysis 104–105
 ions 16, 38–43
 metallic bonding 53
 oxidation and reduction 87, 91
 periodicity 19, 24–25, 30–31
 shielding 30–31
elements 4–5, 14–17, 38–43
 periodicity 19, 22–35

emission spectrography 190–191
endothermic reactions 112–113, 115–119
end points, titrations 74–75
energy changes 112–125
 bond energy 117–119
 chemical cells 120–121
 energy transfers 114–115
 fuel cells 122–123
 greenhouse gases 198
 reaction profiles 116–117
 temperature changes 113–115
energy level of electrons 13, 18–19
energy transfers 37, 140–141
enhanced greenhouse effect 198–201
equilibria 98–99
 dynamic 142–143
 pressure 144
 rates of reactions 128–129
 reversible reactions 138–145
 temperature 145
errors 267
esters 161, 164, 170–171
ethanoic acid 164–165
ethanol 159, 160, 162
ethene 159, 168
evaluation 270
evaporation 9–10
evidence 270
evolution of the atmosphere 196–197
exothermic reactions 112–113, 114–119
extraction of metals 88–89, 106–107, 212–213

fair tests 266
fermentation 162
fertilisers 228, 232–235
fibreglass 227
filtrates/filtration 8
finite resources 206–207
fixed points 180–181
flame emission spectrography 190–191
flame tests 186–187
flammability of hydrocarbons 150–151
formulations 181
fossil fuels 196, 200–203
fractional distillation 10, 150–151
fractions of crude oil 149–151
freshwater 208–209
fructose 172
fuel cells 122–123
fuels 148–157, 196, 200–203

fullerenes 50–51, 58–59
functional groups 158

galvanised metals 221
gases 6, 36–37
 analysis 184–185
 atmosphere 194–205
 greenhouse effect 198–202
 pressure 36
 volume 78–79, 129
general formula of alkanes 149
giant covalent structures 45, 48–51
giant ionic structures 42–43
giant metallic structures 54–55
glass 226
global climate change 199–202
global dimming 202–203
global warming 199–202
glucose 172
glycine 173
gold alloys 222
graphene 51
graphite 49
graphs 268–269
green chemistry 70–71
greenhouse gases 198–201
group 0 24–25
group 1 26–27, 30–31
group 7 28–29, 31

Haber process 119, 228–231
half-equations 87, 104–105, 107, 108, 123
halide tests 188–189
halogens 28–29, 31, 158, 188–189
hand warmers 114
hazards 265
HDPE see high density poly(ethene)
heat 36–37
heating 37
high density poly(ethene) (HDPE) 224
history of the atom 12–13
homologous series
 alcohols 160–161
 alkenes 158
 carboxylic acids 161
 esters 161
hydration 140–141
hydrocarbons 148–155
 alkanes 149, 160
 alkenes 154–155, 160–161, 170
 bromine test 155, 158

Index

combustion 154–155
cracking 154–155
distillation 148–151
properties 150–151
hydrogen 28, 86, 88–89, 122–123, 159, 184
hydrogen ions 99, 108
hypothesis 265

impurities 180–181, 208–209
incomplete combustion 152, 202–203
independent variables 265
industrial fertilisers 234–235
infrared radiation 198–199
insoluble bases 92–93
instrumental analysis 190–191
intermolecular forces 46–47, 225
investigations 265–267
iodides, tests 189–190
ionic bonding 38–43
ionic compounds 27–29, 33, 38–43, 92–93
ionic equations 86
ions 16, 38–43
electrolysis 102, 104–105
periodicity 40–41
pH scale 99
tests 186–191
transition elements 33
iron 216–217, 220–221, 223
isotopes 17

lattices 42–43
Law of conservation of mass 6
LCA see Life Cycle Assessment
LDPE see low density poly(ethene)
leachates 213
Le Châtelier's principle 143
Life Cycle Assessment (LCA) 214–215
light measurement 129
limestone 134
limiting reactants 67
line of best fit 268–269
line graphs 268
liquids 6, 36–37
litmus 138, 185
low density poly(ethene) (LDPE) 224

macromolecules 45, 48–51
macro nutrients 234
making bonds 117–119
malachite 212–213

mass
balanced equations 64–67
decreases 128
gases 79
law of conservation 6
solutes 73
mass numbers 14–16
matter, states 36–37
mean 268
measurement 266–267
accuracy and precision 266–267
gases evolved 129
mass changes 128
precipitation 129
resolution 267
medicinal drugs 181
melting points 36–37, 47
alkali metals 26
halogens 28
purity analysis 180–181
transition elements 32
Mendeleev, Dmitri 23
metal carbonates 95
metal halides 27
metallic bonding 52–55
metal ores 88–89, 106–107, 212–213
metal oxides 88–89, 106–107
metals 24–27
acid reactions 85, 90–91
alloys 54–55, 222–223
bonding 52–55
coloured ions 33
extraction 88–89, 106–107, 212–213
flame tests 186–187, 190–191
ions 40–41
reactivity 26–27, 84–89, 220–221
recycling 216–217
reserves 207
rusting 220–221
salts 90–91
sodium hydroxide tests 186–187
spectrography 190–191
transition elements 32–33
methane 44, 46, 194, 197, 198, 201
methanol 160, 162
methylated spirits 162
miscible liquids 10
mixtures 8–9, 148–149, 180–181
molecules 5, 38–51
moles 62–63
molten ionic compounds 42–43

monomers 168–169, 224
monosaccharides 172–173

nanoparticles 56–59
nanotubes 50, 58–59
nanowires 59
natural gas 196
natural polymers 172–175
negative ions 39, 188–189
neutralisation 74–77, 92–97, 232–233
neutrons 13–17
nickel-steel alloys 223
nitrates 90
nitrogen, Haber process 119, 228–231
nitrogen-based fertilisers 228, 232–235
nitrogen oxides 202–203
noble gases 24–25, 197
non-metals 24–25, 27–29, 31, 40–41, 45, 48–51, 86
NPK fertilisers 234–235
nucleotides 174–175
nucleus 5, 13–17
nylon 171

observation 265
oil 148–157, 196
OILRIG 91
order of discharge at anodes 105
organic compounds
alcohols 159–163, 170–171
alkenes 154–155, 158–159, 168
carboxylic acids 161, 164–165, 170–171
esters 161, 164, 170–171
saturation 159
organic reactions 158–167
outliers 267
overall energy change 118–119
oxidation 87, 91, 104–105, 152–153, 163, 220–221
oxides of metals 212–213
oxygen 184, 194–195, 197

paints 181
paper bags 215
paper chromatography 10–11
particle model 36–37
particulates 202–203
patterns, identifying 268–269
percentage yield 68–69
periodicity 24–25, 30–31
periodic table 4–5, 19, 22–35, 40–41

255

Index

phosphorus fertilisers 234–235
photosynthesis 194–195
pH scale 96–99
phytomining 213
plastic bags 215
plywood 227
pollution 202–203, 217
polyesters 170–171
poly(ethene) 168–169, 224
polymers 168–177
   addition 169, 224
   condensation 170–171
   forces between chains 225
   natural 172–175
   properties 224–225
polypeptides 173
poly(propene) 168
polysaccharides 172–173
positive ions 38, 186–187, 190–191
potable water 208–209
potassium salts 234
precipitation 129, 186–187
precision 266–267
prediction 265
pressure
   equilibria 144
   gases 36
   Haber process 230–231
   rates of reactions 134, 230–231
products 6–7
   mass calculations 63–67
   measurement 128–129
   rates of reactions 128–129
   reversible reactions 138–139
   yield 68–71
propene 168
proteins 173
protons 13–15
purification of water 208–209
purity 180–181

random errors 267
range of data 268
rates of reactions 128–147
   catalysts 136–137
   collision theory 130–135
   concentration 134–135
   equilibria 128–129
   pressure 134
   reversible reactions 138–145
   surface area 130–131
   temperature 132–133

reactants 6–7
   atom economy 70–71
   limiting 67
   mass calculations 63–67
   rates of reactions 128–129
   reversible reactions 138–139
   yield 68–71
reaction profiles 116–117, 136
reactivity
   alkali metals 26–27
   metals 26–27, 84–89, 220–221
   periodicity 19, 30–31
reactivity series 84–89, 120–121
recycling 216–217
redox 120–121, 123
reduce, reuse, recycle 216–217
reduction 87, 89, 91, 104–105
reinforcement 227
relationships between variables 265, 268–269
relative atomic mass 62–63
relative formula mass 62–63
renewable resources 206–207
repeatability 264
repeating units 169–171
reproducibility 264
resolution 267
resources 206–245
   alloys 222–223
   composites 227
   fertilisers 228, 232–235
   finite and renewable 206–207
   glass and ceramics 226
   Haber process 228–231
   life cycles 214–215
   metals 212–213
   polymers 224–225
   recycling 216–217
   rusting 220–221
   using 220–245
   water 208–211
retention factors 183
reverse osmosis 209
reversible reactions 138–145, 159
risk 59, 265
rusting 220–221
Rutherford, Ernest 13

saccharides 172–173
sacrificial protection 221
salts
   acids and carbonates 95

displacement reactions 29, 31
   formulae 92
   insoluble bases 92–93
   metals 90–91
   neutralisation 94
salt water 209
saturated hydrocarbons 149
saturation of organic compounds 159
scatter graphs 268
sedimentary rock 196
separation of mixtures 8–9
sewage treatment 210–211
shells, electrons 13, 18–19
shielding 30–31
silicon 226
silicon dioxide 48
silver nanoparticles 56, 58–59
simple molecules 44–47
sinks of carbon dioxide 198–199
size of atoms 16
size of nanoparticles 56–57
sludge 210–211
smelting 212, 217
soda-lime glass 226
sodium, alcohol reaction 163
sodium hydroxide 109, 186–187
solids 6, 36–37
solutions
   concentrations 72–73
   electrolysis 103
   ionic compounds 42–43
   mass of solutes 73
   titrations 74–77
solvents 11, 162
soot 202–203
spectrography 190–191
stainless steels 223
standard notation 18–19
starch 172–173
states of matter 36–37
state symbols 6–7
steam, ethanol synthesis 159
steel 216–217, 223
sterilisation of water 209, 211
stick and ball models 42, 46
strong acids 98–99
structural formulae 161
sub-atomic particles 13–17
sucrose 47, 172
sugars 172–173
sulfates 90, 189
sulfur dioxide 202–203

Index

surface area 130–131, 136
sustainability 70–71, 206–207
symbol equations 6
systematic errors 267

tables 268
temperature
   changes 113–115
   climate change 199–202
   energy transfers 114–115
   equilibria 145
   greenhouse gases 198–200
   rates of reactions 132–133
thermal decomposition 139, 154–155, 212
thermal radiation 198–199
thermosetting polymers 224–225
thermosoftening polymers 224–225
thinking scientifically 264–265
Thomson, J.J. 12

titrations 74–77
transition elements 25, 32–33
tungsten 89

uncertainty 270
universal indicator 26, 97
unsaturated hydrocarbons 154–155, 158–159
using data 268–269

variables 264–265
vinegar 164–165
viscosity of hydrocarbons 150–151
volatility of hydrocarbons 150–151
voltage 120–121
volumes of gas 78–79, 129
volumetric flasks 72

warming up 114–115
washing-up liquids 181
waste water 210–211

water 44–45
   alkali metal reactions 26–27
   alkene additions 159
   desalination 209
   electrolysis 104–105
   potable 208–209
   reactions with metals 84–85
   sewage 210–211
weak acids 98–99, 164–165
word equations 6
working scientifically 264–270

yield 68–71

zinc 221
zinc-carbon dry cells 121
zinc chloride 102
zinc-copper cells 120